DATE DUE

MAR 2 0 1993		
MAY 1 8 1994		
JUN 0 6 1994		
SEP 1 1 2000		

DEMCO 38-297

HARMLESS ENTERTAINMENT

Hollywood and the Ideology of Consensus

by RICHARD MALTBY

The Scarecrow Press, Inc.
Metuchen, N.J., & London 1983

The author gratefully acknowledges permission to reprint the following:

Lyrics on pages 3-4 from "Hooray for Hollywood," by Johnny Mercer and Richard A. Whiting. © (Renewed) Warner Bros. Inc. All rights reserved. Used by permission.

Lyrics on page 170 from "You Made Me Love You," written by Joseph McCarthy and James V. Monaco. © MCMXII Broadway Music Corp.; © renewed MCMXL Broadway Music Corp.; © 1973 Broadway Music Corp.; © 1981 Broadway Music Corp. International Copyright Secured. All rights reserved. Used by permission.

Lyrics on page 182 from "'Tain't What You Do (It's the Way That Cha Do It)." Words and Music by Sy Oliver and James Young. © Copyright 1939 by MCA Music, A Division of MCA Inc. Copyright renewed 1967 and assigned to MCA Music, A Division of MCA Inc. and Warock Corporation for the U.S.A. MCA Music, A Division of MCA Inc., New York, N.Y. for the World outside U.S.A. Used by permission. All rights reserved.

Lyrics on page 218 from "Now and Then It's Goina Rain," by John Reid. Used by permission of House of Gold Music, Inc.

Lines on page 304 from the poem "The Second Coming," by W. B. Yeats. Reprinted by permission of Macmillan Publishing Co., Inc. and A. P. Watt Ltd. from Collected Poems of W. B. Yeats. Copyright 1924 by Macmillan Publishing Co., Inc.; renewed 1952 by Bertha Georgie Yeats.

Library of Congress Cataloging in Publication Data

Maltby, Richard, 1952-
  Harmless entertainment.

  Bibliography: p.
  Includes index.
  1. Moving-picture industry--United States.
2. United States--Popular culture. I. Title.
PN1993.5.U6M2295 1983   384'.8'0979494   82-10244
ISBN 0-8108-1548-6

CONTENTS

ACKNOWLEDGMENTS

However isolated a writer may feel when confronting the existential fact of the blank piece of paper in the typewriter, every book is a communal endeavour, and this one is certainly no exception. Its faults are entirely mine, but the help of friends and colleagues have helped me eliminate its worst excesses. My greatest debts are to Simon Arrowsmith and Ian Craven, with whom I have spent many hours discussing the American cinema and formulating the central ideas of this book. Mick Gidley, Mike Weaver, Brian Lee and Eric Moon have kindly read my manuscript at various stages, and their advice has been invaluable in shaping the final product. Douglas Pye and Martin Pumphrey have discussed some of the material with me, and Lavinia Lubbock, Anthony Fothergill, Nicole Irving and Willow have provided much needed encouragement. Over the years my ideas have been refined and frequently revised through the experience of teaching, and I am grateful to all my students at Exeter University for the contributions they have made.

I would like to thank David Horn and the staff at Exeter University library, Anne Schlosser and her staff at the American Film Institute Library in Beverly Hills, Robert Knudsen and the staff of the Special Collections Department of the University of Southern California, and Gillian Hartnoll and the staff of the British Film Institute library, for the assistance they have provided. I am grateful to the Exeter University Research Fund Committee for their financial assistance. Angela Day and Lyn Longridge braved the unenviable task of converting my manuscript into a comprehensible typescript with patient good humor.

Finally, this book is gratefully and affectionately dedicated to my parents.

PART 1

THE CRAP-GAME

"You've got to gamble. The
movie industry isn't a slide-
rule business and never will be.
It's the world's biggest crap-
game."

Richard Zanuck

CHAPTER 1

TAKING HOLLYWOOD FOR GRANTED

"METROPOLIS OF MAKE-BELIEVE"

(Title describing Hollywood in the credits of A Star Is Born, 1937)

> The film industry probably knows less about itself than any other major industry in the United States.
>
> Eric Johnston[1]

> The truth is they don't know as much about Hollywood as they believe they know.
>
> Daniel Fuchs[2]

Hollywoodland, the sign said, announcing another country whose boundaries extended from Los Angeles to the 20,000 movie theatres in America. It was the fantastic land over the rainbow where bluebirds flew and dreams came true in Schwab's drugstore. Or else it was the Locust-land of lost content where the dreams turned sour and fan magazines, or even the Hollywood Sign itself, became Instruments of Death for the debris of Tinsel Town who failed to find their crock of gold.[3] Beyond the films it made, Hollywood was itself an American fantasy, for sale on every newsstand and cosmetic counter. The main ingredients of its fantasy were beauty and easy success.

> Hooray for Hollywood,
> Where every office boy or young mechanic
> Can be a panic
> With just a good-looking pan,
> And any shop girl

> Can be a top girl
> If she pleases the tired businessman. [4]

It offered a seemingly effortless version of the Horatio Alger myth, in which a star could be made by a self-made man, and hard work was replaced by talent, good looks or merely good fortune. Hollywood was a citadel of conspicuous consumption, described in its fabulous mansions, parties, clothes and marriages. The fantasy of consumption was also a fantasy of availability. The people who lived in Hollywoodland were just like their audiences, except that they had been chosen by a kindly fate to act out the dream of happiness through material abundance.

> "I do want to assure you," writes the editor of one of the more elegant fan magazines to a worried reader, "that we do try conscientiously and constantly to give you these gallant people as they really are --living, experiencing human beings, who, underneath all their glitter and beauty, are very much like you and me." [5]

In compensation, these gallant ideal types also acted out their audiences' envious fantasies of suffering for rewards insufficiently earned. In David O. Selznick's 1937 version of A Star Is Born, benevolent studio head Adolphe Menjou tells Janet Gaynor, "You'll find out you have to pay for anything you really want, and usually with your heart." "The Price They Pay for Fame"[6] was the other side of Hollywood's fantastic currency. Exhaustion, divorce, alcoholism and, worst, the loss of fans' loyalty were as much part of its mythology as were its pleasures. Fostered by such dissenting novelists as John O'Hara and Budd Schulberg, The Price They Paid secured Hollywood as no more than a fantasy for its audience. It was safer to stay home and sample the Hollywood melodrama by proxy.

Hollywood's melodramatic fantasy compensated luxury with distress, and balanced the availability of its dreams against the mystery of their production. Its contradictions were its essence: a closed community of world-famous people, Hollywood could be taken for granted but not comprehended by those outside it. In The Last Tycoon, Cecilia Brady explains, "It can be understood ... but only dimly and in flashes."[7] She sees Hollywood as itself a movie, perceived in the flashes on the screen of a dimly-lit theatre. For Cecilia, who is "of the movies but not in them,"[8] the

Dream Factory is to be comprehended through its dreams, not as a factory.

It is a policy that has been pursued by fans and film critics alike, engaging in their differents ways with the individual products of the Hollywood system and, like Cecilia, taking that system for granted. Broadly, criticism has taken the line that Hollywood is to be read through its products, making no more than brief introductory acknowledgements that its objects of study were manufactured for commercial purposes, and concentrating almost exclusively on recovering the meanings of those objects. All too frequently the aesthetic or political nature of a film is discussed without reference to the commercial and industrial system which produced it, as if it had simply sprung, fully formed, into existence on the silver screen. Whether this critical activity describes itself as thematic criticism or textual deconstruction, its privileging of film over system, text over context, tells only half the story and actively encourages interpretations which reinforce Hollywood's projected self-image. Hollywood and its critics proclaim together that movies, like stars, are born and not made, and that the secrets of the womb are not to be delved into. The task of criticism, it seems, is psychology, not obstetrics, while the patient can be the film, its producers, its audience, or the society that nurtured it.

This critical practice is, I think, the result of a number of influences. Perhaps the most formative has been the desire to elevate films to the status of a bourgeois art form, comparable to painting or literature. From such motives critics have imposed models of the creative process derived from other media, and have offered, in the various versions of the auteur theory, an individualist interpretation of film production more appropriate to European habits of filmmaking than to the American industry. A second influence has been the novelty of film's aesthetics. "The Seventh Art"[9] has been theorized repeatedly, without conclusions--except, perhaps, that it is all too easy to write film theory. The issues are by now well-defined: the ambiguity of the film-audience relationship; the inconvenient semiological fact of the image's mimetic relation to external reality; the collaborative nature of film production and its resultant confusions of authorship and intention. In addressing these questions, film theory has all too often preferred the universalities of an analytical discourse foreign to the medium--whether it be the language of literary criticism or psychoanalysis--rather than attend to the specific problems of formulating terms by which the cinema, and the American cinema in particular, can be discussed as a social, economic, political and aesthetic institution.

The tendency to take film theory on detours through European metaphysics in search of a common critical language has been exacerbated by the mystifications practiced by filmmakers themselves. After her filmic image of cinematic understanding, Cecilia Brady continues, "Not half a dozen men have ever been able to keep the whole equation of pictures in their heads."[10] To comprehend Hollywood apparently requires a rare diversity of skills: "the whole equation of pictures" involves tax law and optics, marketing systems and costume design. If the task is well-nigh impossible for the filmmakers, who instead resort to a complex division of labor, how much more so is it for the critic, who must also take on board contemporary Marxism, linguistics, and Freud? No wonder, then, that students of popular culture anxious to defend their own activity against the established academic hierarchies of elite bourgeois art have chosen the convenient route of obscurantist theorizing. Like the Hollywood they criticize, they are insulated by their incomprehensibility, and discourse only among themselves. Hollywood has compounded this critical preference by making itself available for study mainly in the disreputable forms of anecdote and autobiography. Its publicists' enthusiasm for preserving "the magic of the movies" and the reluctance to open its archives for examination have reinforced critical preferences for attending predominantly to the fully-formed text. Academics unwilling to soil their hands with economics have elevated the inaccessibility of factual information into a critical discipline which disposes of the areas it finds most difficult. Confronted with John Ford's refusal to accept responsibility for the thematic consistencies in the films he directed, auteur-structuralists have invented the critical construct of "John Ford," who exists as "the shifting relations between antinomies"[11] in the films he directed, and who can be examined with no more than incidental biographical reference to John Ford the one-eyed Irishman who stood on sound stages telling actors what to do and argued with producers in story conferences.

I am not suggesting that such critical practices are mistaken, nor that the critical construct "John Ford" is a figure without value; indeed, I shall be using him myself. But he is an incomplete figure, and the creation of such figures has been a selective and somewhat arbitrary process in the history of film criticism. For example, "John Ford" can also be critically constructed as a matrix of compositional and lighting codes preferring slanting light, chiaroscuro and compositions along the diagonals of the frame. These perceptual practices are as "Fordian" as the antinomies of wilderness and garden, and, indeed, are probably more specific to films "signed" by John Ford than the thematic motifs. It is, however, much more difficult to ascribe a specific meaning to them, and this elusiveness has tended to confine discussion of them to the ghetto of incidental paragraphs beginning "Stylistically, ... "[12] Critics have recognized authorship overwhelmingly in the literary terms of a director's thematic consistency, producing an orthodox hierarchy of "texts" which has been adhered to even by those theorists who wish to revise authorship out of existence. [13]

This process of canonization is selective not only in the qualities it expects of its authors, but also in the figures it selects for its accolades. The final scene of The Grapes of Wrath provides an example. In summary of the film's thematic impetus, Ma Joad declares,

> "Rich fellas come up an' they die, an' their kids ain't no good, an' they die out. But we keep a-comin'. We're the people that live. They can't wipe us out. They can't lick us. We'll go on forever, Pa, 'cause we're the people. "[14]

Auteurists have often taken this speech as a concise articulation of Ford's populist beliefs. [15] Such a claim, of course, is perfectly viable if authorship is unproblematically assigned, a priori, to Ford, or, for that matter, to any of the other available candidates. The speech does have both a summary function and a concluding, optimistic message, and its sentimental populism is in keeping with the thematic content of other films directed by Ford. It is also in keeping with the thematic content of other films written by Nunnally Johnson, who revised and relocated the speech from an earlier part of Steinbeck's novel, giving it a significance as Ma's considered reflection that it does not have in the book. [16] Equally, the film's conclusion is both thematically and structurally in keeping with many of the "social consciousness" films produced by Darryl Zanuck. The Jeffersonian ideal of good will and the ethical centrality of work and family are consistent values in Fox films of the 1930s and 1940s, while the narrative device of ending with

an explicit thematic summary is one which Zanuck's films
have consistently employed. [17] Attributing the theme to Ford
on the basis of the completed film alone has no more inherent merit than attributing it to Johnson or Zanuck; certainly
the critical constructs "Nunnally Johnson" and "Darryl Zanuck" could be established, and the latter will recur throughout this book. An examination of the film's production history indicates that responsibility can be allocated more precisely.

Zanuck was responsible for buying the book for Fox
and for bringing the film into production, despite some reported opposition from the studio's financial controllers,
Chase National Bank. He assigned both Johnson and Ford
to the project, and supervised Johnson's adaptation, which
shifts attention away from the novel's concern with the disintegration of the Joad family. The film follows the published script[18] fairly closely, the only major expansion being the dance scene at the government camp, in which rec-
ognizably "Fordian" business is introduced. Deletions from
the script, including the reply to Tom's question, "What is
these reds?", seem more likely to have been made during
editing (at 129 minutes the film was still noticeably longer
than average) rather than shooting, since the omissions
leave plot details unresolved. Zanuck supervised the editing of the film, while Ford was apparently on vacation in
Honolulu, [19] and all sources agree that the idea for the
single accordion on the music track was his. There is
some dispute over who actually provided the ending. Ford
acquiesced in Bogdanovich's proposal that he wanted to end
the film with Tom walking up the hill, [20] while Gussow
claims Zanuck wrote the final scene himself, and that it
was filmed after Ford left the project. [21] Stempel's more
authoritative evidence seems conclusive in establishing that
Johnson actually wrote the scene, and that while Zanuck and
Ford were in some doubt as to which end to use, Johnson
was not. [22] However, such a significant decision would not
have been taken without Zanuck's approval, and the fact that
he was closely involved in editing the film, while the others
were not, makes it clear that the ending was Zanuck's preferred choice.

The available evidence, then, does not support the
"Fordian" claim, nor does it entirely endorse a straightforwardly collaborative interpretation of the emergence of
the film's thematic emphasis. The discussion was not
among equals. Clearly this was a sensitive project, heavily

criticized both before and after production, and Zanuck, of
necessity, maintained a close supervision over it. Rather
than seeing it as a collective enterprise, it would be more
accurate to propose that the controlling intelligence behind
the film was its producer's, inflected by the performances
of writer, director and, for that matter, cinematographer
Gregg Toland and the actors. The notion of inflection provides a less rigid means of establishing the relative weight-
ing of authority for both thematic and visual motifs within
the production system, without displacing the arbitrary but
obviously useful notion of the critically constructed creative
personality. It also serves to point out the anomaly within
auteurist criticism by which the men who in practice had
most influence over the films made in Hollywood--the studio
heads*--have hardly been examined as critical entities. The
moguls, who were most responsible for the mystification of
Hollywood, have to date mystified themselves out of the
critical arena.

        And yet, to understand Hollywood, we could do little
better than follow Cecilia Brady's advice "to try and understand one of those men" who kept the whole equation of pictures in their heads. Whether Russian immigrants or Ne-
braska Episcopalians, the moguls embodied the Horatio Alger
myth as fervently as Carnegie. In their success, they constructed an industry that at one time claimed to be the
fourth largest in America, and spread its products around
the world. No evidence of our failure to comprehend Hollywood can be clearer than the simple fact that we know very
little of what they did. Our knowledge of the studio heads
is clouded by the mists of publicists' hagiographies and
screenwriters' denunciatory anecdotes. Mayer, we know,
could cry on cue, Goldwyn could whip Mrs. Malaprop with
both hands tied behind her back, and Harry Cohn's ass was
the best judge of an over-length movie on the West Coast.
Beyond that, they were sentimental, ignorant, philistine,
"shrewd businessmen," brutal autocrats, crooks, overgrown
hucksters and insatiable despoilers of starlets. The extent
to which the moguls are still shrouded in a corrupt version

---

*"About six producers today pass upon 90% of the scripts
and cut and edit 90% of the pictures." Frank Capra, then
President of the Screen Directors' Guild, New York Times,
April 2, 1939. Quoted in Richard Glatzer and John Raeburn,
eds, Frank Capra: The Man and His Films, Ann Arbor,
1975, p. 15.

of their own mythology is indicative of how much Hollywood has been taken for granted and how little it has been taken seriously.

The central proposition in this book is straightforward: that the American cinema should be understood for what it is: primarily a commercial institution, engaged in manufacturing and selling a specific product in a capitalist market-place, and only incidentally a species of art, a political statement, a sociological document, a cultural product or an object of theoretical speculation. I do not dispute that the American cinema is all of those things, but I want to suggest that, before it can be treated as cultural history or sign system it must be comprehended as a commercial commodity. Only by acknowledging the explicit primary purpose of every act of cinematic production within Hollywood--to make money--can we properly place the subsidiary intentions or incidental consequences of any particular film.

"MOVIES ARE YOUR BEST ENTERTAINMENT"

(Industry promotional slogan of early 1950, hastily withdrawn when it was pointed out that its initials spelt M. A. Y. B. E.)

"What do you go for, go see a show for?"--lyrics to Dames[25]

... entertainment is a type of performance produced for profit, performed before a generalised audience (the "public"), by a trained, paid group who do nothing else but produce performances which have the sole (conscious) aim of providing pleasure.

Richard Dyer[26]

The American cinema was a commercial institution, and its films were commercial products. Any assessment of those products must acknowledge this economic fact of life, and not merely because Hollywood took an industrial attitude to its own activities. Film, by its very nature, proposes a symbiotic relationship between the commercial and the aesthetic. It exists simultaneously in two states. Materially, it is a roll of celluloid, wound onto a metal spool and stored in a tin can. In use, it is a progressive series of "moving pictures," evanescent shadow images projected onto a blank white screen. Unlike books or paintings, film undergoes a material transformation when it is viewed or experienced. This transformation is engineered by a combination of mechanical and optical processes needing complex projection equipment as well as a large space across which the magnified image is thrown. The economics of these material prerequisites forcibly encourage film to project itself before as large an audience as possible. The evolution of viewing apparatus, from the Kinetoscope and peepshow to the nickelodeon, picture palace and Cinerama, traces a history and an economic logic of larger pictures projected in front of larger audiences. The institution of the cinema is first of all a physical institution of the buildings in which it takes place.

In its inert, tin-can state, film is purely a trading commodity of no intrinsic value or use. As an economic entity it depends on its potential existence as a spectacle offering its consumers an aesthetic experience. It can only perform both its commercial and aesthetic functions when being exhibited to an audience. While showing a film need not involve a financial exchange between customer and exhibitor, the cost of projection, and for that matter of production, must be borne by someone. In capitalist practice, the consumers have conventionally paid for their experience, binding the material requirements for cinema's existence to a commercial system of exchange.

We might, however, consider what it is the spectator actually buys in the cinema. It is nothing tangible or permanent. Film offers the illusion of motion by projecting an uninterrupted flow of sequential images, and the temporal continuity of their projection is essential if the illusion is to be maintained. Each image has a place in this flow, but is of necessity only on temporary exhibition, replaced in a fraction of a second by the image that follows it. The temporary nature of the cinematic experience, which is a material condition of film's existence, again differentiates it from stable aesthetic forms such as books or paintings. The spectator does not actually buy anything in the sense that he

or she leaves the cinema with a material object at the end
of a screening. He or she merely rents a seat in the cinema for the duration of a performance, a process we might
call buying time. The aesthetic experience that has been
purchased ends with the expiry of the commercial transaction that has predicated it. You leave the cinema behind
you when you leave the movie theatre.

This transitoriness is a quality common to aesthetic
experiences commonly described as "entertainment"; for example, the circus, vaudeville, or playing a pinball machine.
It is, of course, an inevitable condition of any performing
art, since the act of performance itself is impermanent.
But it may also be seen as a determining condition of entertainment as a sub-species of leisure. Sociologically, leisure
can be approximately defined as a non-work activity that is
relatively self-determined; that is to say, leisure time is
segregated from time spent at work, and is occupied by activities undertaken voluntarily. Such a concept of leisure is
a product of an industrial society which segments work as
separate from other activities. 27 Within a capitalist economy, leisure time can be regarded as a possession, purchased through the expenditure of time at work. At the
same time, however, an industrial society turns the provision of leisure into a commercial activity, and what is
categorized as leisure for one section of the population becomes work for another: professional sports or the theatre,
for example. Leisure thus becomes an activity of consump-
tion--consumption of time if nothing else--and, in consequence, is attached to production.

> Leisure is therefore a type of activity which can
> be recognised through its dependence on commodi-
> ties, the audience is entertained through the ob-
> jects it chooses to possess. In the sense of con-
> spicuous consumption this process is easily recog-
> nised, it is less easy to grasp in relation to the
> complementary sense of "spending time. "28

In an economic system which treats time as a commodity (the eight-hour day, leisure-time, etc.), the buying
and selling of time are normal activities, constantly expressed in the economic metaphors of "spending time, "
"time-consuming" and so on. Nineteenth-century industrial-
ists regarded their labor force as simply a necessity for
production, but in the early twentieth century it was recognized that capitalism must put labor to work as consumers

as well. One mechanism of this process was to reduce working hours and increase leisure time. In 1926 Henry Ford argued, "It is the influence of leisure on consumption which makes the short day and the short week so necessary."[29] Terms such as Show Business and "the entertainment industry" make semantic associations between amusement and commercial activity and describe entertainment as a subject of economics. Historically the development of commercial mass entertainment--preeminently the cinema-- and consumer capitalism are closely related.

Hollywood's self-description as "the entertainment capital of the world," and its happy acceptance of its goal of producing "escapist entertainment," acknowledged that its function was to amuse and distract. The American cinema was, indeed, legally defined as both a business and entertainment by the Supreme Court in 1915,[30] which declared films not to be vehicles for ideas. For fifty years Hollywood acquiesced in this opinion of itself, and provided the primary example of an industrial system devoted to what Lasch describes as "the organisation of leisure as an extension of commodity production."[31] From its establishment as an industry (at the latest by 1922 with the founding of the MPPDA), the American cinema committed itself absolutely to the business of entertainment. Throughout the Classical Age of Hollywood (which lasted until the 1950s) the industry saw itself as manufacturing and merchandising a non-durable consumer commodity, which was the experience of "going to the movies," rather than the specific articles it produced. The picture palaces of the 1920s, the development during the 1930s of longer programs including newsreels, Screeno and other participant activities, indicate that what was being proffered by the cinema was a way of spending part of the "leisure dollar." Individual films were simply the principal manifestation of the mode in which it provided entertainment, but show business embraced such other forms of leisure as fan magazines, fashion and children's toys, as well as promoting consumerism and offering stars as celebrities for public consumption.

The debates over "Mass Culture" arose from the occupation, by commercial enterprises such as the cinema, of territory previously segregated from economics by its appellation as "Art." The cultural distinction between art and entertainment is far from precise: we may not know what entertainment is, but we recognize it when we see it. Its determining characteristics are negative: that which fails to

be art is entertainment, as is that which lacks a socially or
politically significant meaning. "Mere entertainment" is an
idea frequently implicit in the term's use, and its connotations are triviality, ephemerality, and an absence of seriousness. Unlike art, entertainment is not "about" something
outside itself, but is self-enclosed. Ernest Lindgren suggests entertainment is

> In the form of fiction, at least, ... the use of
> representation to create make-believe situations
> which are designed to arouse emotion for its own
> sake, and for the mere pleasure of having it
> aroused. It is not intended that the emotion shall
> be carried forward into the practical affairs of
> life. The emotion is both aroused (titillated is
> perhaps a better description) and satisfied within a
> self-contained framework. [32]

This self-contained quality, with its inevitable connotation of a lack of seriousness, is the most frequent charge
by which entertainment is indicted. Even though their language and their political precepts are at odds, both the elitist critics of "Mass Culture" and the theorists of the Frank-
furt School argue the existence of what Dwight MacDonald
termed "Gresham's Law in Culture,"[33] in which mass entertainment drives out Art by mimicking and debasing its forms.
Mass culture, it is alleged,

> pre-digests art for the spectator and spares him
> effort, provides him with a short-cut to the pleas-
> ures of art that detours what is necessarily diffi-
> cult in genuine art. [34]

At the same time, it forces Art to compete on its vulgar
economic terms, or else encourages its ghettoization into an
Avant-Garde protected in one way or another from market
forces. For Adorno and Horkheimer, who saw this process
not simply as a matter of cultural debasement but as an
ideological instrument for repressing the difficult, subversive
qualities of art, the shallowness of entertainment reduced it
to a commodity of consumption which reinforced the exploitative pattern of bourgeois systems of production. "Amusement
under late capitalism is the prolongation of work."[35]

These analyses investigated the function of entertainment and, however they phrased it, generally agreed that
entertainment was an ideological commodity. But definitions

of entertainment have, in the main, tended to be affective rather than formal, and describing entertainment as that which is not art in a society which professes pluralism gets you nowhere. One man's meat is still another man's poison. As a function of leisure, entertainment is "deliverance from boredom." As a particular kind of leisure activity, however, entertainment must be defined by its specific formal features. Kaplan distinguishes between entertainment and Johann Huizinga's view of play by suggesting that play involves the subject actively, while entertainment is passive and controlled by others.37 Such a definition fails to elucidate distinctions that exist in ordinary usage about the relative cultural value of different forms of leisure.

Among the arts of performance, there is a broad, commonly assumed distinction between the performances of High Culture, consisting in performances of musical or dramatic texts which exist independently of any production of them, and the performances of entertainment, in which the text does not have the status of a fixed referent but may be infinitely revised with cultural impunity. Clearly, this distinction between "official" and "unofficial" cultural forms can only be regarded as a tendency, and not as in any sense absolute. However, the sacredness of a "text" by Shakespeare or Tchaikovsky bears on any particular production of it in a way quite different from the responsiveness a stand-up comic brings to his performance of routines before any particular audience. Implicit in the contrast are distinctions related to the durability of the "text" and between two understandings of the concept of performance. Theatrical performance, in the Grand Tradition of the English theatre from Kean to Olivier, is essentially a matter of interpretation and convincing imitation. In discussing Olivier's Hamlet, there is an implicit assumption that "Hamlet" is a fixed entity, inscribed in the words on the pages of The Complete Works of William Shakespeare. In this sense, performance is primarily a matter of inflecting a given object. Kaplan illustrates both this point and the absence of a sociological distinction between entertainment and art when he says,

> The entertainer does respond to his audience, but fundamentally it is a one-way communication; no serious violinist would cut Bach's "Chaconne" in half because of a restless audience.38

The stand-up comic, on the other hand, is obliged to respond to his audience in exactly the way Kaplan suggests

the violinist does not.   To carry on regardless would be, in
the vernacular of vaudeville, to "die" before the audience.
We can, then, distinguish between two types of performance:
that of the actor, whose primary relationship is with a pre-
existing text, and that of the entertainer, whose primary
relationship is with the audience.   Where the actor performs
the text, what the entertainer does is to perform himself,
to enact himself as a fiction constructed in collaboration
with his audience.   The theatrical actor attempts to disguise
his presence in the act of performance, immersing his own
existence and the audience's suspended disbelief in the character he portrays rather than his portrayal of that character.
The entertainer, by contrast, asserts his presence in the act
of performance, constantly reminding his audience of his actuality, whether it be in the spectators' knowledge of the
tightrope walker's physical vulnerability (if she falls she will
break her neck) or in the comic's asides directly addressed
to his audience.   It is this latter sense of performance as
self-assertion that I shall employ from now on.

The cinema might seem to occupy an ambiguous position in this typology of performance.   It is in itself a fixed
text, which appears to deny it the flexibility of response possessed by audience-related performances, while at the same
time it does not provide the opportunity for variable interpretation provided by theatrical performance.   To clarify its
position, it will be necessary to examine the relationship the
cinema posits between a film and its audience.   Before doing
that, however, it is worth pointing out that two conditions of
entertainment are particularly appropriate to the material
form of film.   First is the idea of transitoriness, which is
implicit in the ephemeral nature of the cinematic image.
The other is the proposition that entertainment is self-
contained: "going to the movies" is an event, marked off
from other activities by a sustained set of segregations.   It
takes place in a separate building, which conventionally has
this exclusive function and a unique architecture.   Its accommodation and lighting are arranged to reduce extraneous sensory perception to a minimum, while the film itself is formally isolated by the strong caesuras of the house lights going down at the beginning and coming up at the end, and the
internal device of its opening and closing credits.   This experience was, of course, intensified by the grandiose decor
of the picture palaces, which impressed even more forcefully
on audiences the sensation of being in another world, but the
formal devices that insulate the spectator are the same in
any cinema.   However well-worn the metaphor of the Dream

Factory may be, the dreaming state remains the most evocative analogy to the cinematic experience, suggesting as it does the contradictory position of the spectator as participant witness to a fantasy not under his or her control.[39] What is perhaps most important about the familiar cinematic sensation of being awake in the dark is the way that it is separated off from other activities, protecting both itself and its spectators for a while from the world outside. This separation, which V. F. Perkins describes as a "public privacy,"[40] constitutes it as a self-contained event, formally immune to and removed from events outside the cinema.

David Chaney suggests that

> There is a recurrent paradox that as metropolitan provision swamps regional variation, so that we seem to live more in a world of shared forms, there is an increasing emphasis upon retreating from public civility to private individual experience.[41]

The formal arrangements of the cinema serve to insulate the audience from each other at the same time that they expose them to an identical apparition. When compared to the audience's experience of theatre, these arrangements precisely chart Chaney's paradoxical movements towards shared forms and private experience. Television, of course, extends both movements even further.

THE CINEMATIC CONTRACT

> "The Cinema exists in the distance between the audience and the screen."
> Jean-Luc Godard

Recent critical theories of film, developed out of the rarified atmosphere of Marxist semiotics and Lacanian psychoanalysis, have proposed a model of the cinema that locates the spectator as an essentially passive figure acted on by the film. The individual subject (the spectator) is deprived of his or her centrality by a theoretical assertion that he or she is constituted in a prior existing system, which may be identified as "a linguistic system,"[42] "the imaginary,"[43] or "ideology."[44] The integration of these theoretical discourses by their originators and disciples suggests that we can take these various terms to apply to different aspects of "the system of ideas and representations which dominate the mind of a man or a social group."[45] The individual subject, deprived of such false bourgeois attributes as free will by his or her restriction within a system of language which determines his or her consciousness, is seen as a receptacle for the various manifestations of this pre-existent and determinist system. The correlative of such a theoretical construction is that the primary object of study is seen to be the language system rather than any particular language event. Despite its immense complexities as a theoretical and analystical discourse, such an approach to the cinematic experience seems to be somewhat simplistic, reducing the audience to a passive amalgam of individuated but not individual receivers of pre-determined messages.

This approach has two weaknesses, which ultimately derive from its origin as a theoretical systemic model. Firstly, it discards Chaney's paradoxical relationship between shared form and private experience by describing the form as a system and singularizing the audience into separate spectators, to whom the system is applied. This singularization is the exact reverse of the cinema's optical process. The camera records a field of vision from a singular point of view, which is itself spatially contiguous to the space it records. In projection, however, the camera's point of view is abstracted from its original spatial context and universalized for the audience, who, wherever they are sitting in the cinema, see the field of view from the same, by now abstracted, point of view. By this process of spatial abstraction and universalization the camera/projector does not so much constitute the spectator as its subject as indicate the difference between perception inside and outside the camera. The single perspective is pluralized by its presentation to a plural audience.

> Unmistakably, reproduction as offered by picture magazines and newsreels differs from the image seen by the unarmed eye. Uniqueness and permanence are as closely linked in the latter as are transitoriness and reproducability in the former.[47]

In the third quarter of the seventeenth century, Samuel van Hoogstraten, a Dutch painter and theorist of perspec-

tive, constructed a peepshow in which the spectator, looking
through a hole in the side of the box, would see a three-
dimensional view of the interior of a room. The painting,
on five of the interior surfaces of the box, presents its illusion of monocular perspective only from the point at which
the peephole is cut, and the box is designed so that it can
be viewed from that point alone.[48] Such an artefact, perhaps the archetypal product of the optics of bourgeois individualism, can precisely be said to constitute the viewer as
its subject, since it obliges the spectator to adopt a precise
geographical position in relation to the image. The cinema,
on the other hand, does the very opposite in the way it establishes the spectator's spatial relationship to the screen.
The camera records the scene before it from a unique optical position, which the projector then pluralizes and makes
equally available to every spectator in the theatre. This
pluralization of the image in part accounts for the experien-
tial differences between cinema and theatre, and also emphasizes the distinction between the spectator's perceptions within the cinema and those he or she experiences outside it.
The result is to mark a distinction between the fiction of the
image and the corporeal, material reality of the spectator,
which, Walter Benjamin suggests, "permits the audience to
take the position of the critic, without experiencing any personal contact with the actor."[49]

One example of this distinction is an audience's reaction to point-of-view shots taken through car windshields in
chase sequences, or the switchback ride sequence in This Is
Cinerama. The audience will react physically to such
scenes, jumping up and down in their seats as the car hits
bumps. But at the same time that they are most obviously
viscerally associating with the image before them, the spectators are most concretely aware that they are watching an
illusion. The motion might make them sick, but they do not
think themselves in danger of falling off the rollercoaster.
Chaney describes this "feature of the spectacle" as fulfilling
the audience's "desire for vicarious authenticity," and providing "an opportunity for a member of the audience to participate in and yet be distanced from someone risking his
life crossing the Niagara Falls, an organization spending
many millions of pounds, and Christians actually being eaten
by lions."[50] It is not a matter so much of the camera/
projector's imposing a point-of-view on the audience as a
question of their adopting the camera's perspective. The
distinction is between a diktat and a voluntary agreement,
but the distinction is essential. If the individual spectator

is irredeemably fixed in position by the image, then the possibilities of his or her relation to its signification are at best limited to what Stuart Hall describes as "preferred," "negotiated" or "subversive" decodings or readings.[51] If, on the other hand, the audience's role of participant witness is a voluntary one, then their relationship with the image is open to much wider, polyvalent, interpretations. I am suggesting that such polyvalence is implicit in the pluralized nature of the cinematic image as presented to the audience, and that attempts to describe the cinema as constituting its subject misinterpret the nature of the exchange between the audience and the screen.*

To this description of the audience's relation to the image as polyvalent it might be objected that they in fact have no choice as to what they look at. The film pre-exists its audience in its selection and ordering of images. But in that selection and ordering, it also offers the audience a multiplicity of fictional perspectives. Within any sequence of the most conventional Hollywood fiction the camera may cut among half a dozen distinct spatial placements and provide as many different viewpoints on the events. The cut, for which there is no literary or linguistic equivalent, is an even more obvious instrument to distinguish between the process of cinematic and non-cinematic perception. Only in the cinema can we move our viewpoint without moving physically. The task of the spectator-- which is an active task, and a necessary one for even the most basic comprehension of film--is to correlate the separate visual viewpoints, comprehend their spatial relationship, and construct a fiction out of their juxtaposition. Those who propose that the cinema constitutes its subject are in a sense giving no more credit to the audience's capacity than the producers who objected to the introduction of the close-up because the spectators would be confused as to what had happened to the rest of the character. Rather than convert it into a determinist relationship between film cause and spectator effect, we should try to preserve the paradox that the camera's presentation encourages the view-

---

*It is worth noting that detailed analyses of the proposition that the film constitutes its audience subject have concentrated almost exclusively on the atypical visual rhetoric of the direct point-of-view shot.[52] Even from its own theoretical position, this approach has a great deal more of the image stream to account for than it has yet done.

er's participatory identification with the performances it presents at the same time that it demonstrably reveals itself as artificial. *

It might be more useful to offer a model of the film-audience relationship based on a model of contractual relations. There is, of course, a legal contract established between spectator and exhibitor by the sale of an admission ticket; that is why box offices display notices announcing that "the management reserves the right to...." The obligations under this contract are, however, limited: try demanding your money back on the grounds that you didn't like the film! However, the broader notion of a contractual relationship between film and audience serves first of all to make the point that the audience's commitment to the film is a voluntary one, particularly since they have already fulfilled their part of the contract by paying the price of admission before seeing the film. ** In one sense, the cinematic contract may be taken to be the arrangement by which the filmmakers consent to provide the sequential materials necessary for the construction of a fiction, and the spectator consents to undertake its construction, remaining free to determine significance wherever he or she may choose to locate it. David Bordwell and Kristin Thompson's distinction between plot and story may make the point clearer:

---

*Walter Benjamin concisely expresses the paradox of the camera: "In the studio the mechanical equipment has penetrated so deeply into reality that its pure aspect freed from the foreign substance of equipment is the result of a special procedure, namely the shooting by the specially adjusted camera and the mounting of the shot together with other similar ones. The equipment-free aspect of reality here has become the height of artifice; the sight of immediate reality has become an orchid in the land of technology."[53]

**We can distinguish two levels of performance participation (negotiation). The first is those social skills displayed in buying tickets, finding one's seat, observing the conventions of attention and applause and managing exiting. The second level is only analytically distinguishable from the first, but it relates to the development of identity involved in attending performances of a distinct style.... By patronizing a certain type of performance an individual is asserting a conception of self with distinctive aesthetic tastes and communal commitments. [55]

> The story, then, is a mental reconstruction we
> make of the events in their chronological order and
> in their presumed duration and frequency. The
> plot is the way in which these events are actually
> presented in the film. [54]

I will elaborate on this distinction and add other terms to it
later, but for the moment it is enough to observe that it is
obviously possible to construct a wide variety of stories from
one plot, simply by varying the emphasis placed on different
plot events. Anyone who has ever tried to tell someone else
the story of a film, or, even worse, tried to explain "what's
happened so far" to someone who has come in late, will know
what I mean. The process of constructing a fiction is formally retrospective: it requires a distance between the fictional events and the spectator who puts them to use. In
practice, the audience construct the fiction as they go along,
relying on their individual powers of memory and observation to locate the material the film provides them with in the
overall pattern of the fiction they construct.

Two things should by now be clear. First, the spectator is not a passive recipient of the film. He or she is
assigned a task which must be performed if he or she is to
elicit any meaning from it. The audience, then, have to
work at their entertainment; they have, in fact, to entertain
themselves from the material provided on the screen. *

The work involved may not be very hard, and a knowledgeable spectator performs it as unconsciously as he or she
might perform a simple task on a factory production line,
but the fact that the cinematic contract does provide the
spectator with a task to perform if the fiction of the film is
to be brought into being is empirically demonstrated every

------

*They may, for example, choose to do this in "deviant"
ways quite contrary to the filmmakers' expectations: the
Camp appreciation of B-movies is one example; the repeated viewings of cult films like The Rocky Horror Picture Show, in which audiences dress up as their favorite
characters in the film and recite the dialogue with them,
is another; tearing up cinema seats during screenings of
Rock Around the Clock is a third; and adolescent sexual
experimentation in the back row or the drive-in is obviously an extreme possibility in constructing your own entertainment in the cinema.

time a cinematic convention is ruptured and the spectator
has to negotiate a new spatial or character relationship. *

My second point is that an alternative description of
the audience's activity is to call it a process of performance.
Entertainment is not a system or a material object, it is an
activity. The product the American film industry sold in its
movie theatres was entertainment, but that commodity was a
process in which the audience was contractually obliged to
perform a function. Kaplan's distinction between play and
entertainment does not, in this analysis, hold. Applying my
earlier definition of performance as an act of self-assertion
the audience becomes not simply an active presence in the
process of cinematic articulation, but necessarily a self-
conscious presence. I shall argue later that the cinema of
the consensus (which to some extent coincides with what is
now commonly, if vaguely, called "the classical Hollywood
narrative") seeks to construct a mode of articulation in which
the self-conscious role of the audience is reduced to a minimum so that its cinematic fictions may be consumed with as
much ease and as little work as possible. To a degree this
makes my empirical interpretations of the effects of the consensual mode on fictional construction similar to the conclusions of the theorists I am criticizing. But there are, or at
least there seem to me to be, several crucial points of methodological difference, which reveal themselves in terminology.
I shall argue that the cinema of the consensus effectively restricts its products to a unilateral mode of communication,
in which the spectator is encouraged to construct the fiction
intended by the filmmakers because of the conventional arrangements of the fictional material. But I emphatically do
not accept that such a procedure is inherent in the cinematic
process, or within the Hollywood cinema. The Interludes on
Dissent exist precisely to make this point: that it was and

----

*Recent developments in the theory of motion perception
have invalidated the idea that the cinematic illusion results
from persistence of vision, and suggest that the spectator
is involved in a much more complex unconscious process.
"Just as film theorists have supplanted naive notions of
cinema as a simple copy of the world with an attempt to come
to grips with the medium as a system of representation and
signification, so too must the naive notions of persistence of
vision and of direct perception be replaced with an effort to
understand visual perception itself as a transformational and
representational process."[56]

is possible to make films that contest the assumptions of the consensus by questioning, breaking or exposing its conventional arrangements--and still remain within the Hollywood system.

My second point of disagreement with the systematizers is a discrepancy in the objects of our inquiry. I am much less concerned with the language system of cinema than I am with the language event; that is, with the film as experienced by its audience and as located in its specific historical and ideological context. I am unconvinced that the cinema is either a language or a language system because its production of meaning is both too mimetic and too connotative to be systematized. A science of connotations strikes me as an inherently contradictory proposition. I do not deny the value of a great deal of recent semiological analysis, and it will, I hope, be clear that my own methodological techniques have been influenced by formalist and structuralist approaches to film. But I am inclined to think that the study of the cinema is at the moment more in need of historical and textual research than it is of further theoretical speculation.

Finally, I disagree with the assumptions about ideological intention and effect in much recent theoretical writing. European presumptions about ideology cannot be imported unproblematically into the analysis of a culture which has so steadfastly refused to acknowledge their existence. Of course, American society can be subjected to class-based European modes of analysis, but in the process, some acknowledgment should be made of the fact that American institutions do not recognize themselves in these terms. The concept of a dominant ideology fits more readily into a society that consciously operates class divisions than it does in one which propounds its egalitarianism. America's Great Refusal of Marxism is a curious cultural fact the ramifications of which go far beyond the scope of this book. But while the English or French cinemas can clearly be seen to be operating class-based ideologies, I am less convinced that such assumptions can be readily recognized in Hollywood. Equally, the conventional structures of Hollywood which determine its unilateral mode of communication cannot automatically be regarded as hegemonic in purpose even if they achieve that effect. The evolution of the mechanisms of consensus cinema was not concerned with the establishment of an ideological hegemony or the imposition of a particular, ideologically conditioned perceptual system. It was rather a technological evolution geared to the production of more efficient entertainment. * Hollywood sought to minimize its audience's effort both because it was economically more effective for it to do so, and because that was what it presumed its audience wanted. Within the contractual framework I have proposed, there is good reason for thinking that it was correct in its presumption. The development of Hollywood's fictional conventions was a gradual process, conducted progressively in film after film, and took the form of an economic dialogue between filmmakers and audience at the box-office. Innovations in form or content were negotiated by their financial success or lack of it; a crude mechanism of consultation, no doubt, but a mechanism nevertheless. **

My proposition, then, is that while the American cinema of the consensus may have established itself as a hegemonic and unilateral system of communication, it did so not out of a conscious or unconscious desire to impose a dominant ideology on its audience, but with the active participation of that audience, which was also maintained through its products. If Hollywood films governed the perception of their audiences, they did so with "the consent of the governed. "

---

*In contrast to Europe, the private business sector in American history has been a more and more important factor in affecting activities, attitudes, and tastes for leisure ... education or quality are not primary goals of business. The leisure dimension of American life, inasmuch as a portion of it is dominated by goods or services provided for financial profit, is efficiently served instead of purposefully elevated. 57

**I am, of course, making certain assumptions about the legitimacy of capitalist procedures that many Marxist critics would dispute. This seems to me exactly the problem in much critical analysis of the American cinema. I do not seek to defend monopoly capitalism as an economic or ideological institution. I merely intend to acknowledge that that was the condition within which the American cinema operated. Any analysis of its products must place it within that condition rather than insisting against history that it ought to have operated under different conditions.

THE CANNING BUSINESS

> "After all, pictures are shipped
> out in cans. We're in the can-
> ning business. "
>
> Sammy Glick[58]

Having considered the responsibilities of the audience
under the cinematic contract, it is now time to examine the
obligations imposed on the product they consent to buy.
Joseph Breen, administrator of the Production Code, articulated the duties of Hollywood in a letter to Will Hays:
"There is ever present the obligation to entertain those who
pay the price for what they believe will be entertainment. "[59]
Breen's job was to ensure that Hollywood produced "entertainment which tends to improve the race, or at least to recreate and rebuild human beings exhausted with the realities
of life. "[60]

As well as this prescription, the movies were also
expected to contain a number of known or anticipated ingredients, which can be characterized in several ways. In fulfilling its "obligation to entertain" the Hollywood movie had,
like any other non-durable consumer product, to meet certain standards of quality. Predictable quality was indicated
by the same criteria as might be employed by a manufacturer
of canned food: the reputation of the producing company's
brand name (MGM, Warner Brothers), and the quality of the
product's ingredients (starring Cary Grant and Jean Arthur,
directed by Frank Capra, screenplay by Ben Hecht and
Charles MacArthur, based on the novel by Margaret Mitchell,
etc.). Commercially, film, like canned food, required that
its customers could anticipate enjoying it by contemplating
the mixture of known and reliable ingredients.

On the other hand, while one can's contents should
taste exactly like another's, a film needed to present at
least the illusion of being distinct from every other film.
Even the most formularized B-film entailed a separate act
of production and had to supply its spectator/consumers with
an element of novelty to keep them engaged in its consumption, as well as the predictable ingredients which would initially lure them to the cinema. Advertising slogans often
sought to make this joint appeal. "M. G. M. 's most lavish
production ever" traded on the studio's established reputation

for extravagance and suggested that new heights would be
reached.   Campaigns mounted around a star--along the lines
of "Bogart/Cagney/Brando as you've never seen him before!"
--offered the audience a novel experience from a familiar,
reliable source, an idea perhaps most concisely expressed
in the advertisements for Ninotchka, which simply announced,
"Garbo laughs. "

      According to legend, Brian Foy, "The Keeper of the
Bs" at Warner Brothers, kept a large pile of scripts permanently on his desk.   A completed film's script would go
to the bottom of the pile, and after it had worked its way up
to the top, it would be remade with a different cast, setting,
period, or alteration of other details.   Whether or not the
story is apocryphal (and Foy did once boast that he had made
the same film eleven times), 61 it illustrates an important aspect of Hollywood production techniques: the development of
archetypal structures through industrial pressures.   The
most common criticism of the American cinema, that it is
repetitive and formulaic, is in a sense an acknowledgment of
its effectiveness as a commodity, as well, of course, as being a tacit declaration in favor of a particular bourgeois individualist notion of art.   The operation of such archetypal
structures is most clearly visible in B-features because they
operated under the most stringent economic restrictions.   A
typical Republic budget of 1951, for one of its cheapest
"Jubilee" category of films with a total production cost of
$50, 000, shows an expenditure on story and script of $1, 800,
less than the cost of the unprocessed film to shoot the picture. 62   Operating within such tight financial limits, the cost
of developing new material was prohibitive.   It was cheaper
to keep a stable of contract writers to revamp familiar plot-
lines. 63   The pressure of a fixed budget exerted a similar
influence at all stages of production, encouraging the employment of stock companies and stock shots, existing sets and
pre-arranged lighting and camera set-ups.

      While most acute in B-features, such economic pres-
sures existed in all areas of Hollywood production.   The
system, as Harry Cohn explained to Robert Parrish, was
geared to volume production.

> Now, let me give you some facts of life.   I re-
> lease fifty-two pictures a year.   I make about
> forty and buy the rest.   Every Friday, the door
> of this studio opens and I spit a movie out onto
> Gower Street....   If that door opens and I spit

and nothing comes out, it means that a lot of people are out of work--drivers, distributors, exhibitors, projectionists, ushers, and a lot of other
pricks. [64]

Standardization was as much an economic necessity in film
production as in any other industrial process, and it appeared in the form of conventional or formulaic structures.
Warner Brothers, which prided itself on its cost efficiency,
was the studio most inclined to remakes. It produced, for
example, three versions of The Maltese Falcon in ten years.
Throughout Hollywood a standardization of budgeting, sched-
uling and casting (two stars per A-feature) was the norm.*

This standardization was the means by which predictable quality could be guaranteed to the audience. Its effect
was evident in the two most advertised mechanisms of its
operation, the film genre and the star system. Both functioned as practical and prior operating indexical systems upon
which the audience could base their consumption decisions. A
knowledgeable audience would have expectations of a film
starring Clark Gable or of a gangster movie, and would decide to go to it or not depending on their past response to
identifiably similar products. Although much less considered
either by audiences or, in the main, by subsequent criticism,
equivalent mechanisms operated within the film itself, to provide conventional patterns by which the audience decoded the
representation of plot, character, movement, space and time.
These various mechanisms, examined in more detail later,
formed a matrix of conventional structures within which a
fiction comprehensible to its audience could be constructed.
Although not immutably fixed, such fictive conventions provided the predominant source of predictability in a Hollywood
film, while the equally necessary element of novelty was
supplied by the particular story the film narrated.

The audience's principal activity in the cinema is the
construction/consumption of the story the film is telling.

*Jeanne Thomas Allen argues that "Standardisation is pri-
marily the outcome of the interchangeability of parts made
possible by the development of precision tools to replicate
identical component systems," and suggests that it might be
possible to extend this notion beyond its application to technological development into "the standardisation of film products for marketing efficiency." [65]

That this is so can be empirically demonstrated by looking at the volume of film criticism that concerns itself only with examining story and theme, as easily as it can be done by asking an audience what the film they have just seen is "about." (Not many people will tell you that it's "about" the dialectical relationship between sound and image track, although every film is "about" that.) This is partly the result of the functional system of film production: the story is the simplest and cheapest ingredient to change and therefore the cheapest form of novelty. Partly, it is simply a matter of societal habit: the ritual consumption of particular, frequently repeated stories is an activity largely reserved for children. The elderly woman who went to <u>The Sound of Music</u> more than 200 times was regarded as such a freak phenomenon that the cinema she patronized took her out of the economic system by giving her a free pass! While the movies clearly do supply frequently repeated fictions describing the same social arenas and presenting the same moral/ideological conclusions, the details of their stories vary. The audience is always buying a new product. The primacy of the story as the object of consumption is also, however, guaranteed by the nature of the fictive conventions used to present it. The mechanisms of these conventions seek to efface themselves, allowing the audience to assume their operation without taking particular notice of them. Eyeline matching is one convention the audience is likely to take for granted, the iconography of a Western is another. The process by which conventions are assumed and disregarded concentrates the audience's attention on the story. It is, in the main, the superstructure of a film that we observe, while the continuity of its deep structures are taken for granted.

> "I hope you realize that you're making a perfect spectacle of yourself," Katharine Hepburn to Cary Grant in <u>Bringing Up Baby</u>.

If a binary opposition between novelty and predictability, the familiar and the original, can be proposed in the Hollywood product, an overlapping opposition, between narrative and the spectacle of performance, can also be argued for.* While the primary object of consumption is a film's

---

*In film and literary criticism, "narrative" tends to be used in two senses, corresponding to its adjectival and noun forms. Bordwell and Thompson define a narrative as "a   (cont.)

story, a second, and sometimes competing, source of audience pleasure is in witnessing spectacular events or the performances of favorite stars. The star system not only provided its audience with commodities other than films to consume, it also provided them with an alternative way to consume the films. The "star vehicle," as Frank McConnell
says, existed "primarily, if not solely, for displaying its
leading players in as many of their famous postures as possible."[67] Sneak preview questionnaires asked their audiences
to comment on the principal performances separately from
the story.[68] The audience's consumption of film as spectacle
was accepted by Hollywood's production and advertising alike,
as an alternative to engaging the narrative.

One source of pleasure in viewing The Oklahoma Kid
(Warner Bros., 1939) comes from following the story of Jim
Kincaid as he avenges his father's lynching and gets the
Girl--that is, in watching the interplay of character relationships within a developing narrative. An alternative
source of pleasure, in tension with that, is in witnessing
James Cagney performing himself in the unfamiliar iconography of the Western, something which constantly reminds
us of the presence of Cagney in the role, and distracts us
from Jim Kincaid. At times, Cagney takes over completely,
as in a scene, entirely without narrative purpose, where he
sings "Rockabye Baby" in Spanish to a Mexican infant we
never see again. The product on offer here is Cagney's
performance, rather than his functioning as a figure within
the narrative.

This tension between narrative and performance is a
constant, and perhaps determining, feature of the American
cinema. In its largest terms a consensual Hollywood fiction is engaged in both activities at the same time. It

---

chain of events in cause-effect relationship occurring in
time,"[66] which is straightforward enough and overlaps considerably (as the dictionary definition of the noun permits)
with story. As an adjective, however, narrative refers to
the activity of telling a story, rather than that which is told.
This ambiguity is inconvenient, and I shall try to keep my
use of the term to its second, adjectival, meaning. It
should then be clear that narrative refers to something distinct not only from "story," but also from "fiction," which
is a larger entity which will encompass both narrative and
performance structures.

performs its conventional articulations--of genre, star persona, space--in the process of narrating its story. They
are closely related by separable activities, and the audience
can selectively direct its attention towards either or both.
While consuming the story spectators may also admire (and
later imitate) the gestural codes of their favorite performers, or the other codes of spectacular performance that the
film offers, such as dress codes in fashion. The codes of
the film's performance, both internally (the conventions of
the film's construction) and externally (the film's references
outside itself to performance codes in the everyday world),
operate as a framework in which the act of narration can
take place. But the individual spectator may choose to concentrate his or her attention on the conventions themselves:
there is an inevitable sense of ritual in watching The Oklahoma Kid's operation of Western conventions, which is inextricably bound up with their effect on the narrative. It is
clear from very early on that the film will climax with Cagney shooting it out with Bogart; it is clear that Bogart will
be killed, and it is also clear that either Cagney or his
brother (Harvey Stephens), who are both in love with the
Girl (Rosemary Lane), must die to leave the way free for a
romantic resolution. It is not, however, clear which brother will be killed, since the various conventions at work conflict with each other. Cagney is quite used to giving up the
Girl to someone more respectable and dying at the end of
the picture (The Roaring Twenties, Angels with Dirty Faces),
but an outlaw hero can get away with more reprehensible
conduct than a gangster, since the frontier offers more possibility than the city for redemption by a good woman. The
spectator can be interested in how the story turns out, or
in how the film solves the problem of its conflicting conventions. Equally, he or she may view the individual image as
a unit of the story, concentrating on the narrative relationships between objects in the frame, or as a spectacle in itself, looking at the objects within the image as separable
elements. 69 Neither of these modes of audience behavior is
aberrant; both are sanctioned by the way the film is constructed, although different films will find different points of
balance. Ultimately the choice of emphasis, for film, audience and critic, is political, since to stress the performance
of a film is to signal its artificiality, while privileging its
narrative affirms its continuity and holistic nature.

Some generic conventions allow performance to interrupt or fracture narrative more readily than others; musicals and comedies, for example, expect the disruption of

their narrative progression by separable acts of performance
where epics contain their spectacle within the larger narrative framework. A particularly schematic distinction between narrative and performance takes place in the Warner
Bros. musicals of the early 1930s: 42nd Street (1933) and
Gold Diggers of 1933 divide rigidly into straightforward back-
stage narratives interrupted by separate musical spectacles
which, as Richard Dyer has pointed out, [70] operate different
conventions of spatial presentation. This explicit bifurcation
of space into separate areas for narrative and performance,
work and play, practiced as rigorously by Chaplin in Modern Times (1936) as by Busby Berkeley and his co-directors,
is not necessary for performance to be disruptive. Gene
Kelly's roller-skate dance in It's Always Fair Weather
(M. G. M. , 1955), for example, provides a transformation of
space by performance, rather than by the perceptual conventions through which it is depicted. Instead of being passively integrated into a narrative space as he has been in the
previous sequences, Kelly forcibly asserts himself against
it, insisting, by his movements, that the audience's comprehension of the space and the object relations within it be revised. He glides along the street singing to himself, una-
ware either of the peculiarity of his movement or of his being an object of attention for passers-by. His performance
of the song, essentially a private act shared with the film
audience, creates a safe performing space free from narrative pressures (he is at the time being pursued by three
thugs). Once Kelly becomes aware of his performance, he
celebrates the safety it provides by dancing on the skates,
drawing a crowd and even stopping the traffic, whereas his
narrative identity would insist that he try to be as incon-
spicuous as possible. As long as he is dancing, in an
arena made safe by his performance, he cannot be affected
by narrative forces: the three thugs will not find him.

Within the consensus, tradition performance, although
always available for consumption, is normally subordinated
to and contained by narrative. M. G. M. 's 1936 production
San Francisco provides a number of illustrations. Within
the framework of a linear narrative built around a triangu-
lar relationship involving Clark Gable, Jeanette MacDonald
and Jack Holt there are two kinds of suspending performances. MacDonald sings a number of songs and arias, presented as events within the narrative (by devices such as
intercutting between her singing, audience reaction, and one
or both of the men), which propose a narrative development
continuing at the same time as the performance, although

such developments are never in themselves sufficient to justify the songs' duration in the fiction. They supply a separate
kind of audience pleasure while remaining firmly placed within the narrative. The other performance is more disruptive
of the narrative, since, like the Berkeley numbers, it operates a different set of spatial codings. The spectacle of the
earthquake is introduced at a climactic moment of the plot:
MacDonald has just renounced Holt for Gable (establishing
this by performing a song), and Gable has rejected her. At
this level the earthquake has the conventional melodramatic
function of the external, natural manifestation of the characters' tempestuous emotions (more frequently signaled by a
thunderstorm). But the sequence of the earthquake itself is
performed in a manner stylistically quite at odds with the
rest of the film. The soft-focus quality of the narrative
image is exchanged for a hard-edged, sharp-focus clarity,
the previously exclusively eyeline-height camera level is replaced by extreme low and high angles and canted shots.
Objects, rather than people, occupy the frame, with a concentration on selected details, such as the detached wheel of
a crashed carriage, which is photographed spinning to the
ground in three shots. The editing tempo is radically increased. It is not simply a montage sequence, nor a performance of special effects, although it is, obviously, both
of those things. It is a sequence constructed along lines of
expressive articulation quite different from the rest of the
film, based on concepts of composition and rhythm, recognizable to the contemporary spectator as influenced by
Eisenstein, and in fact the work of Slavko Vorkapich. [71] In
much the same way as the other sequences I have mentioned,
this three-minute episode self-assertively marks itself off
from the rest of the film, and claims a separate existence
for itself within the fiction so long as it lasts. The end of
the earthquake produces a reassertion of the narrative, which
is then concerned with its own resolution as Gable searches
for MacDonald. The fiction, however, has not been unaffected by this sequence, and the presentation of spectacle
competes with the Gable-MacDonald narrative for fictive
centrality during the remaining fifteen minutes of the film--
to the extent that in occasional shots Gable, who is the narrative guide through the second earthquake and its aftermath,
is abandoned both by the soundtrack suppressing his dialogue
in favor of incidental figures (usually screaming), and by the
camera's retreating from its usual distance of medium or
full shots of him to a repeated placing of him as one among
several figures in a long shot.

There is, then, an inherent tension within Hollywood fictions between the activities of narrative and performance. Supplying a range of commodities from which the audience could, within limits, construct its own entertainment, the American cinema potentially allowed for a considerable diversity of political expression. That, in practice, it promulgated a consensual conservatism was the result not of its formal conventions so much as of its social function. But the containment of performance within narrative by most Hollywood film neither eliminated the possibilities for formal experimentation nor prevented the audience choosing the objects of its consumption within the fiction on offer. Those critics who argue that Hollywood film is essentially a realist narrative form conflate the dialectical relationship between narrative and performance into a unilateral emphasis on story, and restrict the polyvalent possibilities of the film-audience relationship. In terms of a political analysis, such a diagnosis assumes that ideology has a prior existence external to the film, whose operation of it can be seen as a hegemonic activity by the dominant bourgeoisie. If, against this, we see both film and audience as active,

> if we see representational force as deriving from the process of becoming, being made, rather than from our contemplation of an object of accomplishment, then this has major implications for the relevance of a vocabulary of communication. [72]

If we see the film as an enactment, rather than a container, of ideology, then the process of inscription becomes central to the comprehension of ideology within any given film/text. For the critic to presume the existence of an ideologically preconditioned perceptual system--whether derived from a literary or a psychoanalytic aesthetic--is to drastically restrict the possibilities for the act of inscription.

It is (as they say) beyond the scope of any single book to revise the critical treatment of the American cinema. In what follows I am not seeking to rewrite the history of Hollywood, although I hope that eventually more of the material needed for such a task will be made available, and that the anecdotal information on which so much of our present knowledge is based will be replaced by the primary sources other historians take for granted. Rather than a history, I am proposing a context and a method for such a history, and offering speculations as to what that history might be. These speculations seek to confront and examine

the self-sustaining mythologies of Hollywood, locate and
analyze them within a larger tradition of ideological assumptions, and suggest, in the Interludes on Dissent, the possible
areas available for reassessment and revision that the Hollywood system provided. Unlike much recent film criticism,
this book is offered as schematic rather than proscriptive,
and opportunist rather than exhaustive. In this respect, at
least, it seems to me to operate along similar lines to the
objects which it is examining.

REFERENCES

Part I Title-page note--quoted in David Pirie, ed., Anatomy
of the Movies (London, 1981), p. 40.

1. Eric Johnston, Annual Report to the Motion Picture
Association of America, March 25, 1946, p. 12.

2. Daniel Fuchs, quoted in Tom Dardis, Some Time in
the Sun (London, 1976), p. 1.

3. In Horace McCoy's I Should Have Stayed Home (1938)
Mona blames the suicide of her friend Dorothy on the
failure of her dreams of success in the movies. When
a photographer wants a photograph of the instrument of
death, Mona scatters fan magazines over the corpse.
In the 1930s, at least one unsuccessful actress attempted suicide by jumping off the Hollywood sign.

4. Lyrics of "Hooray for Hollywood," composed by Johnny
Mercer and Richard Whiting, in Hollywood Hotel (War-
ner Bros., 1937; prod. Sam Bischoff, dir. Busby
Berkeley).

5. Margaret E. Thorp, America at The Movies (London
1945), p. 54.

6. Marquis Busby, "The Price They Pay for Fame," in
Silver Screen (no date), reprinted in Martin Levin,
Hollywood and the Great Fan Magazines (New York,
1970), pp. 94-97.

7. F. Scott Fitzgerald, The Last Tycoon (Harmondsworth,
1974), pp. 5-6.

8. F. Scott Fitzgerald, letter to his publisher, September
25, 1939, in The Last Tycoon, p. 166.

9. V. F. Perkins, Film as Film (Harmondsworth, 1972), p. 11.

10. Fitzgerald, The Last Tycoon, p. 6.

11. Peter Wollen, Signs and Meaning in the Cinema (London, 1969), p. 102.

12. e. g. Peter Wollen (Lee Russell), "John Ford" New Left Review 29, reprinted in John Caughie, ed., Theories of Authorship (London, 1981), p. 106.

13. e. g. the editors of Cahiers du Cinéma chose to inaugurate their psychoanalytical re-reading of "classic" texts with Ford's Young Mr. Lincoln. Stephen Heath's article "Film and System: Terms of Analysis," in Screen, Vol. 16, No. 1, selects as its subject Welles' Touch of Evil.

14. Quoted in Warren French, Filmguide to The Grapes of Wrath (Bloomington, Indiana, 1973), p. 36.

15. e. g. Andrew Sarris, The John Ford Movie Mystery (London, 1976), p. 97; Jeffrey Richards, Visions of Yesterday (London, 1973), p. 275; Warren French, Filmguide to The Grapes of Wrath, p. 53. Janey Place, in "A Family in a Ford," Film Comment, Oct-Nov 1976, p. 54, sees it, rather improbably, in more Marxist terms.

16. Although Johnson claimed that Steinbeck told him he had considered ending the novel with those lines. See Tom Stempel, Screenwriter: The Life and Times of Nunnally Johnson (London and New York, 1980), p. 82.

17. I Am a Fugitive from a Chain Gang, Gentleman's Agreement, Viva Zapata! and Che! are four random examples. See Russell Campbell, "The Ideology of the Social Consciousness Movie," Quarterly Review of Film Studies, Winter 1978, pp. 49-71.

18. The script is published in John Gassner and Dudley Nichols, ed., 20 Best Film Plays (New York, 1943).

19. Mel Gussow, Zanuck: Don't Say Yes Until I Finish Talking (London, 1971), p. 92.

20. Peter Bogdanovich, John Ford (London, 1968), p. 78.

21. Gussow, Zanuck, p. 92.

22. Stempel, Screenwriter, p. 83.

23. See Russell Campbell, "The Ideology of the Social Consciousness Movie," pp. 52, 58; Stempel, Screenwriter, p. 84; French, Filmguide to The Grapes of Wrath, p. 61.

24. Fitzgerald, The Last Tycoon, p. 6.

25. Lyric to "Dames," composed by Al Dubin and Harry Warren, in Dames (Warner Bros., 1934; prod. Robert Lord, dir. Ray Enright and Busby Berkeley).

26. Richard Dyer, "Entertainment and Utopia," Movie 24, p. 2.

27. Kenneth Roberts, Contemporary Society and the Growth of Leisure (London and New York, 1978), Ch. 1.

28. David Chaney, Fictions and Ceremonies: Representations of Popular Experience (London, 1979), p. 98.

29. Henry Ford, quoted in Max Kaplan, Leisure: Theory and Policy (London, 1975), p. 4.

30. Mutual Film Corp v. Ohio, 236 US 230, 244-247. See Richard S. Randall, Censorship of the Movies (Madison, Wisconsin, 1968), pp. 18-19.

31. Christopher Lasch, The Culture of Narcissism (London, 1980), p. 217.

32. Ernest Lindgren, The Art of the Film (London, 1948), p. 180. Lindgren is summarizing ideas in R. G. Collingwood, The Principles of Art (London, 1938), pp. 57-72.

33. Dwight MacDonald, "A Theory of Mass Culture," Diogenes No. 3, Spring 1953. Reprinted in Bernard Rosenberg and David Manning White, eds., Mass Culture (New York, 1957), p. 61.

34. Clement Greenberg, "Avant-Garde and Kitsch," in Rosenberg and White, Mass Culture, p. 105.

35. T. W. Adorno and M. Horkheimer, "The Culture Industry: Enlightenment as Mass Deception," in Dialectic of Enlightenment (London, 1973). Reprinted in James Curran, Michael Gurevitch and Janet Woolacott, eds., Mass Communication and Society (London, 1977), p. 361.

36. Max Kaplan, Leisure: Theory and Policy, p. 45. Kaplan is quoting Joffre Dumazedier, Towards a Society of Leisure (New York, 1967), pp. 16-17.

37. Kaplan, p. 152.

38. Kaplan, p. 309.

39. See V. F. Perkins, Film as Film (Harmondsworth, 1972), Ch. 7.

40. Perkins, p. 134.

41. Chaney, Fictions and Ceremonies, p. 58.

42. Roland Barthes, Mythologies (London, 1973), p. 115.

43. Daniel Dayan, "The Tutor Code of Classical Cinema," Film Quarterly, Vol. 28, No. 1. Reprinted in Bill Nichols, ed., Movies and Methods, (Berkeley and Los Angeles, 1976), p. 442.

44. Louis Althusser, "Ideology and Ideological State Apparatuses (Notes Towards an Investigation)," in Lenin and Philosophy and Other Essays (London, 1971), p. 149.

45. Althusser, p. 149.

46. See Christian Metz, Film Language (New York, 1974); "The Imaginary Signifier," Screen, Vol. 14, No. 2; and Stephen Heath, "Film and System," Screen, Vol. 14, Nos. 1 and 2.

47. Walter Benjamin, "The Work of Art in the Age of Mechanical Reproduction," in Illuminations (London, 1973), p. 225.

48. Hoogstraten's "wonderlijke perspectifkas," as he described it, is on view in the National Gallery, London.

The date of its construction is uncertain: the earliest estimate is 1662, the latest 1678. Perspective boxes were probably first developed in Italy in the fifteenth century; some sixteenth-century examples survive, and peepshows similar to Hoogstraten's may well have been common in seventeenth-century Holland. See Neil Mac-Laren, The Dutch School (National Gallery Catalogue, London, 1960), pp. 192-195.

49. Benjamin, p. 230.

50. David Chaney, Fictions and Ceremonies, p. 130. Charles Barr describes the audience's physical reaction to sequences such as the Cinerama switchback ride as a "circus effect." Charles Barr, "Cinemascope: Before and After," Film Quarterly, Vol. 16, no. 4. Reprinted in Gerald Mast and Marshall Cohen, eds., Film Theory and Criticism: Introductory Readings (New York, 1974), p. 128.

51. Stuart Hall, "Culture, Media, and the Ideological Effect" in Curran, Gurevitch and Woolacott, eds., Mass Communications and Society, p. 344.

52. Daniel Dayan, "The Tutor Code of Classical Cinema," is a case in point; as is Raymond Bellour, "The Birds," Cahiers du Cinéma, no. 216, (Oct 1969). An alternative approach, which offers a rebuttal of the notion that the direct point-of-view shot is protypical of the relationship between audience and image, can be found in Nick Browne, "The Spectator in the Text: The Rhetoric of Stagecoach," Film Quarterly, Vol. 29, No. 2.

53. Walter Benjamin, Illuminations, p. 235.

54. David Bordwell and Kristin Thompson, Film Art: An Introduction (Reading, Massachusetts, 1979), p. 52.

55. David Chaney, Fictions and Ceremonies, p. 117.

56. Joseph and Barbara Anderson, "Motion Perception in Motion Pictures," in Teresa De Lauretis and Stephen Heath, eds., The Cinematic Apparatus (London, 1980), p. 93.

57. Max Kaplan, Leisure: Theory and Policy, p. 264.

58. Budd Schulberg, What Makes Sammy Run? (Harmonds-worth, 1978), p. 223.

59. Joseph Breen, letter to Will H. Hays, March 1, 1936. Quoted in Raymond Moley, The Hays Office (New York, 1945), p. 98.

60. Martin Quigley and Father Daniel Lord, S. J., "Reasons Supporting the Preamble of the Production Code of the Motion Picture Producers and Distributors of America, Inc." (1930). Reprinted in Garth Jowett, Film: The Democratic Art (Boston, 1976), p. 471.

61. Roy Pickard, The Hollywood Studios (London, 1978), p. 194.

62. Charles Flynn and Todd McCarthy, "The Economic Imperative: Why Was the B Movie Necessary?" in Todd McCarthy and Charles Flynn, eds., Kings of the Bs (New York, 1975), p. 26.

63. Nathanael West and Horace McCoy were employed in this kind of activity by Republic in the 1930s. See Tom Dardis, Some Time in the Sun, pp. 167-169.

64. Robert Parrish, Growing Up in Hollywood (London, 1976), p. 187.

65. Jeanne Thomas Allen, "The Industrial Context of Film Technology: Standardisation and Patents," in De Lauretis and Heath, eds., The Cinematic Apparatus, pp. 29, 32.

66. Bordwell and Thompson, Film Art: An Introduction, p. 50.

67. Frank D. McConnell, The Spoken Seen: Film and the Romantic Imagination (Baltimore, 1975), p. 171.

68. See Christopher Finch and Linda Rosenkrantz, Gone Hollywood (London, 1979), p. 343.

69. "The revelation of what the cinema of the future can be came to me one day; I retain an exact memory of it, of the commotion that I experienced when I observed, in a flash, the magnificence there was in the relationship of a piece of black clothing to the grey wall of an

inn. From that moment I paid no more attention to the martyrdom of the poor woman who was condemned, in order to save her husband from dishonour, to give herself to the lascivious banker who had previously murdered her mother and debauched her child." Elie Faure, The Art of Cineplastics (Boston, 1923). Reprinted in part in Daniel Talbot, ed., Film: An Anthology (Berkeley, 1969), p. 6.

70. Richard Dyer, "Entertainment and Utopia," Movie 24, pp. 8-9.

71. See Slavko Vorkapich, "Cinematics: Some Principles Underlying Effective Cinematography," in Hal Hall, ed., Cinematographic Annual (Hollywood, 1930). Reprinted in Richard Koszarski, Hollywood Directors 1914-1940 (New York, 1976), pp. 253-259.

72. David Chaney, Fictions and Ceremonies, p. 68.

CHAPTER 2

THE BUSINESS OF FANTASY

THE CONDITION OF CRISIS

> "Film Biz Dips to Only Ter-
> rific," from Used-To-Be
> "Sensational"   Variety[1]

One of Hollywood's most persistent myths was that it
was always in crisis. "Crisis," producer Maurice Bergman
declared, "is the backbone of Our Industry"

> Existing as we do on the people's hopes and mak-
> ing films evocative of these hopes, we just can't
> let a crisis affect our creative efforts. We have
> to function in our own atmosphere of crisis. Bet-
> ting $400,000,000 or so a year that the pictures
> will please is what we term a crisis ab initio. [2]

Gambling, of course, is a much more predictable economic
activity if you happen to own the casino. Hollywood's melodramas of financial crisis, however real they may have been
to their participants, were an economic fiction. From its
beginnings until the late 1940s the American film industry
was a consistently profitable enterprise, securing around one
per cent of total personal consumption expenditure, and taking in more than 80 per cent of all money spent on spectator amusement. [3] Cinemagoing was a regular social activity
with predictable earnings. The film industry's task was to
supply the product that would sustain the moviegoing habit,
and to allocate the financial returns from this activity among
its various branches. Investing in a large motion picture
company involved in production, distribution and exhibition
was a safe enough thing to do with your money. Putting
cash into a particular production, on the other hand, was a
great deal more risky.

As an economic activity, film production is analogous to ship-building. Both produce very expensive single articles requiring individual design, large investments in plant and material, and the employment of a wide variety of different craft skills in their manufacture. However, film merchandising bears no resemblance to the selling of a finished individual ship to a customer who will have ordered the vessel to his specification. Rather, films are marketed as low-cost consumer goods, aimed at a wide audience, seen once and then discarded by the individual consumer. Since consumer approval of each article could not be guaranteed, this distinction between production and merchandising methods ensured that the production of any particular film would always be regarded as a high-risk activity, however stable the overall market was. The ever-present possibility of failure provided a strong impetus to Hollywood's maintenance of a perpetual state of crisis. It also provided an incentive for the industry as a whole to develop mechanisms for stabilizing what was assumed to be an inherently unstable enterprise--to make costs, receipts and profits as predictable as possible in an industry which assumed that the tastes of its audience were beyond prediction.

By the late 1920s the industry had assumed the shape it would maintain for the next twenty years. It was dominated by five major companies which produced and distributed films, and exhibited them in their own theatres. This system of vertical integration had been pioneered by Adolph Zukor at Paramount, and the 1920s saw Fox, Loews', First National and Universal establishing large theatre chains to complement their production and distribution systems. The enormous capital expansion of these companies was funded by some of the largest investment houses and financial institutions on Wall Street, partly because of the proven profitability of the industry, and partly because the heavy capital investment in real estate stabilized the companies' activities. After a series of mergers and take-overs, four organizations, Loews', Paramount, Fox and Warners, emerged to dominate the market. In 1928 they were joined by RKO, an enterprise owned by RCA and assembled to challenge the Western Electric monopoly in film sound systems. These companies--the Big Five--between them effectively controlled American film production, distribution and exhibition. The Crash and the early years of the Depression revealed that much of the investment in theatres and the conversion to sound had been over-optimistic, and resulted in several major companies declaring bankruptcy, while all of the Big Five except Warner Brothers relinquished financial control to their Wall Street investors, and ultimately to Morgan or Rockefeller interests. [4] But the upheavals of the early 1930s did not interrupt production or markedly alter the pattern in existence before the Crash. When, in 1935, the Fox theatre chain merged with the Twentieth Century production company, the Big Five assumed the final forms in which they would administer the American cinema.

The majors' decision, in the late 1930s, not to further expand their theatre holdings, amounted to a declaration that the system had achieved a formal completeness, secure from external disruption. The purpose of vertical integration was economic security: distributing and exhibiting its own products, each of the Big Five had guaranteed consumer outlets for its films. The existence of a block of five such companies gave them together an influence greater than merely control over what happened to their own product. Their ownership of the most important and prestigious theatres in the United States combined with their control, as distributors, of the bulk of the film product available gave them a monopoly power over the rest of the exhibition sector. Having dissolved the conventional distinctions between buyer and seller through their domination of production and exhibition, the major companies could manipulate the relative profitability of each sector, not merely for themselves but for the entire industry. Keeping the cost of production high and its profitability low, for example, was one means of maintaining their hegemony and preventing the development of competition.

Prior to 1948, the Big Five had effective control over exhibition in 95 per cent of American theatres. They actually owned only 17 per cent, but they had concentrated their ownership on key theatres, particularly first- and second-run houses in the major metropolitan centers. [5] Getting the newest films, and charging the highest prices, these theatres could expect to take at least 45 per cent of the total earnings of any film. [6] The Big Five controlled the exhibition policies of 80 per cent of the first-run theatres in the country, and that control was the key to their monopoly strength. Not only did they dominate the most profitable sector of the exhibition market, but that dominance in itself gave them control over the exhibition policy of the rest. Exhibitors and audiences alike assumed that any good picture would have an initial release in a first-run theatre in New York or Los Angeles. A New York premiere was a newsworthy event, and a successful New York run would have a decisive effect on a film's bookings in early-run theatres in

other areas. On top of this, the majors had effectively divided the rest of the country into geographic areas as far as
their ownership or other direct control of exhibition outlets
was concerned, so that there was little overlapping of major
companies' theatres in any region. Their pooling arrangements over distribution consolidated their oligopoly position,
by making them mutually dependent for both product and outlets.

As exhibitors, the Big Five could grant or deny a
film the opportunity of commercial success, by allowing or
refusing it access to the most profitable sector of the market. As distributors, they controlled the availability of
product to those theatres they did not directly influence.
They used their market strength to impose a uniform system of classification on all the theatres with which they
dealt, grading them as first-run, second-run, and so on,
down to ninth- or tenth-run houses. This rating dictated
the order in which theatres could book films, and the rental they were charged for them. On occasion, it even governed the admission price they were required to charge the
public for a particular film. The system of classification
operated in combination with "clearance" arrangements
whereby a certain length of time had to elapse after the
showing of a film at a higher-run theatre before it could be
released to a lower-run house in the same area or "zone."

Along with classification, zoning and clearance the
distributors imposed two other practices on theatre opera-
tors. Block booking was a procedure whereby the exhibitor was offered a preselected block of between five and fifty
films, rather than being permitted to book films individually.
Normally block-booked pictures were bought "blind," without
the exhibitor having a chance to see them, or knowing more
about them than, at most, a skeletal plot outline and the
names of the stars. Both practices were arranged primarily for the convenience of the distributor, who could thereby
guarantee exhibition for all his studio product, regardless of
its individual quality. Small independent exhibitors had little opportunity to cancel or choose films within the block
and could not prevent distributors from including films of
dubious commercial quality in the package. The main purpose of much of the majors' low-budget production, indeed,
was to occupy exhibition time, foreclosing entry into the
market by independent distributors and maintaining their own
monopoly. [7] All these control mechanisms, ultimately sanctioned by the majors' monopoly power over distribution and

first-run exhibition, amounted to a means of standardizing
the post-production merchandising of the product, and of
maximizing the profitability of those sectors of the industry
most in the hands of the monopolists. The operation of
these mechanisms at the peak of their development in the
late 1930s and early 1940s ensured that seven Hollywood-
produced films out of ten would show a profit on exhibition
in the United States. [8]

PATTERNS OF INVESTMENT

> Of course, he talked all that
> double talk to Wall Street about
> how mysterious it was to make
> a picture.
> Fitzgerald, The Last Tycoon[9]

As a producer of consumables, the film industry was
differentiated from other manufacturers not only by the unique
properties of its product, but also by the pattern of its investment. Film production was extremely expensive in
terms of cost per unit, involving not only heavy capital expenditure in plant and facilities, but also a large outlay on
the individual costs of each film. Production, however,
was the least profitable of the three areas of merchandising.
RKO, financially the least stable of the Big Five, lost money
on its production and distribution branch in every year of its
operation except the war boom years of 1942-1946, and
1951. [10] While the other major companies did better, prior
to the Paramount decision none of them made more than half
of their pre-tax earnings from production, distribution and
related subsidiary activities such as music publishing. [11]
This meant that there was a significant imbalance in the relation between earnings and investment. At the time of the
Big Five's various executions of the divorcement decree,
only Warner Brothers had larger assets in exhibition than
in production-distribution. Taken together, the five companies had 57 per cent of their total capital investment in
production and distribution facilities, although these activities
produced only 40-45 per cent of their total profits. [12]

The relative imbalance in the profitability of the
various sectors can be indicated by looking at the profits

made by the smaller studios in comparison to those of the
Big Five. In the industry's most successful year, 1946,
Loews' Inc. made a profit of 17.9 per cent, Paramount's
profit was 39.2 per cent and the other three majors fell
between these figures. By comparison, Universal made a
profit of 4.6 per cent, Columbia of 3.5 per cent, Republic
of 4.5 per cent, and Monogram of 6.4 per cent.[13] Profitability was closely linked to theatre ownership, and the pick-
ings at the bottom end of the production market were slim.
In its best year, 1947, Monogram made an average profit on
its 29 productions of a mere $13,000,[14] and the slightness
of the margin for error on Poverty Row was graphically illustrated by the frequency with which the B studios changed
their names and their owners.

   The explanation of this imbalance in profitability was
that it served the monopoly interests of the majors to siphon
profits to those branches of the industry they dominated most
completely. Directing profits to early-run exhibition and,
relative to its costs, to distribution* reinforced their stran-
glehold on supply. Noncompetitive pricing policies among
the majors ensured their mutual cooperation in a stable system in which production was geared to and controlled by the
demands of the first-run exhibition market. Their control
over that market was almost absolute. In the 1943/4 season,
the eight major distributors received 94 per cent of total domestic rentals,[17] while the Paramount Findings revealed that
pooling and clearance arrangements over exhibition were so
efficient that

> There appears to have been little, if any, compe-
> tition among the five [theater-owning] defendants
> or any of them in 97 per cent of the towns and in
> respect to 95 per cent of the theatres in which they
> had an interest.[18]

   To maximize the profitability of the most secure sectors, production was made into an inconvenient economic
necessity rather than a profitable activity in its own right.
The New York-based distribution offices dictated the volume
of production to Hollywood to ensure that there was not a

---

*The operating costs of a nation-wide distribution system
were estimated to be between $80,000 and $125,000 per
week in 1945.[15] Total costs incurred in distribution
amounted to about 30 per cent of gross rentals.[16]

wasteful glut of movies to be rushed onto the market before previous films had achieved their maximum earnings.

The final bastion of the Big Five's oligopoly was the inflated cost of production itself. The fabled extravagances of film production were central to the myth of Hollywood the Dream Factory, but they also had the practical effect of restricting the number of companies which could afford to mount A-feature productions. The overwhelming bulk of "quality" films was produced by the five major companies: in his fourteen years with United Artists, Sam Goldwyn, the most prodigious of the independent A-feature producers, made 50 films, approximately the annual output of each of the Big Five. Only the majors were sufficiently heavily capitalized to be able to invest large sums in individual products: in 1949 Monogram, one of the most successful minor studios, had assets amounting to $7,000,000, while Loews' Inc. had assets worth $230,000,000, of which an estimated 63 per cent ($145,000,000) was in production-distribution. [19] The Big Five took the best films for themselves, and left the rest for the minor studios and the independents. With a few exceptions, the minors were obliged to concentrate their production on medium-budget productions and particularly on cheap B-features. Since B-pictures were rented for a fixed sum, they had a low but predictable earnings ceiling. In comparison to A-features, the return on investment in facilities and personnel was insufficient for the majors particularly to concern themselves with this bottom end of the market. Their lower-budget productions served to keep plant in full use and as a training and testing ground for new talent. *

Production costs were high in large part because the majors recognized that it was in their interests that this should be so. Approximately 50 per cent of film production costs was accounted for by salaries in the 1940s. [20] Hollywood's high salaries were usually explained as a means of

---

*Perhaps not surprisingly, it is these films, frequently representing the early work of subsequently established actors and directors, which constitute much of the B-film material currently readily available for study. Unsurprising but to a degree unfortunate, in that they represent the exception rather than the rule of B-feature production, and as a result, large areas of the Hollywood product are substantially closed off to detailed critical examination.

rewarding unique talent, but they also served other, more circuitous purposes. The incomes of stars, directors and particularly studio executives were a form of profit-sharing, diverting financial rewards from shareholders and investors into the hands of those responsible for profitable production. More significantly, by inflating the cost of film production, they reduced its profitability while ensuring that the personnel involved were well-rewarded. Keeping production both expensive and marginally profitable, the majors could discourage others from attempting to break their monopoly over the supply of films, which in turn guaranteed their profitable monopoly over distribution and exhibition. Hollywood's extravagance not only ensured its publicity, it also preserved the Big Five's oligopoly. This direction of profitability, with its consequent inhibitions on the scope for independent production, was a policy developed among the majors at the time they became involved with Wall Street, and amounted to a conservative preference for the financial stability of the oligopoly as a whole, rather than an entrepreneurial attempt to maximize profits.

Within the industry, there were two distinct forms of investment. The capital investment in theatres, in distribution networks and in studio facilities provided the Big Five and their owners with a strong incentive to long-term commercial stability, secured by millions of people regularly going to the movies. Investment in production, on the other hand, involved committing substantial proportions of a company's total assets to the manufacture of a very small number of products. The thinly capitalized B studios, which did not have the protective net of theatre ownership, frequently invested more than the amount of their total assets in annual production. Monogram, for example, spent $11.3 million on producing approximately 40 films in 1949, more than half as much again as the company's assets were worth.[21] The comparable figures for the majors were not so dramatic, since their assets included theatres, but they regularly invested as much as 25 per cent of their total assets in annual production. In 1949, for example, Twentieth Century-Fox produced 24 films at a cost of $28.5 million, which represented 25.6 per cent of its total assets, and 39.6 per cent of its assets in production and distribution.[22] The investment of such substantial proportions of a company's resources made them heavily dependent on a rapid turnover. Return on investment had to be rapid as well as fairly consistent. The dependence of production on a pattern of high short-term investment in a small number of products sustained belief in the enormous riskiness of film production, and perpetuated Hollywood's atmosphere of continual crisis. It also led inevitably to short-term accounting procedures, by which studios wrote films off their books after at most two years, regarding any further earnings as windfall profits.

Procedures of this kind, which were favorably regarded as conservative economic policies by Wall Street, [23] fixed production as an economic system in which very large sums of money chased small and frequently elusive profits. Protected by the more stable returns from the other sectors, the majors could tolerate the economics of the system they had created with more equanimity than companies that were solely dependent on income from production. Nevertheless that system fostered attitudes towards the industry as a whole that the majors, and particularly the studio executives, were more than content to perpetuate. Part of the glamorous attractiveness of Hollywood lay in its apparently inherent instability, and whatever else may have resulted from the majors' decision to keep production only marginally profitable, it served to divert public attention from the cartelized areas of the industry which provided its long-term stability and to concentrate it on the competitive insecurities of filmmaking. This process was facilitated by the geographical schism between production, based in Los Angeles, and the distribution and exhibition offices, headed by different personnel and centered on New York. The relatively consistent earnings of the East Coast activities were concealed behind the dramatically fluctuating fortunes of production. In the public eye, at least, the unpredictable economics of Hollywood production were mirrored by even more drastic variations in individual rewards. Mae West, for example, earned $326,000 in one year, and could not get a studio contract the next. [24]

This pervasive atmosphere of insecurity was not inherent in film production, and certainly did not accurately reflect the economic situation of the major companies. Concentrating attention on the short-term economics of production was a strategy employed by the majors to divert attention from their oligopolistic practices. It did, however, have a number of significant side-effects that markedly affected the balance of power within the industry and its attitude toward the way in which it created its products.

THE SEAT OF HARRY COHN'S PANTS

The industry as a whole needed the stability of predictable box-office earnings to guarantee the production and
advertising pattern of large-scale short-term investment.
This was a division of interests which corresponded to the
requirements for novelty and predictability of the films themselves. Movie economics resembled those of the fashion industry in their dependence on stable consumption of a product which was constantly being modified, and in their ambiguously determining and dependent relationship with audience
"taste." Many of Hollywood's moguls had worked in clothing
trades early in their careers and may have acquired the particular skills which entrepreneurial success in both industries
required: in particular, "the ability to suspend one's own
tastes and calculate the desires of others. "25

The promotion of fashion as a mechanism for the
superficial alteration of a fundamentally consistent product
was as important to the workings of the film industry as it
was to the garment business, because it attached unnatural
limits to the durability of the product in question. Films,
like clothes, went out of fashion before they were worn out.
This imposed an attitude towards the product on the part of
the producers that influenced their manner of distribution.
The felt need to be fashionable reinforced the notion of the
product having a short commercial life, and being worthless
after expiry. Fashion had to be latched on to quickly; producers, like dress designers, had to stay one step ahead of
public taste, anticipating it by at least a year in order to
have product ready for the market.

The studio heads' claim to control over production
was in part based on the assertion that they had unique intuitive abilities to gauge and predict audience reaction to the
individual films their companies produced. In their interven-
tions over story development, characterization, casting or
costume design, all the moguls insisted on their mediating
role as arbiters of the Common Taste, though few were as
terse in expressing their peculiar gift for judgment as Harry
Cohn:

> When I'm alone in the projection room, I have a
> foolproof device for judging whether a picture is
> good or bad. If my fanny squirms, it's bad. If

> my fanny doesn't squirm, it's good. It's as sim-
> ple as that. 26

The claim to insight, whether exercised in Cohn's manner of
demanding nineteen minutes cut from a completed print because his fanny started to squirm nineteen minutes from the
film's end, or in the extensive and detailed control over productions maintained by Thalberg or Selznick, was a crucial
element in the moguls' power over their employees. It provided a rationale one step short of naked authoritarianism
for their intervention in creative matters, and served as a
constant reminder to writers and directors that their objective was to produce profitable entertainment, not art.

The moguls' claimed abilities to predict audience
taste were also central to their relationship with their financial overlords in New York. It amounted to a justification
of autonomy for production, by providing a further mechanism for stability. Industry economics dictated that films
should be designed to appeal to the widest possible audience
as the most reliable guarantor of profitability. The mythology of Hollywood constructed by the moguls insisted that
audience taste was inherently unpredictable and that, as a
result, film could not be subject to simple financial expedients. Film production did not require conventional accounting abilities so much as a capacity to manage the irrational
and the unpredictable, skills to which the moguls laid an exclusive claim. Rather than encouraging programs of audience
research which might undermine their claims the studio heads
promoted their own image as predictors of the public taste as
a means of securing their independence from East Coast financial pressure. The effectiveness of this strategy, and the
extent to which it was endorsed by their parent companies,
was confirmed by the enormous salaries the studio executives
were paid.

The moguls made themselves the men who gave the
public what the public wanted. What the public wanted was
in large part revealed by what they went to see, but the
studio heads secured for themselves the vital position of
determining what it was about any successful film that had
appealed to audiences, and that could therefore be capitalized upon in later productions. The moguls' mediating role
was, therefore, not only between their companies' creative
employees and New York executives, but also between audience reaction and subsequent product. Their attitudes per-
meated everything Hollywood produced, and those attitudes

were chiefly influenced by a commitment to short-term profitability which geared production to the repetition of successful ingredients via generic formulae and the star system, and
by an equal commitment to the ideal of "harmless entertainment" which structured the expression of ideology in the
American cinema.

Hollywood's existence as a major industry, and its
need for long-term economic stability to provide a secure
base for its short-term financial adventurism encouraged its
acceptance of the existing status quo.   The moguls defined
their activity as responding to audience tastes rather than
formulating them, and hence saw their product as reactive,
not innovative.   This essentially conservative definition of
the cinema's ideological function allowed films to reflect
changes in social and political attitudes by fitting them in as
topical, novel elements in basically stable patterns.   A new
idea introduced as a superficial variation on an established
theme or plot structure no more disturbed the overall ideology of the combined studio product than a new star disturbed the mechanisms of the star system.   A superficial
and topical radicalism was always permissible if it could be
bracketed into a stable and already comprehensible narrative
structure.   The attitude was neatly summarized by Darryl F.
Zanuck, head of production at Twentieth Century-Fox, in a
memo of May 1940 to Ernest Pascal, a writer working on
the script of How Green Was My Valley:

> This is a revolutionary type of story; therefore,
> our treatment should not be revolutionary.   Now
> it fumbles around and I get the impression that we
> are trying to do an English Grapes of Wrath and
> prove that the mineowners were very mean and
> that the laborers finally won out over them.   All
> this might be fine if it were happening today, like
> Grapes of Wrath, but this is years ago and who
> gives a damn?   The smart thing to do is to try
> to keep all the rest in the background and focus
> mainly on the human story as seen through Huw's
> eyes. 27

The conservatism of this attitude blended perfectly
with the entertainment ethic, to which the studio heads adhered until, at the earliest, 1940.   Under the questioning of
their political impartiality by the 1941 Nye-Clark Senatorial
Investigating Committee, a few members of the Hollywood
community, including Zanuck, proposed a defense of such

cinematic social comment as there has been by arguing that
the cinema's social responsibility obliged it consciously to
enter contemporary political debates.   But, among senior
studio personnel, this opinion was held only by a small minority, and its influence over production was slight, even
for Zanuck, who managed without difficulty to combine it
with a wholehearted endorsement of the entertainment ethic:

> If you have something worth while to say, dress it
> in the glittering robes of entertainment and you
> will find a ready market ... without entertainment
> no propaganda film is worth a dime. 28

Zanuck did not question the extent to which making a political statement correspond to the requirements of entertainment as understood by the studio formulae might distort its
message, any more than the question bothered him during
the supervision of The Grapes of Wrath and How Green Was
My Valley:

> In The Grapes of Wrath we had to make a very
> vital decision ... whether to tell the story of the
> Okies as a whole or the story of one isolated fam-
> ily.   This meant the elimination of the flood ...
> the elimination of the fights with the police ... the
> dropping of certain characters very important in
> the book and writing an entirely new last act....
> When I think what I got away with [on How Green
> Was My Valley] ... and won the Academy Award
> with the picture, it really is astonishing.   Not
> only did we drop five or six characters but we
> eliminated the most controversial element in the
> book, which was the labor and capital battle in
> connection with the strike. 29

In both cases, Zanuck was effectively taking potentially controversial material and rendering it safe by placing it
within an established context for a socially conservative Hollywood narrative.   Both films endorsed the stabilizing influence of the family as a cohesive unit, and presented the
tragic element of their stories as being the fragmentation of
the family, without digressing into a consideration of the
underlying causes of that fragmentation.   While Zanuck did
not strip the films completely of a political context, he
nevertheless drastically altered their political implications
by fitting them into a narrative that depicted "nice people
involved in heartbreak, "30 defusing their radical potential.

This was less the deliberate imposition of a conservative viewpoint than ideological censorship by default. The Grapes of Wrath was nevertheless sufficiently "political" to earn the condemnation of Martin Quigley, the influential editor of the Motion Picture Herald and co-author of the 1930 Production Code. While Zanuck argued that the movies could educate through pleasure, Quigley firmly maintained the extreme conservative version of the entertainment ethic: "The entertainment motion picture is no place for social, political and economic argument."[31]

The entertainment ethic provided for social and political conservatism in two ways. Firstly, it proscribed an area of human activity, going to the movies, as being detached from political significance. Movies were, according to the accepted wisdom of their manufacturers, mere "harmless entertainment," at most influencing only fashion and such inconsequentialities as whether or not men wore undershirts. They might aspire to "Art" so long as it was defined along the narrow middle-brow lines of Goldwyn's adaptations of "the classics of literature." In discussing the Production Code, Joseph Breen maintained:

> Entertainment, then, is the keynote of the Code, in its practical application to the production of motion pictures.... With the artistic character of pictures the Production Code Administration is not seriously concerned. But it is concerned with the attempts to justify immoral themes and indecent scenes by the sophistry of the excuse of beauty.[32]

Similarly, the Legion of Decency did not concern itself with "art," but with "immorality," even if its definition of that term was rather broad.

But this definition of films as mere entertainment required that the range of human activities presented by the movies must be taken as devoid of any political consequence. In 1938 the Institute for Propaganda Analysis criticized common value-judgments in motion pictures:

1. That the successful culmination of a romance will solve most of the dilemmas of the hero and heroine.
2. Catch the criminal and you will solve the crime problem.
3. War and preparation for war are thrilling,

              heroic and glamorous.

4.   The good life is the acquisitive life, with its emphasis on luxury, fine homes and automobiles, evening dress, swank and suavity.[33]

What they objected to was what the industry and the majority of its critics regarded as the beneficent conventions of an escapist entertainment. Moreover, industry heads presupposed that such value-judgments accorded with the contemporary consensus. Their reactive cinema reinforced attitudes that were presumed already to exist, while also providing a mechanism by which these attitudes could be permitted to reflect upon topical issues or subjects of debate.

    Secondly, the entertainment ethic, bolstered by the economic necessity the studio heads saw in appealing to the mass audience, encouraged the tendency, implicit in the idea of entertainment as it was then understood, to appeal to the lowest common denominator of public taste. This did not necessarily mean appealing to the spectator's baser instincts; rather, it proposed that the films it produced should be as inoffensive as possible in order to keep them available to the largest possible audience. Since the righteous were more vocal, if not more numerous than the prurient or the permissive, once the industry had begun to seek respectability in the early 1920s, it expressed a more or less consistent willingness to cooperate with the most morally conservative elements of society.

SHORT-TERM THINKING

    The ideological conservatism of the Hollywood product ought not to be seen simply as a political decision, even an unconscious one. In almost every area of its activities, the industry was curiously reluctant to adopt new techniques, and displayed a consistently conservative attitude to change. It declined most of the opportunities offered by audience research and was invariably hostile to independent investigations of the cinema's effects on its public. It remained committed to conservative accountancy in spite of indications that some films, at least, could continue to make profits long after their first release. These attitudes indicated the strength of the industry's attachment to the short-term economic interest promoted by the financial structure of production. The implicit conservatism of this dominant short-term preference was perhaps most clearly revealed in Hollywood's attitude to technological innovation.

Few industries can have as poor a record in research, not only into the composition of its market but also in investigating ways of improving the product. All the major innovations in film technology were developed not by the major studios, but by organizations outside the cinema industry. Sound, the largest technical change, was pioneered by Warner Brothers and Fox, neither of which was a major vertically integrated company at the time (although both became so in part as a result of the profitability of sound production).[34] Neither of them was involved in the technical development of the sound film process, which was undertaken by the leading companies in the radio industry, Western Electric and RCA, which constructed its own vertically integrated company, RKO, to exploit its sound system. The reluctance of the major companies (in 1925 First National-- eventually taken over by Warners--Loews', and Famous Players-Paramount) to adopt the technological innovation was one reason Warners and Fox were able to challenge and join their oligopoly.

One explanation commonly advanced for the industry's failure to adopt technical improvements was the hostility of exhibitors to the introduction of innovations that required expenditure on their part; such an explanation is usually offered for the abandonment of large-screen systems used occasionally in the 1920s and '30s.[35] Cinerama failed because exhibitors claimed that the cost of converting their projection facilities was prohibitive. The 3-D process met similar resistance in the early 1950s, and CinemaScope benefited from the comparative cheapness of the modifications to projection systems that it required. Even so, it was not widely adopted until Fox announced that all their future product would be made using the system, and that they had also persuaded M. G. M. , Columbia and Universal to adopt it, guaranteeing theatre-owners a large enough supply of films to make conversion worth their while.

Exhibitors' unwillingness to install new projection systems without a guarantee of product seems a reasonable economic response. The attitude of the major production companies, however, needs further elaboration. The failure of the 3-D system provides a case in point. Its brief life-span was largely the result of the attitude the studios adopted towards it. Having been presented with a working system, they made little attempt to improve it or overcome its defects, which often resulted in substandard presentations. Production in the new process was concentrated on cheap, quickly-made films with poor plots, few stars, and little drawing-power other than the 3-D effects. Within a couple of years of its introduction, as studio executives had predicted, the public tired of the cardboard Polaroid glasses, and the system was abandoned as another gimmick which had briefly helped stave off the crisis of falling audiences. 3-D failed because of the purpose to which the studios had put it.

A similar approach was initially brought to the introduction of both sound and widescreen. They were seen as being useful primarily as added attractions that would have a short-term effect in promoting the occasion of going to the film theatre from a routine occurrence to a special event. The companies exploited the new techniques as a means of drawing audiences largely separate from the subject matter or quality of the film, and as far as possible waited until they had proved their potential for holding audiences before committing themselves to them. The technology of Cinema-Scope had been available since 1930 but, like 3-D, widescreen was only adopted by the studios under the financial pressure of declining audiences.[36] Sound was originally used by Warner Brothers to make shorts which would replace vaudeville routines in first-run houses, and by Fox for newsreels.[37] Even for the pioneers, feature production came only after sound had proven its substantial commercial value. Even color was fairly reluctantly adopted, and was not brought into common usage until twenty years after a successful three-color process had been patented. Partial explanations for the delay can be provided: Technicolor's long insistence on their close supervision of color films; the chronological accidents of a color system being developed shortly after the industry's conversion to sound; the economies imposed on production by the Second World War; the cost and technical problems of lighting color films in the 1930s. None of these explanations, however, can entirely account for the industry's delay in using color, nor for their sudden adoption of it in 1952-3. In the late 1940s 30 per cent of Hollywood productions were being made in color, with MGM, for example, filming 12 of its 34 releases in Technicolor. In July 1952 Film Daily announced that 78 per cent of current productions were in color.[38] In 1953, 28 of MGM's 36 films were in color, which, like the widescreen processes, was being used as a way of holding audiences against the competition of television and as an instrument of the majors' move into prestige productions. For the majors the widespread use of color processes was not related to a technical development (Technicolor Monopak had been available since 1942), but to an economic imperative, the declining audience. *

The studios preferred to stick with a technologically inferior product for as long as it could retain its commercial viability, rather than invest in research and possibly risky conversion to an improved system. Instead, they bought the rights to systems once they had been invented, and adopted major technological advances such as color and widescreen only when forced by external economic pressures, and only in order to reap what were generally regarded as short-term benefits in increased or maintained audience size. In part their resistance to change was justified by the increased cost of production caused by the new devices; sound, for example, doubled production costs. But the studios' reluctance to invest in research and development of their product and its production equipment, and their hostility to fundamental innovations in it, reflects the same economically-induced conservatism witnessed elsewhere: a preference for the short-term advantages of rapid recoupment of investments in production over the long-term possibilities of product development.

REFERENCES

1. Headline in Variety, April 9, 1947. Quoted in Hortense Powdermaker, Hollywood the Dream Factory: An Anthropologist Looks at Hollywood (Boston, 1950), p. 35.

2. Variety, January 18, 1948.

---

*Although the Technicolor laboratories were working to capacity by 1948, and signing contracts for films as much as three years ahead of their scheduled release,[39] this demand ought to have been an incentive for the majors to develop alternatives to the Technicolor system, such as Thomascolor[40] in the 1940s. They were certainly prepared to undertake such research in the next decade, when several studio variants of color processes (Metrocolor, Warnercolor, Trucolor, Fox Lenticular Color, Columbia color) appeared.

3. Garth Jowett, Film The Democratic Art, p. 473.

4. F. D. Klingender and Stuart Legg, Money Behind the Screen (London, 1937), pp. 74-78. Mae D. Huettig, Economic Control of the Motion Picture Industry (Philadelphia, 1944), pp. 106-108.

5. Michael Conant, Antitrust in the Motion Picture Industry (Berkeley, 1960), p. 49.

6. Conant, p. 50.

7. Conant, p. 79.

8. Conant, p. 37.

9. F. Scott Fitzgerald, The Last Tycoon, p. 35.

10. Conant, p. 131.

11. Conant, p. 131.

12. Conant, p. 134.

13. Jowett, p. 483; Charles Flynn and Todd McCarthy, "The Economic Imperative: Why Was the B Movie Necessary?" in McCarthy and Flynn, Kings of the Bs, pp. 25, 32.

14. Flynn and McCarthy, p. 24.

15. Variety, May 30, 1945. Quoted in Conant, p. 47.

16. Variety, May 4, 1955. Quoted in Conant, p. 120.

17. Conant, p. 83.

18. United States v. Paramount Pictures, 85F Supp. 881 (S. D. N. Y. 1949). Final Findings of Fact by the United States District Court, dated February 8, 1950. Paragraph 153 (f). Quoted in Conant, p. 55.

19. McCarthy and Flynn, p. 24.

20. Leo Rosten, Hollywood, The Movie Colony, the Movie Makers (New York, 1941), pp. 79 ff.

21. McCarthy and Flynn, p. 25.

22. Conant, p. 124.

23. Halsey, Stuart and Co., "The Motion Picture Industry as a Basis for Bond Financing"; Prospectus, May 27, 1927. Reprinted in Tino Balio, ed., The American Film Industry (Madison, Wisconsin, 1976), p. 189.

24. Rosten, p. 40.

25. Lary May, Screening Out the Past: The Birth of Mass Culture and the Motion Picture Industry (New York, 1980), p. 171.

26. Quoted in Philip French, The Movie Moguls: An Informal History of the Hollywood Tycoons (London, 1969), p. 78.

27. Quoted in Mel Gussow, Zanuck: Don't Say Yes Until I've Finished Talking, p. 94.

28. Darryl Zanuck, Address to the Writers' Congress in Los Angeles, October 1943. Quoted in Roger Manvell, Films and the Second World War (New York, 1974), p. 203.

29. Quoted in Gussow, p. 95.

30. Charles Higham and Joel Greenberg, Hollywood in the Forties (London, 1968), p. 8.

31. Martin Quigley, Motion Picture Herald, January 27, 1940. Quoted in Russell Campbell, "The Ideology of the Social Consciousness Movie: Three Films of Darryl F. Zanuck," Quarterly Review of Film Studies, Winter 1978, p. 58.

32. Quoted in Raymond Moley, The Hays Office, p. 98.

33. Quoted in Ruth Inglis, Freedom of the Movies: A Report on Self-Regulation from the Commission on the Freedom of the Press (Chicago, 1947), p. 5.

34. Douglas Gomery, "Towards an Economic History of the Cinema: The Coming of Sound to Hollywood," in Teresa Di Lauretis and Stephen Heath, eds., The Cinematic Apparatus, pp. 38-46.

35. e. g. James L. Limbacher, Four Aspects of the Film (New York, 1968), p. 87.

36. Limbacher, p. 107.

37. Gomery, in Di Lauretis and Heath, pp. 40-44.

38. Quoted in Limbacher, p. 35.

39. Dudley Andrew, "The Post-War Struggle for Colour," in De Lauretis and Heath, p. 69.

40. Limbacher, pp. 59-60.

CHAPTER 3

MIXED ECONOMIES

DIVORCE--AMERICAN STYLE

The period 1947-1952 is crucial to an understanding of the forms that the American cinema has taken since then. In those five years a series of events took place that would lead to the disintegration of the studio system of production that was synonymous with Hollywood. For the first time in nearly ten years box-office receipts dropped in 1947. They would continue to drop more or less steadily for the next decade, before leveling off in the early 1960s with a weekly attendance of half that of the early 1940s.[1] The immediate post-war period saw the start of the escalating importance of foreign sales and overseas production to the American industry. The number of television sets in use in the United States grew from 14,000 in 1947 to 32,000,000 in 1954.[2] The beginning of the Cold War coincided with a vicious and extensive inquisition into Hollywood's political allegiances and a jaundiced examination of the relationship between film and political expression. In 1948 and 1952 the Supreme Court pronounced two judgments which led to drastic alterations in what was regarded as permissible film content, and a complete restructuring of the industrial and commercial system that was the American cinema.

The consequences of the 1952 Miracle case censorship decision will be discussed in Chapter 5. The Court's verdict, four years earlier, in the "Paramount case" was the main cause of the subsequent collapse of the studio system. The case resolved a legal dispute which had been conducted, in a variety of forms, for 27 years. The suit settled by the 1948 verdict had itself been brought by the Department of Justice ten years earlier, but its underlying assumptions were identical to those first presented by the Federal Trade Commission in 1921. The government maintained that, in

breach of the Sherman and Clayton Antitrust Acts, the Big
Five companies operated as a monopoly controlling exhibition
throughout the United States. The charge was irrefutable,
and in May 1948 the Court unanimously upheld the earlier
verdict of a district court requiring the five companies to
divorce their production and distribution activities from
their theatre outlets.

    The divorcement of theatres would have been enough
to bring about the abandonment of the studio system by itself, since that method of production, with its heavy investments in the overheads of studio plant and contract lists,
was economically viable only so long as the profitability of
the bulk of its product was guaranteed. Once the studios
could no longer be sure of widespread and preferential exhibition for their films, the economic excesses of Hollywood
production became liabilities they could no longer afford.
The decline of the studios was slow and reluctant, marked
by occasional attempts to revive the old production methods,
and obscured by the companies' continuing successful operations as distributors of independently produced films. But
it was also inevitable once the Paramount decrees took effect, because they drastically altered the basis on which
films were sold for exhibition.

    After divorcement producer and distributor alike were
no longer assured of their market. They were forced to
sell each film on its individual merits, and so had to present more attractive merchandise to the exhibitor. Production values and production costs rose to ensure sales.
M. G. M. 's production of Mogambo in 1953 was far from being the most extravagant of the studio's products for that
year, but it featured three of their highest-salaried contract
stars--Clark Gable, Ava Gardner and Grace Kelly--as well
as being directed largely on location by John Ford. One
consequence of promoting and selling films individually was
the gradual disappearance of distinctive "studio styles" which
had been so evident in the 1930s. Another was the ever-
increasing emphasis on the "prestige" production and the
development of the "blockbuster" phenomenon, by which profits were concentrated more and more on a shrinking number of films. Prior to 1950, only 100 films had grossed
over $5, 000, 000 worldwide. In 1953 and 1954 30 films
grossed that much. A-feature budgets of well over
$1, 000, 000, rare in the 1940s, became the norm after
1953, as talent and finance were concentrated on a smaller
number of productions intended for long spells in early-run
theatres.

In their oligopolistic position prior to the Paramount decrees, the majors had been able to regard production as a marginally profitable activity necessary for the continuation of the exhibition outlets where they reckoned to make the majority of their profits. Their whole system of production was thus geared less to the product than to its marketing, and the retionalization of distribution procedures was of central importance to their calculations about the required amount of production. This system was thrown out of gear by the Supreme Court's decision that these rationalizations--block booking, clearance arrangements, and so on--were illegally in restraint of trade. Divorcement forced producers and distributors to seek a greater degree of profitability than they had during the industry's peak of success, at the same time that they were subject to increasingly severe competition from television. It was hardly surprising that conservative economic solutions--cutbacks in production and personnel and concentration of resources on prestige productions--should have been adopted. For the companies themselves, the policy was initially successful: with the exception of R.K.O., under the erratic control of Howard Hughes, the majors maintained healthy profits in the early and mid-1950s. Even so, their profits were made on a declining share of the market. Not only were they losing audiences to television, they were also, through their production policies, failing to maintain their dominance over American production.

TELEVISION AND THE NEIGHBORHOOD THEATRES

It is not possible to attribute the subsequent developments in the American film industry wholly to the effects of the Paramount decrees, but their influence was of greater consequence in the restructuring of the industry in the postwar period than any other single factor. By comparison, the impact of television on the studios has been exaggerated. Undoubtedly, the main reason for the decline in audience attendance over the period from 1947 to 1962 was the availability of television as an alternative form of entertainment. But during those fifteen years the methods of American production underwent a major reorganization which was only in part the consequence of falling attendance. It is more accurate to suggest that the effects of the Paramount decrees were exacerbated and accelerated by the immediate financial pressures imposed on the studios by audience defections.

The initial decline in audience attendance in the immediate post-war period had little to do with television.
After the peak attendance year of 1946, a fall to pre-war
levels was perhaps to be expected, independent of other influences.   That natural fall in audience numbers was aggra-
vated by the post-war restructuring of the national economy,
as wartime production resources were diverted into the manufacture of consumer goods.   Returning servicemen married,
started families, and acquired consumer durables, which
both reduced the amount of money available for leisure-time
spending and tied families to their homes.   When box-office
receipts began to decline in the 1947 season, there were
fewer television sets in America than there were cinemas.
Television, indeed, was one of the major beneficiaries of
this redirection of the economy into the production of consumer goods, as the movies suffered from its concomitant
concentration of financial resources on the nuclear unit, the
suburban family home.   The growth of television sales, television's enormous penetration of the American market in the
ten years after 1948, and the nature of its content intensified
the already existent tendency of the family audience to find
its entertainment at home rather than going out to the movies to find it.   That this tendency was, however, independent
of television itself can be seen in the rise of book sales and
the growth of the magazine industry in the immediate post-
war period.

Most of the misconceptions about the relationship between the American film industry and the society in which it
operates stem from the widespread acceptance of the myth of
the undifferentiated mass audience.   In the discussion of television's effect on audience decline this myth has been particularly important in imposing a simplistic causal relationship
where in fact a much more complex process of interaction
was taking place.   By 1957, the "mass audience" had ceased
to exist.   An Opinion Research Corporation survey in that
year found that only 15 per cent of the American public attended the cinema as often as once a week, and that this
group accounted for 62 per cent of total admissions.   But if
the audience was no longer a mass, it still seemed to be
socially heterogeneous.   Apart from establishing that 72. 2
per cent of cinema-goers were under 30, the survey failed
to find significant variation in attendance on the basis of income, education or sex.[3]   However, even without precise
demographic statistics to locate exactly which sections of the
audience stopped going to the cinema, conclusions can be
drawn from, for example, the pattern of theatre closures.

Viewed from a distance, the statistical evidence would appear to indicate a severe general decline in film attendance and in theatre seating in the first post-war decade. There was a drop in seating capacity of 18 per cent, from 12.5 million seats in 1948 to 10.6 million in 1954.[4] In the decade after 1946, 4,120 theatres closed altogether. Another 5,200 theatres were operating at a loss by 1956, while 5,700 were breaking even. Of the 19,000 cinemas operating in the United States, 56 per cent were failing to make a profit, and it was estimated that, as a whole, the exhibition sector was making a net loss of $11.8 million.[5]

Frederic Stuart[6] argues cogently that television was responsible for 80 per cent of the decline in audience attendance between 1948 and 1956, basing his conclusion on a state-by-state study of box-office receipts and theatre closures. While the evidence he presents would appear overwhelming, his statistical data conceal the extent to which the theatre closures constituted a structural reorganization of the exhibition industry, and the way the production companies' response to the Paramount decrees and the threat of television exacerbated the initial decline in overall attendance. The vast majority of the theatres that closed, and a very high proportion of those doing poorly, were small, late-run houses in neighborhood areas, used to changing their programs at least twice a week and gaining their support from a small proportion of the local community who attended regularly. These were the theatres that had made two staple Hollywood products--the family film and the B-feature--profitable concerns. They catered to the middle-class family audiences who had "gone to the movies" once or twice a week, rather than specifically going to see an individual film. But despite their numbers and the size of their audiences, these theatres had not, even in the 1930s, comprised a particularly important source of revenue to distributors, because of the relatively low rentals they were charged. In the post-war economic atmosphere, their share of the market was steadily diminishing. In 1951 the 8,000 small theatres at the bottom of the exhibition ladder produced only 20 per cent of gross domestic rental income.

Even the demise of the small neighborhood theatre cannot be attributed entirely to television. Rather, it was the result of a set of interlocking and cumulative pressures --of which television was one--and has to be seen in the light of other developments in exhibition. The closing of four-wall theatres between 1946 and 1956 was matched

almost exactly by the opening of drive-ins: 4,200 were
opened in the period, and by the mid-1950s they accounted
for 22 per cent of admission grosses. [8]   The growth in the
drive-in circuit reflected a change in the composition of the
American audience.   As the family began to go to the cinema less frequently, teenagers and young adults replaced
them as the most frequent attenders.   More obviously,
drive-ins drew a more mobile audience, able and prepared
to travel further to see a film.   For drive-ins to compete
with city center theatres for this audience, they needed to
be able to show more recent films than the late-run neighborhood theatres could offer--in other words, they needed a
higher clearance classification.   Replacing the "nabes" with
drive-ins increased the number of early-run exhibition outlets.   This in turn meant higher rental fees, and higher profits for successful films.   In response, the industry geared
its production policy to the most profitable--and expanding--
sector of the market.

Exhibitors claimed that one major reason for their
inability to survive was the increased rental costs of prestige productions, but this change was vehemently denied by
the distributors.   At the Senate Committee hearings on
Small Business in 1956, Y. Frank Freeman, Vice-President
of Paramount Pictures Corporation, stated that his company's 7,000 smallest accounts paid an average rental per film
of less than $25. [9]   It was argued that these theatres would
fail even if films were available to them rent-free.   Whether
this is true or not, it certainly reveals the extent to which
the majors were prepared to abandon the low-run theatres.
Before the Paramount decision distributors had quite regularly
adjusted their rental fees to small independent theatres,
keeping them in profit as a means of preventing them from
filing antitrust actions. [10]   These concealed subsidies disap-
peared after 1948.   Revenues from the theatres that closed
were small enough to make their loss a matter of little
consequence to distributors in comparison to the advantages
to be gained from an increase in the number of first- and
second-run houses equipped to show the more costly prestige productions.   The gradual change that was taking place
in exhibition during the early 1950s was an alteration in the
attitude towards cinema-going, as the prestige production in
the well-appointed first-run theatre made it more of an
event and less of a regular family activity.   Drive-ins, with
their lower overheads, could in any case compete in admission prices with small four-wall houses.   By providing an
informal family means of entertainment, television acted as

a contributory factor to the speed at which this alteration took place, but it was not the primary cause of the change.

Changes in exhibition led to changes in the kinds of films Hollywood produced, and these in turn reinforced the new patterns in the theatres. Wartime restrictions had reduced the volume of the majors' film production from 388 in 1939 to 252 in 1946, [11] and the post-war fall in revenues prevented a return to pre-war levels of production. At the same time increased wartime demand had led to longer theatrical runs, and higher grosses for the films which were made. Average rentals per film increased from $400,000 in 1939 to $1.3 million in 1946, [12] and such figures encouraged the conclusion that production funds could be more effectively invested in fewer, more expensive films. The earliest casualty of the industry's recession was the middle-budget picture, revenues from which declined by up to 40 per cent from 1947 to 1950. [13] The initial effect was to reduce the length of these films' theatrical runs, and the Big Five responded by increasing the volume of their production from 132 films in 1949 to 172 in 1951. [14] The capital available for production was spread more thinly; each individual film had less to attract the audience, and as a result was less able to hold its own at the box office. In response to this failure, the majors turned to technical novelties like 3-D and, more permanently, committed themselves to prestige productions. In 1956 they produced only 116 films. The fall in production meant that there was a shortage of films for those smaller theatres that were financially dependent on a regular audience seeing programs which changed twice or three times a week, a problem exacerbated by the majors' partial conversion to CinemaScope. Small theatres unable to afford the cost of conversion to the new projection methods were deprived of the most profitable section of the industry's product, while audiences who wished to see Bwana Devil or How to Marry a Millionaire were driven away from the neighborhoods by advertising campaigns that stressed the novelties only available in the more expensive early-run theatres.

The dramatic decline in the production of two-star middle-budget pictures led to a fall in demand for B-features as well. Prestige films could be released without a supporting program on the first- and second-run circuits, and these films consumed more and more of the total box-office gross and theatre playing-time. The economics of B-movie production, as a result, became unsound. Since

B-features were rented for a fixed sum, their financial viability depended on the number of theatre rentals they obtained, not the number of people who came to see them.
The B-picture studios could operate on small but consistent
profits so long as there were enough theatres to rent to.
Because the profits per film were small, a high number of
B-pictures had to be produced for the studios to remain
economically viable. When the demand for their staple
product declined, studios like Republic and Monogram were
unable to sustain their operations in the face of the sharply
rising production costs of the late 1940s and early 1950s.
This decline in B-studio production meant that fewer double-
bills were available to the small neighborhood theatres. On
top of the problems they incurred as a direct result of the
major studios' emphasis on prestige productions, they were
subjected to ever-greater difficulty in finding material with
which to fill the four- or five-hour program their family
audiences had come to expect during the years of factory
production. While the small exhibitors pleaded for studios
to return to producing B-picture staples like Francis the
Talking Mule, Joe Palooka or Sunset Carson, the economic
state of the industry militated against it.

For the studios, then, it was not a simple matter of
television taking away a segment of their potential audience.
While it was true that much of the content of the B-pictures,
and later in the decade many of the films themselves, appeared on television, * that in itself was not what prevented
the films being made and drawing audiences. Television's
substantial effects on attendance cannot be denied, but those
effects were somewhat more circuitous than simply direct
competition. The majors' principal response to television
was to concentrate on offering the public what television did
not give them: color, the big screen, extravagant sets and
lavish production values. The studios invested much greater
effort than they had in the past in attracting the audience to
an individual picture, and those people who had just "gone to
the movies" found Hollywood was actually making fewer
films for them.

----

*Francis the Talking Mule, in one of the more transparent
and amusing examples of B-feature series characters transferring to the smaller screen, became Ed the Talking Horse
on television. Other B-movie stars, like Gene Autry and
Roy Rogers, kept their own names when they made the
move.

A DISTRIBUTION OF INFLUENCE

The B-studios, Monogram and Republic, sold their pre-1949 films to the television networks almost immediately the rival for audiences appeared in the early 1950s. The majors held out for some time, since the fall in their market was less immediate. However, when R. K. O. abandoned production in late 1955, the studio sold off its film library to a television programming syndicate for $15,000,000. Once the boycott had been broken, the other companies followed suit, Warner Brothers selling its library to Associated Artists in February 1956 for $21 million. By February 1958 all the majors except Paramount and Universal had sold or leased some of their product, mostly pre-1949 vintage, to television; 3,700 features were released to television for $220 million, a sum equivalent to one year's total remittances to distributors. [15] The sale took place at the same time that the companies began to move into production for television, but while it was profitable in the short term, it had a noticeable effect on theatrical box-office receipts. A 1956 survey indicated that out of the 71 million daily television audience, 25 million watched televised films for $10\frac{1}{2}$ hours a week. [16] The films sold to television became a prime-time viewing staple, with almost every channel screening at least one feature per evening. Theatre admissions fell by 20 per cent in 1957, wiping out in one year the small gains made in each of the previous three. [17] Much of this decline may be directly attributed to film sales to television, which could now offer a comparable alternative to the movies. The sale had also taken place at the time when the initial impact of widescreen was beginning to tail off, and the cycle of novelty technical devices was exhausted. The majors' decision to sell, the result of a desire to gain profits from otherwise useless product, came at an unfortunate time. The industry's first attempts to ignore or deride television, and to make their alternative much more impressive, had not affected the development of their rival, and had merely slightly delayed the impact of television on the size of their future audience. But, coming as it did at the same time as the majors decided to enter television production, the sale was one significant factor in improving the quality of the television product.

In the mid-1950s the majors substantially conceded the battle over audiences by default and by their preference for their short-term economic interests. Earlier in the

decade, exhibitors had noticed a pronounced drop in box-
office receipts on particular nights when audiences stayed
home to watch the Milton Berle show or other popular programs.   By 1956 television now provided sufficiently attractive programming all week round--and particularly over the
weekends--substantially to eliminate the family audience.
Until 1955 Universal had responded to the neighborhood
theatre-owners' pleas for family entertainment of an elementary kind, and had kept their profits healthy with cheap
series productions like the Ma and Pa Kettle films.   In
1956 they began to move this large portion of their output
to their television subsidiary, United World Films, Inc., an
action which had a predictably severe effect on the neighborhood circuits they had been supporting.

     If by the later 1950s television was a qualitative com-
petitor, and if the film industry had exhausted the currently
available stock of technical improvements which might have
a novelty value in boosting revenues, it was clear after the
majors' move into television that they were going to have to
adopt other measures as a means of drawing audiences.   The
prestige production, and the associated blockbuster phenomenon, continued as the dominant economic trend, but the nature
of the films' content began to alter.   The musical, for example, which had gained a new impetus from the widescreen
processes, fell victim not only to rising costs but also to the
regular provision of "spectacular" musical entertainment on
TV.   Those that were produced shifted their emphasis from
large-scale dance numbers to definitive versions of an already established theatrical score.

     The majors' poor performance in competing with tele-
vision can in part be attributed to their refusal to abandon
the undifferentiated mass audience which they believed to
have been the mainstay of their economic prosperity in the
past.   The more unpredictable nature of the post-Paramount
audience might have encouraged them to handle more uncon-
ventional and controversial content.   To a limited extent
this did happen, but largely in the work of independent producers.   The studios maintained their innate, economically-
induced conservatism, enhanced by the intense desire of
production chiefs and distributors alike to re-establish the
predictability of formulaic financial success that had governed the industry's economic operations in the 1940s.
Television's erosion of the mass audience for family entertainment guaranteed the failure of such a strategy.   MGM
in particular suffered from L. B. Mayer's unwavering

attachment to obsolete values. In the last three years of his reign as head of production, (1949-1951) MGM lost $9 million, [18] which at least some commentators ascribed to Mayer's conservatism over film content. *

The move into prestige production was to some extent compromised by this conservatism over content. The blockbuster alternative to the old and unprofitable generic formulae was to adapt successful plays or books for the screen. These already popular properties had the advantage of being "pre-sold" to their audiences, which appeared to make them somewhat safer investments. But the adaptation of popular books provided as many problems as it solved, since their content frequently conflicted with the studios' inclination to preserve the family film. Producers, distributors and financiers alike maintained their belief that a successful film was obliged to appeal to the widest possible audience, and therefore had to be rendered suitable for the entertainment of juveniles--even if this ran counter to the likelihood of a film adaptation appealing to the same market as the novel on which it was based. The works of Jones, Williams, Mailer, or for that matter Grace Metalious required substantial alteration of plot and theme before they could conform to the requirements of family entertainment embodied in the Production Code. The majors had absorbed the lessons of Will H. Hays that the way to profit and respectability was through the appeal to a conservative mass market. The Production Code defined that policy in its detailed stipulations over film content, and the studios were reluctant to abandon its guarantees to the family audience. As a result, in adapting pre-sold material for the screen they found themselves caught between a felt need to bring the salable elements of The Naked and The Dead or Peyton Place to the film and a desire to avoid offending conservative moral powerbrokers by prurient description. Assailed by the increasing permissiveness of the culture around them and by the ever more risqué nature of the works they adapted, their overall reaction was a reluctance to embrace such dubious content and a hearty enthusiasm

---

*This was somewhat too sweeping: MGM was also slow to rent out studio space to independent producers, a decision which was less Mayer's than Nicholas Schenk's. The company was also overproducing in the period 1950-53, and thus failing to deal with the problem of studio overheads as effectively as the other majors.

for then rendering it "safe." Designing their product for a
dwindling share of the market, and working under the constant scrutiny of bodies like the Legion of Decency, the majors were compelled to remain "far behind ... the trend to
break down accepted standards ... and proud of it,"[19] while
nevertheless exploiting the publicity given to books in the
forefront of that trend.

To a degree, the majors' attempts to reach an unsatisfactory compromise between these two polar positions
resulted in their comparative decline in economic importance. Their attachment to the family film was more than
an emotional preference for certain types of subject matter. It involved extensive capital outlays on permanent
sets, costume departments and other facilities, including
contracts with actors who had built up typecast reputations.
They continued their adherence to films suited to an undifferentiated and unclassified audience long after the commercial viability of films designed to appeal more specifically
to the new pluralist urban audiences had been demonstrated
by the growth of the "art house" circuit. Their choice of
the epic and the musical as their initial blockbuster genres
indicated the extent to which they were hoping to preserve
the family as their basic audience unit, even if they were
no longer trying to lure them to the cinema as often as
they had in the past.

Only in 1956 did they consent to amend the Production Code, after it had been strained by their own adaptations and openly breached in a commercial success by the
leading American independent distributor, United Artists.
By then the position of the Big Five had been seriously
weakened in relation to independent producers in general
and the Little Three in particular. Much less encumbered
by the consequences of divorcement, Columbia, United Artists and Universal greatly promoted their status in the
post-war decade, and by 1957 were actually together releasing more pictures than the Big Five combined. Successfully exploiting the Paramount decrees' stipulations
that the major exhibition chains deal impartially with all
distributors, Columbia and United Artists had expanded
their share of large-budget A-feature production, while
Universal and two of the smaller studios had cornered
profitable areas of the market left vacant by the majors'
programming policy. Universal continued a steady stream
of low-budget films aimed at the neighborhoods, while
Allied Artists and American-International produced cheap-

budget double-bills oriented specifically towards the youth
market at the drive-ins. The more established and conservative companies suffered by comparison.

Along with a greater willingness to accept a fragmentation of the market and to shape content accordingly, the
minor companies showed a greater willingness to employ
new methods of production. * As with many of the changes
in the 1950s, the way to independent production was led by
United Artists; it was, in fact, the way the company had
always operated, acting as a distributor for production companies run by its members.

Independent production was, by its nature, somewhat
more amenable to experimentation and risk-taking than the
entrenched studio system. It began its significant development, despite studio opposition, in the early 1940s, as a
result of wartime tax law revisions which allowed individuals
to retain more of their money if it came from capital gains
rather than income. ** Actors, directors, and particularly
producers found it more profitable to form their own companies, often for a single production, and to operate on
small salaries and percentages of the profits. The restrictive practices of the majors retarded the growth of independent production and post-war tax revisions reduced the economic incentive by making it more difficult to claim as capital gains profits which substituted for salary.

However, the Paramount decrees resulted in increased
opportunity for independent productions to secure favorable
first-run releases, and a number of other economic factors
encouraged the independents. Since they generally undertook
only one production--or at most a few--at a time, they were

_____
*With the exception of Universal, which, because of the
nature of its production systems, clung to the contract system longer than any of the other studios, eventually turning
it over, with the bulk of its production activities, to television in 1956.

**An individual in the top income bracket could cut his taxes
from 81 per cent of income to 60 per cent by operating as a
corporation. If his interest in a completed picture could be
sold, for example to a studio or distributor, as a capital
asset, his income from such a sale would only be taxed at
25 per cent.

not burdened with the upkeep of extensive studio facilities.
Compared to the majors, their overhead costs were minimal, little more than rentals on office space and the salaries of a small number of permanent employees. They
leased facilities and staff only so long as they were employed on any given production, rather than maintaining long
contract lists. By comparison, the cost of studio upkeep
was obliging the majors to add substantial amounts to the
cost of any film in the form of "studio overheads" for the
maintenance of facilities, whether the production in question
used them or not. Underused studio space was an economic
liability that hindered the majors' capacity to compete with
the independents, which could offer more favorable distribution deals since their comparable productions were brought
in at lower cost. In May 1950 Business Week estimated the
average cost of an independent A-production at $800,000. [20]
Twentieth Century-Fox's 28 productions in that year cost an
average $1,634,000, and while that reflected the studio's
high production values, a minimum of 50 per cent of the
added costs was incurred by studio overheads. Paramount's
25 productions averaged a cost of $1,144,000, with the ex-
tra expenditure being almost entirely attributable to the cost
of studio facilities. [21] In consequence, there was a steady
rise in the number of independent producers from 40 in 1945
to 93 in 1947 to 165 in 1957. Meanwhile, the majors' cut-
back in production left them, as early as 1950, with unused
studio space. They could reduce their overheads, and hence
their cost per production, by leasing facilities to the independents whose rise they had earlier so opposed. By 1951,
most of the majors were renting out studio space to independent producers at rates of between $100,000 and $150,000
for an A-feature.

Both parties saw benefits for themselves in the absorption of independent production units into the studios.
The independents needed the distribution facilities of the
majors, and also relied on them for a proportion of their
financing. The studios acquired a cheaper product of comparable quality, and took less financial risk, since they
rarely provided more than 40 per cent of the film's production costs. They also had studio facilities occupied, which
reduced the size of their standing operating costs. The first
deal between a studio and a self-operating independent production company was concluded in March 1951, between
Columbia and Stanley Kramer Productions. For a variety
of reasons, it was unsuccessful. One reason was that
Kramer was hired as a potential successor to Harry Cohn,

with detrimental effects on their personal relationship. The principal cause of the failure, however, was the inclusion in the contract of a production schedule beyond Kramer's capacity. Expected to produce 30 films in five years Kramer left in 1954 having made only eleven. Of those, ten had lost money. But the nature of the already firmly rooted blockbuster phenomenon was such that Kramer's one successful picture at Columbia, The Caine Mutiny, was sufficiently profitable to wipe out his deficit with the studio, although not until after he had left. 22

It was on an economic model such as this that the studios came to operate in the late 1950s. Of the 382 films released from October 1956 to October 1957 by the twelve largest distributors, 219 (57.3 per cent) were independently produced. 23 Of those twelve companies, only Universal had no involvement with independent production. They were also, with M.G.M., the only one of the eight majors to retain a stock company that in size came anywhere near resembling the contract lists maintained by all the studios in the 1940s. * The majors' position as large distributors, which had always been central to their success, was enhanced by the blockbuster phenomenon. The enormous profitability of an ever-decreasing percentage of the mainstream industry product was sufficient to support the mechanics of a distribution system, but the assumed unpredictability of public taste ensured producer dependence on an established distribution network. Moreover, since the mass audience seemed to select a film for its overwhelming support with ever-decreasing regard to those factors which had made profitability relatively predictable in the 1940s, the distributors required a constant but varied flow of product. The growth of independent production in fact strengthened the position of the major distributors considerably, since independents had no alternative distribution system, and no capital to establish one.

As production became more diffuse, the centrality of the distributor's role as a necessary point of economic stability increased. If only one production in ten made profits --a statistic which would have been incredible in the 1940s and unfortunate in the 1950s, but was increasingly normal by the mid-1960s--the power of the distributor was increased.

---

*M.G.M.'s contract list was, however, only 31 strong in 1957, compared to 89 in 1952. Of the 31, only 13 were established stars. 24

Releasing, say, 50 films a year, a distributor could count on five films to make sufficiently large profits to cover the losses on the other 45. But an independent producer, making anywhere from one to ten films a year, might miss out on profits altogether. Since most of the producer's financing came from bank loans, not from the distributor, the gap between the profitability of the two concerns was further widened. The distributor was bearing no more than 40 per cent of the loss on an unsuccessful production, while the producer had not merely to provide the rest, but to find the interest payments on the bank loan too. Independent production companies and the personnel composing them frequently found themselves heavily mortgaged to the distributors for productions they were more or less forced to undertake in order to recoup previous losses. As a result, the balance of power between producer and distributor moved substantially towards New York and away from Hollywood; a move encouraged by the death or retirement of the remaining first-generation studio heads, and the growing tendency to shoot on location away from Los Angeles. Far from adding to the producers' power over their films, the demise of the studio system merely inserted more layers of authority between the producer and those who financed him, decreasing the probability of his final control over his product.

FOREIGN BODIES

When the Motion Picture Producers and Distributors of America became the Motion Picture Association of America in 1945, * it also changed the title of its Foreign Department to the Motion Picture Export Association. With the altered name came a major reorganization. The Second World War had closed some markets, particularly the profitable European sector, to American films. Others, notably in South America, had been opened up. The end of the war offered opportunities both for the continued exploitation of the recently developed areas and for the re-opening of markets in Europe. The M. P. E. A. was organized specifically for the exploitation of these markets, operating as a kind of legal cartel with considerable government support. The

---

*At the same time that Eric Johnston replaced W. H. Hays as President.

market monopoly which was prohibited at home by antitrust laws was encouraged abroad by the Webb-Pomerene Export Act of 1918. Not only did the Paramount decrees on theatre divorcement not apply to cinemas owned by the major companies in other countries, but legislation actually encouraged firms supposedly in competition to combine for the purpose of fixing prices and dividing up the foreign market.

With the decline in American revenues after 1946 foreign sales came to play an increasingly important role in distribution financing. Prior to World War II, the American market had more than recouped production costs, making it possible for American films to dominate the European market because, having already gone into profit, they could be distributed more cheaply than their native competitors. In the immediate postwar period, the backlog of available features permitted the flooding of some European markets, particularly in Italy, where nearly 3,000 American films were released in the period 1946-1950.[25] By the early 1950s most of the major European governments had stopped this flow by establishing quota systems restricting the number of American films that could be imported, or imposing restrictions on current exports. This left American distributors with surplus amounts of foreign currency.

The logical thing to do with this money was to invest it in production, although a variety of other expedients, including ship-building and distilling, were used as a means of exporting profits to America.[26] Europe had certain obvious advantages as a base for production. It offered reduced labor costs and, after 1950, the possibility of capitalizing on government subsidy schemes. An influence in European production helped the home industry since this partial colonization impaired the development of national cinemas in Europe, and kept overseas markets open for penetration by the American product. Including European locations and stars in American productions made Hollywood films more attractive to European audiences, as well as adding a touch of exoticism for the domestic market. Economic circumstance encouraged American films to become more cosmopolitan in their surface appearance. One American exhibitor complained to a Senate Committee in 1956 that

> American producers now rarely make pictures especially adapted to American audiences.

His argument that the producers' policy of appealing to foreign as well as American audiences

> has virtually eliminated the American family-type
> pictures and those featuring familiar American
> sports and customs[27]

oversimplified the case, but American exploitation of the
international market certainly contributed to the shortage of
suitable material that small exhibitors complained of. Hollywood's declining production in the 1950s was also mainly
responsible for the limited penetration of the American market by European films, but such success as European films
did have in the U. S. was dependent on their distribution by
a major American company.

The M. P. E. A. was legally empowered to act as the
sole exporting agent for the member companies of the
M. P. A. A. , and, because of its size and domination of the
market, it was also in a position to negotiate over quotas
for American imports, tariffs and currency restrictions with
foreign governments anxious to revive their own film industries.   In such negotiations it was directly aided by the
State Department, which in the post-war and Cold War periods continued the policy fostered by the Office of War Information that American films were useful ideological exports.
Not only did their depiction of the American Way of Life encourage consumer demand in foreign countries for other
American products and hence act to reinforce Coca-Coloniza-
tion, but they also served as what both Roosevelt and Truman somewhat ambiguously described as "ambassadors of
good will. "[28]   The government's principal interest in promoting American film exports was derived from their value
in the ideological war it saw itself waging under Truman
and Eisenhower.   The American intervention in the 1948
Italian election campaign, when the State Department count-
ered communist electoral propaganda with U. S. information
programs supporting the Christian Democrats, encouraged
the flooding of the Italian film market with backlogged American films as a useful extension of its policy.   The American film industry, because of its propaganda value, found
itself a covert beneficiary of the Marshall Plan.

The motives of the American distributors were undoubtedly less conspiratorial.   It is unlikely that they were
at all politically motivated, except in the sense that the
first- and second-generation American executives of the
major companies were pleased to seem patriotic, especially
where their own interests were so well served by cooperation with the government.   Deftly combining economics with

ideological bluster, Spyros Skouras, President of Twentieth Century-Fox, declared forcibly in 1953,

> It is a solemn responsibility of our industry to increase motion picture outlets throughout the free world because it has been shown that no medium can play a greater part than the motion picture in indoctrinating people into the free way of life and instilling in them a compelling desire for freedom and hope for a brighter future. Therefore we as an industry can play an infinitely important part in the worldwide ideological struggle for the minds of men and confound the communist propagandists.[29]

But the industry's more general tendency was to play down its overt ideological role. Eric Johnston maintained that

> Hollywood is not in the business of grinding out pictures neatly labelled for use as weapons in the propaganda war.... Hollywood is in the entertainment business, and that's precisely why our films are loved and believed by people abroad.[30]

Although cooperation with the State Department was extensive, it was tempered by commercial interests. The post-war Military Government in West Germany found its plans to use films as a tool of democratic indoctrination substantially thwarted by the companies' refusal to supply films in any quantity unless they could use the profits they made to penetrate the German film industry. The Military Government's opposition to this attempt at colonization limited German access to American product until 1948, when the State Department established a scheme by which American films deemed to have propaganda value were permitted to convert their German earnings into dollars.[31]

The M. P. E. A. permitted the major companies to operate abroad the kind of cartel policies that the Paramount verdict had declared illegal at home. Impelled by economic self-interest, they refrained from competing over quotas for much the same reasons that they had previously concurred in a uniform system of clearance. The stability of the international market was by 1955 as essential to the majors' well-being as the stability of the home market had been in the 1930s. By then, foreign distribution accounted for approximately half of their income, a level which has remained fairly constant ever since, with the European market com-

prising 80 per cent of the foreign total. American investment in European production simply became a logical concomitant of this situation. European government restrictions ensured that American firms would not be permitted
to colonize European industries, even if they had wanted to.
Their subsidy schemes, however, encouraged American production in Europe by providing a capital incentive on top of
the cheaper costs, particularly of labor. By 1960, 35 per
cent of American films were produced abroad and towards the
end of the decade these runaway productions accounted for as
much as 60 per cent of total American output,[32] although
this figure rapidly declined with the fall in the value of the
dollar and rising European costs in the early 1970s. Although cultural nationalists deplored the Americanization of
their industries made possible by the loose definition of what
counted as a "national" film, governments recognized the extent to which their film industries were sustained by American investment. The British government, for example, was
perfectly happy to acquiesce in the apparent anomaly that,
in 1965, 80 per cent of its Eady fund subsidy, amounting to
$10 million, went to the British subsidiaries of American
companies[33] on the basis that American investment provided
capital and employment for the British industry.

That the move into foreign markets took place at the
same time as television appeared as a home market compet-
itor was not, of course, coincidental. Expansion of foreign
interests was a less problematic alternative source of income than finding ways to maintain home audiences. The
industry's notable failure to resist the encroachments of
television on their potential audience in part provoked, and
was in part permitted by, the exploitation of an underde-
veloped market elsewhere. By its actions in the mid-1950s
the industry declared its intention of preserving the attitude
towards its product that had prevailed under the studio system. The introduction of foreign stars and locales was,
like the adaptation of pre-sold material, simply a modification of the product in the face of new market circumstances.
Hollywood remained committed to its policy of providing
long-term security for the exploitation of its short-term
economic advantages. As before, stability continued to be
sacrificed for immediate gain, even if at times this emphasis threatened the entire structure of the M. P. E. A.[34] The
post-war industry, confronted by increasing economic uncertainties, confirmed its pre-war assumptions about its own
activity. However much the masses stayed at home, film
was mass entertainment, designed for a now internationally

undifferentiated mass market. Its costs were high, and could be expected only to continue rising. Its profitable economic life was short, and the available evidence suggested that profits would continue to be concentrated on an ever-decreasing percentage of films. The economic obligation therefore remained one of finding a fashionable formula and riding it hard for as long as the market would stand. Michael Conant's observation that

> The motion picture market, like commodity markets, seems to have over-speculation in any product that shows early success[35]

became, if anything, more true in the post-war period than it had been in the 1930s. The confirmation of film's status as entertainment determined that the industry would continue to operate in the years after 1950 on its traditional basis of quick profits quickly reinvested.

REFERENCES

1. Garth Jowett, Film The Democratic Art, p. 475.

2. Tino Balio, ed., The American Film Industry, p. 315.

3. Variety, January 22, 1958. Quoted in Michael Conant, Antitrust in the Motion Picture Industry, p. 5.

4. U. S. Bureau of the Census, Census of Business: 1954, Vol. V, pp. 8-12.

5. U. S. Congress, Senate Select Committee on Small Business, Hearings on Motion Picture Distribution Trade Practices, 1956. Quoted in Conant, p. 149.

6. Frederic Stuart, The Effects of Television on the Motion Picture and Radio Industries (New York, 1976).

7. Variety, July 25, 1951. Quoted in Conant, p. 119.

8. Conant, p. 147.

9. Senate Select Committee on Small Business, p. 353. Quoted in Conant, p. 151.

10. Conant, p. 75.

11. Conant, p. 46.

12. Conant, p. 47.

13. Variety, May 28, 1947. Quoted in Conant, p. 122.

14. Conant, p. 124.

15. Balio, ed, p. 322.

16. Variety, September 26, 1958. Quoted in Conant, pp. 13-14.

17. Jowett, p. 473.

18. Conant, p. 133. See also Bosley Crowther, The Lion's Share: The Story of an Entertainment Empire (New York, 1957), pp. 296-308.

19. Motion Picture Association of America, pamphlet of early 1955, quoted in Andrew Dowdy, The Films of the Fifties: The American State of Mind (New York, 1975), p. 88.

20. Conant, p. 116.

21. Conant, p. 124.

22. Bob Thomas, King Cohn: The Life and Times of Harry Cohn (London, 1967), p. 158.

23. Conant, p. 118.

24. Variety, February 6, 1957.

25. Thomas Guback, "Hollywood's International Market, " in Tino Balio, ed. , The American Film Industry, p. 398.

26. Eric Johnston, in testimony to the U. S. Senate Committee on Foreign Relations, 1953. Quoted in Thomas Guback, The International Film Industry: Western Europe and America since 1945 (Bloomington, Indiana, 1969), p. 121.

27. Senate Select Committee on Small Business, 1956. Quoted in Guback, p. 12.

28. Thomas Guback, "Hollywood's International Market, " in Tino Balio, ed., The American Film Industry, p. 396.

29. Variety, January 7, 1953. Quoted in Guback, The International Film Industry, p. 125.

30. Variety, January 28, 1953. Quoted in Guback, p. 126.

31. Guback, pp. 124-141.

32. Guback, in Balio, pp. 403-404.

33. Guback, p. 170.

34. See Guback, p. 93.

35. Conant, p. 7.

INTERLUDE

An American definition of a
first-class intelligence:
The ability to hold two opposed
ideas in the mind at the same
time, and still retain the ability
to function.
F. Scott Fitzgerald:
The Crack Up

"PRODUCTION FOR USE"--HOWARD HAWKS

You work your side of the
street, I'll work mine.
Steve McQueen in Bullitt

The imperatives of Hollywood production set strict
limits on both the possibilities and the need for thematic
sophistication in its individual films. These commercial
restrictions are the first and largest hurdle confronting the
auteur critic, desperately trying to convince himself and
others that the apparently simple is secretly, subversively
profound. Howard Hawks is a test case.

Hawks' films may be the models of thematic density
that Robin Wood and others take them to be. But if they do
reveal a consistent morality through their plot development
and dialogue, it is no less rooted in nineteenth-century precepts than Ford's or Chaplin's. More importantly, earnest
discussions of the high moral tone of Rio Bravo, dotted with
caveats about the film's unpretentious and relaxed good humor, miss the point. The self-evident fact that Hawks'
films whole-heartedly accept that their goal is to entertain
is the first observation that must be made about them. For

86

Hawks, working within the limitations of that perspective--
acknowledging the film as product and accepting the status
quo of the production system--is not a necessary evil but a
positive virtue. It is his very recognition of these limited
objectives which gives his practice of cinematic entertainment an emphasis so significantly different from that of his
more orthodox contemporaries.

As practiced by Hollywood, entertainment relied on a
balance between the familiar and the novel, the familiar being provided by the audience's recognition of conventional
characters, situations, and so on. The idea of genre, as
providing a stock of this familiar material, is thus central
to an understanding of how the American cinema worked.
It may be more useful to consider Hawks as a genre rather
than an auteur, even if only briefly; the Hawksian hero and
Hawksian woman have distinctive qualities that set them
apart from other, conventional figures in much the same
way that the generic archetypes of the Western are set
apart from those of the crime film. Rio Bravo is more
a re-make of Only Angels Have Wings than it is a Western.
The Bogart-Bacall relationship in The Big Sleep presumes
on their previous relationship in To Have and Have Not.
Hawks' films repeat themselves, both inside and outside the
single narrative, and this repetition provides a sense of enclosure within conventional modes of expression that informs
the reactions of characters and audience alike. Looking at
the dead Thomas Mitchell's meager possessions in Only Angels Have Wings, Cary Grant says: "Not much to show for
twenty-two years." It is the second time he has said it in
the film, and it is a line already familiar from Ceiling Zero
which will be used again in Air Force. Hawks knows it,
and Grant knows it, and he says it as if he knows it, so the
audience know it, too. The scene, which makes a point
about the necessary limitations of expressing emotion, is--
like a generic configuration--transposable from film to film
as a substantially intact block.

In keeping with this pattern of construction, the pleasures for the audience in a Hawks film are all incidental
ones: whether they be the delights of unlikely engineering achievements (Pocket's rocket in Hatari!), the game-playing
of characters within a scene (Bogart and Bacall all the time,
Wayne and Clift in Red River, Martin and Brennan in Rio
Bravo), or the enforced realization of the irrelevance of the
linear plot (the song sequence in Rio Bravo). They are incidental in several senses. They are tangential to the plot.

They are separate incidents in themselves, whose entertainment value derives from their performance--how they happen, not why they happen. They are, like the cinema itself, transitory: they give immediate pleasure, and then they're over. In Hawks' narratives, the scene itself, and what happens within it, are more important than the scene's contribution to a developing plot. As a result, there is no imperative for his plots either to make sense or to progress.

If it mattered who killed Owen Taylor, The Big Sleep would collapse. The implausibilities of the story are accepted because attention is diverted elsewhere. The situation simply exists. The town in Rio Bravo is completely cut off. Statement. Narrative fact. This is the point from which the film tees off. The coincidence of Richard Barthelmess' arrival at Barranca in Only Angels Have Wings is not up for examination, it is simply the means of engineering the situations Hawks wants to make his film about. There is no need to explain why Carmen Sternwood walks into Joe Brody's apartment pointing a gun at him when Marlowe and Vivian are already there. Her entry is justified by the new elements she brings to the scene and by what happens after she arrives. Hawks plays on the immediacy of the audience's experience of film in his narrative construction, replacing plot logic with the pressure generated by one piece of film coming after another. The Big Sleep is sustained only by the passage from incident to incident, a completely internal narrative pressure which has no point of reference outside the film itself. The spatial tension of his framing or the a-temporal pacing of his scene transitions substitutes for exegesis. Because each scene works independently as a dramatic set-piece, we always seem to be where we ought to be, and never mind how we got here or where we're going next. With Hawks, you do not suspend your disbelief, you entirely disengage the faculty, because plausibility is not a requirement or an ingredient in his narratives. The plot is the final construct, built from the characters and situations that inhabit it. It comes last, not first, and its development is determined by the situations Hawks wishes to explore, not by a continual narrative pressure towards resolution. It may be more (Rio Bravo) or less (The Big Sleep) coherent, but the plot is never of primary importance. We are never in doubt of its outcome, only of the route.

Hawks' films are not progressive. They are self-contained exercises, and Hawks is a volunteer inside his own limitations. As a result, his aims are always limited and tactical. Scenes are frequently about the tactics of the situation they describe (Martin's entry into the Burdett saloon in Rio Bravo). It is not just that Hawks shoots in a deceptively simple visual style in which the camera rarely deviates from the eye-level shot of several characters forced into narrative relationship by their spatial proximity. Nor that this style of shooting emphasizes the claustrophobia of his interiors, establishing a pattern of tension and release between them and his fluid exteriors, where the capacity for expansive movement becomes a celebration of action and performance as their own rewards. Nor is it merely a matter of the way characters relate to each other, relying on conventions of cinematic narrative that allow their relationships to be presented in a form of shorthand, an indexical system of gesture and monosyllabic dialogue that permits the complicit audience to flesh out these skeletal figures.

Within any given scene, Hawks makes his audience work harder than any of his contemporaries. Whether it is a question of keeping pace with the machine-gun dialogue of His Girl Friday, or picking up on the sexual innuendo of Bogart and Bacall, or following the dual illogic of a Grant-Hepburn conversation in Bringing Up Baby, or interpreting a sentimental motive into the rigidly unsentimental action of Only Angels Have Wings, the spectator has to work to keep up and must participate in the scene if it is to function. It is one half of Hawks' dual approach to the question of his audience's passivity. He makes them work to read a second, unstated, layer of meaning within each of his scenes, and achieves their complicity by never making this process of participation explicit through explanation. Either you get the joke or you don't.

This, I take it, is what Hawks meant when he suggested that the director's primary skill was the ability to tell a story. But telling a story (narrative) is not the same as the story itself (plot). One of the things that makes Hawks such a supreme manipulator of narrative is his fluency in persuading the audience to ignore plot incongruities. It is by the very artificiality of his plots and settings that he operates the second, suitably contradictory half of his narrative equation, which emphasizes the passivity of the audience. Their inability to affect the passage of the film is stressed by the illogic of the plot development, by the refusal of Hawks' stories to make sense, to explain themselves, or even to progress.

Hawks endorses the limited aim of entertainment, but by his practice of it he not only provides a different basis for entertainment and a different narrative model, he also negotiates a different relationship between film and audience. Like the most thoughtful of genre directors, he substitutes economy for realism--a point which should be obvious from the first five minutes of any of his films. The real world outside the cinema does not intrude into the artificiality of his entertainments. Hawks accepts the idea of the film as product, and the status quo of the production system, but he does so overtly, never purporting to present his films as anything other than a diverting illusion. This acknowledgment of limitation makes both the balance and the effect of his narratives differ from those of consensual directors who seek to offer their audiences an illusion of reality.

Instead, Hawks presents us with a fixed artifact, held together by the arbitrary juxtaposition of pieces of film of the same set of characters in different situations, and allows us to engage it at whatever level we choose. The option of presuming that the plot makes sense, even the option of pre-suming that His Girl Friday is about The Lure of Irresponsi-bility, is left open to us. By himself acknowledging the ar-bitrary nature of the film as closed text, and by permeating his films with that acknowledgment (embarrassing his char-acters by abandoning them in the middle of a two-shot for longer than they can comfortably find a reason to be there), he provides a text which thereby becomes open for the au-dience to manipulate for themselves. That acknowledgment comes through Hawks' acceptance of the status quo as the initial fact; he accepts the conventions of the cinema because that is a requirement of his industrial position. As he is interested in professionals because he regards competence as more interesting than incompetence, he sees his competent acceptance of convention as no more than the required pro-fessionalism of his job. But as a professional, he doesn't make films for amateurs. He does not disguise those con-ventions or seek to beguile his audience into believing in his films and characters as anything but fictions whose existence is limited to the spectator's experience of the film. Hawks dissents from the consensus by embracing the artificiality of the American cinema, and thus permitting his audience to acknowledge this artificiality at the same time that they ac-quiesce in the arbitrary nature of his narrative.

With Hawks as a starting-point, it is possible to propose a distinction between two strands of the American cinema: the Cinema of the Consensus, and the Cinema of Dissent. That dissent is sometimes, but by no means invariably, overtly political, but that is never its defining quality. What categorizes the Cinema of Dissent is its renegotiation of the relationship between film and audience, as the Consensus is categorized by its failure to do so. That process of renegotiation must always begin with the director's acceptance of the limitations of his position, both in relation to the system of production and in the nature of the unilateral communication he practices with his audience. That is why these Interludes on Dissent will consistently deal with directors who exploit the conventions of Hollywood cinema as a starting-point for their subversion.

PART 2

THE LINE OF LEAST RESISTANCE

Too many girls follow the line
of least resistance--but a good
line is hard to resist.

Mae West, in Klondike Annie (1935,
Paramount; dir. Raoul Walsh)

CHAPTER 4

SENSE AND CENSORSHIP

CHIEF INVESTIGATOR STRIPLING: Mr Menjou,
if a picture is produced, as for example Mission
to Moscow, which gives a false portrayal or which
has propaganda in it, who do you hold responsible
in your own mind as a veteran actor in the motion-
picture industry?

MR. MENJOU: Well, I believe that the manufacturer of any product is responsible in the end for
the quality of his product.

MR. STRIPLING: In other words, the producers
should be held responsible?

MR. MENJOU: They should be.

House Committee on Un-American Activities,
October 1947. [1]

The producers, the studio executives, never attempted
to deny their public responsibility for the quality of their
product, nor for its content.   Their films, of necessity,
existed in the public domain, and were therefore subject to
the critical comment not only of their audiences, but also
of the socially opinionated.   As a pervasive mass entertainment, the cinema was exposed to a more intense examination of its social implications than either more conventional
non-durable consumer goods or forms of expression generally seen to operate independently of commercial pressures
and the responsibilities of the mass audience.   The unique
position of the film industry made it vulnerable to a particular kind of public threat.   Film was a mass consumption
commodity that traded publicity in ideas and social conventions.   As a result its producers were obliged to acknowl-

edge their accountability for the value-systems they pur-
veyed. They were forced into poses of responsibility by
the manner in which other groups interpreted the commodity
they offered for sale.

In dealing with those who took an undue interest in
their merchandise, the producers invariably placed a pre-
mium on their own financial interests. The crucial threat
to the majors' interests came from the raising of the antitrust issue; compared to the maintenance of their economic
hegemony, questions of the political or artistic freedom of
the screen dwindled into insignificance. The only threats
industry leaders took note of were financial ones. Nothing
else could persuade them to act in concert, and nothing
would make them acquiesce so fast as a threatened boycott.
Equally, they saw no purpose in challenging a status quo
which worked to their financial advantage. Any stable system of internal or external control over expression could be
tolerated; so long as it did not work to the economic detri-
ment of the majors, they would not repudiate it. The emphasis on purely economic considerations in their attitude to
external pressure is well illustrated by their behavior on the
issue of censorship: since both the most severe restriction
of the cinema's freedom of expression and the greatest opportunity to expand that freedom took place at times of financial crisis in the industry, the majors' preference for
their short-term economic interest was never revealed so
clearly.

WILL H. HAYS AND THE PRACTICE OF BETTER BUSINESS

The constitutional position of film as a medium of
expression was defined by the Supreme Court in a ruling on
the case of Mutual Film Corp. vs. Ohio in 1915. In ruling
on the issue of the legality of state prior censorship, Justice
Joseph McKenna denied the cinema the protection of the Ohio
State guarantees of freedom of speech--and by default the
protection of the First Amendment--on three grounds.

> The exhibition of motion pictures is a business,
> pure and simple, originated and conducted for
> profit ... not to be regarded ... as part of the
> press of the country or as organs of public opin-
> ion. They are mere representations of events,

> of ideas and sentiments published or known; vivid,
> useful, and entertaining, no doubt, but ... capable
> of evil, having power for it, the greater because
> of their attractiveness and manner of exhibition. [2]

That judgment determined the legal status of film for the
next 37 years. It also delineated the terms of the debate
over accountability. The movies were entertainment, not
vehicles for ideas, but because of the particularly affecting
nature of the medium, they were deemed to have a peculiar
capacity for evil influence. Not only, therefore, did they
not qualify as constitutionally protected speech; those responsible for the maintenance of public order and morality
were bound to regard them warily because of their potential
for harm.

The producers had to don a cloak of respectability
not as a direct result of this decision, but because of its
consequences: the rapid proliferation of state and local
prior censorship boards, which would either cut sections
they deemed offensive from prints or ban the exhibition of
some films altogether. The studios' consciences were
reached through their pockets, the potential losses in revenue forcing them to seek a solution that would not interfere
with their business. If their companies could be made to
appear respectable in the public eye, their products would
be less liable to hostile scrutiny, and hence more profitable.
They needed to escape the unwelcome attentions of the reform lobby which had established prohibition and then turned
to the movies as an ideal target for its next crusade. The
production companies' eager response to the oppotunities for
more permissive subject matter provided by the dawning of
the Jazz Age in 1921 lent weight to the reformers' demands
for a system of federal censorship in the name of public
morality. The Arbuckle and Taylor scandals exacerbated
the public's increasing hostility towards Hollywood's decadent extravagances in a period of economic recession. Un-
contested, that hostility would damage box-office receipts as
well as imposing sanctions on content. To maintain their
business freedom the companies needed a cosmetic gloss
that would make them appear as conventional businessmen.

It might be argued that the company heads, as individuals, felt a similar need. The studio moguls were almost all of extremely humble origins, and had little or no
formal education. None of them were White Anglo-Saxon
Protestants, the majority being immigrants or the sons of

immigrants, and further hampered in their strivings for the trappings of social respectability by being Jewish in a period when anti-Semitism was a common business practice and a respectable belief. Whatever incentives their original circumstances might have given them in the first twenty years of the industry's history, when it grew from nothing to having a gross annual box-office income of $500 million, Loew, Mayer, Zukor, the Schenks and the rest may well have comprised the most socially disadvantaged group of industrial magnates in the economic history of America. By 1921 the industry was moving out of its initial phase of meteoric expansion, in which business ethics were a polite irrelevance, into a period of consolidation, stabilization, the formation of vertically integrated companies and the establishment of the film factory. But corporate respectability was not yet theirs.

> Business generally looked down a sensitive nose at its new companion. The world of banking sniffed at it. The royalty of industry regarded it as something faintly unsavoury, untoward, hooliganish, though it could not be brushed aside as unimportant. [3]

When they founded the Motion Picture Producers and Distributors of America in March 1922, the industry leaders chose as their figure-head the most respectable man their money could buy. Will H. Hays was then Postmaster General, had been Chairman of the Republican National Convention that had elected Harding, and claimed to have originated the maxim that what America needed was "more business in government and less government in business." For $100,000 a year he became "the spokesman for the Association in all communications to the public,"[4] but he was also in a position from which he could, to a degree, impose his political outlook upon the producers. Faced on the one hand with the growing censorship lobby and on the other with the intransigence of the producers in their mutual dealings, Hays worked to implement his maxim with the ultimate intention of converting the film industry into a model of business self-regulation.

Initially, at least, he was considerably more successful in restraining external opposition--particularly in preventing the establishment of further state censorship boards-- than he was in controlling the internecine disputes of his employers. The evident failure of Prohibition, Republican policies of minimal government implicit in the return to "nor-

malcy," and the semantic hostility the word "censorship"
aroused (particularly in Hays' persistent use of the phrase
"political censorship") weakened the reform lobby.   The
producers, however, were reluctant to accept even self-
imposed limitations on their freedom of content.   Their
rhetorical interest in freedom of expression failed to disguise their principal objection: the assumption that the
most obviously censorable content was also the most profitable.   Frequently during the 1920s they passed what
amounted to good resolutions promising

> to establish the highest possible moral and artistic
> standards of motion picture production[5]

and

> to prevent the prevalent type of book and play
> from becoming the prevalent type of picture ... [6]

but they never required themselves to take more than token
notice of these resolutions.

It was this failure on Hays' part that led the reform
groups to link the questions of censorship and antitrust legislation in the proposals they brought before Congress.   In
1928 the Brookhart Bill attempted to combine censorship with
an attack on the system of block booking and blind selling,
alleging that these two mechanisms of distributor control
forced inferior material on the exhibitor and the public.
The assumption that block booking forced theatres to show
films of questionable morality was a consistent feature of
subsequent legislative proposals.   The Hudson Bill, first
introduced in 1930 (and re-introduced several times there-
after), combined a prohibition of block booking with elaborate standards of morality affecting film content, a rigid
licensing system, and controls over production.   The Neely-
Pettingill Bill of 1936 (revived as the Neely Bill of 1938,
and introduced for a third time by Senator Harvey M. Kil-
gore in 1943) used the Motion Picture Research Council
Payne Fund Studies on the harmful effects of screen content
to justify the outlawing of block booking and blind selling.

The legislative relation of antitrust and censorship
questions, however, provided Hays with evidence to support
the strategy he was attempting to impose on the M. P. P. D. A.
It involved accepting the validity of public concern over content, but avoiding interference by the adoption of a code of

self-regulation as stringent as that which the moral conservatives in the vanguard of the reformers would themselves wish
to implement.   Such a restrictive policy, the argument ran
had substantial commercial benefits.   It would undermine the
antitrust lobby, which was the principal enemy, by removing
the ammunition of alleged evil influence.   Even more, if the
M. P. P. D. A. companies could be seen to be enforcing a respectable code of conduct in their choice of content, they
could claim not only that they were providing adequate evidence of self-regulation; they could also argue that block
booking helped to keep films of dubious moral quality, made
by non-affiliates of the M. P. P. D. A., out of the theatres.
The loss of creative freedom was a small price to pay for
the enormous advantages of monopoly profit.

Hays' strategy received its first articulation in the
list of "Don'ts and Be Carefuls" adopted in June 1927 by the
Association of Motion Picture Producers. * Compiled by officers of the A. M. P. P. and Colonel Jason Joy (Hays' appointee as liaison officer between the studios and the public), the list was based on material about which objections
had been received by the M. P. P. D. A. Department of Public Relations, or which had been cut by local censors.   The
determining principle behind the inclusion of each item was
not a consideration of morality or public taste, but the practical application of Hays' argument.   If the moral watchdogs
had nothing to bark at, they would have no reason to bite,
either.

The working abstract of the 1930 Production Code
made the rationale behind Hays' actions even more apparent.
As originally written by Martin Quigley and Father Daniel
Lord, S. J., ** the Code was an argument in Catholic moral
philosophy which contained no specific catalog of material
deemed unsuitable for the screen.   When the Code was
adopted as binding by the M. P. P. D. A. in 1934, what Quigley and Lord had written was designated as "The Reasons

_____

*A West Coast organization of the major producers, estab-
lished in 1924, the A. M. P. P. was a separate body from the
M. P. P. D. A., but in practice had much the same membership.   Policy seldom varied between the two Associations.

**Martin Quigley was the staunchly Catholic editor and pub-
lisher of the Motion Picture Herald.   Father Lord was Professor of Dramatics at the University of St. Louis.

Supporting the Preamble of the Code, " and was, for all
practical purposes, ignored. The Code itself was Hays'
compilation of the prohibitions in Quigley/Lord together
with those of the A. M. P. P. "Don'ts and Be Carefuls" that
they had omitted. It was dominated less by a specifically
Catholic moral stance than by Hays' requirement that it
should preclude the necessity of any further censorial controls. *

It was not an easy strategy to sell to a group of men
who had made their fortunes in exploitation. Neither their
own good resolutions nor the threat of legislation gave it the
force to become more than a paper policy. Col. Joy complained to Hays in January 1929 that his Studio Relations
Committee, in charge of the administration of the "Don'ts
and Be Carefuls, " was dealing with only 20 per cent of
A. M. P. P. companies' productions. Some companies did
not require production supervisors to take any notice of his
decisions about debatable material. In any case, since he
did not screen release prints, he had no means of determining whether the others were incorporating his suggestions
into their final scripts or not. M. P. P. D. A. members successfully resisted attempts to have the Production Code included in the 1933 National Recovery Administration Code of
Fair Competition for the Motion Picture Industry, which
would have made violation of the Code subject to the punitive clauses of the N. R. A. code. ** Their reluctance to
accept self-regulation gave support to charges that the industry would not and could not control itself in the public
interest, and to Senator Brookhart's allegations that

Mr Hays has done nothing towards improving the

---

*For example, nothing in Quigley/Lord required a prohibi-
tion on the depiction of miscegenation, which was carried
over from the "Don'ts and Be Carefuls, " since it would
obviously be excised by local censors in the Southern States.

**The NRA Code merely acknowledged the existence of the
Production Code in terms reminiscent of the industry's previous pledges of good behavior:
  The industry pledges its combined strength to maintain
  right moral standards in the production of motion pictures
  as a form of entertainment. The industry pledges itself
  to adhere to the regulations made within the industry to
  attain this purpose. [7]

> moral tone of the movies.... The truth is that
> Hays was employed primarily as a "fixer" to pro-
> tect the industry against any sort of regulation
> through public action. [8]

The companies' refusal to adopt the Code in the early
1930s was based on economic circumstance. While the post-
sound expansion had carried the industry over the first years
of the Depression, it had involved them in expensive conversion of facilities, and had doubled production costs. The industry's slump came in 1932-1933, when both Universal and
R. K. O. were in receivership and Paramount was near bankruptcy as annual audience attendance figures declined for the
first time in the industry's history. Only a direct and severe economic threat could cause the studio executives to
abandon sensational content policies that all their experience
inclined them to believe would secure the highest audiences.
Hays recognized their financial problems and relaxed his
internal campaign for self-censorship for the duration of the
crisis. But if he was forced to accept this situation, others,
less concerned with the economic well-being of the movies,
were not.

In particular, the Catholic Church reacted strongly to
the industry's failure to observe the Catholic-composed Code.
During 1933 there were a number of moves by Catholic
clergy threatening boycotts of films and theatres, and in
December a committee of bishops was set up to examine
the question of the church's attitude to motion pictures.
Their conclusions resulted in the formation, in April 1934,
of the Legion of Decency, whose members were pledged "to
remain away from all motion pictures except those which do
not offend decency and Christian morality. "[9] The threat of
mass boycott, which gained additional support from Protestant, Jewish and other voluntary organizations, was astutely
timed. It came at a period of economic insecurity, when
movie stocks were at their lowest, and it reached its peak
of activity--including a total boycott by Catholics in Philadelphia, which caused a reported 40 per cent drop in box-
office receipts[10]--while plans for the new production season
were being made. The producers capitulated immediately.
In June Martin Quigley and Joseph Breen (since November
1933 head of the Studio Relations Committee) met with the
Catholic bishops to request a relaxation of the boycott in
return for a strict enforcement of the Code. On July 1 the
Studio Relations Committee was replaced by the Production
Code Administration, which would vet all script drafts and

release prints of every film produced, distributed or exhibited by the member companies of the M. P. P. D. A. , who
contracted not to distribute or exhibit any film not bearing
the P. C. A. Seal of Approval.   The appeals procedure against
any P. C. A. decision was demolished, and conformity was
further enforced by a statutory $25, 000 fine for any viola-
tion of the Code's provisions.

KINDER CUTS

        In conceding as they did, the M. P. P. D. A. members
had provided the clearest example to date of the sanctity of
their short-term economic interest.   They took to the Code
not because they believed, as Hays claimed to, that audiences had been gradually educated to accept higher moral
standards in their entertainment, but because of the threatened boycott.   And in giving in to a threat, they also accepted the principle by which Hays had constructed the Code's
working abstract.   The strength of the entire system of prior
censorship was that it operated on the basis of a series of
undefined relationships, rooted in the producers' acknowledgment that the P. C. A. was a necessary intermediary to give
them protection from the undesirable assaults of organizations more morally scrupulous than they themselves might
care to be.   The P. C. A. in practice operated as a mechanism for the maintenance of a necessary predictability in the
subject matter of movies and the manner of its handling, in
much the same way that the formulae of genre pictures did.
The difference was merely in the manner of audience response reaching the producers: a Western formula would
prove its value in box-office returns; a censorship formula
proved its value in not provoking concerned organizations to
action.   The undoubted power over film content which was
vested in the hierarchy of the Legion was based on its
proven or threatened economic sanction.   Concern about the
movies went well beyond the merely censorable, and Hays
frequently had to deal with protests from trade associations
over a film's representation of their business.   The industry's response to such complaints was strongly related to
the amount of economic pressure the complainant might
exert, either directly or through influence in Washington. [11]
In early 1933 Hays was sufficiently concerned about the new
Administration's intentions to express his fear that the hostility generated in Congress by Gabriel Over the White House

might provoke punitive tax or censorship legislation. Political films which caused "affront" ought to be avoided.[12]
Above all the industry wished to manufacture an acceptable product: since its audience was undifferentiated, and since the product had to achieve mass consumption before it became profitable, it seemed to make economic sense to pitch film content fairly consistently at the lowest common denominator of its audience, and equally, to adopt the line of least resistance in dealing with protests about content, insofar as these were compatible with successful corporate economics.

In such circumstances, it would have been naive to expect the M. P. P. D. A. to challenge governmental prior censorship institutions. The Production Code was one element of a diffuse censorship system that involved Federal, state and municipal organizations and opinion-making groups such as the Legion. As far as the majors were concerned this diffuse system operated as an integral whole, as a means of imposing pressure on filmmakers to handle only broadly acceptable subject matter. To challenge the legitimacy of one element in that system was to challenge the whole construct. Since that construct came to serve the economic interests of the majors, challenging it would serve neither their short- nor their long-term interests. They cooperated with local censorship boards because they wanted to appear both responsible and responsive to pressure, and because of their economic requirement that their films receive the widest possible distribution, regardless of the restrictions on content or the excisions they might occasionally be forced to make as a result. Much the same attitude, filtered through the P. C. A., affected their response to the Legion of Decency and other pressure groups. This attitude reaped its rewards in the form of a greater reciprocal cooperation from the censors in their dealings with the major distributors. The preferential treatment afforded to the majors made up for the occasional inconvenience brought on by erratic censorship decisions. Equally, the Legion had at least a tacit interest in the preservation of oligopoly. In his 1945 thesis on the Legion, Paul Facey observed,

> The Department of Justice has tried to break up the monopoly of the film industry. Should it carry its attack to the point where it would force the dissolution of the Hays Office, the Legion of Decency would face a situation fraught with real problems. Instead of a single focus for its pressure, the Hays Office, it would have as many as there are producers.[13]

The maintenance of this loosely defined censorship system, with the Production Code as its focus, served a pwerful economic interest at the same time as it upheld the public image of respectability the major companies sought to preserve. * The Code was a means of standardizing content and restricting audience expectations as to what constituted entertainment in the cinema. For an industry acutely sensitive to the pressure of public opinion the Code functioned as a means of eliminating content that might inadvertently stir up controversy, and of neutering such controversial content as might be deliberately included. [15] The system of control was enhanced by the practical operation of the Code, which was frequently accused by independent producers and distributors of showing a greater leniency in its decisions over the content of films produced or distributed by the major companies than in cases involving independent productions. Since provisional P. C. A. approval was a vital factor in obtaining the outside financing necessary for independent production, this alleged bias helped ensure that the independents were unable to compete on equal terms with the studios.

The majors also found the P. C. A. Seal of Approval a useful additional tool in maintaining their effective exhibition monopoly. ** It was, for example, helpful in restricting the

---

*The coincidence of the Production Code's implementation shortly after most of the major companies were taken over by Wall Street interests has not yet been examined in any detail. Although evidence to establish a direct causal relationship would be almost impossible to obtain, the Code's standardization and neutralization of film content would be likely to appeal on both economic and ideological grounds to Morgan and Rockefeller interests. It is also the case that, in the later stages of their negotiations with the M. P. P. D. A., the Legion of Decency abandoned their dealings with the producers and concentrated their attention on the executives in New York. On June 15, 1934, Variety reported,
Switch of all moral problems from the West to the East is revealed to have been motivated by an understanding that the crusaders have lost patience with the studio heads, but still believe in the judgment and good intentions of the Eastern executives. [14]

**Prior to 1948, films distributed by M. P. P. D. A. companies, all of which had to have a P. C. A. Seal, accounted for 97 per cent of films obtaining releases in the United States.

import of foreign films. The distribution companies, reluctant to handle product that was partially outside their economic control (and hence less profitable), used the Code as a weapon with which to question their suitability for American audiences. Though not originally responsible for associating European films with dubious subject matter, they were content to allow the relationship to permeate the public consciousness. Raymond Moley, in his laudatory account of the Hays Office, published in 1945, concluded his final chapter by emphasizing Hays', and the M. P. P. D. A. 's, intention of adhering to the standards laid down in the Code:

> There will, of course, be critical questions of enforcement to meet, since the present standards prescribed by the Code are the highest in the world. These high standards are now so completely taken for granted by American public opinion, in fact, that little or no public pressure is any longer exerted to support them.... Of course there will be demands from some countries for more piquant entertainment than the Code allows, but as far as present prospects indicate, these countries will have to supply their own spice.[16]

At best, the M. P. P. D. A. 's ostentatiously-held high moral standards coincided with their economic self-interest. For the previous ten years the P. C. A. 's version of wholesome family entertainment had proved eminently profitable for the major companies, and there seemed little reason for them to upset their vested interests in innocuousness, particularly when the direct opposition from foreign films could be held in check by maintaining moral values.

A LIMITED EXPRESSION

> "It is therefore evident, gentlemen, that there never was a real issue in this controversy."
>
> Government mediator at the end of Black Fury.[17]

The Code enshrined in its prohibitions the common

wisdom of Justice McKenna's 1915 ruling that film had a special capacity for evil. It stated, in "General Principles. 1. ":

> No picture shall be produced which will lower the moral standards of those who see it. Hence the sympathy of the audience shall never be thrown to the side of crime, wrong-doing, evil, or sin. [18]

That regulation, more than any other, controlled the nature of the subject matter, plot and characterization available to the filmmakers. In practice, Breen and his staff would analyze stories primarily in relation to their theme.

> For such evaluative purposes, the theme of a picture can be determined by asking what problem confronts the leading characters and stating how the problem is solved. If the characters find their answers in moral ways, the theme of the picture is usually acceptable. If the characters find it necessary to steal or commit adultery or break some other social taboo or law, the story is unacceptable unless proper and compensating moral values and element of punishment are present. [19]

"Compensating moral values" were defined by Breen in a letter to Hays in March, 1936:

> Time and again there occur in the decisions of the P. C. A. the words: "Compensating moral values." The Code demands "that in the end the audience feels that evil is wrong and good is right." To satisfy this requirement of the Code, stories must contain, at least, sufficient good to compensate for any evil they relate. The compensating moral values are: good characters, the voice of morality, a lesson, regeneration of the transgressor, suffering and punishment. [20]

The bulk of the P. C. A. 's activities was concerned with the detailed administration of the Code, which operated on the principal of judicial precedent, cases being filed by subject, from "abdomen" to "zipper." But since none of the correspondence or decisions of the P. C. A. were published, the Code was open to re-interpretation, and special dispensations might always be granted, as in the case of Clark Gable's last line in Gone with the Wind, which specifically contradicted Part V of the Code, as amended November 1, 1939. [21]

There was, further, a large peripheral area of the
P. C. A.'s work which involved making suggestions about material not specifically forbidden by the Code itself, but liable
to incur the displeasure of either local or foreign censors
(such as the British Censor's persistent practice of deleting
the Lord's Prayer from any film), or of interest groups.   It
was in this context that comment about the overtly political
content of films might occur.   Such advice was not infre-
quent among the potentially socially controversial films of
the 1930s, at least.   Colin Shindler cites the case of the
drastic altering of the story line of Black Fury (1935,
Warner Bros.; dir. Michael Curtiz), from an indictment of
working conditions among Pennsylvania coal miners to a
gangster melodrama about an innocent's exploitation by rack-
eteering union leaders. [22]   Walter Wanger, producer of
Blockade (1938; dir. William Dieterle) was advised that it
might be as well not to identify his characters with either
side in the Spanish Civil War, and that even to identify the
locale as Spain was dangerous. [23]   Olga Martin stated explicitly in 1937:

> Nothing subversive of the fundamental law of the
> land, and of duly constituted authority, can be
> shown.   Communistic propaganda, for instance,
> is banned from the screen. [24]

Ruth Inglis quotes from a letter from Breen to Samuel Goldwyn regarding Dead End (1937; dir. William Wyler):

> We would like to recommend, in passing, that you
> be less emphatic, throughout, in the photographing
> of this script, in showing the contrast between the
> conditions of the poor in tenements and those of
> the rich in apartment houses.   Specifically, we
> recommend you do not show, at any time, or at
> least that you do not emphasize, the presence of
> filth, or smelly garbage cans, or garbage floating
> in the river, into which the boys jump for a swim.
> This recommendation is made under the general
> heading of good and welfare, because our reaction
> is that such scenes are likely to give offense. [25]

Inglis' conclusion, borne out by Shindler, "that, upon occasion, the Production Code Administration does try to exert
a conservative influence,"*[26] would almost certainly not

---

*"The tribulations of Black Fury, Gabriel Over   (continued)

have been contested by Breen. Moley quotes him as saying:

> Without going into the philosophical discussion of whether or not revolution or violence are ever desirable, and without raising the question of the role which the arts may or may not have played in the dissemination of political ideas, the Code Administration maintains that it is unwise for any producer to expose the industry to the charge of fomenting political and social unrest. It emphasises the point that when this is done by a book, the reader who takes violent exception to the content is merely outraged at the author, not at the publisher or at the entire art of the printed word. But the motion picture spectator, when he is annoyed, is annoyed at "the damned movies," and, likely as not, at the theatre where he saw the offending picture. [28]

He defended the P. C. A against charges that its moral, social or political conservatism interfered with the artistic potential and social responsibilities of the American film by claiming that it was protecting the industry and its workers as a community because it prevented them damaging their own public esteem. Its rigid standards were necessary because large forces of articulate and powerful opinion threatened economic sanction if they were not adhered to. Because the industry was particularly vulnerable, it had to take particular care. The Code Administration was merely the industry's mechanism for establishing the exigencies, restrictions, and conventions within which the medium's artists might legitimately operate. If the limitations on narrative development imposed by the system of "compensating moral values" prevented the forceful articulation of explicit social criticism, it merely reflected the public will of Justice McKenna and the Legion of Decency that the cinema should ensure that its mass entertainment was "harmless."

Despite its predominantly conservative effects, the Code was a rich source of contradictions. Its impact on the crime film was immediate. Gangster films, which had

---

the White House, of Dead End and Blockade, are clear indicators of the political bias and crucial deployment of the power of the Hays Office." [27]

been one of the principal objects of the reformers' criticism, had been closely modeled on the genre's first success, <u>Little Caesar</u>. They depicted the flamboyant rise and abrupt fall of a figure usually modeled on Al Capone, usually of Italian or Irish extraction, usually deriving his income from bootlegging, and always limited in his area of operation to a city, usually a thinly disguised studio version of Chicago or New York.* Despite their inevitable morally compensating violent death in the streets, the films' protagonists were presented as heroic in their assertiveness and determination to get to the top, offering an attractive if left-handed version of the myth of Success. By its stipulation that

> Crimes against the law ... shall never be presented in such a way as to throw sympathy with the crime as against law and justice, or to inspire others with a desire for imitation.[30]

the Code obliged the studios to convert their individualist outlaw heroes into equally heroic embodiments of benevolent federal authority, but it failed to remove the moral ambiguities of the genre. Warners remodeled <u>Public Enemy</u> James Cagney as a G-Man, but left his behavior unmodified: despite a specific prohibition in the Code against the law resorting to unlawful means to gain the ends of justice,[31] Cagney's previous violence against the law was simply replaced by an equal violence in the name of the law. A 1935 amendment to the Code, that

> Crime stories are not to be approved when they portray the activities of American gangsters, armed and in violent conflict with the law or law-enforcing officers,[32]**

---

*It is, however, worth noting Capone's personal hostility to gangster movies. "They ought to take them and throw them in the lake," he declared. "They're doing nothing but harm to the younger element of this country. I don't blame the censors for trying to ban them.... These gang movies are making a lot of kids want to be tough boys and they don't serve any useful purpose."[29]

**In large part this Amendment was designed to prohibit films about Dillinger, Bonnie and Clyde, and the Public Enemies of J. Edgar Hoover.

directed against G-Men and its sequels, appears to have
been less than strictly enforced as the cycle continued into
1937, to both praise for its responsible presentation of governmental power and condemnation for its devious circum-
navigation of the spirit of the Code.

    The contradictions inherent in the studios' solution to
the prohibition on gangster films were most concisely indicated in a title change by which Warners' second G-Man
film, Public Enemy's Wife, was renamed G-Man's Wife for
its British release. The depths of the contradictions, however, emerged with their next film, Bullets or Ballots, in
which "Edward G. (Little Caesar) Robinson moves in on the
modern mobs."33 The Robinson character, Johnny Blake,
is a New York detective who joins a crime syndicate in order to discover who its secret bosses are. The film man-
ages to follow closely the established plot structure of the
gangster film, depicting Robinson's rise in the criminal
hierarchy and his battle with Humphrey Bogart for control
of the rackets. It even provides him with the archetypal
gangster's ending: fatally wounded by Bogart, he staggers
out of his last meeting with the bosses to die in the street.
At a plot level, the contradictions are apparent. As a cop,
Robinson denounces racketeers and declares, "I don't like to
see decent people pushed around." As a gangster, he introduces the numbers racket to New York. There is, too, a
contradiction between the moral fervor with which the film
denounces the rackets and the corruption that permits them,
and its generic impulse to provide an individualistic, heroic
solution to the problem it poses. On the one hand, Robinson is depicted as a thoroughly honest man, made very uncomfortable by the duplicity of his role as undercover agent
where he has to "double cross" criminals rather than give
them the "even break" he has always done in the past. His
moral qualms are made a central issue by the presence of
Joan Blondell, who loses faith in him when he takes the
numbers game away from her. In tension with the film's
foregrounding of Robinson's conscience is the strident attack
on the racketeers contained in the imitation March of Time
documentary with which the film opens, and expressed with
particular clarity in an early script treatment:

>   The purpose of the picture is to arouse public
> indignation and to stop public support of every
> racket chronicled herein, for without public sup-
> port, the rackets will die!... Besides presenting
> entertainment the picture's mission will be to

leave a flaming question mark in the minds of
American audiences.　What can be done to stamp
out rackets and racketeers as effectively as Re-
peal stamped out bootleggers and rum-runners?[34]

In its advertising the film avowed the educative purpose which
came with its acquisition of a documentary mode of expression.　One ad declared,

Watch the cops crack down on the Secret Friends
of the Public Enemies ... the higher-up Dictator-
ship of Modern Gangdom that's still sticking up
America to the tune of $15,000,000,000 a year!

But having proposed a factual basis behind the story, both
the advertising and the film itself abandoned documentary for
the individualist moral concerns of its plot.　The same ad
asked,

Will "Little Caesar" rat on this secret Syndicate
of Crime? ... can he save his own skin by turning in the Big Bosses?[35]

Although the individualist narrative was Hollywood's conventional mode of expression it was rarely placed in such direct tension with an explicit use of the documentary form,
even in "social consciousness films."

Bullets or Ballots is clearly a fissured film, in the
category that Comolli and Narboni argue should be examined
because their cracks expose the ideology they express.[36]
What is noteworthy about it is that the film's internal tension is directly attributable to the operation of the Hays
Code:　from the visual details by which a man firing a gun
and the man he shoots are not presented in the same shot,
to the underlying stress between the objective of entertainment and the claim to social consciousness, the film's contradictions are products of its obligation to abide by the
Code rather than arising from any creative tension in its
production.　Its presentation of its principal villains is
particularly revealing.

The film's Secret Syndicate of Crime is actually run
by a Wall Street banker, an ex-Senator, and a third man
unidentified in the film but described in the script as "a
young millionaire, socialite and clubman."[37]　This elite
triumvirate appears in evening dress, and there is a clearly

established contrast between their refined manners and dress and those of Robinson and Barton MacLane, the leading racketeer. The Bosses are identified as members of the Establishment, but whether that position is defined by their economic and political power or by their social performance is left open. They appear in only a couple of scenes and have little opportunity to be more than ciphers of the plot, an explicit, conspiratorial version of the "Big Boy" figure present in the genre since <u>Little Caesar</u>. The film's implicit suggestion is that the American elite are corrupt, and exploit "decent people." It leaves ambiguous the question of whether that corruption is because they are decadent socialites or because they are bankers and monopoly capitalists.

In similar vein, the film presents its racketeers as a species of businessmen. Their headquarters is a vast accounting house, and their supervisor, MacLane, describes and conducts himself as a businessman.* He tells the hotheaded Bogart,

> Someday, you're going to get wise to the fact that strong arm gangster stuff went out with prohibition! You're not running liquor any more ... you're in big business![40]

While this change in the personality of the gangster obviously bore some relation to external events, the presentation of the racketeer as a species of businessman was also encouraged by the Production Code. Writing in 1937, Olga Martin suggested that the Code's stipulations meant that

> the tough type of individual formerly used to portray a gangster is no longer allowed for screen presentation. This means that the hard-looking, foul-speaking type, eager to kill, is banned from screen stories. He has been replaced with a new type of criminal suggestive of the racketeer rather than a "gangster." Instead of being hard-looking, he appears to be a gentleman with at least a surface polish. Instead of using foul speech, he is

---

*In this he echoes Capone himself, who once remarked, "Everybody calls me a racketeer. I call myself a businessman."[38] In a significant reorientation of the conventional analysis, Shindler remarks on the essential conservatism of the gangster as a public figure.[39]

soft-spoken and businesslike in his conversation rather than "tough." Finally, instead of showing an eagerness to kill, he is eager to avoid killing, preferring to use his wits to gain his ends rather than to use weapons, to resort to scheming rather than violence. The danger of building up the racketeer as a central character, dominating his group, is avoided by making him more or less anonymous --as one of a group of associates who operate as partners. [41]

The objective was clear enough: to present criminals in a way that would not make them appear glamorous, or which could be easily imitated. But the effects were less clear-cut: the criminal figure became outwardly more respectable, and much less readily distinguished from the society around him. If racketeers were presented as businessmen, the distinction between the two activities was reduced, and business, particularly Big Business, acquired a dubious moral status. This was emphasized by the recurrent motif of disguise in crime films: in Bullets or Ballots Robinson is a cop disguised as a racketeer, the Bosses are criminals purporting to be decent citizens, MacLane's organization is concealed behind the offices of the Metropolitan Business Improvement Association Inc., and even Bogart insists, "I'm doing a legal wholesale business here."[42] The Code replaced one form of moral ambiguity with another, for however ambivalent the audience's response to Little Caesar was, at least it was clear where everyone stood. The early crime films' emphasis on loyalty was replaced by an atmosphere described by Joan Blondell:

> Around this town the only reason friends pat you on the back is to find an easy place to break it![43]

Duplicity, deception and concealment became dominant motifs, proposing that the genre's urban environment was an inherently unstable and unpredictable place, where recognizable boundaries between law and crime could easily disappear: in Bullets or Ballots policemen and criminals are paralleled by their chafing against the restraints of their organizations, and the moral impropriety of Bogart's murder of a newspaper publisher is lessened by the enthusiasm with which Robinson, in the next scene, throws a minor criminal through a plate-glass door.

The contradictory tensions between documentary and

generic convention, community responsibility and individual
direct action, social consciousness and entertainment, that
permeate Bullets or Ballots and leave it open in detail to a
wide range of ideological interpretations are largely present
because of its conformity to the Production Code. The ambiguity of Robinson's status, in particular, was revealed by
the ending. He dies, as a gangster must, in the street, but
in doing so he contravenes a Code regulation that "law-
enforcing officers should not be shown dying at the hands of
criminals. "44* The Code provided a restrictive framework
for film narrative that was not only in tension with the generic impulses of much of Hollywood's product but itself
contradicted its conservative purposes. The conflicting elements within individual narratives can in retrospect be used
to point up the films' implicit ideologies, while the Code itself can be seen as the source of Hollywood's confused solutions to such problematic areas of content as crime, sexual-
ity and ethnicity. In having to avoid offending any group and
compensate for immorality, Hollywood perpetrated stereotypes and made a fetish of "glamor" that corresponded only
obliquely to the world outside itself.

REFERENCES

1. Quoted from Eric Bentley, ed. , Thirty Years of Trea-
    son: Excerpts from Hearings before the House Com-
    mittee on Un-American Activities, 1938-1968 (New
    York, 1971), p. 121.

2. Mutual Film Corp. vs. Ohio 236 U. S. 230, 244 (1915).
    Quoted in Richard Randall, Censorship of the Movies:
    The Social and Political Control of a Mass Medium
    (Madison, Wisconsin, 1968), p. 19.

3. Raymond Moley, The Hays Code, p. 23.

4. "By-laws of the M. P. P. D. A. , Article IX, Section 1. "
    Hays' salary was later increased to $150, 000.

5. By-laws of the M. P. P. D. A. , Article XIV.

---

*An alternative ending, in which Robinson survives, and is
rewarded by Blondell's attendance at his hospital bedside,
was filmed but apparently not used. 45

6. M. P. P. D. A. Resolution passed February 26, 1924.

7. National Recovery Administration Motion Picture Code, Article VII, Part I. Quoted in Jowett, p. 245.

8. Senator Smith W. Brookhart, speech in the Senate, February 1932. Quoted in Ruth Inglis, Freedom of the Movies, p. 89.

9. Original Pledge of the Legion of Decency, 1934. Quoted in Cobbett Steinberg, Reel Facts (New York, 1978), p. 585.

10. Inglis, p. 124.

11. For an effective example of such pressure, see Colin Shindler's account of the National Coal Administration's campaign to modify Black Fury (Warner Bros., 1936). Colin Shindler, Hollywood During the Great Depression (unpublished Ph. D. thesis, Cambridge University, 1974), pp. 323-338.

12. Will H. Hays, letter to James Wingate, February 14, 1933, in Gabriel Over the White House file, Association of Motion Picture and Television Producers, Inc., Los Angeles. Quoted in Shindler, p. 210.

13. Paul W. Facey, The Legion of Decency: A Sociological Analysis of the Emergence and Development of a Pressure Group (New York, 1974), p. 190.

14. Quoted in Olga G. Martin, Hollywood's Movie Commandments (New York, 1937), p. 35.

15. Shindler includes several detailed case studies of the Code's operation to this effect. See in particular his account of Blockade (1938), pp. 172-177, and of several Warner Bros. films, pp. 301-339.

16. Moley, p. 222.

17. Quoted in Shindler, p. 334.

18. "Code to Govern the Making of Talking, Synchronized and Silent Motion Pictures," General Principles, 1. Quoted in Moley, p. 241.

19. Quoted in Inglis, p. 161.

20. Quoted in Moley, p. 98.

21. For correspondence, see Rudy Behlmer, ed. , Memo from David O. Selznick (New York, 1972), pp. 268-270.

22. Shindler, pp. 327-330.

23. Letters from Joseph Breen to Walter Wanger, February 3 and February 22, 1937, in Blockade file, A. M. P. T. P. Quoted in Shindler, pp. 172-3.

24. Martin, p. 118.

25. Quoted in Inglis, p. 181.

26. Inglis, p. 181.

27. Shindler, p. 364.

28. Quoted in Moley, p. 177.

29. Quoted in Kenneth Allsop, The Bootleggers (London, 1961), p. 344.

30. Production Code, General Principles, 1. Quoted in Moley, p. 242.

31. Martin, p. 117.

32. Quoted in Martin, p. 132.

33. Publicity booklet, Bullets or Ballots, at Department of Special Collections, University of Southern California, Los Angeles, p. 16.

34. Script draft titled And the Home of the Rackets, no author shown (Martin Mooney?), dated November 23, 1935, at the Center for Film and Theater Research, University of Wisconsin, Madison. Title page.

35. Publicity booklet, Bullets or Ballots, p. 14.

36. Jean-Louis Comolli and Jean Narboni, "Cinema/ Ideology/Criticism (I)," Screen, Vol. 12 No. 1. Reprinted in Screen Reader (London, 1977), p. 7.

37. Seton I. Miller, Bullets and Ballots, Final Script,
dated February 5, 1936 (with revisions to March 28,
1936), p. 32. At Center for Film and Television Research, University of Wisconsin, Madison.

38. Quoted in Eugene Rostow, Born to Lose: The Gangster
Film in America (New York, 1978), p. 88.

39. Shindler, p. 238.

40. Miller, Bullets and Ballots final script, p. 29.

41. Martin, pp. 133-134.

42. Miller, Bullets and Ballots final script, p. 79.

43. Miller, Bullets and Ballots final script, p. 54.

44. Martin, p. 123.

45. References are made to this ending as having been
used in the United States in British newspaper reviews
of the film on its London release. See Clippings file,
Bullets or Ballots, British Film Institute, London.

CHAPTER 5

DOUBLE MEANINGS

> Some of these lines have innu-
> endos and double meanings, and
> things like that, and you have
> to take eight or ten Harvard
> law courses to find out what
> they mean.
>
> Jack L. Warner: Testimony to
> the House Committee on Un-
> American Activities, October
> 1947.
>
> There is not a single film com-
> pany of any importance which
> has not been in the red since
> the last quarter of 1947.
>
> Eric Johnston, February 1948.

PUBLIC OPINIONS

In the manner of its adoption and in its specific formulation the Hays Code had demonstrated the extent to which
the major producers and distributors were committed out of
what they saw as economic necessity or convenience to an
endorsement of the social and political status quo.   The
débâcle of the House Committee on Un-American Activities
hearings indicated quite how far their accommodations would
go under difficult financial circumstances.

The Production Code's implementation had drawn the
string of Hollywood's more overtly anarchic elements (the
Marx Brothers, Mae West) by the same process that tamed

118

James Cagney from the abrasive Tom Powers (in The Public Enemy) to the bland Rocky Sullivan (in Angels with Dirty Faces). But since the studio heads found themselves obliged to don mantles of public responsibility, they saw less reason, as the first decade of sound progressed, to regard that responsibility as entirely passive. The studios' one venture into explicit propaganda, the short anti-Sinclair films produced by Irving Thalberg for the California gubernatorial campaign of 1934, was not repeated. But Warner Brothers fostered their reputation for a "social conscience" throughout the 1930s; if that reputation sat a little uneasily on Jack Warner's shoulders, his discomfort was eased by the profitability of those mild indictments of injustice and fate the studio produced after 1934.

Apart from a brief attachment to the Blue Eagle of the N.R.A., Warner avoided public discussion of his political affiliation or that of the films he produced. His former protégé, Darryl Zanuck, was more enthusiastic about entering political controversies. The architect of Warners' "Headline News" stories in the early 1930s,* and one of the few moguls to involve himself actively in politics, Zanuck was in 1940 and 1941 a forceful advocate of intervention in the European war. His advocacy was carried beyond a personal level: productions such as A Yank in the R.A.F. (1941; dir. Henry King) and Manhunt (1941; dir. Fritz Lang) called unambiguously for American involvement, while he also took charge of the production of Army training films in Hollywood. As important was his public attitude toward the isolationist criticism that Hollywood was fostering interventionist thought.

---

*Zanuck, in fact, produced almost all the films on which Warners' "social conscience" reputation was initially based. He produced Little Caesar in 1930, and followed its success by inaugurating the gangster cycle with The Doorway to Hell (1930), The Public Enemy (1931), Smart Money (1931), and The Mouthpiece (1932). He also began the cycle inspired by newspaper headline stories with Illicit (1931), about premarital sex; Five Star Final (1931), about yellow journalism; and I Am a Fugitive from a Chain Gang (1932). It might reasonably be argued that Warners' retreat into more conservative content began with Zanuck's departure in April 1933, rather than with the implementation of the Hays Code a year later.

> If you charge us with being anti-Nazi you are
> right, and if you accuse us of producing films in
> the interest of preparedness and national defense
> you are also right. [1]

Zanuck not only accepted the isolationists' assertion that the
cinema was publicly accountable for its political viewpoint,
he insisted that it had a right to express specific opinions
on political matters.

The War amplified claims to responsibility. The
government's eager recognition of the cinema's usefulness
for propaganda purposes was apparent in its employment of
Hollywood personnel. While Zanuck, Ford, Capra, Huston
et al. departed to the Office of War Information or the Field
Photographic branch of the U. S. Navy for the duration, the
War Activities Committee was established to assist motion
pictures to "usefully serve the National Defense effort." To
this end, the government proposed six areas to which films
might direct the nation's attention or boost its morale:

> (1): The Issues of the War: what we are fighting
> for, the American Way of Life; (2): The Nature of
> the Enemy; his ideology, his objectives, his meth-
> ods; (3): The United Nations: our allies in arms;
> (4): The Production Front: supplying the materi-
> als for victory; (5): The Home Front: civilian
> responsibility; (6): The Fighting Forces: our
> armed services, our allies and our associates. [2]

With these suggestions came an acknowledgment that in
handling these subjects the screen would be accorded the
same degree of freedom as the press.

That state of affairs, and the resulting plethora of
movies dealing with the war, gave rise to the two central
issues in the American right's post-war attack on Hollywood:
the extent of the industry's cooperation with the dubious ideological policies of the Roosevelt administration, and the
cinema's right--or lack of it--to the same guarantees of
freedom of expression as the press and other forms of the
written word. But it was not mere coincidence that a Congressional investigation of "Communist Infiltration of the
Motion Picture Industry" should occur at the same time that
the movies were cautiously developing their wartime freedom
of expression into areas of social controversy. The Committee and its volunteer associates pursued a strategy of

selecting individuals as targets for their accusations, but the backlash they provoked was intended to affect the expression of opinion by a much larger group. The more active social conscience of the post-war American cinema was in part the product of the industry's cooperation with the Roosevelt administration, and it was hardly surprising that its most prominent figures should be chosen as early victims of the attack on that administration's achievements. Even the suggestion that the movies might compromise their status as entertainment by a representation of social problems was a by-product of the kind of liberalism that had led to the New Deal. The encouragement the industry and the Roosevelt administration gave each other during the war was enough to guarantee that the right-wing opposition would take its opportunity to indict Hollywood along with the government.

However, contrary to the assertions of the Hollywood Ten, an attack on the cinema's emergent liberalism was not the main intention of the 1947 Committee. One object was simply publicity. Hollywood had long been a fantastic place; the Committee redirected that fantasy into its own paranoid vision, and achieved palpable success when its "unfriendly witnesses" were christened the "Hollywood Ten" by the press. The film industry's synonym for itself was indicted in the public consciousness along with the ten men actually cited in contempt of Congress. The Committee's other goal was to establish that a hardcore group of card-carrying Communists in the Screen Writers' and Directors' Guilds had made pro-Russian propagandist films during the war under the direct or indirect sponsorship of the Roosevelt government. Their early line of questioning indicates that they hoped to establish a direct link between Roosevelt and the "subversive" films via Lowell Mellett, FDR's personal appointee as head of the War Activities Committee. The complete collapse of this line of attack was masked by the cooperative behavior of the Unfriendly Ten in conveniently diverting attention away from the fact that the Committee had failed to establish a case for its investigation.

Neither individually nor as a group were the producers directly intimidated by the Committee; in their testimony Warner, Mayer, Schary and the rest expressly denied that there was any Communist propaganda in their films--largely, they claimed, because of their own vigilance. Warner retracted some of the allegations he had made at the Committee's closed sessions in May, because he found he did not have the evidence to substantiate them. Both the M. P. A. A.

and the A. M. P. P. protested the hearings before they began and during the early sessions. The A. M. P. P.'s statement complained,

> We are tired of being the national whipping boy for Congressional committees. We are tired of having irresponsible charges made again and again and not sustained. If we have committed a crime we want to know it. If not, we should not be badgered by Congressional committees. [3]

On October 19, 1947, the eve of the hearings, Eric Johnston publicly denied Committee Chairman J. Parnell Thomas' claim that the producers had offered to institute a blacklist in exchange for an abandonment of the hearings. Even War- ner, who had fired a number of the Unfriendly Nineteen* for their political activities during and after the 1945 and 1946 strikes at his studio, refused to consider a blacklist.

> MR. WARNER: Of course, I don't believe it would be legal--speaking only personally--to have the As- sociation or any other men band together to ob- struct the employment of any other man. I don't believe the Association would have anything what- soever to do with that type of operation. I would not be a party to it and neither would any of the other men, from my knowledge of them. [4]

---

*The Hollywood Ten were, in order of their court appear- ance: John Howard Lawson (writer), Dalton Trumbo (at the time one of the three highest paid writers in Hollywood), Albert Maltz (writer), Alvah Bessie (writer), Samuel Ornitz (writer), Herbert Biberman (writer, director), Adrian Scott (producer, writer), Edward Dmytryk (director), Lester Cole (writer), and Ring Lardner, Jr. (writer). The eleventh wit- ness called was Bertolt Brecht, who elected to answer ques- tions in the mistaken belief that as an alien he was not pro- tected by the Constitution. He denied membership in the Communist Party. Dmytryk was later a friendly witness whose method of rehabilitation became the model for "clear- ance" procedures. The eight who did not then appear were Richard Collins (writer, later a friendly witness), Gordon Kahn (writer), Howard Koch (writer), Lewis Milestone (di- rector), Irving Pichel (director), Larry Parks (actor, later a friendly witness), Robert Rossen (writer, director, later a friendly witness), and Waldo Salt (writer).

The producers' stance was demolished by the behavior of the Ten on the stand, and by the public reaction to it. John Howard Lawson, in particular, fulfilled every expectation the Committee might have had of him. The first of the Unfriendly Nineteen to appear, he was called by Thomas on October 27 in place of the scheduled witness, Eric Johnston. Expecting Johnston, the Committee for the First Amendment* had sent a delegation of its most famous members to the hearings "to see whether they would be fair," and also to steal back some of Thomas' publicity thunder. By calling Lawson instead, Thomas completely out-maneuvered them. Engaging in shouting matches and repeatedly rising to Thomas' bait, Lawson made the Chairman's case for him. Hollywood's liberal celebrities had been publicly associated with a display of intransigence which demolished the basis of sympathy they had hoped to use as a weapon against H. U. A. C. Bogart, Bacall, Garland, Huston et al. returned to Hollywood the next day completely demoralized. In following Lawson's example, the other unfriendly witnesses played into Thomas' hands, and alienated the public and industry support they undoubtedly had at the beginning of the hearings.

"YELLOW TRAVELERS"

Communists are killing Americans in Korea. Fellow travelers support Communists. Yellow travelers support fellow travelers. Don't be a yellow traveler.

Wage Earners Committee picket sign against a film produced by Dore Schary.

---

*The Committee for the First Amendment was a liberal group formed by John Huston, William Wyler and Philip Dunne shortly before the hearings began, which presented a petition for redress of grievances to the House of Representatives, and sponsored two celebrity radio programs to protest the hearings. Membership of the Committee was later regarded as sufficient grounds for blacklisting.

Although Thomas' abrupt abandonment of the hearings
on October 30 (after only eleven of the Nineteen had been
called) revived rumors that the producers had secretly agreed
to a blacklist, there is no evidence to support such a conclusion. The Chairman, however, closed the Committee pro-
ceedings with a threat he hardly bothered to veil:

> It is not necessary for the Chair to emphasize the
> harm which the motion picture industry suffers
> from the presence within its ranks of known Com-
> munists who do not have the best interests of the
> United States at heart. The industry should set
> about immediately to clean its own house and not
> wait for public opinion to force it to do so. [5]

While industry leaders issued no more aggressive statements
denouncing the hearings, they did not act until the House of
Representatives had confirmed the contempt citations on the
hollywood Ten. On November 24, the same day that the citations were confirmed by 346 votes to 17, the A. M. P. P.
began a two-day meeting in New York's Waldorf Astoria
Hotel to discuss what action they should take. At this point,
they reverted to type. Aware of the hostile treatment the
case had received, particularly in the Hearst press, fearful
of the effects of adverse public opinion, * and as sensitive to
threats as they had been in 1934, they capitulated.

"Deploring" the behavior of the Ten, they declared,

> We do not wish to prejudge their legal rights, but
> their actions have been a disservice to their em-
> ployers and have impaired their usefulness to the
> industry.

They would discharge any of the Ten who were under contract, and not re-employ them until they had been cleared
of contempt and declared themselves not to be communists.
Further, they professed their intention not to

---

*A Gallup Poll published on November 29 in large part con-
firmed the executives' misgivings. Eighty per cent of those
questioned had heard of the case--more than knew of the
United Nations or of the Marshall Plan. Of those, 37 per
cent approved of the way the hearings were being conducted,
while 36 per cent disapproved. Forty-seven per cent thought
the Ten should be punished, 39 per cent thought they should
not.

knowingly employ a Communist or a member of any
party or group which advocates the overthrow of
the Government of the United States by force, or
by any illegal or unconstitutional method. [7]

The Waldorf Statement was released as the unanimous opinion
of the executives, but privately a number of them--in particular Dore Schary, Walter Wanger, Eddie Mannix and Sam
Goldwyn--expressed their disquiet.   The document reflected
the producers' underlying anxieties.   As a body, they were
less concerned about the implied loss of a free screen than
they were about being trapped in a situation where, however
they acted, they could not escape criticism.   The Statement
echoed Mayer's plea at the hearings to have the burden of
responsibility placed on someone else's shoulders:

> The absence of a national policy, established by
> Congress, with respect to the employment of Com-
> munists in private industry makes our task diffi-
> cult.   Ours is a nation of laws.   We request Con-
> gress to enact legislation to assist American indus-
> try to rid itself of subversive, disloyal elements. [8]

Failing that, they sought the cooperation of the talent guilds

> ... to work with us to eliminate any subversive;
> to protect the innocent, and to safeguard free
> speech and a free screen wherever threatened. [9]

Dore Schary was selected to present the M. P. A. A. 's plea to
cooperate in the preparation of blacklists to the Screen Writers' Guild.   Schary, the most conspicuous of the liberal producers (he was later accused of being a "serious Red sympa-
thizer" by Hollywood Life) had argued that anyone in the industry had the right "to think politically as he chooses," and
had told the Committee that he would continue to hire staff
on the basis of ability alone.   By being forced publicly to
implement the Waldorf Statement, he became the first victim
of the punitive requirement for "clearance" before the sys-
tematization of public atonement was even contemplated.

    In every respect, the producers' reaction epitomized
their response to any external pressure.   The publicity necessary to promote their products kept the people who made
them in the forefront of public attention.   The maxim that
any publicity is good publicity holds only up to a certain
point; for figures constantly under public scrutiny bad publicity has no attraction.   Under the economic pressures of

the period it was hardly surprising that the producers should
close ranks, and that Schary, Zanuck, Goldwyn, and whoever
else would later claim a troubled conscience should bow to
the majority argument in favor of unanimous action for the
general good of the industry.   Nor was it surprising that
they should, under the same banner, attempt to enlist the
support of the talent guilds.   Personal politics entered into
the issue hardly at all; they were a luxury that could only
be afforded in times of economic prosperity.

Moreover, the producers were so inured to reacting
to external pressure, to responding to an issue only when it
had been raised by factions outside the industry, and then
responding in whatever way would be to their most immediate advantage, that they appeared almost incapable of taking
a stand on a matter of principle.   There was no profit in
principle, and the war had demonstrated that even a substantial number of leading figures could be removed from the
talent pool without an adverse effect on box-office revenues.
The producers' reaction to the political offensive of 1947
mirrored their predecessors' reaction to the censorship
campaign of the early 1920s: the figures involved in the
scandal were punished, less for their political affiliation
than for damaging the industry's image.   The letters sev-
ering R. K. O.'s contract with Scott and Dmytryk contained
the sentence:

> By your conduct [in refusing to answer questions]
> and by your actions, attitude, public statements,
> and general conduct before, at and since that time,
> you have brought yourself into disrepute with large
> sections of the public, have offended the commun-
> ity, have prejudiced this corporation as your em-
> ployer and the motion picture industry in general,
> have lessened your capacity fully to comply with
> your employer agreement, and have otherwise vio-
> lated your employment contract with us. [10]

The industry took its revenge impartially.   Several
friendly witnesses of lesser consequence found their careers
abruptly curtailed: Richard MacAuley and Morrie Ryskind,
both writers, did not receive a screen credit after 1947.
Adolphe Menjou also found parts more difficult to come by,
although this may have had as much to do with his increasing age as it did with his political convictions.   Certainly
there was no organized policy against these people, as there
had been no organized blacklist against right-wingers in the

early 1940s, but there was a general feeling of antipathy
towards them, a sentiment that they, like the Ten, had be-
trayed the industry.   In the prevailing atmosphere, if there
was someone else who could do the job as well, there
seemed little reason to employ someone you weren't likely
to get on with.

Those of the Ten who were employed by the studios
were dismissed for having breached the morals clauses of
their contracts.   Several brought law suits questioning the
legality of this or the Waldorf Statement.   All were settled
out of court, a procedure the producers found much simpler
than contesting the finer points of law in a public arena.
Money solved the immediate problem of principle, as it had
consistently done in the studios' relations with labor in Hollywood. *   Those of the Nineteen who had not testified and

---

*"Through the years of Hollywood's turbulent labor troubles,
it must be said, the studio-union relationship was uncommon-
ly corrupt and venal.   In every jurisdictional fight, either
the I. A. [International Alliance of Theatrical Stage Employ-
ees] or the craft unions opposing it broke the strike by making private deals with the producers.   Until quite recently
[1965] the studios maintained a policy of handling labor relations on a personal "deal" level.   The cosy tête-à-tête between movie czar and labor leader replaced the formidable
conference table in Hollywood. "11   The extent of the corruption emerged in the trial in 1941 of Willie Bioff and
George Browne on charges of extorting $550,000 from War-
ner Brothers, Loews', Inc., Paramount and Twentieth
Century-Fox.   Bioff was an ex-Chicago racketeer, and the
international representative of I. A. T. S. E.   Browne was the
I. A. union president.   The payments, which were considerably less than the total made to Bioff, were in exchange for
restricted wage claims and Bioff's prevention of labor disputes.   Bioff had also levied a two per cent assessment on
the wages of all Hollywood I. A. members as contribution to
a non-existent union fund.   One producer at the trial ad-
mitted that the arrangement with Bioff had saved the companies in excess of $15 million.   After his removal, the op-
posing faction, the left-wing Conference of Studio Unions, a
C. I. O. -affiliated group led by Painters Union leader Herbert
Sorrell, became the dominant labor organization.   Jurisdictional disputes between them and the I. A. continued throughout the war years, and erupted into the violent and prolonged
strikes of 1945 and 1946.   The abusive division   (continued)

were under studio contract were required to sign statements
saying they were not members of the Communist Party, and
were then allowed to continue working.

The studios displayed an initial reluctance to introduce
a blacklist, particularly if the names were to be provided by
individuals outside the industry. They stalled the issue for
more than two years, but their palliative measures, including the program of explicitly anti-Communist films, failed to
appease extremist groups. The outbreak of fighting in Korea
in June 1950 coincided with the publication of Red Channels,
which cataloged "subversives" in the entertainment industry.
In the heightened Cold War atmosphere, pressure to put the
Waldorf Statement into effect was intensified. The American
Legion and the Motion Picture Alliance for the Preservation
of American Ideals were insistent in their demands for some

---

between the labor organizations, in which each accused the
other of being either "Commies" or "Racketeers," was the
source of much of the underlying conflict between left and
right in Hollywood; although neither of these strikes directly
involved any of the talent guilds, they did offer an opportunity for both left-and right-wing factions to express their opinions in the form of resolutions before Guild meetings, and to
act by reinforcing or attacking picket lines. Roy Brewer, a
former president of the National Federation of Labor and
member of the War Labor Board, was brought to Hollywood
in October 1945 as a "trouble shooter" by Richard Walsh,
president of I. A. T. S. E. Brewer, who later became a major
figure in the Motion Picture Industrial Council, and who
founded and chaired the A. F. L. Film Council, broke the
1946 C. S. U. strike with the aid of the Teamsters, and repeatedly accused the C. S. U. membership of Communist affiliation. That victory greatly strengthened the I. A. 's--and
Brewer's--position, and while he did not exploit his union
presidency for financial gain as Bioff had done, he did adopt
a policy of personal negotiation with the studio heads. He
became a central figure in the process of "clearing" black-
listed personnel--and, it was claimed, in the institution of
the blacklist in the first place: one writer called him "the
strawboss of the purge" in 1947. Cogley suggests "Brewer
dominated the motion picture industry more than any other
individual had ever succeeded in doing."[12] But in 1955 he
failed in an attempt to unseat Richard Walsh as International
President of I. A. T. S. E. , and became a New York executive
for Allied Artists.

response from the studios: the Legion through a policy of
public protests, articles in their magazine and occasional
picketing of individual films; Alliance Chairman Roy Brewer
through persistent personal contact and a quiet line in almost rational argument. The studio executives recognized
Brewer as a man who understood their problems, but they
remained reluctant to concede power over employment within
the industry to anyone as detached from its activities as the
Legion. By March 1952, when studio representatives and
Eric Johnston met with officials of the Legion to discuss the
question of the employment of "controversial" personalities,
the major companies were already operating their own investigations procedure into the past records of company employees.

The definition of "controversial" grew broader as
blacklisting procedures became more institutionalized. * The
appearance of one's name in a list published by the Legion's
Firing Line, Counterattack, the publications of AWARE, Inc.,
or any of the even more obscure Red-baiter groups was all
that was needed. Figures without studio protection who had
past "controversial" allegiances found it increasingly difficult,
and finally impossible, to obtain work. The studios were
careful to avoid providing grounds for any possible charges
of conspiracy, so that there was never an industry-wide
"blacklist" as such. There were almost certainly minor
variations in policy between studios, with less pressure on
independent producers. These inconsistencies as well as the
lack of written evidence on the subject, the general pattern
of declining employment in the industry, and the reluctance
of any but the victims to discuss the issue, make it almost
impossible to determine accurately how many people were
affected by blacklisting, or the resulting impact on film production. 13

The studios' adoption of blacklisting practices can,
however, be explained, and largely in non-political terms.
The economic crisis provoked by falling audiences and the

---

*By 1952 the "controversial" category covered not only the
324 names cited by co-operative witnesses at the H. U. A. C.
"mass hearings, " but also brief membership of the 194 organizations deemed "subversive" by Counterattack, or a list-
ing in the notorious Appendix IX of the 1945 H. U. A. C. report, which even the Committee had ordered destroyed on
the grounds of its inaccuracy.

Paramount decrees left the majors anxious to avoid any
further criticism that might have repercussions on their
financial position.   They conceded to the anti-Communist
lobby for the same reasons that they had conceded to the
Legion of Decency in 1934, and if the influence of the anti-
Communists was disproportionate to their numerical strength,
the financial crisis facing the industry was more severe.
Moreover, the increase in relative authority that the crisis
had given distribution executives in New York encouraged
the timid solution.   After 1947 the position of the studio
production heads was seriously and permanently weakened.
Louis B. Mayer was forced out of M. G. M., Darryl Zanuck
was pressured into resigning from Twentieth Century-Fox,
and two of the Warner Brothers sold their interest in the
company.   Hughes' sale of R. K. O. to a branch of the General Tire and Rubber Co. in 1955 may have predated by ten
years the submergence of other film companies in disparate
conglomerates, but it did indicate in dramatic terms that the
era of the all-powerful production head was over, and that
the dominant voice in studio policy would from now on belong to those in charge of distribution and finance.

     The changed nature of the right-wing attack on liber-
alism in the early 1950s also encouraged the institutionalization of blacklisting.   Earlier attempts to rescind hated pieces
of New Deal legislation through Congress or the courts had
failed, and the enormous success of the Alger Hiss case had
shown the reactionaries that the most effective way to destroy Rooseveltian influence was through victimization of individuals.   This policy was applied to Hollywood in the "mass
hearings" of 1951 and 1952.   The Committee's new line of
attack permitted the industry the face-saving rationalization
that they were not abandoning the freedom of the screen,
which had been the primary issue during the 1947 hearings.
The situation in the early 1950s, it was argued, was that
certain specific individuals were no longer acceptable to
sections of public opinion because of their private politics.
The more stringent policies adopted by radio and television
companies and their sponsors in the name of the political
purity of their consumer products forcibly affected the employment policies of the majors.   A studio employing an
actor too "disloyal" for television would be bound to come
under heavy fire from the anti-Communists who had secured
his original unemployment.   And, as ever, but particularly
as in any period of financial crisis, the industry executives
were unwilling to alienate any section of the public who
might decide to boycott, picket, or refuse to show their
product.

ON NOT WORKING MIRACLES

The self-interested conservatism the film companies
displayed over blacklisting also explains their reluctance to
deal with the question of censorship. For any of the companies publicly to challenge the continuing censorship lobby
in the atmosphere of growing political and cultural conservatism in the early 1950s would be offering their critics another rod with which to beat the industry's back. The Production Code was not primarily a political document, and the
major censorship issues were concerned with morality rather
than politics. But it was imperative that the thin dividing
line between the moral conservatism of the Catholic Church
and a corresponding political conservatism be maintained.
If the Legions were to unite, the movies would appear both
indecent and un-American. For the unlikely benefits of gaining the support of minority audiences, the risk was simply
not worth contemplating. Between 1950 and 1968, there were
19 court cases concerned with film censorship. Only five
involved major American distributors. In three of these
cases, [14] producer/director Otto Preminger obliged United
Artists to go to court by refusing to make cuts to conform
to the Production Code or local censorship practice. The
other two cases, [15] and a sixth case involving a low-budget
Hollywood production, [16] all took place between 1950 and
1952, and concerned films dealing with race. In every
case, the court action was provoked by an outright ban on
the film by a local board of censors.

The Supreme Court opinion in the Paramount decision
suggested that it would be prepared to reconsider its 1915
ruling excluding motion pictures from protection under the
First Amendment. Since then it had given a number of
rulings that invited the abridgment of free speech by prior
censorship and extended the protections of the First Amendment to material normally considered entertainment. However, the Court declined to hear the first two cases sub-
mitted for its consideration after 1948, without offering any
explanation. That both Curley and Lost Boundaries dealt
with the contentious issue of racial integration, and had been
banned in Southern cities because they might endanger the
"good order" of the community was, however, the probable
cause. The case they did elect to hear, New York's ban-
ning of Roberto Rossellini's The Miracle on the grounds that
it was "sacrilegious," presented a much simpler legal issue
as well as avoiding an area of specifically political contention. A work protected by the First Amendment could not

be banned on the grounds that it was sacrilegious, whereas
the extent of governmental power to prohibit activities constituting a threat to public order was more debatable. The
Miracle had the additional advantage of having had its artistic credentials established. As part of the trilogy Ways of
Love, it had won the New York Film Critics award for best
foreign language film of 1950. Since the film's dispute was
with the Catholic Church, the majors found it convenient to
play no part in the controversy.

While the Court had made clear its theoretical attitude
to the motion picture's status under the First Amendment in
1948, [17] its opinion in Burstyn vs. Wilson on The Miracle
and in the six other censorship cases it heard in the following ten years indicated a clear lack of unanimity among its
members as to how to implement this position. Its verdict
in the Miracle case was unanimous, but there were three
consenting opinions. The majority opinion, given by Justice
Clark, sought to answer Justice McKenna's 1915 verdict.
He restated the dictum of the Paramount decision,

> ... it cannot be doubted that motion pictures are a
> significant medium for the communication of ideas,

and consequently guarantee the protections of free speech
under the First and Fourteenth Amendments regardless of
the fact that they were exhibited for profit and designed to
entertain as well as inform. However, Clark failed to re-
fute the conservatives' most frequent line of defense. The
"hypothesis" that films possessed a greater capacity for evil
was deemed

> ... to be relevant in determining the permissible
> scope of community control, but it does not auth-
> orize substantially unbridled censorship. [18]

By concentrating on what constituted "substantially unbridled
censorship, " the judgment left open the question of how
broad "the permissible scope of community control" might
be. The decision established a precedent, whereby the limits of censorship were narrowed on a case-by-case basis,
as the Supreme Court or a lower court ruled that particular
grounds for refusing to license a film for exhibition were
unconstitutional. The burden of proof now lay with the censors, although the Court's ruling did leave them some freedom of action. In remarking that each medium of communication presented its own individual problems of control, and

in stressing that the Court regarded obscenity as valid grounds for censorship, Clark's decision permitted a prior censorship system to remain in existence. That in itself inhibited the majors since they remained reluctant to have their films involved in court cases.

The studios' continued acceptance of the vaguely defined censorship system, and their invariable caution, created a gap between what was legally permitted on the American screen in the early 1950s and what the industry produced. In spite of Preminger's somewhat willful protests against censorship, the Hollywood film stayed well inside the boundaries of "acceptable" content, while the issues were debated on other people's money. The Miracle ruling had effectively placed the power to define the limits of film censorship in the hands of the film proprietors, since they could decide to contest any censor's verdict in courts which took freedom of speech as the norm. In the 1950s the main battleground of the censorship debate was the art film, gradually replaced during the next decade by the sex film. The markets for these products were not large enough to interest the major distributors, who were as unwilling as ever to risk capital in films likely to incur censorship problems. They maintained a discreet and respectable distance from the litigation, which was left to the small independent distributors catering to the art-house circuits. They had no wish to share in the air of disrepute that clung to the predominantly European films involved in well-publicized court cases, and were certainly not harmed by the resulting public identification between "art films" and prurient interest in sexual matters.

REFORM BY PERMISSIVE NEGLECT

The narrowing-down of the grounds for censorship as a result of the Miracle case weakened the rest of the system for controlling content. The influence of the P. C. A. was perforce reduced because it could no longer claim that disregarding its advice would lead to difficulties with local censorship boards. Its remaining strength as an instrument of restraint rested on the dominance of the industry by the major company members of the M. P. A. A., who were in theory obliged to uphold the Code. But the Code itself was clearly outmoded by the Supreme Court's decision, and as a result it was more open to manipulation or alteration. It could even be ignored. Preminger's The Moon Is Blue and The Man with the Golden Arm were both released without P. C. A. Seals, and the fact that both made considerable profits undermined another prop by which the Code had been supported: that a Seal was necessary if any major American production was to be financially successful. Other M. P. A. A. producers employed non-affiliated distribution companies to release films containing material contravening the Code. The weakening of its various foundations made it easier for the majors to pressure the P. C. A. into passing material it would previously have rejected.

Nevertheless, the size and dominance of the majors' economic operations involved them in censorship conflicts from which the smaller distributors were exempt. Few art- or exploitation-film distributors bothered to submit their product to the Legion of Decency, either because a rating would have little effect on the financial prospects of a film, or because they knew it would be condemned. Neither of these considerations applied to the majors' movies. The standards they sought in their products had much more in common with those of the Legion, the Film Board of National Organizations and similar reviewing bodies than they did with the standards applied by censorship boards, mainly because these organizations had a sizable influence on potential audiences. The P. C. A. 's long-established ties with the Legion were little affected by the Miracle decision: Warner Brothers' A Streetcar Named Desire (released in March 1952) had the deletions demanded by the Legion made despite the protests of Elia Kazan and Tennessee Williams. The countervailing pressures of the new opportunities provided by more permissive censorship laws placed some tensions on the relationship, but only in five cases during the 16 years following the Miracle decision did the Catholic reviewers give a condemned rating to a film passed by the P. C. A. [19] More frequently, they issued B-ratings (morally objectionable in part for all) to major company films, particularly where their plots touched on suicide, divorce, abortion or religion. [20]

The industry's attempts to keep the Production Code in being were perhaps the final struggles of the old, moribund, Hollywood system. It was revised first in 1956, when the prohibitions against the depiction of miscegenation, prostitution and the use of narcotics were withdrawn after the Code's debacle over The Man with the Golden Arm. In 1961 the restriction on the presentation of homosexuality and other "sexual aberrations" was withdrawn, an indication of the extent to which the Code was increasingly regarded as open to alteration at the convenience of the majors: at the time, three of them were involved in productions whose plots in part dealt with homosexuality. [21] But the P. C. A. 's major test case over nudity came over a briefly flashed shot of a black prostitute's breasts in one of Hollywood's ostentatiously "serious" films, The Pawnbroker (1965); that this occurred eight years after the Supreme Court had declared that "immoral sexual behaviour with or without nudity"[22] was not obscene indicated how far the M. P. A. A. continued to lag behind the courts. Similar controversies in 1966 over profanity in Who's Afraid of Virginia Woolf (1966) and abortion in Alfie (the P. C. A. 's decisions over which were reversed on appeal) indicated that the distance between what was stated in the Code and what the producers found to be commercially acceptable was as wide as it had been in the period 1930-1934. The granting of a P. C. A. Seal to The Pawnbroker after it had been condemned by the National Catholic Office[23] resulted in a breakthrough in exhibition bookings.

In spite of the commercial triumph of innocuous entertainment signaled by The Sound of Music in 1966, the M. P. A. A. in that year conceded that the existing Production Code was unworkable, and abandoned it for a much shorter and less specific formulation that could be adapted to changing circumstances, in the legal definition of obscenity, for example. [24] In itself, the redrafting of the Code was more significant symbolically than materially: it evidenced the industry's final and reluctant acceptance that it could no longer profitably purvey a specified form of harmless entertainment to an undifferentiated mass audience. In one particular, however, the 1966 revision made that acceptance concrete. It specified that some films should be labeled as "suitable for mature audiences," and thereby introduced a system of classification which the majors had consistently resisted much more vehemently than they had opposed censorship. Film classification had been the main issue of dispute between the M. P. A. A. and censorship boards since 1952. Boards had taken more and more to restricting certain films, including some of the majors', as unsuitable for children. Their right to do so had been upheld by the Supreme Court, and some boards were operating exclusively on this practice, rather than attempting to enforce bans. The industry had fought any attempt to restrict audiences, particularly in the light of its knowledge that a large and growing proportion of movie audiences were under

17.   As before, the producers accepted classification only in
the face of a growing censorship lobby, pressure from exhibitors who were concerned that they might again fall prey
to community protest, and the forceful arguments of M. P. A. A.
President Jack Valenti[25] that such a system was in their
long-term self-interest.   Even so, the system introduced in
1966 was, at best, half-hearted.   It went no further than
requiring that some films carry the label "Suggested for
Mature Audiences" (abbreviated to S. M. A.) on their first-
run advertising.   This minimalist system did not quell the
censorship lobby either inside or outside the industry, and
was replaced in 1968 by a four-category classification system[26] that finally abandoned the Code altogether.

The revisions of the Code during the 1960s amounted
to a belated and reluctant acknowledgment by the member
companies of the M. P. A. A. that a significant change had
taken place in the composition and tastes of the movie audience.   The classification system represented the institutional abandonment of the myth of the undifferentiated mass
audience.   But the tardiness and hesitancy with which these
changes were implemented indicated even more clearly the
extent to which distributors and major producers clung to a
conservative economic definition of their product.   The
P. C. A. was replaced by the Code and Rating Administration
(C. A. R. A.), but the philosophy with which the new organization operated did not differ from that of its predecessor.
Instead of excising material by declaring it prohibited, the
new administration achieved the same result by threatening
producers with an X rating, which the major companies were
not prepared to have attached to their product.   Although
some independent producers consciously pursued the publicity value of an X rating, the majors, committed as they
were to blockbuster economics, continued to ensure that
with very few exceptions their films were accessible to audiences under eighteen.   Despite the increasing evidence to
the contrary, they persisted in practicing the restrictive and
conservative attitude to their product that the classification
system appeared to have breached.   That attitude continued
to predominate because neither the political nor the economic
events of the post-war period, disturbing as they were for
the industry, caused the majors to alter their fundamental
assumptions about the nature of film as a commercial commodity.

REFERENCES

1. Darryl Zanuck, Speech to the American Legion, September 1941. Quoted in Mel Gussow, Zanuck: Don't Say Yes Until I've Finished Talking, p. 105.

2. Quoted in Lewis Jacobs, "World War II and American Film," Cinema Journal, Vol. VII (Winter 1967-68), p. 10.

3. Quoted in John Cogley, Report on Blacklisting: I: The Movies (New York, 1965), p. 3.

4. Warner's testimony, quoted in Gordon Kahn, Hollywood on Trial: The Story of the Ten Who Were Indicted (New York, 1948), p. 22.

5. Eric Bentley, ed., Thirty Years of Treason, p. 224.

6. Kahn, p. 174.

7. Quoted in Kahn, p. 184.

8. Quoted in Kahn, pp. 184-185.

9. Quoted in Kahn, p. 184.

10. Quoted in Kahn, p. 191.

11. Cogley, p. 53.

12. Cogley, p. 160.

13. For example, Dalton Trumbo's volume of Letters, Additional Dialogue, ed. Helen Manfull (New York, 1970), excises the names of other writers working under pseudonyms and through "fronts."

14. The Moon Is Blue (1952), The Man with the Golden Arm (1956), Anatomy of a Murder (1959).

15. Curley (1949), Pinky (1949; prod. Darryl F. Zanuck, dir. Elia Kazan).

16. Lost Boundaries (1949, dist. Film Classics; prod. Louis de Rochemont, dir. Alfred Werker).

17. Justice Douglas' decision included the dictum, "We have no doubt that motion pictures, like newspapers and radio, are included in the press whose freedom is guaranteed by the First Amendment." United States v. Paramount Pictures, 334 U. S. 131, 166 (1948). Quoted in Richard Randall, Censorship of the Movies, p. 23.

18. Burstyn v. Wilson, 343 U. S. 495, 501-2 (1952). Quoted in Randall, p. 29.

19. The five films were: Son of Sinbad (1955, R. K. O.; dir. Ted Tetzlaff); Baby Doll (1956, Warner Brothers; prod./dir. Elia Kazan); Kiss Me, Stupid (1964, United Artists; dir. Billy Wilder)--this despite extensive deletions to bring it into conformity with Legion standards (Wilder's previous film, Irma La Douce, had had an alternative ending shot to make it passable by some censorship boards); The Pawnbroker (1965; prod. Landau-Unger, dir. Sidney Lumet)--when the nude scene was edited out the film was passed A-3 (morally unobjectionable for adults); and Hurry Sundown (1966, Paramount; prod./dir. Otto Preminger).

20. One such film was John Ford's last movie, Seven Women (1966, M. G. M.), rated B because it made suicide appear as a heroic gesture.

21. The films were Advise and Consent (rel. Columbia, June 1962; prod./dir. Otto Preminger), The Best Man (rel. United Artists, 1964; dir. Franklin Schaffner), The Children's Hour (rel. United Artists, 1962; dir. William Wyler).

22. Richard Randall's classification, in Randall, p. 62. The film in question was Game of Love.

23. The Legion of Decency changed its name to the National Catholic Office for Motion Pictures in 1966.

24. Compared to the 1934 Code, which ran to over eight pages, the 1966 Code was an exercise in brevity. It is worth quoting in full, since it is also a careful exercise in vagueness.
    "The basic dignity and value of human life shall be respected and upheld. Restraint shall be exercised in portraying the taking of life.

Evil, sin, crime and wrong-doing shall not be
justified.
Detailed and protracted acts of brutality, cruelty,
physical violence, torture, and abuse, shall not be
presented.
Indecent or undue exposure of the human body shall
not be presented.
Illicit sex relationships shall not be justified. Inti-
mate sex scenes violating common standards of decency shall not be portrayed. Restraint and care
shall be exercised in presentations dealing with sex
aberrations.
Obscene speech, gestures or movements shall not
be presented. Undue profanity shall not be presented.
Religion shall not be demeaned.
Words or symbols contemptuous of racial, religious
or national groups, shall not be used so as to incite
bigotry or hatred.
Excessive cruelty to animals shall not be portrayed
and animals shall not be treated inhumanely. "
The Motion Picture Code of Self-Regulation, The
Motion Picture Association of America, 1966,
pp. 5-6.

25.   Valenti succeeded Eric Johnston as president on the
       latter's death in 1963.

26.   These are: G (general audience); PG (parental guidance
       suggested, indicating that some material may not be
       suitable for pre-teenagers); R (restricted, those under
       17 admitted only if accompanied by an adult); and X
       (no-one under 17 admitted).

INTERLUDE

I WAS A COMMUNARD FOR THE F. B. I. :
GENRE AND POLITICS--ANTHONY MANN

> "There's a revolution going on.
> Don't stay out late. "
> Arnold Moss (Fouché) in Reign
> of Terror

What constitutes a political cinema? A dissenting
film within the commercial cinema may choose to make
statements about politics as a force outside the institution
in which it operates (plot politics), or it may expose the
mechanisms of manipulation and exploitation within its
economically determined forms (political narrative). In
Hollywood these possibilities have consistently functioned
as alternatives, obliging a conventionality in one discourse
in order to permit opportunistic subversion in another.
The limitations of a superficial radicalism in content are
apparent: Jack Warner and Louis B. Mayer were quite
justified in their claim that no Communist propaganda had
ever sullied their studios' output, although it is perhaps
debatable whether that was entirely due to their unceasing
vigilance. The possibilities of formal subversion are more
ambiguous, since such a strategy involves a side-step into
areas not normally recognized as political. A challenge to
conventional modes of representation is, however, a pre-
requisite for a politically subversive cinema, particularly
in Hollywood where highly developed narrative codes circumscribed and recuperated the radical elements of a
film's subject matter. To succeed in either political or
aesthetic terms a dissenting film was obliged voluntarily
to subjugate itself to the immediate demands of its status
as a commercial product. By, for example, accepting the
conventions of genre and plot development, a subversive
film might create a free space for itself through its overt

140

conformity. Working below the surface level of plot perception is exactly what makes such films subversive; they generate a tension between plot event and its performance, which
offers the audience a choice as to the level on which it wishes
to read the film. Manny Farber's description of these movies
as "Underground Films" captures their essential quality precisely.

The generic puritanism of Budd Boetticher's Westerns,
for example, so emphasizes the ritual in the patterning of
plot events that the conventional moral lessons of those events,
so evident in Ford, cannot be drawn except by an unreflective
reading of the plot as sole text. Rather, this rigid, ruthless
adherence to generic conventions uses irony to turn the usual
implications of the plot on their heads. The sympathetic villain is hardly unique to Boetticher's miniaturist approach, but
rarely has evil been more personably personified than by
Claude Akins in Comanche Station, nor has righteousness, the
central tenet of Randolph Scott's performance, seemed more
absurd.

Thus the paradox: in order to create a political cinema, you have to create a non-political cinema. Which is to
say, you have to create a cinema which expresses its politics
in terms other than those already labeled political. The divisions within Hollywood over H. U. A. C. in a way defined this
contradiction. Those people who took positions on either side
of the issue were accepting the terms of the debate, even if
they denied the existence of common ground between them
and their opponents. Both groups were, in a sense, more
fundamentally in opposition to those individuals attempting to
define the political in a new manner than they were to each
other. An alternative politics was not to be defined through
positions on issues as such; rather, it was bound into films
by their makers' attitude towards the act of filmmaking itself.
For those who wished to practice an existential politics,
specific issues were irrelevant. Their films contained an
implicit acknowledgment that narrative cinema could not
democratically present a political content before it had redefined the political implications of its style. The first task
for filmmakers of Dissent was to reorganize their attitudes
towards the narrative conventions within which they were obliged to work.

To make an overtly political film--a film which took
politics as its subject matter--in 1949, two options were
open. Either choose a contemporary subject matter in
which good and evil could be readily identified, and didactically

bludgeon the audience with the dramatic logic of the central
character's corruption (<u>All the King's Men</u>) or redemption
(<u>I Married a Communist</u>).   Or eschew message cinema
through the use of generic and stylistic conventions to create a political cinema.   <u>Reign of Terror</u> practices what it
preaches: in describing the unstable realpolitik of the French
Revolution Anthony Mann employs a barrage of film noir
techniques and gangster movie conventions to present his
audience with a cinematic world they can comprehend.
<u>Reign of Terror</u> is a conscious exercise in displacement:
gangster archetypes in eighteenth-century dress--Robespierre
the grotesque homosexual city boss making a show of opulence ("I didn't know such prosperity went with the Revolution," says DuVivier to him on their first meeting); St. Just
the brutal dandy whose spiritual corruption is measured by
his physical beauty; Fouché the deformed sardonic intellectual
who plots to kill his master; Madeleine the film noir fatal
woman (kissing DuVivier, she murmurs, "I could kill you");
DuVivier himself, the hero who is a double agent--exchange
the dialogue of a hundred crime movies: "Fouché, why don't
you go take a walk?" ... "Don't tempt me, I still have a
gun. "

All the stylistic devices used to create the insecure
urban landscape of the film noir are employed to endow
eighteenth-century studio Paris with an instability of circumstance and morality: cross-lighting; the threatening use
of extreme close-ups; the expressionist play with shadows
(several characters talk to shadows); persistent composition
against the natural balance of the subject; the definition of
space as solid and three-dimensional through the use of high-
or low-angle shots, but still capable of sudden distortion by
a cut to an unexpected camera position.   Mann carefully
sculpts his space, using deliberately positioned people and
objects to establish depth in detail and precisely define the
space in any shot--frequently to prove to the audience how
deceptive appearances are: mirrors conceal doors, a book
which turns out to be hollow then turns out to be no more
than a container for dog food.   His use of camera movement stresses his ambiguity: violence is directed either at
or from the camera, implicating the audience or threatening
it.   In beginning the film with an extreme high-angle long
shot, which pans down to a direct overhead shot of the first
scene, and cutting occasionally to similar long shots throughout the film, Mann establishes a distance between himself
and the audience.   He reserves the power to withdraw from
the action when he wishes, but forces his audience into participation, bewilderment and suffering with the characters.

Mann's manipulation of the audience parallels Robespierre's and Barrat's manipulation of the crowds. "I created the mob ... where else would they find a leader?" declares Robespierre. This is a world of realpolitik, where the issue at stake is the control of the elements of power (here the mob, but also an object, the Black Book). What makes Reign of Terror's politics so distinctive is that it assertively defines the difference between good and evil as lying not in tactics but in purpose. The Barrat faction manipulates the mob at the Assembly to destroy Robespierre at the end of the film in precisely the same manner as Robespierre manipulated it to destroy Danton. Mann reinforces the point by the similarity with which he shoots the two scenes, in the same set with the same lighting, using the same camera setups.

Hero and villain are closely related: at one level of the plot, Barrat and Robespierre; at the other DuVivier and Fouché. At one point the latter are paired in a two-shot, facing each other in profile on either side of the frame, making a partnership by their mutual occupation of space, their mutual acceptance of each other's role and their mutual respect for each other's competence. They share the same aim, to find the Black Book and use it for their own ends. They share the same willingness to discard the other when he ceases to be useful. And they share the same duplicity: neither intends to fulfil the bargain they have just struck. By the end of the scene they are trying to kill each other. The moral distinction between them is offered to the audience only on a purely iconic level: DuVivier (Robert Cummings) is the film's ostensible hero because of his physical stature, because of his involvement in the romantic subplot, and because the plot draws us into his conspiracy--we can comprehend its motivation as well as its purpose. Fouché (Arnold Moss) is the villain because of his appearance--crooked, beak-nosed, invariably dressed in black--and because he is a natural dissembler. But almost the first thing we see DuVivier do is to murder a man with his bare hands. Significantly, Fouché has others perform all his butchery.

Mann's political methodology thus involves taking a conventional form and displacing its conventions. But in displacing them he does not violate them--unlike, for example, Abraham Polonsky in Force of Evil, where film noir criminal protagonist John Garfield turns renegade in the final scenes, reneging on his relationship with the audience and perhaps providing a model for the ex-Communist witnesses to H. U. A. C. Reign of Terror uses its generic and stylistic borrowings to create a world which is familiar enough for its unfamiliarities to be disturbing. The sets are made familiar by their lighting, the costumes by their inhabitants. What is unfamiliar is the extent of the film's realpolitik ambivalence. By making its hero a political assassin who will, at the film's end, compromise in a balance of power with its personification of evil, it persistently denies that a fixed morality of action exists. That denial is made generically possible by the film's position, at the same time inside and outside the conventions of the film noir.

Reign of Terror's narrative fits the pattern of Mann's later Westerns. The action of the film is a neutralizing movement towards compromise and control. But it is more explicit in its discussion of power as morally ambiguous than the Westerns were to be. They assume the territory Reign of Terror travels, and employ more independent reified symbols of the ambivalence of power--the rifle in Winchester 73. They also seek resolution at a different point. By concentrating on the obsession or dilemma of a single character, they articulate the politics of an introverted individualism, and at the plot's conclusion leave the central character a good deal less interesting than he was at its beginning. Reign of Terror, because it is not so clearly focused, can abandon its characters in the middle of a balance of forces no more stable than that with which it began; the untenable joint governance of Barrat, the "honest man, " and Fouché, the "disloyal, unscrupulous, deceitful, treacherous, cunning" embodiment of studied malevolence. It is an apt enough commentary on the two worlds of Hollywood politics it describes.

PART 3

"I'D RATHER HAVE MANDRAKE FALLS"

"Welcome to Mandrake Falls
Where the scenery enthralls,
Where no hardship e'er befalls,
Welcome to Mandrake Falls."

Sign in Mr. Deeds Goes to Town

CHAPTER 6

THE AMERICAN WAY:
THE EVOLUTION OF A POPULIST ARCHETYPE

>"It is not the easy way, but the
>American Way, and it was Lin-
>coln's way."
>
>Herbert Hoover, radio broad-
>cast, February 1931.
>
>"Hip Hooray, The American
>Way"--lyrics of "That's Enter-
>tainment"[1]

THE DREAM FACTORY

The industry leaders, and in particular the first- and
second-generation studio heads, accepted the limitations imposed on their product by the Production Code in large part
because they could accommodate these limitations within their
own vision of the commodity they dealt in. That vision was
the product of three factors which conveniently knitted together and reinforced each other: their attitude towards
their audience; their conception of their own role as mediators between that audience and the filmmakers who worked
for them; and the set of social and political assumptions
which they, as a group, had in common.

The "movie moguls"--the small group of men who
brought "Hollywood" into being and dominated the studio system from the 1920s to the beginnings of its decline--shared
a narrow perspective on the expectations of their audience.
The commercial nature of their product dictated that they
seek to appeal to the widest possible spectrum, and in attempting to do so they assumed that there existed a broad
consensus of taste little affected by regional or class varia-

tion. Part of their marketing conservatism was the result
of their low estimation of their audience's flexibility. Commercial experience, however, confirmed the validity of this
assumption. Although Sticks might occasionally Nix Hick
Pix, box-office failures and successes did not, in the main,
vary greatly from region to region, while the available sur-
veys indicated that movies attracted all socioeconomic groups. [2]
The economic need to appeal to the undifferentiated mass audience was reinforced by the profitable success of that appeal and, once established as a credo, it became almost impossible to challenge. The studios conducted little research
into the composition of their audience because there seemed
no need for it.

Such research would in any case have questioned the
security of the role the moguls had defined for themselves.
Expanding from their assumptions about the audience, they
prescribed their product as being socially and politically reactive, a mirror reflecting attitudes already in common currency, not a beacon guiding its public to new opinions.
Their own role was to angle this two-way mirror from behind it; as mediators between the creators and their public,
they made sure the public got what they thought it wanted.
Their apparent ability to predict the erratic taste of their
mass audience guaranteed that their decisions would determine the nature of their studio's content, and that as a result
they would define the personalities of the studios they ran.
Only by asserting their own opinions and preferences on
their product could they be seen to be doing their jobs.
The function of the studio executive was to make decisions
about what films were to be made, who would write, direct, and act in them, how their plots would be shaped,
and so on. These decisions, which were the practical applications of their role as mediators between public opinion
and creative activity, at the very least set the limits on
the potential for political expression available to the creative personnel, and arguably exerted a much more determining influence on their films' political sentiments.

Yet it was rarely their individual political opinions
that influenced their actions. Certainly Zanuck was more
likely to make The Grapes of Wrath than California State
Republican Party Chairman Louis B. Mayer, but the populist sentimentality that infused Zanuck's vision of Ameri-
cana in the late 1930s would not have been out of place in
Mayer's own small-town idyll of American perfection, the
Carvel of the Andy Hardy films. Privately, most of the
moguls were Republicans, antipathetic to the policies of the

later New Deal. But publicly their industry was a beneficiary of Rooseveltian liberalism, at least until the enactment of the Paramount decrees. As Business Week put it in 1935,

> Though not all of them favored the re-election of Roosevelt, his social program, so they say, plays right into their pockets. The President seeks higher wages, shorter hours, unemployment insurance and old age pensions. Wrap that into one small capsule and it means to the motion picture mentality more money to spend on movies and more leisure in which to spend the money. 3

The divisions of conventional party politics had little effect on the way the moguls ran their studios, and there is little to suggest that they deliberately and consciously attempted to influence their audiences' party political preferences through the films they produced. *

---

*The one clear exception to this general rule was the notorious campaign against Upton Sinclair and his EPIC (End Poverty in California) program in the 1934 gubernatorial election. The studios' anti-Sinclair propaganda and other actions, including compulsory contributions to the Republican candidate's campaign fund, were probably more important in providing an impetus to unionization and other forms of political activity among resentful employees than they were in influencing the outcome of the election. Certainly the experiment was not repeated.

The Cahiers du Cinéma editors' suggestion that Young Mr. Lincoln was a piece of Republican propaganda does not stand up to detailed examination. Their contention that Lincoln was, in the context of the 1940 election, a specifically Republican mythic figure is dubious, to say the least. Although Zanuck was involved in the 1940 election campaign in support of Wendell Wilkie, Wilkie had not announced his candidacy at the time of the film's release, let alone at the time of the project's inception. Moreover, Wilkie was not the choice of the conservative business hierarchies of the G. O. P.; he secured the nomination substantially because the Republicans were almost certain to lose. The film was released on June 9, 1939, 19 months prior to the election. At the time of shooting, John Ford was a vocal member of the Hollywood Anti-Nazi League, which had already been accused by Martin Dies (then Chairman of H. U. A. C.) of being a "Communist front," and which can hardly be seen   (cont.)

Indeed, political activity was only exceptionally a matter of consequence to them, normally seen as external to their real world, and little more than an alternative form of glamour. They wore their politics as they wore their suits, aiming to produce a public image of restrained respectability, occasionally marred by their tendency to garish overstatement in their choice of ties, their private opulence, or their public protestations of belief in the American Way. From their political affiliations they sought a confirmation of their social status:

> [Harry Cohn] became a Republican--not out of any political conviction, because he was completely apolitical. All rich men were Republicans, hence, Harry Cohn became a Republican. [5]

From their associations with politicians, they sought public acknowledgment that they belonged with the rich, the influential, the powerful. The attraction of power, the recognition of apparently similar personality, and the lack of direct competition drew the moguls to the politicians as their publicity value and the Hollywood mystique drew politicians to them. Prestige was at least as important as business self-interest, and much more important than the allegiance provided by shared opinions.

---

as the natural residence of a propagandist for the Big Business interest. Rather nearer the election date, Ford and Zanuck produced The Grapes of Wrath (released March 15, 1940), which, however compromised a version of Steinbeck's novel it might be, can hardly be called a pro-Republican film. Zanuck was shortly to encounter hostility from right-wing isolationist Senators Nye, Clark and Vanderbilt in their investigations into Hollywood's interventionist bias. He was a liberal Republican who held himself in high esteem for his liberalism and the way it manifested itself in his films. When, in 1944, he did make a film explicitly intended as a statement of his political beliefs, it was a biography of Woodrow Wilson (Wilson, Twentieth Century-Fox; dir. Henry King). At the time of the making of Young Mr. Lincoln, Zanuck was a frequent visitor to Roosevelt's White House. The Cahiers editors suggest "it would ... be wrong to exaggerate the film's political determinism."[4] Not so. It is just that the film's political determinism has very little to do with what they suggest.

> Zanuck has always been politically aware, and at
> least behind the scenes he has usually been politi-
> cally active. But he has no political philosophy,
> except that he usually votes Republican, and likes
> Presidents whoever they are. 6

He saw no anomaly in frequently visiting the White House at
the time he was actively campaigning for Wilkie in 1940.
Most telling of all, perhaps, was the cupboard in Jack Warner's office in which he kept two sets of autographed por-
traits of leading politicans--one of Democrats, one of Republicans. Whichever was appropriate could be exhibited
for visiting dignitaries. 7

    Such curiously anachronistic attitudes to politics
echoed many of the business practices of the film industry,
which were not merely out of step with those of other business concerns, but lagging a generation behind them. * The
moguls saw themselves as benign but autocratic fathers to
their companies. Their hostility to organized labor seemed
to be as much because the existence of the unions questioned
the benevolence of their despotism as because they might demand better pay and conditions. This paternalist self-image
fitted closely the pattern of first-generation capitalist entrepreneurs, as initially modeled by the founders of the English
Industrial Revolution. The moguls' lack of education, the
underlying feeling of inferiority implied by their desire to
avoid personal publicity, their frequently brutally autocratic
behavior towards their employees, and the depth of personal
animosity they exhibited towards each other (best exemplified,
perhaps, by Goldwyn allegedly attending Mayer's funeral "to
make sure he was dead"), present a retrospective image
that appears to have more in common with characters out of
Trollope than with the expected behavior of twentieth-century
industrial magnates.

---

*The idea that one man should alone make major policy de-
cisions had been abandoned by the automobile industry by the
1930s, for example. Henry Ford's refusal to relinquish sole
control of his company is commonly cited as the principal
explanation for its relatively poor performance during that
decade. And it is worth remembering that the Paramount
decrees enforced on the motion picture industry regulations
passed under the Sherman Act of 1890 and the Clayton Act of
1914.

In any orthodox sense, the studio heads were almost without exception poor businessmen: their unwarranted extravagance was one of the causes of the mutual antagonism between them and the men, frequently their relatives, on the East Coast, who might more fairly be called the true entrepreneurial force in the industry. But the moguls were more showmen than businessmen, and perhaps more salesmen than showmen. They conjured up the myth of unpredictable public taste which it took a special ability to prejudge, and reinforced it with each of their successes. Even more importantly, they created something amounting to a private, enclosed world, that in the complexities of its internal relationships resembled some strange tribal society, of which they were "czars" and "emperors." Then they sold that creation to the rest of the world. Hollywood the Dream Factory, acknowledged and to a degree reflected on by almost every writer on the American cinema, was the deliberate creation of a small, often personally as well as professionally interrelated group of men, who fabricated a world and sold it to the rest of America. That their creation grew in large part to be out of their control, and that it attracted others who came to specify and define the myth, is undoubtedly true, but Hollywood, as an empire, as a mythical entity, as an institution, and as a concept governing audience responses to the films it made, was fabricated by the men who founded and ran its studios.

In retrospect, they have acquired an ambivalent commercial heroism, partly because of their improbably antisocial and anachronistic behavior. Neither quite the last entrepreneurs nor the last showmen, the movie tycoons resembled Hughes or Hearst in being fantasists on a grand scale, and more than that, enacting their fantasies in such a way as to make others adopt them as their own. In this none was perhaps more successful than Walt Disney, who, in dominating American film animation, built an empire on the periphery of Hollywood. Not satisfied with that, he built a magical kingdom, Disneyland, and at the time of his death had begun to build a better world--Disney World --in the wilderness of the Florida swamps. Most impressively imperial of all is the fact that his grandiose schemes have survived him, because, like the less enduring creations of the other moguls, his fantasies of innocence were rooted in the commercial reality that, whatever they might signify ideologically, their American Dreams were a salable commodity.

The moguls embedded into the conventions of American film production a trait common to American immigrants: the need to demonstrate oneself as more American than native Americans. Privately, it encouraged them to political conservatism; elsewhere it led them to change their stars' names, disguising their ethnic origins by nominally absorbing them into the dominant Protestant culture. The specifications of the Production Code against giving offense to any group, race or religion reinforced a concomitant tendency, implicit in the rationale of entertainment, to offer the audience a vision of a perfect America, in which the assumptions of its fundamental political doctrines were enacted, while social problems were skirted by invariably couching them in individual terms. Even Warners' "social conscience" films did not so much portray a divided society as one seen to be in the process of achieving harmony through the resolution of invididual conflicts. Here was more than a simple preference for harmless and escapist entertainment. There was, lying obscurely behind the nostalgic and benevolent community fabric of Mayer's Carvel, Zanuck's Old Chicago, and most explicitly Capra's Washington and Shangri-La, an idealistic vision--perhaps not greatly understood and certainly hardly ever articulated--of an essentially unified society, devoted, above all, to the pursuit of spiritual peace through material acquisition and good neighborliness.

By insisting on simple narrative constructions which above all exploited the devices of sentiment, the moguls restricted the range of emotional experience the American cinema might provide its audience. They also limited its possibilities for political expression to the narrow range which they, as first- or second-generation immigrants, saw as being consensual. In embedding their assumptions so deeply in the structures of their narratives, they could at the same time ruthlessly operate an unacknowledged ideology, and systematically deny its existence by insisting that their preference for happy endings was never any more than a concern to give the public what it wanted. Their cinema's conservatism of theme and content was the fulfilment of its social role as reactive affirmation for its consumers' beliefs. As speculative mediators, the moguls presumed on their intuitive understanding of what those beliefs might be. Not surprisingly, perhaps, the virtues of America they thought Hollywood might most profitably celebrate were those reflected by its most persistent tradition of political thought.

HICKS AND STICKS

> "Studios feel that the farmer
> should be edified and glori-
> fied.... One producer ...
> said that such pictures were
> demanded by the public who
> find that small-town atmos-
> phere is much more whole-
> some than that of the met-
> ropolitan area."
>
> Variety, July 31, 1935[8]

A peculiarity of the American political tradition is
its sustained faith in the continued validity of its fundamental documents. The Constitution is the text of the fundamental law. The Declaration of Independence may be seen
as the fundamental article of faith. Both documents have
long been transferred out of the historical contexts of their
framing, and elevated to the status of mythic artifact in the
subsequent history of American political thought. To a large
extent this process has frozen the terms of political debate
open to Americans, for the elevation to mythic artifact has
made the basic assumptions of the two documents unques-
tionable. The truths that Jefferson took to be self-evident
have been taken as being beyond contention ever since, and
while the Constitution has been open to contemporary interpretation, the areas in which it may be interpreted are
limited by the specific ideology inherent in its formulation.

The mythic model of American democracy which the
Declaration of Independence provides is couched in the rhetoric of Locke and Rousseau. It is a bourgeois model, inherently individualistic in its assumptions, and asserting its
egalitarianism in other than economic terms. Rather,
equality between men is seen as the consequence of their
endowment

> by their Creator with certain unalienable Rights,
> that among these are Life, Liberty, and the pur-
> suit of Happiness. [9]

A spiritually derived natural right to individual self-

determination forms the basis for a concise expression of the
fundamental tenet of bourgeois democracy:

> that to secure these rights, Governments are
> instituted among Men, deriving their just powers
> from the consent of the governed.

The American Revolution occurred at a moment in which a
political doctrine of equality could be equated with a social
doctrine of individualism.   The institutionalization of that
equation prevented the ready adoption of nineteenth-century
Marxist theories to an American environment.   Economic
determinism and Marx's theories of class conflict ran counter
to the traditions of a bourgeois individualism which was not
only the legacy of the frontier experience but also the ideological inheritance bequeathed by the Founding Fathers.

Though not Arcadian, Jefferson's vision was nevertheless pastoral.   Agrarian democracy represented an ideal
to be valued above all for its social stability.

> Cultivators of the earth are most valuable citizens.
> They are the most vigorous, most independent, the
> most virtuous and they are tied to their country
> and wedded to its liberty and interests by the most
> lasting bands. [10]

There was an inherent conservatism in Jefferson's vision
that, once achieved, the Revolution would have accomplished
its goal of a society both just and equal.   The Westward expansion of the nineteenth century sustained belief in the ideal
agrarian democratic community, even if practical events
moved the basis of political power ever further away from
the Jeffersonian yeoman farmer to the urban centers.   But
as reality grew more divorced from the ideal, the myth of
the individually self-sufficient farmer, beholden to no man
but loyal to his community and his country out of a natural
beneficence, grew more powerful.   The heroic image of the
farmer as the ideal citizen, which originated as an
eighteenth-century aristocratic and literary idea, became
during the nineteenth century a part of American political
folklore and nationalist ideology.   It fused with a nostalgic
wish among the urban upper and middle classes to pay
homage to an earlier American innocence, while for the
agrarian population it became a defensive armor with which
to cloak their self-esteem in the face of the increasing
realization that economically and politically they had lost

irretrievable ground to the city dwellers. At the same time the agrarian image provided the archetype of the American innocent and became the rallying point for the forces of social conservatism.

Frederick Jackson Turner's assertion that the frontier experience was the formative element in the evolution of the American character and its political institutions was made retrospectively, three years after the frontier was officially declared closed. Turner's argument declined to attach the American dream of abundance to the contemporary urban industrial context, and the widespread feeling around the turn of the century that an era of America's historical development had ended encouraged traditionalists to characterize Jeffersonianism as a conservative belief whose central tenet was the requirement for contact with the land as the almost mystical repository of American democracy and egalitarianism. By the end of the nineteenth century Jefferson's prophecy that

> I think our governments will remain virtuous for many centuries; as long as they are chiefly agricultural; and this will be as long as there shall be vacant lands in any part of America. When they set piled upon one another in large cities, as in Europe, they will become as corrupt as Europe. [11]

seemed in imminent danger of coming true much sooner than he had imagined, and fears for the stability of the social fabric found expression in a consistent if often vague opposition of values between country and city. From the 1880s onwards, a declining and often embittered rural population might see themselves mocked as "rubes" and "hayseeds" in city entertainment, but in conflict with this image was an equally powerful urban nostalgia for the self-sufficient agrarian community. If Progressivism ameliorated the city's depravity and the Jazz Age celebrated the cultural pluralism of the melting pot in a booming consumer economy, the Crash fractured the essentially urban illusion of Twenties sophistication and excess. Rural simplicity, mocked in 1925 at the Scopes trial, emerged again in the Depression as the cultural, if not the economic, bastion of American virtues. The populist mythos of the agrarian community or the small town pervaded the idealized solutions to the Depression; for example, in the Department of Interior's plan for Subsistence Homesteads where farm communities would raise their own food and do their own weaving and woodworking, a scheme which was eventually transformed into the Resettlement Administration's Greenbelt towns.

Some of the decade's most explicitly political films presented precisely this pastoral vision of the country's educative and rehabilitative power. King Vidor's independent production, Our Daily Bread (1934), depicted a young city couple (Tom Keene and Karen Morley) victimized by the Depression in the city, who inherit a small plot of land in the Mid-West and are inspired to return to the soil. At the farm, their inexperience encourages them to take in first a dispossessed farmer (John Qualen) and his family, and then a motley assortment of the Depression's flotsam, who combine their skills in the cooperative venture of constructing a community and making the earth fruitful. The regenerative nature of these twin processes is exemplified by the escaped convict who becomes the community's policeman and later surrenders to the law so that his reward will finance the cooperative. Its educative power is revealed to Keene when, after a vision of the convict, he abandons his flight from responsibility with the unreconstructed city floozy (Barbara Pepper) and returns to inspire the final communal project: digging an irrigation ditch to save their corn crop from drought.

Critics who have remarked on the absurdities of the film's economics[12] miss the point of its ideological thrust as much as the Hearst press did with its accusation that it was "pinko." Our Daily Bread is an expression of populist idealism, and its inconsistencies result not so much from a failure to locate itself in terms of a conventional labeling of left and right as from the contradictions inherent in populism itself. Our Daily Bread contrasts virtuous small independent production with the vicious corporate dependent bigness of the banks and the institutions of the city. It finds no problem in the coincidence that the farm's owner should also be the community's leader, as it is equally untroubled by the cooperative's democratic decision to elect "a strong boss." Like the rhetoric of populism itself, the film's assumptions about property and political power and the relations between the individual and the community appear incoherent only if they are presumed to propose a political practice. Our Daily Bread ignores the real conditions of agricultural overproduction and migration from the land to the cities in articulating an unavailable idealism of what should be. The film's lack of commercial success (no major studio would finance its sustained critique of the banks)[13] does not detract from its

importance as a particularly complete statement of some of
the major ideological motifs of Hollywood production in the
1930s and beyond. The opposition of city and country was
seldom articulated in its entirety within a single film, but
nevertheless pervaded the formulations of such disparate
genres as the Western, the musical and the (invariably urban) crime film, as well as the more obviously idealized
films of Will Rogers, Shirley Temple and Andy Hardy. It
is possible to propose a series of antinomies, along the
lines of that suggested by Jim Kitses for the Western, [14]
which suggest the relative values of country and city, and
which recur, albeit with varying force, in films as disparate as Gold Diggers of 1933 and State Fair.

COUNTRY	CITY
Narrative	Spectacle
Structure	Surface
Emotion	Sensation
Harmony	Discord
Clear Moral distinctions	Ambiguous morality
Violence as disruptive	Violence as endemic
Landscape	Skyline
The Horizontal	The Vertical
Day	Night
Community	Self-Interest
Family	Individual
Fraternity	Competition
Amity	Sexuality
Homogeneous hero	Ambivalent hero
Production	Consumption
Property	Money
Abundance	Deprivation
Sufficiency	Luxury
Tranquillity	Energy
Tradition	Innovation
Stability	Dynamism
Homeliness	Glamour
Purity	Corruption
Fertility	Emptiness

Clearly this grid is heavily biased in favor of the

country's sustenance of virtue, but it does not eliminate the more positive aspects of the city's energy. That, however, seems quite in keeping with the tenor of Hollywood production, particularly after the imposition of the Production Code. The vital role the country has in providing narrative significance to the spectacle of the city is well enough illustrated by Capra's explorations of the redemptive power of yeoman virtue in <u>Mr. Deeds Goes to Town</u> (1936). After two days' experience of New York, small town poet Longfellow Deeds (Gary Cooper) explains to disguised reporter 'Babe' Bennett (Jean Arthur),

> People here are funny. They work so hard at living that they've forgotten how to live. Last night I was walking along looking at the tall buildings and I got to thinking about what Thoreau said. "They created a lot of grand palaces here but they forgot to create the noblemen to put in them." I'd rather have Mandrake Falls.

Arthur's cynicism melts in the face of Cooper's simple purity. She explains to her friend,

> Here's a boy who's wholesome and fresh. To us he looks like a freak.... He's got goodness, Mabel. Do you know what that is? No, of course you don't. We're too busy being smart-alecks, too busy in a crazy competition for nothing.

Later she tells the judge at Cooper's insanity hearing,

> He could never fit in with our distorted viewpoint because he's honest, sincere and good. If that man's crazy, your honour, the rest of us belong in straitjackets.

The judge, of course, concurs in her assessment, upholding Cooper's idealistic agrarian solution to the Depression.

Why should Hollywood choose to promulgate so anachronistic an ideology in response to the Depression? The answer partly lies in its very Utopianism; pastoral fantasies are evidently more available to the urbanites who comprised most of the moviemakers as well as the bulk of their audiences than they are to those confronted with the daily realities of rural life. At least as important, the idealist solutions of populist rhetoric were apolitical precisely because

they were impractical. Cooper's program of self-help with
"10 acres, a horse, a cow and some seed" might appear to
be as critical of the New Deal's federalism as it is reminiscent of the Republican Homestead Act of 1863, but his declaration of the irrelevance of specific political attitudes diffused
the issue into unarguable American generalities:

> From what I can see no matter what system of
> government we have there'll always be leaders and
> always be followers.   It's like the road out in
> front of my house.   It's on a steep hill.   Every
> day I see the cars climbing up.   Some go lickety-
> split up that hill on high, some have to shift into
> second and some shake and slip back to the bottom
> again.   Same cars, same gasoline, yet some make
> it and some don't, and I say the fellers who can
> make the hill on high should stop once in a while
> and help those who can't.   That's all I'm trying to
> do with this money, help the fellers who can't make
> the hill on high. . . .

In this opposition of competition and cooperation, Capra was
expressing the most politically explicit version of an ideology
that guaranteed and was guaranteed by the harmlessness of
entertainment.   It eliminated discord with the harmony of the
happy ending, which demonstrated the beneficent stability of
the moral universe decreed by the Production Code.   At the
same time, Utopian populism contained specific elements
which suited it perfectly to the political requirements and
narrative forms of the American cinema.

MEN OF GOODWILL

> "Lincoln appears and reappears
> in character and portrait
> throughout these films [West-
> erns of the 1930s] as a sort of
> cinematic equivalent of the
> Good Housekeeping Seal of Ap-
> proval. "[15]

A set of rhetorical motifs, inspired by Jefferson's
agrarian preferences, has been a recurrent feature of third

party and extracongressional political movements in American history.   As Donald MacRae suggests, there is bound to be ideological tension "if, like the Americans, one founds a nation on a claim to perfection and yet aspires to progress. "16 While the aims and policies of groups as chronologically diverse as the Jacksonians, the People's Party and the "Radical Right" of the early 1960s prohibit their sharing in any strict sense an ideology, they nevertheless display common emphases in their styles of expression.   Whether they themselves were movements of specific interests or of more general social protest, whether they were radical or reactionary in intent, they shared a rhetoric of social conservatism which emphasized the need to restore the eroded values of an earlier age and which placed its faith in the innate virtuousness of the American people.   Such emphases constitute the materials for, rather than comprising, an ideology, but the consistency of their occurrence is testimony to the endurance of an American political fundamentalism which may as accurately be labeled populism as anything else.

MacRae suggests that

> Populism is not about economics, politics or even, in the last resort, society itself.   It is about personality, and about personality in a moral sense. Populism claims that the individual should be a complete man.... The paradigmatic man of populism is free of any burden of alienation: like his relative, man under communism, he has evaded all the consequences of Adam's fall.   Unlike his communist cousin, however, he is fixed, static, engaged on no Faustian quest to conquer all nature. Because he is perfect he is free....   His freedom ... is not to be different or to change. 17

Like the inhabitants of any Utopia, this idealized figure exists out of time.   His very ahistorical nature may in part explain the persistence with which he recurs.   By the same token, populism

> is therefore profoundly a-political, and no basis for a sustained political party as distinct from a congerie of social movements. 18

The populist tradition has consistently operated tangentially to the main arena of American politics, the two-party system.   Frequently taking the form of a splintering

away by a section of the majority political party who felt
they were no longer adequately represented, populist movements have always failed to become permanent political
forces, coming to grief in the face of their inability to co-
here around specific political policies.   They have often
provided opportunities for the mutually convenient coupling
of what European observers would commonly regard as
strange bedfellows, but then the same may be said for both
the principal political parties.   Indeed, the recurrence of
populist political movements may be traceable to the nature
of the American political party system.   A clear demarca-
tion between the two dominant parties on specific issues has
seldom been a feature of American politics, and the divisions
within the parties have commonly been greater than the divisions between them.   Their existence has been sustained
above all by the institutional weight of the party organizations.   Given such a system, in which party divisions over
issues lacked the coherence provided by the class conflict-
of-interest model of European political parties, the role of
populist movements in effecting a realignment of institutionalized political response becomes apparent.   The shared
rhetoric of such movements, and their recurrent citation of
a number of American political archetypes, emphasize the
idealistic and restorative function of populism.   Its Utopian
purpose places it above the grubby realities of politics and
the inadequate refuges of ideology.   In Frank Capra's <u>You
Can't Take It with You</u> (1938) Grandpa Vanderhof (Lionel
Barrymore) explains,

> Communism, fascism, voodooism, everybody's got
> an ism these days....   When things go a little bad
> nowadays you go out and get yourself an ism and
> you're in business.

As an alternative, he proposes to his daughter,

> Give her Americanism, let her know something
> about America.   John Paul Jones, Patrick Henry,
> Samuel Adams, Washington, Jefferson, Monroe,
> Lincoln, Grant, Lee, Edison, Mark Twain.   When
> things got tough for those boys they didn't run
> around looking for isms.

However anti-intellectual populism in its various manifestations may have been, it has never acquired or required the
services of a theorist.   Grandpa Vanderhof's list indicates
the apolitical nature of its heroes as well as its amorphous-
ness.

Hollywood's representations of the political have followed similar lines. Capra's <u>Mr. Smith Goes to Washington</u> (1939) is exemplary in its complete avoidance of the words "Democrat" or "Republican"--it does not even mention the existence of a President. Jefferson Smith's (James Stewart) scheme for a boys' camp which would

> just get the poor kids off the streets and out of the cities for a few months in the summer and let them learn something about nature and American ideals

is, like Deeds' 10-acre farms, a self-help idea--not, as a journalist tries to make Stewart say, because "the government's putting too much money in too many places," but because "the government's got enough on its hands already." Stewart's filibuster delays the passage of a relief bill, but in the name of the nation's fundamental political principles and to redeem the "sacred chamber" of the Senate from the corrupt betrayal it has suffered. The object of the film's criticism is Bossism and the political machine rather than any aspect of the New Deal. Again, as in <u>Mr. Deeds,</u> the past as repository of moral virtue is invoked by reference to a dead father whose ideals resemble those of the hero: Arthur's in <u>Mr. Deeds,</u> Stewart's own in <u>Mr. Smith</u> (and later, Barbara Stanwyck's in <u>Meet John Doe</u>).

What distinguishes the populist evocation of the American political tradition from the rhetoric of laissez-faire individualism is its emphasis on cooperation.

> Economically, the <u>Idealtypus</u> is a small co-operative.... The essence of co-operation is that the owners are private people, not the state; each owns a share to which there is an upper limit; and each contributes something besides capital. [19]

The farm community of <u>Our Daily Bread</u> is a close cousin to the cooperatives created by the Farmers' Alliance in the 1880s. Both derived their ideological inspiration from Jeffersonian rhetoric, and both rely on the ideal of consensus and its individual embodiment, the man of goodwill. Any democratic institution depends on compromise, but that envisaged by the American democratic model, rooted as it was in an individualist, contractual concept of political allegiance, differed significantly from its European equivalent. Instead of a compromise being achieved between forces with conflicting interests, Jefferson posited an agreement achieved between individuals acting together in good faith.

It is for the happiness of those united in society to
harmonize as much as possible in matters which
they must of necessity transact together. Civil
government being the sole object of forming societies, its administration must be conducted by common consent. [20]

The European notion of enlightened self-interest, as expounded
by Hobbes or Rousseau, equated enlightenment with fear; men
act for the good of society out of a desire to protect themselves. This pessimistic attitude was the product, even
among natural right theorists, of defining the position of the
individual in relation to a prior determined concept of the
state. [21] The individualist orientation of the American view
of enlightened self-interest, however, resulted in an opposite
and optimistic emphasis being placed on the relationship between citizen and state. The interests of individuals and
those of the state were viewed as existing normally in a
state of harmony, rather than conflict, since the state existed to serve the individual, not to restrict the amount of
damage he could inflict on his fellow-citizens. If there is
a political theorist more at odds with the fundamentals of
American ideology than Marx (and whose theories are more
readily demonstrated by American institutions), it is Hobbes.
The American model proposed not merely that men would act
for the good of society as well as for their own good, but
also that at no point in the process of social construction
were the two distinguishable. That the myth of the man of
goodwill was seriously questioned in practice as early as the
framing of the Constitution had no effect on its continued influence. It, too, was a bourgeois concept, incapable of
satisfactorily coping with the emergence of political parties,
but it could be readily incorporated into the construct of Jeffersonian agrarianism, and suitably reflected populist nostalgia for an imagined past of simpler human relationships.

Complete men, living ideally in independent agrarian virtue, would agree with one another. Their
insights would be sound, healthy, bound to appropriate pieties. Their judgements would be free but
would coincide. Their society would be essentially
consensual and uniform. ... Each individual will is
the righteous will, and the sum of these righteous
wills is the general will of the community. ...
[Populism] goes beyond democracy to consensus,
and it sacrifices the freedom it proclaims in the
interest of a moral uniformity. [22]

This archetypal relation between the individual and society
proposed in populist rhetoric suited perfectly Hollywood's
narrative conventions. Capra's protagonists are representative men, propelled by lucky circumstance into extraordinary
positions. To that extent they mirror the star system, as
well as giving voice to what is taken to be the attitudes of
their audience--a voice legitimized by their representative-
ness and their comic vulnerability. But in being representative they are not average: they have not only the opportunity but also what Capra called the "courage"[23] to behave
as their audience would ideally wish to: as independent individuals certain of their rectitude and certain that it is
shared by "the people. " They manage to be both representative and exceptional because they are idealized; their perfection separates them from the people at the same time
that it makes them such articulate spokesmen of the people's opinions. The tension between the individual and the
mass, not only in populist ideas but also in cinematic narrative, is resolved by the idealization of the representative
hero. Capra, among others, lessens the tension further by
his use of reactive characters, such as Vice President Harry
Carey in Mr. Smith, whose predominant role is to watch and
approve, guiding the audience's consensual reactions. Capra,
more vigorously than the other filmmakers who presented less
coherent versions of populist ideas, believes in the charismatic power of example, often combined with the power of
love, to reform the reprobate and restore moral order.

     Such a notion of political good required a correspond-
ingly extreme notion of political evil. The theory of conflicting interests was unacceptable, for the myth of the man
of goodwill proposed that men would normally cooperate for
the betterment of society. The peculiar addiction of Americans to conspiracy theories may be traced to the necessity
of explaining the existence of social or ideological conflict
in terms of the myth of the man of goodwill. When a man
fails to act as a man of goodwill in furthering the social
interest at the same time that he benefits himself, he can
be doing so only because either he or the Power of which
he is an agent (the Money Power, or the Communist Conspiracy, for example) is not merely opposed to the social
interest, but actively trying to destroy it. The social interest is co-extensive with each individual's interest, and
consequently to act against that interest is to act against
each individual's interest, including one's own. Such irrational action can only be explained by the suggestion that the
individual is under the sway of a Power whose aim is the

overthrow of this inclusive political system. A man who
would act thus against his own interest destroys his right to
a place in society, and may therefore be treated as less
than an American, which is to say, less than human. The
Paranoid Style of American politics[24] is merely the logical
concomitant of the central American heroic myth of the man
of goodwill.

The optimistic populism readily identified in the family films of the 1930s and early 1940s found its coherence by
including all its characters within its benevolent vision. Only isolated individuals are marked out as being temporarily
excluded from this idealistic harmony, in order to motivate
the drama, and give it a conflict to resolve. The embodiment of populist demonology, Edward Arnold's pig-eyed mu-
nitions monopolist Anthony P. Kirby in Capra's You Can't
Take It with You, is finally shown the error of his machin-
ating ways and retires to play crises away on his harmonica
in the blissful New York Shangri-La of the Vanderhof household. But the abstract belief in the inclusivity of American
society implied by The Philadelphia Story or the early Capra
films had as its corollary a darker aspect. Those who fell
outside the all-but all-inclusive net of populist optimism were
placed entirely beyond the Pale, victims of its implicit Paranoid Style.

In dealing with those outside, whose covert intention
was invariably the destruction of society, no humanitarian
restraints needed to be exercised, since their aggression
had already demonstrated their lack of humanity. The villain, frequently iconographically identified, was the executor
of unremitting evil, and could be counted on to motivate the
plot while also providing a moral lesson at the film's conclusion, when he received his comeuppance. The Production
Code stated explicitly that throughout the film, the audience
must be made to feel "that evil is wrong and good is right."[25]
Any moral ambivalence had to be presented within the context of that absolute polarization. The location of any character along the line of moral acceptability could be precisely determined by his or her fate in the plot: sins were punished in accordance with the need to suffer at the hands of
the Code's "compensating moral values." The Manichaean
model of populist political thought was converted, through
the strictures of Hollywood's moral accountancy, into a
determinist principle around which plots had to be structured.

THE STATUS OF THE DREAM

> There is nothing Americans
> like so much to be told from
> the screen as that they are
> Americans.
>
> Otis Ferguson[26]

Codified as "harmless entertainment," Hollywood's
representation of politics was both consensual and oblique.
It studiously avoided any discussion of immediate political
issues and promoted its dramaturgy of American fundamentalism, often, in the second half of the 1930s, in the form
of historical hagiographies like Young Mr. Lincoln (1939) or
celebrations of the American spirit in history, such as Ford
and Zanuck's account of Revolutionary pioneers in Drums
Along the Mohawk (1939). Like its populist-inflected rhetoric, the American cinema rose above politics in the declaration of its Americanism, which was both nostalgic and, somewhat perversely, nativist. There was an obvious irony in
the celebration of a white Anglo-Saxon Protestant heritage by
an industry dominated by members of ethnic minorities. But
the Protestant work-ethic, whose hero was the self-made
man, was an American archetype that had appealed anew to
each generation of immigrants, and few had realized its vision of America the golden land of opportunity so fully as the
movie moguls. With the time-honored ferocity of successful
immigrants, they rejected their ethnic origins and asserted
their Americanism. When Ben Hecht attempted to elicit financial support for the Zionist cause from prominent Jews
in the industry, David Selznick responded, "I'm an American
and not a Jew."[27] Their intense desire to demonstrate their
Americanism may well have inspired the M. P. P. D. A. to
choose as their industry spokesman a figure so solidly embedded in the Protestant Establishment as Will Hays. It
combined conveniently with financial self-interest in their advocacy of business "self-regulation" and the Jeffersonian
maxim that "That government is best which governs least. "*

---

*In this respect they could happily cooperate with Roosevelt's
National Recovery Administration, which encouraged the formation of business cartels. The change in policy which led
to the renewed antitrust attacks in 1937-1938 found   (cont.)

In taking to their hearts the ideals of individualist
free enterprise and strenuous Americanism, the moguls and
many of their employees--Capra is only the most conspicuous example--adopted the ideology from which these beliefs
most firmly stemmed. If agrarianism was, by the 1930s,
merely nostalgic, its yeoman virtues remained rhetorically
accessible to the small businessman, while its community
spirit was ideally represented in the life of a small town
like Carvel, where the family survived intact as the essential unit of social and emotional life. Tom Stempel points
out in his biography of Nunnally Johnson that

> Of the six major creators at Fox over a long
> period of time--Zanuck, Johnson, John Ford,
> Henry King, Philip Dunne, and Lamar Trotti--
> all but Dunne came from the same kind of small-
> town, middle-class background. [29]

While such consistency of origin (which itself conceals much
geographical diversity) was unique to Fox, the value system
expressed in that studio's products was not significantly different from that of other studios. In the second half of the
1930s Hollywood maintained a remarkable ideological consistency in its output, which inevitably suggests that these
forms of expression were particularly attractive to their
audiences. In 1929 the Exhibitors Herald World had remarked on rural audiences' lack of sophistication in somewhat scornful terms:

> Perhaps it may be said--for it has been generally
> said--that the inhabitants of large cities regard as
> artistically desirable what people in other types of

---

the film industry a prominent target, and also brought it a
new champion. It is hard to see Raymond Moley's book on
the M. P. P. D. A. as other than a timely attempt to demonstrate that the industry was capable of governing itself. The
Hays Office (published in 1945 but written in 1938-1939, and
revised to include the industry's wartime performance) is
more than a eulogy of Will Hays. It is a concerted argument that government regulation of business generally and
the motion picture business in particular would be both unnecessary and harmful. Self-regulation or self-government,
as Moley variously refers to the practices of the M. P. P. D. A.,
is seen as the only way "business could escape the paralyz-
ing hand of government bureaucracy and politics. "[28]

> communities call smut. The difference in the
> point of view doubtless lies in the fact that city
> life is more varied than that of rural districts
> and it is varied experiences, perhaps, which
> teach discrimination. [30]

Within five years, the movies found themselves much more
inclined to proclaim the virtues of rural simplicity. Stempel's argument, that the assertion of the family, the work
ethic, and the small town were particularly middle class
values, can be extended. Such values also all promoted
social integration on a variety of levels. By presenting a
system of ideas and symbols which pre-existed their expression, the films made their own expression easily comprehensible to their audiences. Choosing those ideas and
symbols which both had the most widespread currency, and
themselves articulated the belief in consensus, secured the
films' operation at the level of their audiences' ideological
lowest common denominator. It was not that the films were
seeking specifically to address a middle class audience, nor,
necessarily, that they were concerned to promote middle
class values. Rather this value-system upheld itself not as
middle class, but as classless, a consensus of beliefs with
which the middle class American audience might most easily
profess their nation's uniqueness while avoiding confrontation
on social and political issues. As Robert Sklar suggests
about Capra,

> the social world Capra created in his movies was
> intended less to represent American society than to
> stimulate and support the ideas and values of his
> audiences. His goal was not to present reality, it
> was to persuade audiences to accept his vision of
> proper belief and behavior, or perhaps to reinforce
> their own. [31]

Despite the Catholic pressure which had forced the implementation of the Code, in the later 1930s Hollywood became what
Protestant reform groups had always sought for: an instrument for the moral endorsement of the status quo, and a
tool to reinforce the cultural authority of fundamental American values at precisely the time they were being questioned
in other media. The cinema, the predominant instrument of
mass culture, was itself committed to a nostalgic critique of
mass society. Capra described the argument of Mr. Deeds
as "fighting for ... the preservation of the liberty of the individual against the mass. "[32] These paradoxes were no

more improbable than a Wall Street-owned monopoly choosing
bankers and monopolists as its principal icons of social evil.
The ideology was itself paradoxical, but unproblematically so,
since it did not seek to articulate a political program. Rather, it managed to express the status needs of both its producers and its audience.

That element in Progressivism which had sought reform to counter corruption and preserve traditional values
had acquired Jeffersonian rhetoric for the devoutly paternal-
istic middle class in their dealings with the urban working
class. From it sprang the Prohibition movement, which
frankly avowed its responsibility for that section of the urban poor which it deemed to be incapable of self-determination. Prohibitionists had dominated the Protestant film censorship campaigns of the 1920s. Each change in objective,
towards a more abstract and therefore more ideological goal,
reflected more explicitly the status concerns of those members of the middle class who felt their values threatened by
urbanization, industrialization and immigration, with its
threat of alternative cultures. Their somewhat improbable
achievement, through the implementation of the Production
Code, was to persuade an industry whose producers were
predominantly of immigrant stock to adopt their morally
conservative values. It was an achievement made possible
by the producers' own status concerns--their desire to demonstrate their own worth as Americans. All coalesced in
the vagueness of a socially conservative consensus of bourgeois values because such beliefs perfectly suited a form of
entertainment that wished to avoid giving offense. Categorized by the Production Code as a moral system, it rose
above politics and persuaded by emotion rather than argument. The American cinema could articulate its ideology
through narratives which relied on their audiences' sentimental attachment to their performers, the stars.

"DEAR MR. GABLE ... YOU MADE ME LOVE YOU"

The star system was the principal tool by which the
individualist narrative acquired its dominant position in the
American cinema's story structure. The introduction of
sound brought an increased psychological realism which required that stars appeal to the public less as a result of
their exotic personalities than through a recognizable

iconography of character type. The coming of sound altered
the relationship between film and spectator, removing an element of participation from the audience role and emphasizing
a more unilateral process of communication, in which the
spectator became merely the receiver of a complete message. A central ingredient of the detached exoticism of the
silent cinema, that had permitted not only much of its content, but also its conscious use of symbolism and non-
naturalistic object relationships, was replaced by a more
obviously "realistic" style in lighting, set design, and performance. The world the cinema offered became less fantastic, and central to this process was the Thirties image of
the star as the perfected common man. The exotic appeal
of Valentino was replaced by the sympathetic identification
that the audience could make with Gable, Stewart or Cooper
as the glamorized relatives of the boy next door.

> Aw, gee, Mr. Gable (sang Judy Garland), I don't
> want to bother you. I guess you've got a lot of
> girls who tell you the same thing, and if you don't
> want to read this, well, you don't have to, but I
> just had to tell you about the time I saw you in It
> Happened One Night. That was the first time I
> ever saw you, and I knew right then you were the
> nicest feller in the movies. I guess it was be-
> cause you acted so, well so natural like, not like
> a real actor at all but just like any feller you'd
> meet at school or at a party. 33

The distancing from an imperfect actuality that came with the
banishment of the minor irritants of ordinary life for the
characters on the screen was implicit in the Hollywood Dream.
With this purification of the physical archetype came a moral
or ethical purification. Characters escaped petty moral dilemmas as they escaped skin complaints; if they had a problem, it was the Problem of the film plot, central to the
story structure. Life in the movies was not perhaps so
much simpler as less cluttered.

The tendency of sound to emphasize the unilateral
process of communication from product to consumer intensified the need for the basis of the relationship between
film and audience to be established by means of an emotional identification with the characters of the drama. The
natural pressure of the need for such relationships was to
focus the narrative on an individual character or relationship. The star system had promoted that tendency; sound

added to its imperative. The focusing of the narrative on the leading players altered the balance of definition between them and the supporting characters. While the stars embodied archetypes, the minor characters became increasingly slight variations on a set of stereotypes: in the R.K.O. Astaire-Rogers musicals, Fred and Ginger's relationship may vary, but Edward Everett Horton is always Edward Everett Horton. The extreme point of this division was perhaps reached by Busby Berkeley in his musical set pieces, in which chorus girls simply become objects moving in a pattern.

The aspirations of the moguls and many of their employees, the commercial requirements of their product to express a consensual ideology, and the limitations on plot development imposed by the Production Code reflected and were reflected by the natural exigencies of a simplified linear narrative. The result of this interplay of forces was a conventional set of narrative structures which, in the process of mutually validating each other, prescribed a unilateral relationship between film and audience. Spectators had provided for them a completely passive position in which they were obliged to accept not only the development of the plot, but also the logic of its development and, behind that, the social and political assumptions which shaped that logic. Above all, those structures invested a moral--and hence a political--authority in the central protagonist of the personalized drama.

The concentration on the individual produced a simplification of narrative possibilities. As Joseph Breen pointed out, the hero is placed in a situation which presents him with a problem. The course of the film consists in him finding a solution to the problem. The role of an individual well-defined figure as the dynamic center of a world of less-defined characters emphasizes the individualist potential: to that extent the construction of the typical Hollywood narrative conforms to the central social assumption of populist sentiment. When the storyline touches upon an area of social or political concern, the attachment is confirmed. Although Hollywood adopted a populist consensus in the second half of the 1930s, the rhetoric and the narrative practices of that consensus are by no means restricted to that period. They persist, often with little modification, throughout the history of the American cinema, and their ahistorical continuity can be as well illustrated by looking at a later, self-sufficient text peculiarly lacking an overall cultural context as it could be by any further consideration of Capra, Ford, or Henry King.

REMEMBERING THE ALAMO

      In the July 4, 1960 issue of <u>Life</u> magazine there appeared a three-page foldout advertisement for <u>The Alamo</u>. Under the headline, "There Were No Ghostwriters at the Alamo," the text of the ad was a commentary on the significance of the Alamo as an event in American history, and a critique of the 1960 Presidential election campaign. It argued that both Presidential candidates were puppets of their party machines, rhetorically asking of either of them,

> Who has written his speeches? Who--or what
> board of ghostwriting strategists--has fashioned
> the phrases, molded the thoughts, designed the
> delivery, authored the image, staged the presen-
> tation, put the political show on the road to win
> the larger number of voters? Who is the actor
> reading the script?[34]

The $200,000 advertisement was signed by Russell Birdwell, publicity director, James Edward Grant, scriptwriter and associate producer, and John Wayne, producer, director and star of <u>The Alamo</u>. The advertisement was a cogent statement of Wayne's widely misunderstood political sentiments, and was indicative not merely of the strong populist spirit that underlay his credo, but of the particular emphasis that the American cinema's presentation of the ethic of individualist self-sufficiency has laid on the definition of character through action. Recognizing that by contemporary assessment his political views were conservative, Wayne nevertheless regarded himself as a "Jeffersonian liberal." His Republicanism stemmed from his Jeffersonian belief in least government and his hawk-like attitude toward American foreign policy from his belief in the Communist conspiracy and acceptance of Manifest Destiny. More importantly, however, his political position was defined by his persona, and his persona was defined by his actions, to a greater extent than any other film actor of comparable stature. The central tenet of Wayne's polity was integrity, and in that he represented not only the Jeffersonian ideal of the integral relationship between personality and politics, but also the propensity of mainstream American cinematic narrative to have its leading characters personify an ideology through their actions.

      <u>The Alamo</u> was an intensely, almost obsessively,

personal project for Wayne, which he had nurtured for over
twelve years before filming began.   He insisted on producing
and directing it himself, despite the resulting eight-year delay in bringing the project to fruition.   At the time of its
production, it was among the costliest films yet made; Wayne
had sunk all his own wealth into it, as well as personally re-
cruiting the remainder of the financing.   As the Life advertisement indicated, it was a film he regarded as being a
deeply personal political statement.   In one interview he
described the film by saying:

> This film is America.   I hope that seeing the Bat-
> tle of the Alamo will remind Americans that liberty
> and freedom don't come cheap.   This picture, well,
> I guess making it has made me feel useful to my
> country.   I think it's important that foreign coun-
> tries know about this aspect of the American strug-
> gle for freedom.   I hope our present generation of
> Americans, our children, will get a sense of our
> glorious past, and appreciate the struggle our an-
> cestors made for the precious freedoms which we
> now enjoy--and sometimes just kind of take for
> granted. 35

The Alamo focuses on an event which unites Western
myth and the political history of American territorial expansion.   The battle of the Alamo is as much a Western myth
as it is a myth of Manifest Destiny or the Monroe Doctrine.
Wayne and James Edward Grant assert the political significance of the myth through the presentation of a Westerner's
comprehension of political independence, the concept around
which American ideas of freedom have consistently been defined.   Independence embraces not only issues of territorial
integrity and political sovereignty, but also a completely
integrated set of ideals of personal freedom.   The purpose
of the Texan War of Independence is depicted as being to
resist the tyranny of Santa Anna, and Houston's intention is
to declare the Republic of Texas. *

It is around the word "Republic" that Wayne, as Davy
Crockett, defines his understanding of freedom as the right

---

*Significantly, Wayne wanted to play the part of Houston him-
self, but was unable to raise the $12 million finance for the
film unless he played one of the leads.   Houston, who makes
only a brief appearance in The Alamo, was played by Richard
Boone.

to say what you want, go where you want, and get drunk
when and where you want. This interrelation of personal
and political ideas of independence, through the embodiment
of a political principle in the actions of an individual, necessarily precludes the possibility of other forms of political
attachment being presented. Only peripherally does The
Alamo concern itself with the historical issue of territorial
aggrandizement, and then principally to dismiss it as motivation for the actions of the heroic characters. Colonel
Travis (Laurence Harvey) suggests that Jim Bowie's (Richard
Widmark) motives for fighting are his possession of two million acres of Texan land, but the spectator is given no grounds
for rejecting Bowie's avowal that he is fighting out of a love
for the country, and above all for the people. The point is
again stressed when the group of Mexicans arrives to aid the
defense of the fort, and are told by Bowie that if they are to
follow him, they may be taken far from their homes and their
own lands. Their leader, himself a large landowner, announces that it does not matter. The function of land, to
hold people to a particular place, and the notion of land as
property, are rejected as bases for political motivation.

The only basis the film proposes for the actions of
its central characters is an idealism based on an exclusive
and direct relationship between the individual and the political
system he is defending. The indissoluble bond between personal and political freedom is established by the slave Jeth-
ro's decision, on being given his freedom by Bowie, to stay
and fight with him. The ideals are the same, whether they
apply to individuals or nations, since their interests are presented as identical. The paradoxes of leaving your land to
fight for it and dying for freedom are not up for discussion.
Nor is the notion of imperialism. The mythic potential of
the Alamo as an event in American history is personalized
by the individual stories told in the film. In the process
the ideology has any mediating levels between the individual
and his allegiance to a political ideal removed from it.
Consequently, the ideology inherent in the heroic situation
is raised to a mythic level again.

This process is centered around Davy Crockett, the
Wayne character. The Wayne persona is the archetypal embodiment of the simple, homogeneous hero, whose self-doubt
is at most limited to tactical decisions, and who is, throughout the film, convinced of his own moral rectitude. This
certainty of outlook forms the basis of his actions, the implied statement being that where right is guaranteed, might

is justifiable.* Wayne, particularly the physically spread
Wayne of the late 1950s and 1960s, is a monolith, both
physically and ethically, acting as the central core of the
films in which he is the undisputed star. Our moral endorsement of Wayne in The Alamo is complete. Contrasted
with Travis, whose arrogant nobility distances him from the
spectator, and who is consequently tainted with a lack of
personal judgment and an exaggerated sense of pride, Crockett's backwoods homespun humor attaches him to the tradition
of populist heroes which is rooted in "the reality of the understanding of the people," and whose archetype is Abraham
Lincoln.** Contrasted with the impetuosity of Bowie (whose
tactics are characterized as "cut, slash and run"), it is his
qualities of level-headed leadership that allow us to see him
as the justified prossessor of the center of our attention.
We know him as a leader not just because of his physical
ability to beat all the others in a fistfight. Nor is it because he is an ex-Congressman and clearly not the simple-
ton he might be taken for. It is because he is, in the tradition of Warshow's Western hero, [36] a whole man, undivided
against himself, secured in his claim to moral authority by
the certainty that his actions and speeches are mutually endorsing, and that both are confirmed by the ending of the
film.

A set of mutually guaranteeing relationships exists by
which the predictability of the ending, Wayne's dominant position in the narrative, and his certainty of himself ensure the
validity of each other for the audience. Each is both cause
and effect, and their consequence is to deny the audience the
opportunity of an ambiguous ideological position with the film,
or any viewpoint which does not endorse the attitudes Wayne
embodies. The film takes the course that Wayne, as Crock-

---

*Both Ford and Hawks have exploited this characteristic of
Wayne's persona to question the nature of audience loyalty,
variously in Red River, El Dorado and The Man Who Shot
Liberty Valance. Typically, Hawks' questioning principally
dwells on the nature of specific actions in relation to his
moral certainty, while Ford displays greater concern with
the consequences of such actions.

**Along with Houston and Douglas MacArthur, Lincoln was
the American Wayne most admired. Unlike the other two,
his desire to portray Lincoln never advanced to as concrete
a stage as a script.

ett, has predicted for us, and by doing so not only upholds Wayne's perspective, but leaves the spectator with no option but to accept the interpretation of events that perspective provides. For Wayne not only determines what happens, but also how much it matters, and the importance of any singular event is revealed to the audience both by Wayne's attitude towards it, and by the style of its presentation. As a result, the political argument of the film becomes self-enclosed and self-validating, irrefutable on its own terms.

Two central components of this system of mutually validating structures are the presentation of violence, and the depiction of sentiment. Consistently Wayne displays a dualistic attitude to the nature of violence. One aspect of his character is expressed by his predilection for horseplay, the harmless bar-room brawl that establishes a basic physical strength and courage and a casual approach to violence and danger. They are unquestioningly assumed to be a part of everyday existence, and consequently to be regarded with the same relaxed approach and lack of self-questioning that might be brought to eating. There is an underlying sense of humor behind the bar-room brawl, which comes most obviously to the surface in Wayne's films for Ford, notably The Quiet Man and Donovan's Reef, and most frequently in the characterization of Victor McLaglen as Wayne's subordinate, stooge, and comic relief. *

The function of such scenes, particularly in their location early on in The Alamo, is to establish Wayne's socially and psychologically adjusted attitude to violence. It is most precisely reflected in his repeated gesture, when picking himself up off the floor in a fistfight, of wiping the back of his hand across his mouth while smiling. The fistfight is a form of physical conversation, implying no animosity in its gestures, a means of harmless fun. We are informed by it of Wayne's willingness to engage in, and enjoyment of, violent activity. We are also given another demonstration of the mutually validating relationship between the attitude he adopts towards a scene and the results of that scene. Since a bar-room brawl is not to be taken seriously, it cannot have serious consequences. When Wayne adopts a different attitude to an impending violent encounter, we recognize that we are about to witness

---

*See particularly McLaglen's role in She Wore a Yellow Ribbon.

something different in kind, a scene of violence in which
people can get hurt or killed. *

    The moral authoritarianism with which Wayne is in-
vested by the mutually validating narrative structures obliges
him to adopt this dualistic attitude to violence. Since he
may dictate the significance of a violent encounter by his
attitude towards it, rather than its significance being the result of its physical outcome, his cinema is--like Ford's and
unlike Hawks'--not of the body, for his is concerned with the
implication of an action, not the action itself. The point is
brought home by Wayne's final action in The Alamo, when he
blows up the arsenal and himself in the process. Such an
action requires a rejection of the idea that the integrity of
an individual rests on the integrity of his physical presence,
the individual's equivalent of the film's rejection of property
relations as a basis for political action. For a director with
a more materialistic outlook, that action would be a demonstration of insanity--exactly the connotation Steve McQueen
brings to it in Siegel's Hell Is for Heroes. But for Wayne,
integrity must rest elsewhere, in the ideas, beliefs and
principles by which a man lives and by which he must die
if necessary. That notion of integrity combines with the
moral authority granted him by the narrative structure, and
permits him to subsume the paradox of dying for freedom
within an ideological viewpoint which allows of the individual's complete ingegration with the ideal for which he dies.
Its singularity also goes far towards explaining Wayne's
narrow-minded political assumptions about the implications
of approval or criticism of his films.

    As The Alamo progresses, it becomes clear that
Crockett has brought his men there neither by accident nor
as adventurers in search of violent fun, but to defend their
ideals. The audience, and the men themselves, become
aware of this slowly, as the action of the film takes its
course. The seriousness of the consequences for them personally, and the related sharp distinction drawn between the

---

*Hence the frequent comments about the unsatisfactory ending
of Red River, in which Wayne's attitude to a violent encounter
is not endorsed by its outcome. The scene does not violate
the dramatic requirements of the narrative so much as the
moral authority that the audience has come to expect from
Wayne's power to predict and provide the dramatic significance of any given scene.

two kinds of violent activity, is emphasized by the amount of
screen time given over to their considering their fate and
their motivation.   Through scenes of sentiment the serious
purpose of action is expressed.   Captain Dickinson's wife
and children, the survivors of the battle, and Smitty (Frankie
Avalon), the young boy sent out with a message for Houston
who returns to witness the end of the battle, not only represent the continuing future at the end of The Alamo; they also
represent the purpose of the sacrifice we have just seen
made.   The freedom that has been fought for is demonstrated
by their ability to walk away alive: they embody victory in
defeat.   The men at the Alamo have died to preserve the two
elements necessary for the continued existence of a society
that wishes to preserve itself: fertility (women) and optimism (children).   In The Green Berets this role of embodying
the ideal is given to the orphan Vietnamese boy, and made
quite explicit.   He is told, by Wayne, that he is "what it's
all about. "   In The Alamo this role falls to Lisa Dickinson
(Joan O'Brien), who, through the device of sentiment, is
appropriately honored by Santa Anna as she rides past him. *

     Sentiment becomes the means of expressing the future,
or the past, within the terms of a form dealing with the
present.   The use of sentiment provides us with an emotional perspective from which to view the film, but since that
perspective is governed entirely from within the film, it acts
merely as another structural device--like Wayne's central narrative location--for ensuring our endorsement of the film's
ideological content.   Sentiment is the tool by which abstract
political ideas can be personified in immediate, emotional
terms, making them available to the constraints of the form
within which Wayne is working.   The result is to disen-
franchise political discussion of the middle ground between
the two extreme points, the individual and the ideals of his
society, that it unites.   Sentimentality is crucial not only to
the cinema of populism, but also to its ideology; its beliefs
are fundamental in part because such beliefs are the ones
most readily expressed by the sentiment of situations.

---

*In connection with the interrelation between Wayne's persona
and his personality, it is worth noting that the Dickinsons'
daughter, for whom Crockett's men provide a birthday party
that is interrupted by the Mexican attack, was played by
Wayne's four-year-old daughter, Aissa.   The benevolent and
paternalist nature of Wayne's authoritarianism has been repeatedly reasserted by his later roles: True Grit, The Cow-
boys.   Siegel captures the point precisely in The Shootist.

REFERENCES

1. "That's Entertainment," by Howard Dietz and Arthur Schwartz, in The Bandwagon (MGM, 1952).

2. See Garth Jowett, Film The Democratic Art, pp. 260-264 for a summary.

3. Business Week, November 9, 1935. Quoted in Colin Shindler, Hollywood during the Great Depression, pp. 91-92.

4. "John Ford's Young Mr. Lincoln," a Collective Text by the Editors of Cahiers du Cinéma. Translated and printed in Screen, Vol. 13, No. 3, p. 11.

5. Bob Thomas, King Cohn (London, 1967), p. 60.

6. Mel Gussow, Zanuck; Don't Say Yes Until I've Finished Talking, p. 115.

7. Philip French, The Movie Moguls, p. 142.

8. Variety, July 31, 1935. Quoted in Shindler, p. 130.

9. Thomas Jefferson, "The Declaration of Independence," in Daniel J. Boorstin, ed., An American Primer (Chicago, 1968), p. 86.

10. Thomas Jefferson, letter to John Jay, August 25, 1785, in Merrill D. Peterson, ed., The Portable Thomas Jefferson (New York, 1975), p. 384.

11. Thomas Jefferson, letter to James Madison, Paris, December 20, 1787, in The Portable Thomas Jefferson, p. 432.

12. See citations in Raymond Durgnat, "King Vidor," in Film Comment, Vol. 9, No. 4, pp. 31-36.

13. King Vidor, A Tree Is a Tree (New York, 1953), pp. 221-227.

14. Jim Kitses, Horizons West (London, 1969), p. 11.

15. Shindler, p. 123n.

16. Donald MacRae, "Populism as an Ideology," in Ghita Ionescu and Ernest Gellner, eds., Populism, Its National Characteristics (London, 1969), p. 157.

17. MacRae in Ionescu and Gellner, p. 160.

18. MacRae in Ionescu and Gellner, p. 162.

19. Peter Wiles, "A Syndrome, Not a Doctrine: Some Elementary Theses on Populism," in Ionescu and Gellner, p. 168.

20. Thomas Jefferson, Notes on the State of Virginia, in The Portable Thomas Jefferson, p. 125.

21. The classic case in point is John Locke's Two Treatises on Government. See in particular the Introduction by Peter Laslett to the Cambridge University Press edition (1960).

22. MacRae in Ionescu and Gellner, p. 162.

23. Lewis Jacobs, "Capra at Work," in Theatre Arts 25 (January 1941). Reprinted in Richard Glatzer and John Raeburn, eds., Frank Capra: The Man and His Films (Ann Arbor, Michigan, 1975), p. 43.

24. Richard Hofstadter, The Paranoid Style in American Politics (London, 1968).

25. Production Code, "Reasons Supporting the General Principles, 1. b."

26. Otis Ferguson, "Democracy at the Box Office" (Review of Meet John Doe), The New Republic 104, March 24, 1941. Reprinted in Glatzer and Raeburn, p. 106.

27. Quoted in French, The Movie Moguls, p. 141.

28. Raymond Moley, The Hays Office, p. 7.

29. Tom Stempel, Screenwriter: The Life and Times of Nunnally Johnson, p. 97.

30. Exhibitors Herald World, July 27, 1929. Quoted in Shindler, pp. 273-274.

31. Robert Sklar, "The Imagination of Stability: The Depression Films of Frank Capra," in Glatzer and Raeburn, p. 128.

32. Quoted in John Raeburn, "American Madness and American Values," in Glatzer and Raeburn, p. 65.

33. "Dear Mr. Gable (You Made Me Love You)," adaptation by Roger Edens of "You Made Me Love You," by James V. Monaco and Joseph McCarthy, in Broadway Melody of 1938 (MGM, 1937).

34. Quoted in Maurice Zolotow, John Wayne: Shooting Star (London, 1974), p. 330.

35. Quoted in Zolotow, p. 316.

36. Robert Warshow, "The Westerner," in The Immediate Experience (New York, 1974).

CHAPTER 7

UNITED WE STAND:
THE CINEMA OF THE CONSENSUS

The social condition and the
institutions of democracy im-
part, moreover, certain peculiar tendencies to all the imitative arts, which is easy to
point out. They frequently
withdraw them from the delineation of the soul, to fix
them exclusively on that of the
body; and they substitute the
representation of motion and
sensation for that of sentiment
and thought: in a word they
put the Real in place of the
Ideal. "--Alexis de Tocqueville[1]

'Tain't what you do, it's the
        way that cha do it,
'Tain't what you do, it's the
        way that cha do it,
'Tain't what you do, it's the
        way that cha do it,
That's what get results.
        Sy Oliver and James
                'Trummy' Young[2]

THE INVISIBLE POLITICS OF STYLE

An ideology which refuses to distinguish between the
good of the individual and that of society discovers democratic compromise not in the resolution of conflict between
opposing interest groups, but in the achievement of a con-

182

sensus among the body of enlightened individuals. Populist
ideology inclines towards status concerns against interest
politics as consensus transcends compromise. While the
progression to a consensus over issues through compromise
is a common democratic activity, once again the individualist orientation of a populist democratic sentiment militates
against so simple a development. Rather, the consensus
appears at a mediated level, that of the terms in which
issue-related political debate can take place. The consensus forms not at the level of opinion over issues, but at the
level of the manner in which that opinion is presented--the
style and rhetoric of political discussion. This mediated
consensus over political style affects more than the manner
of political discourse. By determining the ways in which
politics may be discussed, it also determines the areas of
political discussion, enabling some subjects to fall within its
parameters of tolerable disagreement, and restricting others
from doing so. Welfare provision was a permissible political topic in the 1930s, the institution of the family was not.
A consensus over political style thus allows the maintenance
of the dual illusion on which American democracy is based.
The fiction of the unity of individual and social interest is
upheld by the uniformity of political style, but that uniformity also permits the man of goodwill to disagree over specific issues.

A consensus of style is central to the American political tradition, since only in such circumstances can these
two primary fictions of American democracy be maintained.
Everyone has pledged allegiance to a rhetoric of unity that
at the same time grants the individual the right of dissent
and precludes him or her from institutionalizing that right
of dissent in a political program. Populism practices "a
moderate anarchy"[3] perfectly embodied in the Vanderhof
household of You Can't Take It with You. Asserting the absolute freedom of the individual, the film is nevertheless
committed to a purely apolitical protest. Grandpa demoral-
izes the tax inspector by denying the need for an income
tax, but later announces, "I was only having fun with him,
I don't owe the government a cent." The individual's assertion of his individualism commits him to political ineffectuality, since it restricts the ready emergence of easily
identifiable group loyalties and deprives the individual of the
ideological means of locating himself in relation to others. *

---

*In the American cinema, the particular preoccupa-   (cont.)

The result is to decrease the importance placed on those
areas of disagreement, and emphasize those of already established consensual opinion--in other words to exacerbate
the problem by formalizing and institutionalizing it. Emphasis drifts away from a politics of issues toward a politics of
style. Such a tendency has been recurrent in American political history, and this argument would go far to explain
the severity of the collapse of political stability when it has
occurred. Consideration of divisive issues within the institutions of political debate has been postponed until they
reached extreme points of crisis, when the consensus of
style was destroyed, overwhelmed by the force of events
which carried the arguments outside the normal political
arena, and generally into violent forms of expression.

Since the mechanisms of consensus emphasize status
over interest politics, the maintenance of consensus becomes
most difficult when a change in the balance of economic power is not matched by a change in the balance of political
power. The consensus is assailed--and may or may not
collapse--either by groups who fear for their political or
social position as a result of their economic decline, or by
groups whose economic circumstances are improving without
a concomitant improvement in their political power or their
social prestige. The largest and most conspicuous example
of this phenomenon in American history is the Civil War,
but the rise of Populism and the radical protest of the 1960s
can be seen as having origins conforming to a similar pattern. Since the consensus model is particularly incapable of
dealing with economic issues (because its tenets were framed
before social analysis in economic terms became the norm),
it is predictable that the crises of the consensus should most
frequently occur during alterations in the economic balance
of society: the rise of the Northern industrial states, the
agricultural depressions of the 1880s-1890s, the economic
elevation of the young and the minorities. But once the consensus is upset by the appearance of these economic factors
for which it has not catered, and which assail particularly
the maintenance of the myth of men of goodwill, the main

---

tion of the film noir genre. Bogart's alienated and paranoid
hero in Dark Passage (Warner Brothers, 1947; prod. Jerry
Wald, dir. Delmer Daves) is an archetypal example of such
a characterization, but the presentation of urban settings in
crime films has always tended to stress the element of personal dislocation from the social environment.

force of the assailing movement is commonly directed into
an issue which is only peripherally related to its principal
grievance: slavery, free silver, the Vietnam war.* This
process makes possible the survival of the consensus,**
because it permits the ratification of new patterns of production and consumption, and thus allows the absorption of
the dissenters.

If American history may be seen as a series of attempts to establish a consensus in which the divergent forces
of interest politics can be veiled over by agreement as to
political style, then the re-emergence of an adapted consensus of political style constitutes the re-establishment of political stability. Agreement over the areas and manner of
political discourse places restrictions on the extent to which
disagreement over specific issues is possible within the system operating under the consensus. Such disagreements may
no longer be extreme enough to threaten the disclosure of the
fictions upon which the consensus is based. Invisibility is
essential. The consensus over style must pass unnoticed,
so that neither it, nor the fictions which it sustains, are
available for discussion. In the practical operation of the
consensus, its function is to divert political analysis away
from a consideration of its own workings and towards a consideration of specific issues which do not present a threat to
its continuation. To ensure its own survival, the consensus
prefers to deal only in the small change of political controversy. However, it must also amplify the importance of
those issue-related debates it can accommodate, to route
attention away from its concealed influence. When stable,

---

*Maurice Zolotow comments with a somewhat surprised air
on the level of acceptance that John Wayne's films--with the
exception of The Green Berets--found among young radical
groups of the 1960s. What Wayne and his young audience had
in common was not, clearly, their positions on issues, but
the style of their approach to those issues. Since Wayne's
structural position in The Green Berets--and the political assumptions underlying that position--are actually no different
from those in, say, The War Wagon (1967; dir. Burt Kennedy), True Grit (1969; dir. Henry Hathaway) or The Alamo,
this unexpected example indicates the potential inaccuracies
liable to result from a simple process of labeling by content.

**With the exception of the Civil War, which is the only oc-
casion on which the consensus has collapsed completely.

it operates as a closed system, determinist in so far as it can restrict the areas of controversy it permits. Moreover, by reinforcing its basic assumptions through the mechanisms by which it functions, it can separate off those areas of controversy from each other, and more importantly, detach them from itself. The fact of its determinism is concealed by the flexibility it allows itself over the range of political questions it has deemed permissible.

What, above all, it determines is the relationship individual citizens perceive themselves to have with political institutions. Issues of controversy are, indeed, vital to the persistence of that perceived relationship, since they make it seem active and mutable. Furthermore, the prospect of their successful resolution reinforces the primary fictions of consensus politics. During the New Deal, Roosevelt's use of committees of experts with widely divergent and even opposing views on the issues for which they were supposed to determine policy served less as a useful means of discovering solutions to problems than as a device to present the appearance of unified activity in search of those solutions. It was a precise and shrewd application of the myth of men of goodwill, and its failure to be of practical assistance was less important than its partial success in rehabilitating the myth for the government.

The effect of a closed and individualized narrative structure in films of as varied overt political persuasion as The Green Berets and Guess Who's Coming to Dinner? is similar. The affirmation of the myth of men of goodwill, and the embodiment of the possibility of a solution in the individualist terms of that myth by the specific resolution of the film's narrative, permit the films to avoid an engagement with the issues which their plot situations raise. The film's theme is stated rhetorically in generalized terms, by characters who can resolve its individual formulation in the story. By a concealed but false logic, it moves from the statement of a general issue to a particular manifestation of it, and from the resolution of that manifestation to the proposal of a general solution--a proposal that is never more than: if only we were all as much men of goodwill as Spencer Tracy, Sidney Poitier or John Wayne, the problem would disappear. The issue such films purport to discuss is, by the mechanisms of its discussion, as entirely detachable from the film's narrative as is the message of goodwill with which we are meant to leave the cinema. In relation to the notion of consensus politics, the consistency of both films' stylistic approach to their subject matter is of greater import than the superficial differences in their overt political stances.

PERFECT REPRODUCTION

The primary fiction that the Hollywood cinema of the consensus--to whose aesthetic strategies The Green Berets and Guess Who's Coming to Dinner? both adhere--requires its audience to accept is that they should think of the story a film is telling them as if it were a real event. That is not to say that they are intended to regard, say, the story of The Wizard of Oz as having actually taken place in front of a fortuitously-placed camera. But they are expected to operate a particular suspension of disbelief in which the mimesis of the photographic image reinforces the circumstantial and psychological "realism" of the events those images contain, so that they can presume upon those normative rules of spatial perception, human behavior, and causality which govern their conduct in the world outside the cinema. Thus they may respond to the characters as if they were real people, and regard the story that is told through the characters as if it were unfolding before them without the mediation of cameras or narrative devices. Obviously, this illusion of actuality is a carefully fabricated construct, in which the narrative is a closed, predetermined structure unavailable to the audience's direct manipulation. But there has arisen a consensus between filmmakers and audience which agrees to sidestep those tortuous questions of what constitutes a "realist aesthetic," which so delight and befuddle film theoreticians and critics, by the presumption: as if.

In attempting to come to terms with the nature of cinematic realism, we must first confront, and deconstruct, part of the critical legacy of André Bazin, the Myth of Total Cinema. Describing the goals of Nièpce, Muybridge, and the other precursors of cinema, he argues,

> In their imaginations they saw the cinema as a
> total and complete representation of reality; they
> saw in a trice the reconstruction of a perfect il
> lusion of the outside world in sound, colour, and
> relief.

... The guiding myth, then, inspiring the invention
of the cinema, is the accomplishment of that which
dominated in a more or less vague fashion all the
techniques of the mechanical reproduction of reality
in the nineteenth century, from photography to the
phonograph, namely an integral realism, a recreation of the world in its own image, an image un-
burdened by the freedom of interpretation of the
artist or the irreversibility of time. [4]

The aim accords with the ideology of nineteenth-century
science: the pursuit of objective descriptions of phenomena.
Bazin does not, however, comment on the content of this objective realism, or describe what reality it sought to reproduce. The reality of microbes photographed through a micro-
scope is of a different kind to the reality reproduced in a
Hollywood studio, but Bazin was less than precise in dis-
tinguishing between the technical goal of accurate visual (and
aural) recording, and the aesthetic pursuit of a convincing
illusion. The influence of the myth of total cinema has sustained this confusion between mimesis and narrative in much
of the "Realist debate."

The cinema's central mechanisms, the camera and the
sound recorder, are products of nineteenth-century scientific
inquiry, and demonstrate its quest for objective recording.
As a result, they reproduce the perceptual conventions dominant in the societies in which they were invented: monocular
perspective, for example. Sound technicians in the early
1930s were obliged to evolve such a perceptual convention
in the development of sound perspective. Limited by the
technology of omni-directional microphones, early sound
films tended to present dialogue at a uniform volume regardless of the closeness of the shot. During the early
1930s, a compromise between intelligibility and distance
perception was developed. [5] Technical improvements created an illusion of depth, adjusted to the scale of the image,
without losing sound clarity. The evolution of sound perspective is a paradigmatic example of Hollywood's technical
concerns. While the rhetoric of such research consistently
described its aim as greater "realism," it used the term in
an imprecise and indefinite sense. By one criterion, upheld
since Bazin as fundamental to cinematic realism, the change
from orthochromatic to panchromatic stock was a move away
from a realist aesthetic, since the new emulsion was less
sensitive to light and so restricted the depth of field in the
image. By another criterion, the sensitivity of panchromatic

film to the whole color spectrum produced a more accurate
reproduction of reality, with a greater sensitivity to tonal
variation. In the films of the 1930s the "realism" achieved
by the addition of sound was in some sense offset by the
further reduction in depth of field necessitated by the use of
silent incandescent lights in place of the brighter but noisy
carbon arc lamps used for silent filming. 6 If the motivation
behind technological improvements in Hollywood is to be
labeled as an impulse towards a greater "realism," that
term cannot be ascribed a fixed meaning in terms of a particular constitution of the image. Most certainly, "realism"
cannot be equated, as Bazin sought to, with an increased
depth of field.

On the other hand, technical development was not an
independent objective unrelated to the broader aesthetic
strategies that Hollywood practiced. The myth of total
cinema as a driving force behind technological innovation is
confounded by Hollywood's delayed and reluctant acceptance
of the possibilities offered by color and 3-D. The technical
processes the studios did research (back projection systems,
for example) and the improvements, in areas such as film
stock, which they readily accepted, were geared towards the
more efficient manufacture of a seamless illusion. The
more sensitive Kodak Plus-X stock introduced in 1938 resulted in a reduction in set lighting levels, and hence production costs, rather than an increase in depth of field. 7
The development of effective large-screen back-projection
systems in 1932 greatly increased the amount of material
that could be shot in the controlled conditions of a studio
sound stage rather than on location. 8 Economy, clearly,
was one motivation for technical change. Another, at least
as pervasive and certainly more evident, was the desire
implicit in the ideology of entertainment to conceal the artifice of production. Sound technicians rapidly adopted the
practice of "Blooping"--painting a diamond-shaped area over
a sound splice to transform an abrupt and potentially disruptive sound cut into a smoother and less noticeable rapid
fade. 9 The mechanics of the sound track's construction,
and the heterogeneity of its sources, were concealed behind
the apparent naturalness of its continuity.

In this, of course, the sound track was following the
practice of Hollywood continuity cutting. The evolution of
continuity editing codes--the 180° rule, eyeline matching,
angle-reverse angle cutting, and so on--is again conventionally explained as subservient to some vague aesthetic of

"realism," but it can more satisfactorily be accounted for in terms of Hollywood's preference for narrative and its pursuit of as invisible a technical style as possible. Continuity cutting is above all an efficient way of ordering images into an immediately comprehensible narrative. The 180° rule, for example, ensures that characters maintain consistent spatial relationships within a scene, and allows the spectator to assume the relative position of figures not included in any particular shot. He or she can therefore concentrate more readily on the story being revealed, since the mechanics of its narration can be taken for granted. "Realism," in any sense that implies the reproduction of reality, is a less obvious objective for such a system than effortlessness and ease of comprehension. The elimination of work for the spectator is encouraged by a definition of entertainment and leisure as being non-work activities. The invisibility of the work of production is determined both by the privileging of narrative which directs the spectator's attention away from the mechanics of a film's construction and toward its primary product, the story, and by the logic which dictates that for an audience to be effortlessly entertained, its entertainment must itself appear effortless. Continuity cutting facilitates the audience's willing suspension of disbelief, and disguises the fact of the closed, predetermined narrative, by molding the series of discontinuous events in time and space from which the film is constructed, into a perceptually continuous whole. Through its various codes, editing makes the cut as unnoticeable--as "invisible"--as possible, by cutting, in Bazin's phrase, "according to the material or dramatic logic of the scene."[10]

Such procedures assume the existence of an unstated agreement between film and audience about the nature of the cinematic experience as being primarily to do with the creation and consumption of palatable dramatic narratives whose formal structures were not the object of the audience's attention. The invisibility of the cinematic apparatus, from sound editing to the projectors' reel changes, was part of "the magic of the movies." But the manufacture of a seamless narrative was not bound up with the reproduction of external reality. Hollywood's cinematic contract left the audience aware of the illusion, and aware of its complicity in the creation of that illusion. What it strove to do, through the invisible mechanics of its "realism," was to make the illusion as benevolent, and as effortlessly available, as possible.

Continuity cutting reached its first phase of full

development in sound cinema in the mid-1930s, along with
the image of the star as the perfected common man. Both
can be seen as responses to the "realistic" imperatives of
the new sound technology which, as Peter Wollen suggests,
had renegotiated the contract between film and audience.
With the introduction of sound,

> the role or place of the spectator changes, ...
> from being a spectator watching the action to being
> in the role of "invisible guest. "11

With this increase in the spectator's complicity in the act of
cinematic narrative, the silent cinema's quest for the exotic
was replaced by Lionel Atwill's goal as the mad sculptor in
Mystery of the Wax Museum (Warner Bros, 1933; dir.
Michael Curtiz)--"perfect reproduction. " The phrase har-
monizes the technical pursuit of more convincing illusions of
actuality with the representation of society offered in narratives of the consensus.   Presenting the personalized drama
as if it were a real event served to link the central charac-
ter--the star--and his audience emotionally, at the same
time that it separated them by the star's perfection. It was
a perfection not only of appearance, but also of physical abilities, wit, and most of all timing, which came from the concealed manipulations of the architects of his narrative. In
precisely the same way that Hollywood cutting was obliged to
effect the invisibility of the expertise that produced it, so the
expertise that went into the processing of a star as the glamorized representative of his audience was also required to be
self-effacing. "Perfect reproduction" channeled audience response towards an unquestioning acceptance of the star's emotional, moral, and ultimately ideological authority by providing spectators with a matrix of references to behavior and
circumstance in the external world which they would validate
through their own experience. The cinema of the consensus
thus became a place like the real world, only better. Perfect illusion spoke to imperfect actuality as product to consumer. Cosmetic disguise limited the spectator's self-
awareness during the film, and stressed his or her direct
relation, as receiver, of the film as an organic entity and
of the message that was the film's story. Indissolubly linked
with this process, perfect reproduction emphasized the unilateral system of communication that resulted from diverting
attention away from technique and concentrating it on plot or
theme.

"WHAT IS REAL?" ... PART ONE: COHERENCE

> "Can I tell you a story, Rick?"
> "Has it got a wow finish?"
> "I don't know the finish."
> Bergman and Bogart in
> Casablanca

The dual sense of "perfect reproduction" describes both the intent and the effect of the industry's operation of technology.   The strictures of the Production Code, the obligations imposed by the duty to entertain, and the idealist nature of Hollywood's adopted ideology meant that it represented the world not as it was, but as it should be.   To describe an aesthetic so committed to illusion, artifice, and idealism as "realist" seems a perversity sanctioned only by tradition.   To call The Wizard of Oz a "realist" film seems bizarre.   The aesthetic strategy employed by the cinema of the consensus was not concerned with the philosophical or perceptual presumptions behind its imitation of life, only with the technical expedients necessary to sustain its illusion.   In its presentation of perspective, for example, it was opportunist and inconsistent.   Set design in the 1930s assumed

> That the Long Shots would be taken with a 40mm lens.   For closer shots a 50mm lens was ... the usual choice, and of course for Close-Ups something like 75mm. [12]

The quite visible variation in apparent object relationships between the foreground and background of shots taken with lenses of such different focal length fell within the tolerance levels of a loosely-defined normative perspective, but hardly suggested that Hollywood cameramen recognized realism as a perceptual system governing their work.

However awkward a term it may be, however, realism cannot be altogether discarded.   Perfect reproduction engineered a style which concealed its mediation of the narrative it presented.   However conventional and codified it may have been, it offered itself as natural because it assumed, as part of the cinematic contract, a fixed relationship between film and audience, and did not seek to question that relationship.   If a text and its consumers share the assumption that a fixed and mutually known set of conventions represent external reality, and neither seeks to challenge the efficacy of those conventions of representation, then we may describe the text as "realist," regardless of what perceptual systems it operates. The conventions of representation that Hollywood's consensual cinema employed provided its audiences with the means by which they could treat what they saw as if it were real, and order their emotional responses accordingly. Hollywood's realism operated at two levels. Perfect reproduction effaced the techniques by which it produced a seamless flow, and concentrated the audience's attention on the contents of that flow, the narrative. The spatial construction of narrative placed the spectator in the film, while the ordering of events attached the spectator emotionally to its characters as benevolent sources of meaning and significance. Despite the opportunism of its techniques, the cinema of the consensus was committed absolutely to the maintenance of continuity as the primary ingredient of its realism. As a result it was firmly attached to the articulation of a coherent narrative structure.

The narrative of Casablanca (1943, Warner Bros.; dir. Michael Curtiz)--which may indisputably be regarded as a "classic Hollywood text" of the consensus--is constructed to support and clarify the story of the film, aiming at a coherence in the revelation of the plot in order to concentrate attention on the story as it is revealed. The audience is attached to the film by the process of the revealing of the story, not by the facts of the story's revelations. One example among many is the introduction of Ingrid Bergman, and the establishment of her previous relationship with Bogart. Up to this point the film has concentrated on establishing its locale, Bogart's cynical isolationism ("I stick my neck out for nobody"), and the apparent major plot device of the theft of the letters of transit and the arrival of Resistance leader Victor Laszlo (Paul Henreid). Henreid and Bergman first appear entering Rick's Cafe in a long medium tracking shot, which takes them past Sam (Dooley Wilson) at the piano. Wilson and Bergman seem to recognize each other, and Wilson looks worried and shakes his head. A signal to the audience's attention has been provided, but it is not immediately pursued. Henreid and Bergman are joined first by Berger (John Qualen), a member of the Resistance, and then by Captain Renault (Claude Rains), in conversations about Henreid's situation. Bergman asks Rains about Wilson --"somewhere I've seen him"--a remark whose significance is signaled by its delivery in extreme close-up. Rains

supplies an enigmatic description of Bogart, and its impact
on Bergman is again shown in close-up when the group is
joined by Major Strasser (Conrad Veidt). However, the subject is not pursued and conversation returns to Henreid's
politics and future. But the disruptive influence of Bogart's
presence is registered by the repetition of close shots of
Bergman, detaching her from the men's conversation. When
Rains and Veidt return to their table, a female guitarist begins a song, during which Bergman and Wilson exchange looks
of recognition, and Wilson repeats his concerned expression.
Once more, the cue is left hanging while Henreid joins Qualen at the bar. Bergman calls Wilson over to her table.
Wilson tries to convince her Bogart has another girl, but she
tells him "you used to be a much better liar, Sam." He replies, "Leave him alone, Miss Ilsa, you're bad luck to him."
In its ordering, her next line encapsulates in microcosm the
mechanism of the narrative:

> Play it once, Sam, for old times' sake ... play it,
> Sam, play, "As Time Goes By."

The audience are inveigled into a process of revelation, without discovering, until the end, what the object of that revelation is. The spectator is cued to anticipate an event, the
content and meaning of which has not been disclosed. Wilson's playing of a song whose significance is never explained
is made important by its presentation over an extreme, mel-
ancholic, close-up of Bergman that lasts for 20 seconds,
much longer than any previous shot. The song brings Bogart
to the table, and the existence of a mutual bond is again established by the intercutting of extreme close-ups of their
faces (the first close-up of Bogart in the film), reinforced
by the sudden introduction of violins on the soundtrack. At
this point, with the nature of their involvement completely
unstated by the same means that it has been declared central
to the narrative, Rains and Henreid appear to once again
change the subject, and the couple spend the rest of the
scene exchanging looks and reminiscences of their last meeting ("The Germans wore grey, you wore blue") which provide
the spectator with no more explicit information.

    The process of revelation is continued, at a broader
level, throughout the narrative. The audience witness Bogart's remembering his time with Bergman in Paris, while
her marriage to Henreid, her intention to leave Henreid for
Bogart, and Bogart's final decision to send her to America
with Henreid are all revealed by similar constructions to

that of her introduction. The plot is presented as a linear causal chain, each event located by a relationship of cause and effect to those which precede and follow it, but it only functions if it is correctly placed in the chain. Bogart's memory of Paris is, obviously, chronologically misplaced-- it happened before all the other events of the film. But it is, more importantly, placed at the point in the plot when its partial vision of events (Bergman's explanations will qualify it later) is most emotionally affective.

The linear causal chain of the plot leads inevitably to a point of resolution, but because the spectator is engaged in the process by which the story is revealed, he or she can ignore the determinist causality of such a structure and the restrictions it places on possible interpretations of an event. There is, inevitably, a tension between the plot's determinist pressure towards a resolution of events, and the "realist" objections to an idealist simplicity in the tidy end-stopping of events at the film's conclusion. This structurally insoluble tension in narrative realism (the force that draws realism towards melodrama) is dissipated by the consensus cinema's mode of construction. Guided through the plot by the revelatory narrative, the audience is encouraged to feel unconcerned about the conflict between determinism and normative, unresolved reality by the coherence of what they see and hear. Their acceptance of the story comes not from what they are told, but from the way it is told to them. They can accommodate the contradictions of realist narrative by seeing the events of the film as amounting to a crisis which determines the course of the lives of the characters in it. The typical film of the consensus ends at the point at which another film might begin: in Casablanca, for example, Bogart's adventures with the Free French in Tangiers, or Bergman and Henreid in America.

What holds for narrative structure also holds for scene construction. Because the coherent narrative locates an individual scene at one point in its causal chain, an element of the scene must be reserved for the elucidation and justification of that process of causal linkage. Each scene in Casablanca advances the plot by confirming the knowledge the audience have derived from previous scenes, and adding further information to it. The process of confirmation is enacted through the consistency with which the scenes are presented, a consistency which can be regarded as a form of psychological and circumstantial realism. Consistency of character motivation projects a believable psychology: when Bogart rejects Bergman on her first night-time visit to the café the audience recognize that his drinking has exposed the sentimentality beneath the cynical exterior. When he meets her in the market the next morning and asks for the explanation he turned down the night before, the audience understand that the cynicism ("after all, I got stuck with a railway ticket, I think I'm entitled to know") is only a defensive veneer. Bogart's psychology, along with that of the other characters, is being gradually revealed to the audience, who have to construct it from the information the film provides. Circumstantial realism, similarly, is provided by the consistency with which the film describes and relates its locations and the creation of the seamless illusion hinges, at a level more basic than psychological characterization, on the two fundamental areas of perception most immediately available to cinematic manipulation: the depiction of time and space.

A cinematic narrative is temporally composed of a set of ellipses; it is a distillation of a series of significant events. The presentation of time within a narrative is more immediately apparent than the presentation of space, since the periods not included in the narrative are evident by their omission. We may, for example, see a man getting into his car and driving off, and then cut to his arriving at his destination. The coherent narrative, however, attempts to disguise the elliptical nature of its temporal construction by subordinating both the actual time of a depicted event and the real time experienced by the spectator in the cinema to the artificial, perceived time presented by the narrative. For this purpose, it uses a number of devices to create a continuity in perception of two narratively linked discontinuous events. The most simple device is a passage of "linking" music, which, by its rhythmic or patterned management of the passage of time, provides a suitable vehicle for the presentation of the narrative's temporal continuum. Appropriately enough, the opening bars of "As Time Goes By" have this function in Casablanca. The same purpose, the subordination of external time to the narrative continuum, may be served by the use of "linking" shots, the content of which is unimportant save for their function of relating two consecutive scenes by an association of ideas. For example, one scene may end with a tilt up off the characters onto blue sky, followed by a cut, perhaps imperceptible, to blue sky, which tilts down to the same characters in a different location, different characters, or whatever. The plane to Lis-

bon serves this purpose on more than one occasion in Casablanca, transferring attention from one group of people looking at it to another, or to the scene of its arrival. The
same effect can be achieved by the use of fades or dissolves,
which have their own connotations as accounts of elapsed
time, or, in the extreme assertion of narrative control over
plot events, by a montage sequence. In each case the linkage device establishes a chain of causality which is stylistically asserted by the film, subordinating other perceptions of
time to that of the narrative. The arbitrariness of all these
devices is contained by their conventionality. The attribution
of a distinctive connotation to each of them (a fade implies a
longer ellipsis than a dissolve, while a wipe suggests spatial
rather than temporal alteration) covers their presence as
techniques by emphasizing their function as meaning. The
coherent narrative cinema requires that the scene-to-scene
linkage should be as unobtrusive as possible, since the main
intention is to persuade the audience to assume the connections of linear causality, in order that they focus their attention on the plot or theme. The technical devices of the
cinema of coherence aim to divert the spectator's attention
away from themselves as mechanisms of the illusion, and to
concentrate it the more on the illusion they create--that is,
to divert the spectator's attention away from the film as object to the subject of the film.

   A similar argument may be advanced in relation to
the depiction of space within the scene. A coherent narrative aims to present space in terms which are immediately
recognizable to its audience. This requirement encourages
the construction of images which do not distort conventional
perspective relations, implying that most images will be recorded by lenses in a relatively narrow range of focal
lengths. Equally, it encourages the development of conventional patterns for the juxtaposition of shots: the pattern of
establishing long shot, medium shot, close up is one example; angle-reverse angle cutting is another. When these
conventions of the image are disrupted, the audience is being
signaled: for example, the close up of Bogart when he first
sees Bergman not only takes the camera closer to him than
it has been before, breaking a convention of distance, but is
also shot with a wider angle lens than is used for other
close ups, and taken from an angle above, rather than level
with, Bogart's eyeline. All this communicates surprise and
discomfort without articulating them explicitly, or markedly
disrupting the image stream. Unless aiming for a particular
extraordinary effect such as shock, the coherent narrative

requires the audience to understand the way the space in a
scene works (e. g. , the area in which a character can move),
in the same way that it aims for an unconscious awareness
of the temporal ellipses in the narrative.   They share the
same purpose of convincing the audience of the film's stylistic benevolence in presenting the most readily comprehensible
depiction of events.   We understand by a simple time ellipsis
that nothing important has happened in it, and this process is
made easier by a stylistic device that is self-effacing and allows us to ignore it.   The normal perception of spatial relationships similarly allows us to take them for granted as
comprehensible.   Thus it is possible for us to divert our
energies towards comprehending the events of the plot, rather
than the manner of their presentation.

"WHAT IS REAL?" ... PART TWO: BENEVOLENCE

> Of all the gin joints in all the towns in all the
> world, she walks into mine. --Bogart in Casablanca

     Because it is a system of conventions, the parameters
of realism change.   The depiction of time and space within
the consensus cinema at any particular historical moment is
governed by codes of presentation which determine what is to
be regarded as normative perception.   The evolution of such
conventions is, in turn, governed by the technological developments in recording equipment and by the filmmakers' assess-
ments of what the audience can unproblematically comprehend.
The introduction of the close-up was once resisted by producers because they were concerned that audiences would not
understand what had happened to the rest of the actor's body.
Off-screen music in early sound films was similarly opposed
on the grounds that spectators would demand to know where
the orchestra was.   The emergence of consensual conventions
has consistently been a process of experimentation, originally
causing a perceptual dislocation (and frequently being exploited
for that effect: Citizen Kane being perhaps the most notorious
example), but being gradually accommodated into a readily-
understood code of practice.   The re-introduction of deep-
focus photography in the early 1940s and the extensive use of
telephoto and zoom lenses in the 1960s confronted audiences
with unfamiliar images that were initially difficult to comprehend.   Repeated exposure, however, acclimatized viewers to

the adjustments of perception the images require them to
make, and subsumed these technical strategies within accepted, consensual conventions.

A similar observation presents itself with regard to
the depiction of time within the consensus narrative. Increasing familiarity with the conventions of cinematic presentation reduced the length of time assumed necessary for
the audience to locate themselves within a scene. Thus the sig-
naling devices of scene change have progressively evolved from
fade to dissolve to direct cut, as the audience have been
deemed gradually more capable of following a quicker presentation of events. This, indeed, applies as much to
speeds of cutting within a scene as it does to inter-scene
changes. Contemporary audiences find films of the 1930s
interminably slow by comparison to more recent pictures.
The gaps between dialogue are longer, the camera position
changes much less frequently and according to a more rigid
pattern, and the story, in consequence, appears to be evolv-
ing more slowly. The story itself may well seem simpler
as a result. What contemporary viewers experience is the
gap between the normative perception they have acquired from
films of their own period, and the conventions of presentation operative at the time of the film's creation. Beneath the
superficial difference in appearance, films of the consensus
are united by the attitude they share toward their audience
through the operation of whatever contemporaneous conventions of spatial and temporal delineation are in existence at
the time of their production.

Similar conventions operate with regard to performance. The acting styles of the consensually coherent narrative cinema concentrate attention on the characters rather
than the performer, and consequently psychological realism
becomes an important factor in convincing the audience of
the validity of the characterization. Although approaches to
performance may vary, from the inherently conservative
"reaction" technique of John Wayne's recreation of his political archetype to the Method school of a psychological understanding of the character seeking to obliterate the actor as
performer, the principal objective of both is to provide an
unselfconscious performance, the creation of a character
whose existence the audience can accept as readily as they
can accept the depiction of his or her spatio-temporal
arena. * For the audience, the plausibility of a characteri-

---

*"The simplest examples of Stanislavsky's ideas are   (cont.)

zation must equal the plausibility with which they regard a
room or other location, in order that they can assume the
psychological basis of the character as a set of limitations
on his possible actions, as they assume the spatial basis of
the room as another set of limitations.   With this assumed
knowledge, they may then concentrate their attention on the
events and themes of the film, which will generally be expressed through the development of emotional relationships
between characters.

What the film will have established through its employment of these conventions of acting manner and of presentation is the emotional relationship the audience should
have with the film's characters, and above all with the star.
Capra has defined the goal:

> You can only involve your audience with people ...
> you give them something to worry about, some
> person they can worry about, and care about, and
> you've got them, you've got them involved ... be-
> cause my main objective is to involve the audience,
> to get them when what they're seeing up there ...
> when they begin to believe it, and they become
> part of it and they become interested in what's go-
> ing on up there on the screen. [14]

The audience must identify the hero as one of Us, and thus
accept his problems vicariously as their own.   The typical
coherent narrative presents a personalized drama, in which
the story is told to us through the central character.   As
instigator or victim of events, he or she is the story's protagonist, the reason we are seeing the story unfold in the
pattern that it does.   To make sense of the story, we must
recognize the characters for what they are supposed to be,
and allocate our sympathies accordingly.   Our entrée into
this process is most commonly provided by the star (hero/
heroine), who acts as our benevolent guide to the story's

---

actors such as Gary Cooper, John Wayne and Spencer Tracy.
They try not to act but to be themselves, to respond or react.   They refuse to say or do anything they feel not to be
consonant with their own characters. " (Lee Strasberg)[13]
Whether or not Strasberg's interpretation of Stanislavsky was
correct is an interesting but peripheral issue; it was Strasberg's Method, not Stanislavsky's, which was the pervasive
influence on screen acting from the 1950s onwards.

emotional value-system, by encouraging us to align our character sympathies and antipathies with his.

The complex mechanics of this alignment may be sufficiently illustrated (though not exhaustively analyzed) by drawing attention to two areas in which a given film plays on prior audience knowledge and expectation. The "star vehicle" operates a double-bind on the audience, by which it ties the spectator to the narrative by making star and character interchangeable. The behavior of the star's character is sufficiently close to the public image of the star himself for the star to become credibly absorbed into the story; a point well enough illustrated by the tendency among critics to use actors' names as often as character names when describing plots. The function of a great deal of Hollywood star publicity was to establish an archetypal persona which would refer interchangeably to the actor and to the parts he played; Margaret Thorpe cites the example of William Powell, whose urbane comedy roles at M. G. M. meshed perfectly with a publicity image that emphasized his sophistication and intimacy with "the world of books. "[15] There was sufficient variety of archetypes to provide each member of the regular audience with a close approximation of his or her perfected self-image, which in turn served as the basis by which he or she could transfer his or her allegiance from star to character. A star whose roles corresponded to his or her public image did not seem to be acting, but merely playing out on the screen a possible variation of his or her real life.

Casablanca provides an example. The audience, lured into the story by the process of its revelation, recognizes archetypes and identifies, in Bogart and Bergman, its guiding protagonists. Both enact themselves: Bogart the crumpled isolationist whose verbal cynicism imperfectly conceals his honorable sentimentality, Bergman the mysterious insecure woman wary of her own passion ("I don't know what's right any longer. You'll have to think for us. "). They are separated by their emotional depth from the other characters, three of whom are named after European cars, and all of whom enact stereotypes which are not their own possession. (One might perhaps argue for the individuality of Sidney Greenstreet and Claude Rains, but they are closer to inflecting a stereotype than establishing their own archetypes.) The initiative of the narrative oscillates between Bergman and Bogart; the other characters do no more than establish its circumstances, and then behave according to

the predictable patterns of their stereotypes. Only Bogart
and Bergman are uncertain, and that uncertainty provides
the narrative momentum, since plot development and outcome are dependent upon the choices they make, to an extent that simply does not apply to the actions of any other
characters. At the same time, the larger ideological significance of the story is tied to their actions. Bogart is
explicitly identified as a representative of American attitudes ("It's December 1941 in Casablanca, what time is it
in New York?... I bet they're asleep in New York. I bet
they're asleep all over America"), and both, but particularly Bogart, sacrifice their personal desire for a greater
cause whose moral force they finally recognize. The viewers, then, attach themselves to them (importantly, to both
of them) to find in their performances an emotional and a
political depth of sentiment not provided by the rest of the
film. They are obliged to believe in Bogart and Bergman
as Richard Blaine and Ilsa Lund if they are to accept the
fiction of Casablanca and the abandonment of American isolationism.

The form of believability provided by the star system
is reinforced by another mechanism, by which the sentimental significance commonly invested in objects in the external
world is dwelt upon in the movies as a means of realizing
their material existence, and hence that of the characters
who handled them. In Casablanca this function is implicitly
supplied by the nostalgic force of Dooley Wilson's music.
In John Cromwell's more explicit sentimental tour de force,
Since You Went Away (1944; prod. David O. Selznick), a
series of sentimental transactions takes place in which in-
animate objects are invested with an emotional value by
their past associations. In the opening scene, Anne Hilton
(Claudette Colbert), returning from seeing her husband leave
for the war, wanders numbly about their empty house, touch-
ing objects we can see to be full of emotional significance
now that they are deprived of their familiar context by her
husband's departure. This principle of substitution, by which
emotional attachments between characters are distilled into
the sentimental significance of objects, is clearest in the
transactions around Bill Smollett's (Robert Walker) watch,
which was originally given to him by the Hiltons' boarder,
his estranged crusty old grandfather Colonel Smollett (Monty
Woolley). Bill gives it to Jane Hilton (Jennifer Jones), his
sweetheart, as a keepsake when he goes off to war. After
his off-screen death in action has belatedly made clear to
the Colonel the depth of his affection for his grandson, Jane

gives him Bill's watch for Christmas.   By this stage, almost the conclusion of the film, audience and characters
have invested so much emotional capital in the watch as
symbol of lost possibilities in the past and in the future
that the final transaction, by which it is returned to its
original owner, requires no dialogue explanation for its
emotional effect.   The watch distills the relationships
among the three characters and serves to signal that emotional matrix by its every appearance.   The cumulative effect is here less important, however, than the symbolic
displacement that is involved for the audience.   We are
engaged in the characters' problems by their distillation
into objects onto which we can project our own emotional
responses.   The mechanism opens the narrative to our
participation, but only along the closed and directed lines
of the plot.   We either cooperate with the mechanism, or
we refuse to be affected.   We cannot select our own moments of significance, because the film signals our expected responses too clearly for us to ignore them.   By
building on a common emotional experience, the sentimentally evocative power of objects, the film ties us to the
characters.   We identify with their patterns of emotional
response; hence, we identify with their emotions.

"WHAT IS REAL?" ... PART THREE: SIGNIFICANCE

> It seems that destiny has taken
> a hand. --Claude Rains in
> Casablanca

     Realism in the cinema should not be seen as a per-
ceptual system, but rather as an idiomatic tendency, a
means of providing an opportunity to dramatize.   Since the
rejection of the Expressionist strategies of The Cabinet of
Dr. Caligari, the perceptual conventions of the cinema have
been assumed as being naturalistic: object relations are
presented as inflexible and normative to our experience outside the cinema.   Science fiction films like The Incredible
Shrinking Man (1957) in fact rely on such perceptual conventions for their effect: there is only a distortion of size, not
of the perspective which governs the audience's understanding
of spatial relationships.   The establishment of a normative
perspective is an important initial objective for any film.

It provides a spatial context, a framework within which the audience can view the narrative events. Perspective is established by the consistency of object relationships which define the space within a shot, and particularly by the movement of objects (including characters) through that space as a means of determining its boundaries. The sequences in Rick's cafe in Casablanca generally begin with a shot of the exterior or the sign, identifying the locale, followed by a general shot of the interior before narrowing the field of view to a particular group of characters. What these "establishing" or master shots establish is less the locale of the scene (which is equally recognizable in closer shots) than the spatial borders within which that scene will be enacted. The purpose of such shots is to define for the audience the limits of the scene's possibilities; characters may enter or leave this space, but for the duration of the scene events of narrative importance will take place only within its parameters, and within those parameters objects will obey the normative conventions of perspective.

Since the narrative provides its own causality, it ascribes significance to any event it presents, and makes itself "maximally meaningful."[16] By locating everything it presents in a causal sequence, it makes everything it depicts important to the provision of a context for understanding what happens. This applies not only to the content of a shot, but also to the shot as an act of presentation in itself. The need for normative spatial relations, as a means of reducing the possibilities of interpretation, becomes apparent. If the audience is to understand a sequence as causal, they must be able to connect the events of that sequence through the similarity of their technical presentation. One shot follows another in a causal and significant chain, but the continuity of that chain must be sustained by a consistency of presentation. The structure of a sequence thus becomes dependent upon its gradual focusing on its most important narrative constituent. The pattern of cutting from the establishing shot, which provides the arena for action and locates the characters, to a medium shot, relating the characters to each other, to close-ups related by their viewpoint (e. g. reversed over-the-shoulder shots) is diagrammatically typical of the conventional construction of a dialogue scene. The spatial relationship between the protagonists must be established in order to provide a context within which the audience can place the action. Not only is it significant that a particular line of dialogue be delivered in close-up, but also that that close-up be located within an arrangement of shots providing a spatial continuum that can be immediately understood.

The regular employment of patterns of sequential shots establishes the pattern as a means of understanding the film's manipulation of space, independent of its original purpose of providing a continuity of perspective while allowing the cut to take place. Through their awareness of the pattern the audience can accept shots which distort normative perspective. It is, indeed, this ability on the part of the audience that finally undermines the validity of realism as a perceptual system. The spectator is not baffled by a wide-angle, telephoto, or even a zoom shot: not baffled, that is, to the point where he or she can no longer comprehend the narrative information presented by the shot or integrate it into the story. This achievement is brought about principally by conventional cutting procedures which make it possible to locate a shot independently of its presentation of space, while nevertheless ensuring that that presentation does not lose its significance. A close-up, for example, is spatially the simplest kind of shot because it involves the greatest degree of spatial isolation. Its impact is commonly intensified by emphasizing that isolation by shooting it in telephoto, which by condensing perspective and reducing depth of field can deny the character so presented any spatial relationship with his or her surroundings.

The mimetic power of the film image obviates the necessity for most of the strategies of a literary realism. The need for film to provide an explanation of events, and thus a demonstration of causality, in spatial terms requires instead the development of codes of camera behavior which are comprehensible to the viewer. Such codes, however, comprise only a skeletal aesthetic--a set of common reference points for communication from film to audience. For an individual film, they do not in themselves amount to an aesthetic of intention or an aesthetic of process. They are rather the means towards an aesthetic end, that of convincing the audience that the story being told is a plausible fiction--is, in that sense, "real." While an appreciation of the mechanisms of spatial articulation in the cinema is essential to an understanding of its objectives, including its political objectives, the presentation of spatial relationships cannot be offered as the central tenet of the consensus aesthetic. That lies rather with the cementing of the relationship between film and audience via the establishment of plausible characters in a plausible setting.

To return to the example of the telephoto close-up, the technique of spatial isolation must be employed towards a psychological end in the creation of the spectator's understanding of the character concerned. That isolation occurs in relation to a specific piece of information we are provided with, for example through dialogue, and amplifies it. The close-ups of Bergman, which are commonest at Casablanca's moments of crisis, present her as an object of the audience's emotional attention, detached from her material surroundings, and often from the group of people she is with. Such close-ups oblige the audience to respond emotionally, since they are offered no alternative object for their attention. The significance of any particular spatial articulation cannot be understood outside of its specific narrative context, even if in itself it may be independently recognizable as part of an aesthetic strategy. But that recognition is only useful to the extent that it can be integrated into an interpretation of the narrative as a whole.

The conventional codes of realism primarily comprise a narrative device which provides the story with an implicit guarantee of causality. Its skeletal aesthetic simply offers an opportunity to dramatize within the confines of a comprehensible framework. The spatial logic of conventional scene construction, such as that outlined above, is to present characters in a space in order to isolate them within it, and then to explore their emotional relationship, partly through the scene's manipulation of space. The establishing shot sets the borders, the medium shot further narrows them down in order to define an area of meaningful interaction, in which the characters dominate the space between them and the space between them and the audience. The close-up eliminates space by focusing on an object presented in non-spatial terms (or at least terms which do not seek to relate it to other objects through the way in which they both fill space). The progression from shot to shot produces an expectation in the audience of a dramatic or psychological progression in the characters' actions or relationships. Although the creation of a normative perspective initially serves the purpose of providing the audience with a recognizable system for comprehending the images it is offered, that purpose is bypassed by the process of focusing on smaller spatial units which seek to locate the spectator's interest not in the character as a figure defining himself by movement through space, but in the character as a reactive psychological object whose response to situations is the chief subject of the audience's concern.

Ford, for example, is little interested in the physical
relations between men and objects, or between men and men,
except as they signify their psychological relationships, their
morals or their relative status. Objects exist as unconsidered
props to the depiction of their state of mind, symbols with a
shared meaning for characters and audience (e.g., the cactus
rose in The Man Who Shot Liberty Valance). Attention is diverted from image to significance, and from action to consequence, a device again clearly established by the narrative
construction of The Man Who Shot Liberty Valance. What
makes Ford's work so distinguished within the traditions of
the consensus is his ability to generate a more intense identification between characters and audience than any other
filmmaker.* This he achieves principally by creating areas
of shared significance, which, while not necessarily being
explicitly stated (the symbolic implications of the cactus rose
are never spelled out), are nevertheless readily apparent.
Ford's characters appear always to have read the script in
advance of their performance, to be aware of their destiny
to the extent that their fates are prefigures in the nuances
of their performances. Ethan's inability to reintegrate himself into the community at the end of The Searchers is determined by his inability to pass through any doorway when
shot from inside looking out. Determined, that is, not only
for the audience reading the shots as psychologically symbolic, but also for Ethan, who approaches each such shot
warily and reluctantly, thereby implying its significance for
the audience because of its significance for him. For Ethan,
and thus for the audience, doorways become moral spatial
signifiers.

These "realist" mechanisms of the coherent narrative
can be seen as no more than a logical choice for the rapid
presentation of a quantity of information which the film requires the audience to assume. They provide the common
ground between filmmaker and spectator, working to this end
in the same way as generic codes, of which the "realist"
idiom is ultimately only an example, albeit a very large and
complex one. As a code, it has two effects on the comprehension of the information it transmits. Firstly, it serves

*This I take to be the answer to Godard's question, "Mystery
and fascination of this American cinema ... how can I hate
John Wayne upholding Goldwater and yet love him tenderly
when he abruptly takes Natalie Wood into his arms in the
last reel of The Searchers?"[17]

to divert the audience's attention away not only from the mechanics of the film's constructions, but more broadly away from the action of the film to the significance attached to that action. This is particularly noticeable in its attitude to violence, where the physical nature of the action, the dynamics of one man striking another, for example, is not the subject presented for consideration. Rather it is the consequence or significance of violence which is considered. In the opening scene of The Train Robbers (1973; dir. Burt Kennedy), John Wayne has gathered a group of gunmen together for a purpose which as yet only he knows. When one of the younger men, Christopher George, demands to know what they're going to do, Wayne turns around and unexpectedly punches Rod Taylor, the veteran who brought George along. Before any can ask the obvious question, Wayne growls at the prostrate Taylor, "I thought I told you to find men who could take orders." The violent action dramatizes Wayne's attitude, which is explained after the event. The explanation provides the action with a meaning it lacks in itself. *

In such areas of physical presentation, in which the coherent narrative displaces significance from the events depicted to the meaning of those events, it necessarily works towards a conclusion, a resolution that takes place not within the film, but for the audience after the event. In a perfect coherent narrative (such as Casablanca) the final scene colors previous events, allowing us to tie up the loose ends of the plot and to understand why all the characters behaved as they did. The neatness of this conclusion is inescapable, because the constructions by which events have been depicted have worked throughout to eliminate possibilities for the audience.

----

*This is in clear contrast to the manner in which Clint Eastwood, for example, punches people. As a hero, Eastwood is never one of Us, but is rather, in McConnell's terms, like Keaton and Cagney in "the state of grace,"[18] separated from close audience identification by his complete mastery of space through movement. When Eastwood punches another character, it is not to make a narrative point; invariably, he punches downwards, not as an act of assertion. Anyone punched by Eastwood is already discredited; the punch serves only to portray the dynamic of their relationship. Since the violent action is not burdened with a meaning external to itself, and is therefore redundant to the plot, it can carry its own significance as a purely physical statement.

The film has, for example, consistently employed the visual device of tracking in on characters for significant reactions or lines of dialogue. Bogart's explanatory resolution ("Inside of us we both know you belong with Victor") is cued by an extreme version of this device, a rapid track in from a long medium shot of him and Bergman to a tight close up of their faces. The momentum of the movement confirms Bogart's decision. The spectator functions in relation to a coherent narrative purely as a recipient of a given meaning, offered a preexistent, received method of approaching the events of a film, a method determined by the manner of their presentation. Because of the style's tendency to concentrate on the emotional significance of those events, the spectator is offered only a pre-existent moral or political interpretation of the film, via a process designed to make him or her as little aware as possible of its determinist effect.

Such a unilateral channel of communication can only be established if the film succeeds in inducing the spectator to acquire or sustain an involvement in the primary product, the story. This engagement with the unfolding plot is clearly an effect of the tightly constructed coherent narrative. But it is predicated on the presumption, established through convention, of a resolution. The spectator's uncertainty about how the story will conclude is bracketed within the certainty that a conclusion will draw together the various strands of the plot, thus validating the plot's construction. The bracketing devices in The Wizard of Oz (1939, M. G. M.; dir. Victor Fleming) present an explicit example of the attitude underlying the consensus view of the political function of the cinema. The film is overtly a populist piece about self-discovery and self-realization, but, crucially, this process of self-realization is only ratified by the presentation of a symbol: the Straw Man gets a diploma for a brain, the Lion a medal for courage, the Tin Man a watch for a heart. And while the presenter of the symbols, the Wizard of Oz himself, is a phony wizard, he is nevertheless the architect of the benevolent synthesis, dispensing a solution. For if his magic is mere mechanics the arguments supporting his non-magical symbolic gifts demonstrate that wizardry is not necessary, since the three characters had in themselves what they wanted him to give them by magic. Dorothy's (Judy Garland) realization of this, that

> If I ever go looking for my heart's desire again, I
> won't go looking any further than my own back yard,

> because if you can't find it there, then you proba-
> bly never lost it in the first place.

allows her to achieve her goal, to get back to Kansas, to
escape from the colored fantasy world of the cinematic
dream to secure monochrome reality. The benevolent resolution links self-realization to an incitement to stasis in the
discovery that "There's no place like home, " and in Dorothy's
expressed intention never to go away again. For both Dorothy and the audience, the film's bracketing scenes function as
a means of locating the film as a dream, and its events as
an intensified experience from which a moral lesson may be
gained, but whose excitements and dangers can be enjoyed
because they are located within a framework which defuses
them and makes them safe by explicitly removing them from
actuality.

WISHING ON A STAR

Whether emotionally (Since You Went Away) or physically (the switchback ride sequence in This Is Cinerama) we
the audience realize the illusion as we abandon ourselves to
it, and in doing so we recognize that, as on a switchback
ride, we do not have to assume responsibility for the speed
and direction of the events passing before us. The viewing
circumstances in the cinema work to promote an acknowledgment that the only image registering on our retinas is that
emanating from the screen and thus engulfing us in the experience that is the story of the film. This is the dream-
like quality of the cinema, where we can abandon ourselves
to the illusion, confident that the makers of the dream are
benevolent, and that wherever they lead us, they will have
brought us safely back home by the time we have to leave
the cinema. Of course, the illusion is never total. We are
always liable to disruption from the sound of someone eating
popcorn behind us, or someone intruding into our corporeal
cinematic space by standing up in front of us or pushing past
us. But the extent to which we are inclined to regard these
events as personal intrusions is indicative of the success of
the cinema in selling its all-inclusive illusion.

The ideal of harmless "escapist" entertainment makes
the cinema a place where our dreams might come true.
Through the mechanisms of identification with character, the

coherent narrative cinema encourages us to accept the filmmakers' dreams as our own. The affirmative moral in the
ending of The Wizard of Oz is that if you wish for something
hard enough, you will find within yourself the capacity to
make that wish come true. The construction of films of the
benevolent consensus is to place the audience in exactly that
position in relation to the film's characters, so that what the
audience wishes for them has happened to them by the end of
the film. But while this is a predetermined relationship, in
which the film can affect the audience but we cannot alter the
course of the film, the film can only remain benevolent if it
conforms to our expectations. The consensus is composed of
a series of mutually reinforcing constructions, each restricting the others from functioning in any way that conflicts with
the process of mutual reinforcement. Thus any film must
seek a consistent tone, whether optimistic or not.

     Love Story (1970; dir. Arthur Hiller) opens with a
slow zoom in on Oliver Barrett (Ryan O'Neal) sitting on a
bench in a snow-covered park, while his voice-over announces, "What can you say about a girl who died?..."
This shot-sequence serves no purpose other than to establish
the end of the story before it begins, in order to determine
the tone with which the audience views the events. We are
bracketed into a bourgeois tragedy, the final shot of the film
being a slow zoom-out reverse of the opening shot, stylistically closing a circle and narratively locating the opening shot
in its place in the progression of the story. The foreknowledge of the ending which this shot gives us governs our approach to the characters. Aware that they are fated, we
wish throughout the film for their temporary happiness. Our
attention is diverted away from the inevitable end towards
the obstacles placed in the way of that temporary happiness,
particularly those provided by Oliver's father (Ray Milland).
Indeed, although we know that Jenny (Ali McGraw) will die,
we direct our sympathy less to her than we do to Oliver; it
is, for example, Oliver's reaction to the news of her illness
which we observe at some length--Jenny's we never see at
all. This is only in part because the film is less concerned
with the fact of death than with its emotional effects on those
who survive. Throughout, Jenny is shown as assured and
capable of coping with the problems with which she is con-
fronted--the poverty they suffer after Oliver's father cuts
them off, for example. Jenny is the one who must die because she is emotionally disposable. She is disposable because her strong and capable character presents the audience
with no points of emotional vulnerability onto which they may
latch their sentiment.

The film concentrates on Oliver not only because he is the narrator, our guide to the story, and because we prefer to concern ourselves with the living rather than the dying. Oliver's emotional weakness places him in a position whereby the audience can assume a dynamic emotional perspective toward him. Because we are uncertain of his ability to cope with the situations in which he finds himself, we are led towards a sentimental concern for him. It is his emotional vulnerability which allows the film to re-introduce the element of uncertainty in posing the question of how he will cope with Jenny's death. It also permits a subsidiary uncertainty in what will happen in his relationship with his father. Love Story exposes the redundancy of the resolution of the closed narrative structure in relation to the film's ongoing narrative construction, in that the foreknowledge of Jenny's death diverts attention away from her as a worthwhile investment for audience sympathy and screen time. But it also shows that the narrative resolution does not require the resolution of all elements of uncertainty in the plot; at the end of the film we are presented with too little evidence to draw any conclusion about Oliver's emotional state or his relationship with his father--the perfect basis, of course, on which to build a sequel.[19] The elements of certainty, closure and resolution are thus separated from those of uncertainty and choice by the relationship the film allows the audience to establish with the characters.

That relationship provides the means for maintaining the suspense of a film like Airport (1967; dir. George Seaton), where the ending is predetermined by the film's attitude towards the technology it is depicting. Consistently, Airport asserts man's capacity to cooperate successfully with machines in adverse conditions, as much at a subconscious level, in for example, Mel Bakersfeld's (Burt Lancaster) use of the telephone, as through the overt comments of Joe Patroni (George Kennedy). In this context, it is inconceivable that the aircraft will actually crash. The ending is further guaranteed by the commercial requirements of the product. Clearly the film is a much safer investment if it can fulfill the audience's expectation of the vicarious cathartic experience that turns out all right in the end. Airport's plot is centered on the suspense of whether or not a Boeing 707 damaged by an explosion will land safely, a question to which the solid endorsement of mechanical technology provides the predetermined answer. But in order to sustain the plot, and hence the suspense, the film is required

to filter the spectator's response to the plot through his
sentimental attachment to the characters. It needs to produce a human drama in order that the mechanical inevitability of the solution be disguised, and it is to this purpose
that the various personal sub-plots of the characters prolif-
erate. Mechanical failure is never permitted. Human unpredictability is injected into the story at key points in order
to set up the situation. Pilot error blocks Runway 29, D.
W. Guerrero's (Van Heflin) mental instability produces the
bomb, and the intervention of an obstreperous passenger results in the failure of the crew's ploy to take the bomb away
from him. The sub-plots of Mel Bakersfeld's disintegrating
marriage and Vernon Demarest's (Dean Martin) discovery of
Gwen Meighton's (Jacqueline Bisset) pregnancy serve to concentrate our emotional attachment on the individual fates of
the characters. By the climax of the film, when the aircraft returns to land at Lincoln airfield, the audience is sufficiently concerned with the characters as individuals that the
sequence can function effectively as suspense merely by allowing the mechanical process of landing the aircraft, presented in shots of the airport control tower interior and of
the pilot's view of the approach, to be intercut with individual
shots of the characters, the whole sustained by music. In
contrast, the shots of the crack in the aircraft fuselage, or
the long shots of the aircraft landing, fail to generate tension because the plot has functioned in such a way that the
suspense comes not from doubt as to whether the aircraft
will disintegrate or crash, but from fear that the characters
may not survive; from, in other words, a diversion of concern away from the purported central issue of the drama,
which is mechanical and structurally predetermined, to a concern with the fates of the individual protagonists of the human
dramas. The drawing together of those dramas in the question of whether or not the aircraft will crash reinstates the
centrality of the issue, and allows it access to the suspense
generated by the subsidiary stories.

MUTUAL GUARANTEES

What united the cinematic consensus of Hollywood was
not a particular consistency of plot or theme, or even of
genre, but rather its attitude to narrative. Central to its
assumptions was a particular appreciation of the relationship
between film and audience, and of the reasons that audiences

attended the cinema. Audiences were there to be entertained,
they were passive consumers of a product benignly designed
for their easy digestion. The Hollywood narrative engages
its audience primarily at an emotional level, the majority of
its technical devices being engineered to encourage that level
of engagement over all possible alternatives--a point most
explicitly made by the function of sentiment as the most frequent communicator of the film's "message" in the mainstream fundamentalist tradition (Capra, Ford, McCarey,
Wayne, Andrew McLaglen, etc.).

It is impossible to establish a universally applicable
identification between the consensus style and an overt political persuasion, and it would also be a grave error. For
the identification which might then be made would be one expressed in terms of a parallel between film content and an
already defined external political position. * What is rather
more important, and useful, to determine are the political
implications of the relationship established by the consensus
style between film and audience. The narrative operates as
a closed unit, endorsing particular characters, attitudes and
actions from within the restricted framework which it alone
defines. It is a one-way street, assuming its own causality
by the sequence in which it presents events, and validating
it by the particular information it chooses to include or omit.
It is the spectator's role as passive and unquestioning receiver of the communication, willing to cooperate in an emotional engagement with characters and plot, that the film presumes upon in adopting a unilateral mode of communication.
By doing so it generates a matrix of mutually guaranteeing
structures which channel the audience's reactions into those

---

*Certainly the style is predisposed in favor of certain broad
ideological assumptions, but it could readily accommodate
any position within the spectrum of bourgeois individualism.
Within the context of American politics, that leaves it capable of any, even opposing, stances on any given political
issue: The Green Berets and Coming Home (1978; dir. Hal
Ashby) are both films of the consensus. In any given historical period, the consensual style will be prone to reflect
and therefore endorse prevailing opinion, since it requires
a common ground between filmmakers and audience for its
mechanisms to function. The industrial pressures of the
short-term financial interest ensured that, in the studio system, that common ground would be the fundamental assumptions of the populist tradition of political belief.

forms of response which it has been designed to produce.
So the determinist structure of Airport's narrative is ignored
under the pressure of the plot's revelation.

It is this matrix of mutually guaranteeing structures
which secures the film-audience relationship, and reduces the
channel of communication to a simple, unilateral one, in
which the spectator is denied any context from which to
question the validity of the film's action, causality, or its
interpretation of the events it depicts. A style that conducts its discourse along such a line imposes limits on the
potential for political expression of any film in that style,
since it presupposes, in relation to any individual film, a
particular political relationship between film and audience.
It implicitly denies the audience the opportunity to question
the film's narrative, as it denies the film itself the opportunity to examine its own mutually guaranteeing, mutually
validating structures. The style of the studio consensus
pandered to the requisite social conservatism of its producers, for it provided no opportunity, for example, for
questioning the structured social relationships of its characters, except in the individualist terms of its narrative
(The Philadelphia Story, It Happened One Night).

By assuming a "realist" perceptual mode, the style
presumes to dictate the terms in which the events it depicts
are perceived, as well as the mode of that perception. The
perceptual politics of a film are embedded not merely in its
plot or its thematic concerns, nor simply in the manner in
which it presents its argument. The politics of perception
are governed by the politics of time and space, and the cut
from medium shot to close-up for a particular emphasis is,
in itself, a political comment on both the film-audience relationship and the action of the film. The comment, of
course, does not reside in the cut as such: each shot comprises such a statement, and each juxtaposition may be taken
to be both a statement in itself and a means of commenting
on the two statements made by the juxtaposed shots. The
consensus style chooses to reject these dialectical possibilities inherent in the nature of cinematic construction. Emphasizing an overall coherence, it refuses to disrupt the
revelation of the plot. As a result, the pattern of statement in any shot, cut, and sequence closely resembles that
in any other, and serves to reinforce, by the tool of stylistic consistency, the benevolent, non-dialectical, synthesis of
plot, style, theme and audience relationship that comprises
the inherently conservative message of the film's attitude to
its narrative.

REFERENCES

1. Alexis de Tocqueville, Democracy in America (New York, 1966), p. 172.

2. Sy Oliver and James "Trummy" Young, "'Taint What You Do (It's the Way That Cha Do It)." 1939, MCA Music.

3. Peter Wiles, in "To Define Populism," in Government and Opposition, Vol. 3, No. 2, p. 158.

4. André Bazin, "The Myth of Total Cinema," in What Is Cinema? Volume I (Berkeley, 1967), pp. 20, 21.

5. Mary Ann Doane, "Ideology and the Practice of Sound Editing and Mixing," in Teresa De Lauretis and Stephen Heath, eds., The Cinematic Apparatus, pp. 53-54.

6. Patrick J. Ogle, "Technological and Aesthetic Influences upon the Development of Deep Focus Cinematography in the United States," in Screen, Vol. 13, No. 1.

7. Barry Salt, "Film Style and Technology in the 1930s," in Film Quarterly, Fall 1976, p. 22.

8. Salt, p. 27.

9. Doane in De Lauretis and Heath, p. 50.

10. André Bazin, "The Evolution of the Language of Cinema," in What Is Cinema? Volume I, p. 24.

11. Peter Wollen, Discussion in De Lauretis and Heath, p. 59.

12. Salt, p. 25.

13. Lee Strasberg, Strasberg at the Actor's Studio, quoted in David Zane Mairowitz, The Radical Soap Opera (Harmondsworth, 1976), p. 105.

14. Frank Capra, American Film, Vol. 4, No. 1, p. 44.

15. Margaret Thorpe, America at the Movies, p. 52.

16. Will Wright, Sixguns and Society (Berkeley and Los Angeles, 1975), p. 193.

17. Jean-Luc Godard, in Tom Milne, ed., Godard on Godard (London, 1972), p. 117.

18. Frank D. McConnell, The Spoken Seen, pp. 79, 87.

19. Oliver's Story, 1978; dir. John Korty.

INTERLUDE

> She looked at me in a peculiar
> way
> and told me something I re-
> member yet,
> That if you don't get what you
> want,
> You'd better hope you want
> what you get
>
> J. Reid: "Now and Then It's
> Gonna Rain."

PERFECT TENSION--RAOUL WALSH

> Chase scenes are very easy to
> shoot. Just keep going, keep
> going. Get up on top of the
> mountain, turn around, bring
> 'em down again. Just hope
> there's nobody on the road.
>
> Raoul Walsh[1]

What restricts the cinema of the consensus is not just that it operates as a closed system. It is the covert nature of its closure, its persistent attempt to beguile the audience into accepting the story as if it were a real event, which requires that its narrative seek to conceal its deter- minism at the same time that it unites event and interpre- tation into one act of presentation for the audience. Against this, one option is provided by genre. Genre is no less a conventional structure than those of the consensus, nor are generically dominated narratives any less determinist in the

218

2
2

relationship they establish between plot and audience. But, because they are publicly conventional, and because they consciously rely for their effectiveness on a body of assumed knowledge shared by filmmaker and audience alike, they operate as an overtly closed and limited form. A cinematic genre exists in the cinema, and does not exist outside it. That distinction can be employed by filmmakers who do not wish to use the conventional devices of nostalgia and sentiment for their usual effects. Raoul Walsh is a case in point.

Walsh's films do not step outside themselves. They are, in one sense, purely commercial products carrying a minimum of ideological resonance. They neither pander to their audience nor attempt to exploit it by offering to disclose their meaningfulness. Instead, they adhere to the implicit contract between film and audience that a generic formula provides. Offering self-contained fantasies for the audience's enjoyment, their existence is limited to their time on the screen by the audience's temporary embracing of the artificial and conventional world of their generic presumptions. Walsh's functional, linear narratives do not ask that we believe in his characters as anything more than moving figures. His stories provide neither role models nor social analysis at the level of plot or character. They are solely generic compilations, which do not seek to be taken seriously outside their own limited contractual goal of entertainment. The search for a consistent theme in Walsh is an activity quite in contradiction both to the circumstances under which he worked and to the way his films are constructed. They will not bear the weight of pretensions to external significance that a thematic analysis imposes.

Walsh is an action director; action binds his films together into rigidly linear narratives. They rely on movement rather than sentiment to sustain them. His frame is always in a state of internal motion, as characters pace aggressively across a room, demanding the evidence they need to get out of this scene and on to the next. Explanations are offered impatiently, as if by an athlete having to pause in his stride while his less fit companion catches up and catches his breath.

> I didn't allow any dull moments to develop in my films. I was always afraid that the audience might get ahead of me and say to themselves: "That guy is going to get killed in a minute." Therefore, I had to go faster than them. [2]

That momentum asserts itself with every movement. In his elemental narratives, which rarely run to more than four major characters, his leading players profess their energy with some of the most forceful body language in the American cinema. Minor characters lump across the screen, too circumscribed by their function to impose their individual personalities as significant to the narrow storyline, and falling back on slight variations of the ever-present generic archetypes Walsh provides as safety net for characters and audience alike.

Even as they occasionally rely on the accepted formulae of sentimental devices, Walsh's films are never nostalgic. They use conventions of presentation as they use generic conventions, for their economy in functionally communicating what the audience needs to know. These codes are shorthand, substituting for story coherence by their speed of transmission, and allowing Walsh to exploit not the audience, but the genre or the device, in order to push forward his simple, unlikely plots with a minimum of explanation. His stories conform to their generic requirements without being rooted in them--thus Objective Burma can be transformed without difficulty into Distant Drums, and High Sierra can conveniently lose its sentimental baggage of a sub-plot in becoming Colorado Territory. His films rarely waste time working against the conventions of the genre in which they are located, though they may occasionally (Pursued) extend them.

The pace of his films forces them into a continuous present tense. Even when he uses flashbacks (seldom), there is little interest in the past as a controlling structure for the motivation of character or plot. Rather they are convenient devices to supply necessary information for the furtherance of the linear narrative, which stays with the audience in the present tense. His plots are sustained by the pressure of their events accelerating into each other, and by the intense seriousness with which their participants accept their comic-strip conventions (Edmond O'Brien grimacing his way through White Heat). They omit motivation. They are psychodramas, in which impulse translates directly into momentum, emerging as the sole generative force of conflict in the narrative. Cerebral mediation progressively diminishes because mental processes are defined as primarily defensive or retrospective, and after the plot introduction there isn't time to hang around waiting while you work out why things are happening. A different principle operates.

Analysis is impelled into performance, and it is through performance--through movement and action themselves, and <u>only</u> through movement and action--that the drama can be interpreted. The dynamics of gesture are all there is to understand.

       <u>White Heat</u> is packed full of cardboard characters, stock situations and dimestore Freud. Its dynamism does not come from its originality or its subtlety or its intellectual depth. It comes from the tension Walsh generates from shot to shot of each of his comic-strip compositions, from the mobility and graphic power of his images, and from the vigor of Cagney's performance--which has less to do with the creation of an individual character than with the precise definition of a particular character trait latently present in the generic archetype from which Cody Jarrett springs. The greatness of Cagney's performance lies in its physicality-- the frenetic grace and energy he puts into the simple actions of crossing a room or firing a gun. It generates a nervous dynamism in the narrative; Cagney's manic instability puts the audience on edge, and keeps them on the edge of their seats.

       <u>White Heat</u> is a film about pressure. There is a constant pressure of action, and a constant pressure of narrative. Both in the plot and in their performances each character is under pressure*--mental or physical pressure to complete a task, to restrain an emotion, to beat time. They all take this pressure out on the machines they are surrounded with--their cars, guns, the gas tank at the end. The pressure builds up until it has to escape, in the scalding white heat of the train steam. The motif of pressure is repeated throughout the film. It is how Jarrett works, by putting pressure on everything and everyone around him, including himself, until something breaks down or explodes. This pressure is carried by the film's images, too--the mechanism by which the audience is placed under constant pressure. Each shot makes its own individual point, and is a discrete, separate unit from the shots around it, exactly in the manner of a comic strip, where the compositions are arranged not for their continuity but for what they can individually tell us about the play of power--the play of pressure --between the characters. <u>White Heat</u> is a series of inde-

---

*Appropriately, Walsh made a film called <u>Under Pressure</u> in 1935.

pendent one-shot units bound together only by the pressure of
the skeletal narrative, which requires that each shot carry
its load of the plot, like a set of child's building blocks, to
form the cumulative effect of the plot's progression.

Genre and the linear narrative are in tension, a tension communicated to the audience through performance and
image structure. Walsh's films are held together by the
ruthless, functional economy of his shooting style, which
acts like a generator pushing the plot forward with every
shot, while each shot is held in place only by its capacity
to further the narrative. The goal is circumscribed: Walsh
provides vicarious thrills and tacitly criticizes any objective
external to the cinema. But his model of psychodrama, the
story living off performance in the present tense, binding a
linear narrative together through pressure, provides the basis for subsequent tacticians of the dissenting genre film to
offer a wider political commentary from within an enclosed
world.

REFERENCES

1. Walsh, Action, Vol. 7, No. 6, p. 20.

2. Walsh, in interview with Oliver Eyquem, Michael Henry
   and Jacques Saada, Paris, June 1972. Translated by
   Paul Willemen, in Phil Hardy, ed. , Raoul Walsh (Edinburgh Film Festival, 1974), p. 43.

PART 4

A ONE-WAY TICKET TO PALOOKAVILLE

It was you, Charley. You and Johnny.
Like the night the two of youse come in
the dressing room and says, "Kid, this
ain't your night--we're going for the price
on Wilson. It ain't my night. I'd of
taken Wilson apart that night! I was
ready--remember the early rounds throwing them combinations. So what happens
--This bum Wilson he gets the title shot
--outdoors in the ball park! and what do
I get--a couple of bucks and a one-way
ticket to Palookaville. It was you,
Charley. You was my brother. You
should have looked out for me. Instead
of making me take them dives for the
short-end money.

Terry Malloy (Marlon Brando) in
On the Waterfront (1954)[1]

CHAPTER 8

A LITTLE UNDERSTANDING: LIBERAL
REALISM AND THE POLITICS OF DISPLACEMENT

> The liberals can understand
> everything but people who don't
> understand them. The liberal,
> the true liberal: "I'm so un-
> derstanding, I can't understand
> anyone not understanding me,
> as understanding as I am."
>
> Lenny Bruce[2]

     The Second World War wrought fundamental changes
in the bases of American political thinking--and ultimately,
practice--requiring a redefinition of the boundaries of the
political arena. America's rise to globalism also elevated
a new social grouping to political power: a liberal professional elite whose personal, social and political objectives
were at variance with those of the fundamentalist consensus,
but who, in their acquisition and exploitation of power,
adopted the mechanisms of consensual politics. Liberalism
may be, at least historically, the highest form of thought
developed within bourgeois capitalist society, but its built-
in limitations prevent it from finding expression as a coherent, programmatic political theory. Rather, it is inherently empiricist and pragmatic, reacting to issues as
they arise, and utterly flexible in the range of issues it
can accommodate. This is its uniqueness as an ideology:
it is at the same time progressive and non-dynamic; central to contemporary political structures without dominating
the formulation of contemporary political concerns. In one
sense, liberalism can be seen as a state of mind, a condition to be diagnosed rather than an ideology to be analyzed.

     It is, of course, possible to trace historically the

rise of American liberalism from its modern origins in the
progressive response to industrialization. That, however,
is not the goal of this chapter, which seeks rather to elucidate a number of significant stylistic and structural mechanisms of the liberal thought-process. Most important of
these is the idea of displacement, the means by which the
tensions produced in the liberal consensus by one issue are
transferred--displaced--onto another issue where they no
longer threaten to reveal the contradictions within the liberal attitude. Consequently, this chapter, like liberalism
itself, is non-developmental and non-historical, although it
necessarily uses historical examples for elucidation. It is
not a theory of liberal conspiracy. Liberalism, like populism, is not systematic enough to be conspiratorial; as a
consensual ideology, it absorbs ideas, it does not generate
them. Not only is it reactive rather than instigating, it is
above all a sentimental form of politics, whose reactions
are rooted in an emotional acquisitiveness, which imagines
and then--through the mechanism of displacement--transforms
the world along the lines of its own self-definition.

A WIDER WORLD

        The First World War seriously undermined the
value of nationalism as a belligerent cause. The United
States, never having accepted the nationalist imperative of
nineteenth-century European states, had led the crusade
against that mentality, deemed to have been the cause of
the Great War. Certainly in America the national interest
had become insufficient justification for conflict by the 1930s.
Isolationism was not an inverse kind of nationalism, it was
a denial of its validity. Nationalism required the acknowledgment of other nation states as at least potentially equal
and potentially threatening. For whatever historical, geographical and ideological reasons, the United States failed to
develop a nationalist politics because it could not define its
own interest in opposition to those of other states. The isolationists merely wished to keep the irrelevant issues of
European politics at the safe distance provided by the Atlan-
tic and Pacific oceans. The political conflict in 1914-1917
was between them and those Wilsonian interventionists who
saw the war as an opportunity to spread American democratic principles to a wider world. The entire debate took
place in terms outside a European frame of reference, as

a conflict between alternative versions of Jeffersonian integration and alternative extrapolations from the Monroe Doctrine.

After Pearl Harbor, however, Americans were
presented with a conflict that better suited the implicit polarization of their political fundamentalism. An unprovoked act
of aggression, perpetrated by a global alliance of demonically
evil powers committed to unlimited belligerent expansion,
shattered the isolationist myth of Fortress America. The
Axis powers were exactly the kind of enemy that the ideology
of the consensus could justify retaliating against with all possible ferocity. The totalitarian enemy was the perfect opponent, to be engaged in a total war which could be ended only
by his unconditional surrender.

This vein of thought justified the total mobilization
of the economy for the war effort, and the needs of war production provided the impetus to find applications for the new
scientific discoveries of the previous thirty years. Science,
the heroic quest of the nineteenth century, was converted into
technology for the cause. The Depression had merely produced advocates for planning, technocracy, and the managed
economy. The war, more than any other event could, made
such measures necessary. Needing enormous capital investment and the long-term planning of a controlled economy,
technology acquired a momentum independent of its original
justification as the means towards an end defined by an external ideology. Like a cancer, it contained its own expan-
sionist imperative which took no account of social purpose.
But to justify its financial demands, it required a political
rationale. Since the maintained relationship between technological research and the military purpose was, in time of
apparent peace, insufficient to uphold the cost or the principle of continual expansion, an alternative solution evolved.
The concept of the totalitarian enemy had promoted the
technological ethic; that notion could also sustain it. Since
such an enemy could be brought readily into existence, and
since that enemy could be embodied not in a nation, but in
the vaguer form of an ideology, the wartime expansion of
technology could continue without the economic and social
inconvenience of a war. If the logic of the post-industrial
consumer society dictates that the ultimate consumer is the
enemy soldier, then the Cold War provided the means by
which production could continue without consumption being
necessary.

An ideology had brought into being a mode of production which had become self-validating, and which in turn had given birth to a rhetoric that would provide it with a rationale. As the United States reluctantly accepted its own global imperative during and after World War II, it also accepted, with a much greater apparent willingness, the technological imperative of a commitment to progress. That acceptance was made easier by the evident material advantages technological development brought, particularly in the post-war consumer economy, to the well-being of individual Americans. In the first two post-war decades, as at the height of any consensus grouping, there appeared to be no distinction of interest between the State's need for a continual sophistication of its defensive weaponry in the cause of national security and ideological integrity, and the benefits of mass-produced consumer durables for the average American family. The Space Program was the most spectacular example of this marriage of individual and social drives: Apollo 11 beat the Russians to the Moon and brought back the non-stick frypan.

In the irrational anti-Communism of post-war America there was a meshing of two contradictory impulses. While the projection of an implacable and ultimately intangible foe was a necessary element in the ideological rise of technology, the implications of technological progress for the economic presumptions of traditional fundamentalism should have brought hostility from its supporters. The idea of the free market was undermined by the planned economy. The integrity of the individual and the Jeffersonian ideal of the self-sufficient, homogeneous hero were incompatible with an allocation of role and function according to acquired skill and a concomitant emphasis on expertise and professionalism.

The conflict, however, was avoided by a displacement of the idiom of debate. Those fundamentalists whose ideology was most threatened by the predominance of a technocratic idea of progress were also those most prone to the adoption of a conspiratorial view of history, and hence most likely to accept the notion of Communism as the implacable enemy of their beliefs. The rabid anti-Communism of the right-wing backwoodsmen, from J. Parnell Thomas to John Wayne, was the frightened response of an imperiled species striking out at the only one of their assailants they could recognize. The widely-held theory that McCarthyite anti-Communism, concentrating as it did on the non-existent internal threat, was in reality a displaced and covert attack on the New Deal and the political establishment it had brought into being, may be questioned only so far as it is a theory advanced by members of that elite which it attacked. Lipset, Hofstadter and the other "Radical Right" theorists no more questioned their own rationality than did the McCarthyites. Each group found the other threatening and attacked them with the tools of their trade: the emotive politics of demagogy and inference, or the aristocratic hauteur of academic rationalism. When, in defence of the fundamentalist cause, McCarthy attacked the new liberal East Coast establishment with the Derringer of anti-Communism, he selected the right target, but the wrong weapon. The specter of anti-Communism was nurtured at the cost of a few sacrificial lambs; in due course the reactionary right was discredited for its irrationality while the reality of the Communist threat was relocated in the growth of Soviet weapons technology.

The post-war consensus was born of a materialist optimism, but bound together by an unnatural paranoia. The convoluted mechanisms of its thought were typical of the tendency towards displacement already noted in the earlier discussion of status politics. Lipset et al. detected the status concerns of McCarthyites but ignored their own. Following the time-honored practice of self-interested political theorists, they defined the parameters of legitimate political activity to include themselves and exclude the less rational populist reaction. Yet at the root of both attitudes was the same socio-economic development: the generation of a new industrial technology and the need to reorder social structures and values to accommodate it. While such a tendency was implicit in the emergent consumer economies of the inter-war period, it was progressing at a much slower pace, potentially making possible a gradual social accommodation of the new economy. The Second World War precipitated the crisis, and the Cold War period provided the socio-political rationalization of a response. That the response, the adoption of a totalitarian conspiracy theory, is not rational does not prevent it being a rationalization.

ALMOST THE END OF IDEOLOGY

The new rationalist establishment of American political thought in the 1950s proclaimed their consensus as "The

End of Ideology. " "Few serious minds believe any longer, "
proclaimed Daniel Bell in his statement of the new orthodoxy,

> that one can set down "blueprints" and through "so-
> cial engineering" bring about a new utopia of social
> harmony. At the same time, the older "counter-
> beliefs" have lost their intellectual force as well.
> Few "classic" liberals insist that the State should
> play no role in the economy, and few serious con-
> servatives, at least in England and on the Conti-
> nent, believe that the Welfare State is "the road to
> serfdom. " In the Western world, therefore, there
> is today a rough consensus among intellectuals on
> political issues: the acceptance of a Welfare State;
> the desirability of decentralized power; a system of
> mixed economy and of political pluralism. In that
> sense, too, the ideological age has ended. [3]

Bell articulated the dominant view: there was no going back
on the achievements in social welfare of the New Deal, nor
on the growth of a federal bureaucracy and Presidential power
created by the Roosevelt administrations. William Henry
Smyth's dream of a rule by technicians was to be mediated
through the compromising mechanisms of the democratic free
market. If Eisenhower's warnings about the "military-
industrial complex" and the "scientific technological elite"[4]
were heeded, the engine of social progress might now advance without dispute, but slowly, so that change might be
accommodated without threat to the political and economic
system. Men of goodwill would see that it was so. Yet
the terms of Bell's definition also served to exclude sections of the American political spectrum: in particular, the
reactionary right which had grouped itself around the cause
of virulent anti-Communism, but which was also attacking
the concept of the State that Bell proposed as consensual.
Bell's articulation of "The End of Ideology" excluded this
group from the beneficent consensus of "serious minds" as
it excluded that half of the world still clinging to the rem-
nants of the exhausted, but unfortunately expanding, Communist ideology.

But the premise of anti-Communism was still not
questioned, and remained a governing doctrine. On its
foundation in 1951, the American Committee for Cultural
Freedom, which numbered Bell among its liberal associates,
accepted the assertion of such intellectual McCarthyites as
Arthur Koestler that the communist issue simply over-rode

the conventional political distinctions between left and right.
Only after the defeat of McCarthy did the liberal establishment overtly attack him and the style of his rhetoric. The
association, however, was already made, and the central
importance to the liberal consensus of the Communist conspiracy was restated over and over again, whether in Leslie Fiedler's arguments that liberals must accept some of
the blame for the crimes of Alger Hiss, 5 or Sidney Hook's
assertion that Communism was a conspiracy by its very
nature. The intellectual acceptance of anti-Communism was
the abstract concomitant of the post-war political consensus
that social welfare had progressed far enough, and that the
options of the Second New Deal were not to be taken up. In
their pessimistic expressions, the liberal establishment be-
rated themselves with failing to recognize the objective evil
of Communism in the 1930s and 1940s, and thus helping "to
weaken the case of Western democracy against Communist
totalitarianism"6--the obverse side of the new anti-
ideological coin of the consensus.

The limits of the "cultural freedom" that the liberal
intellectuals lauded were defined by their acceptance of anti-
Communism. McCarthy and his disreputable ilk might be
condemned as "cultural vigilantes," but such condemnation
managed to gloss consensual anti-Communism with the more
beneficent confections of official and moderate respectability.
As long as McCarthy picked peripheral targets he provided
a convenient focus of attention against which liberals could
assert their moderation. But when, in the Army hearings,
he chose to criticize official anti-Communism directly, he
stepped over the line, and the charade on which his political
power was based had to be dismantled. Attacking the Voice
of America was simply going too far.

The liberal orthodoxy was tied to support of the interests of the United States government. "A Government contract," Eisenhower declared with little apparent sense of
irony, had by 1961 become "virtually a substitute for intellectual curiosity."7 Those who questioned its policies,
McCarthy or Oppenheimer, were open to condemnation for
failing to adhere to the appropriate idioms of political
expression--what the A. C. C. F. called "sincerity." The
focusing on McCarthy and the "cultural vigilantes" indeed
served to direct criticism away from any suggestion of official government repression of cultural freedom. More
importantly, such figures were attacked because they embarrassed the United States abroad and hindered "the very

possibility of the United States embarking on a program of
psychological warfare against world communism."[8]

Nowhere, however, was the fallacy of Bell's argument
that the end of ideology was an acknowledged fact more evident than in the basis on which U. S. foreign policy was conducted. The U. S. had entered the Second World War as a
satisfied power, with no war aims except a return to the
status quo ante bellum.   But that objective was clearly not
possible; the defeat of Germany was bound to enhance Russian power.   The objective thus had to be the post-war establishment of a stable system that would provide world
peace.   The American dispute with her wartime allies was
over a means of achieving this.   Statements of good intentions and the United Nations were insufficient protection for
the American commitment to a rejection of the imperialist
politics of spheres of influence.   Post-war Russian policies
caught the Americans without a satisfactory means of retaliation and without an ideological basis for recognition of
Soviet de facto acquisitions.   The resultant American policy
combined a pragmatic attempt at containment with an ideological crusade against unprincipled Communist aggression.
The Truman Doctrine expanded American political naïveté
into the governing principle of its foreign policy.   National
security was threatened because world peace was endangered
by an irresponsible Power which would not play by the
American rules of the game.   Those rules, however, dictated that the United States could not acknowledge an overt
political or economic interest as the determinant of their
policy.   America, after all, had never gone to war; instead,
it had gone on crusades.   The ideological argument was
necessary to justify American involvement in the containment of Soviet expansion.   Only by such convolutions could
national security be equated with the defense of Western
Europe or, later, South East Asia.

Basing foreign policy on ideological hostility made it
enormously difficult to end the Cold War, because it drastically inhibited compromise, or even tactical withdrawal.
It also ensured that there remained a contradiction between
stated and actual aims and effects of American policy: containment in practice established and enforced conflicting
spheres of influence, which, however, could not be referred
to as such.   The semantics of an inflexible anti-Communism
had to cover the gap: until a third was discovered, there
were two polarized worlds--that of the Communist aggressors
behind the Iron Curtain, and the Free World.   Neutrality had

to be condemned; states and individuals alike were either anti-Communists or fellow-travelers. No ideological quarter was given.

In such a context, Bell's proclamation of "The End of Ideology" is explicable as part of a necessary intellectual camouflage of the fundamental tensions within the Cold War liberal orthodoxy of cultural thought, part of a process of divorcement and compartmentalization of intellectual spheres of influence. At the same time that politics was being divorced from ideology, the "new criticism" was divorcing art from politics, and "academic freedom" was being defined in terms of "pure research" and "value-free judgments." The cultural freedom being propagated by the A. C. C. F. was offered only to those who adopted the correct, "objective" attitude to their creation, as something essentially divorced from external, particularly economic or political, determination. Anyone who refused to regard their work in the correct light had thereby declared themselves on the other side of the great divide. The definition was self-validating, with the added advantage of permitting political repression of dissidents, even if such distasteful activities were left, at least in public, to the "cultural vigilantes" who might also be criticized.

THE CORPORATE ELITE

Implicit in these intellectual orthodoxies was an expression of the real basis of the new establishment's power. What each of them covertly expounded was the expanded influence of an expert elite, which was laying claim to greater powers. The enormous growth of technology, the expansion of government and the extensive development of education provided fields in which an expert technical or bureaucratic knowledge was required. A narrow professional expertise became ever more necessary as the subjects of scientific study grew increasingly complex. The social value of scientific research was legitimized in material terms by technological applications, and the scientific model was adopted for other fields. As knowledge expanded and social structures appeared to grow more complex, specialization became a sine qua non. The entrepreneurial basis of earlier industrial development was replaced by the ideal of the expertly planned course to an infinitely expanding economy and the

Utopia of material well-being. All of this required the elevation of the expert to an unprecedented position of unchallengeable authority, in whatever field he operated. Only by making his activities independent of a larger context could he be freed from the hindrances of public scrutiny. Hence "pure research," and even "pure technology." Hence the "new criticism." Hence "The End of Ideology." All sought to divorce previously interrelated fields of activity in order to legitimate the autonomy of an intellectual elite whose authority was guaranteed by its specialized knowledge. The private language of the new professionals made their decisions impenetrable to nonexperts and intimidated the uninitiated from questioning the validity of their actions.

The process of specialization involved a separation and categorization of talent, requiring distinctions to be made between individuals according to their ability. The liberal consensus required individual equality, democracy as a political principle, to be redefined in relation to this process. A system geared to the exploitation of manifest personal inequalities needed for its own sustenance an illusion of political equality unless it was to assume totalitarian political forms. Specialization of labor necessarily produces an alienation from the forms of production; the democratic illusion is a necessary device to prevent the alienation from productive power spreading to an alienation from political power. Such an illusion requires that the individual define himself politically in terms other than those of his position in the productive system, so that the increasing cycle of specialization and alienation can be excluded from the political model.

This process, however, entails an increasing separation between the actual location of power in a political system, which moves towards the centers of specialized power (equated by the capital needs of a complex technology with the holders of financial power and the military-industrial complex), and its supposed location in the democratic process. As the democratic model grows ever less relevant to the location of political power, its forms of expression change, moving away from an emphasis on the politics of issues, towards the politics of style, as a means of further disguising its loss of political power. The principal mechanism of this change of emphasis has been one of focusing attention on individuals, people as recognizable and comprehensible entities in an increasingly complex social and organizational structure. The individual politician or corporate executive functions as

a figurehead assuming apparent responsibility for the decisions of his organization. If the democratic illusion is to
be sustained, it must be possible to portray its instruments
as controllable. And once these instruments reach a point
of sufficient complexity that they cannot clearly be comprehended by the citizen at large, it becomes necessary, in
order to sustain the illusion of democratic control, to present to the citizen spectator a figurehead performer as being in control of them. The complexity of the instruments,
however, means that their workings are not in themselves
up for consideration, and consequently the debate turns away
from them towards the comprehensible area--the nature,
character, and personal style of the figurehead. Politics
thus becomes predominantly a matter of performance, and a
unilateral form of communication where the citizen spectator
is given a choice only in whom to invest his political and
emotional capital, his vote. The growing prominence of
television as a political medium has exacerbated this process
and made it more conspicuous, but television is more symptom than cause, itself operating as a model of a technologically complex medium which requires the arbitrary installa-
tion of figurehead performers--known as "anchormen"--whose
function is to provide an individual focus to an otherwise apparently incomprehensibly complex structure.

     Once established in practice, the "New Mandarins"[9]
adhered of necessity to a conservative viewpoint. Since the
status quo of the division of political and economic power
preserved their spheres of influence and social status, their
self-interest dictated that they should seek to maintain the
new order. The drift to conservatism was gradual, however,
occurring as part of the legitimizing process, through a
series of displacement mechanisms. Anti-Communism created an artificial unity of ideological purpose at the same
time that it denied it was an ideology at all. The adoption
of the idea of progress ensured that the future could only
look brighter for one and all, while the way to progress was
decreed to be too complex for the ordinary citizen to comprehend. Knowledge became the basis of power only by acquiescing in the fictions of existing power structures, and
converting them to its own use. Narrow specialization of
interest and concern necessitated a belief in interdependence
among the expert elite. Loyalty to the group, the company,
the institution, based on loyalty to the power structure, thus
came to replace individual integrity as a measure of worth,
reaching perhaps its apotheosis in the activities of John
Mitchell, John Dean, Bob Haldeman and John Ehrlichman.

The decision, right or wrong, had to be defended by the elite in order to protect the decision-making process which ensured their social status. The self-validating circle of what Mailer aptly calls "liberal totalitarianism"[10] was complete.

THE POWER OF PRINCIPLE

The "bright young men who are born with silver spoons in their mouths," and "who have had all the benefits that the wealthiest nation on earth has had to offer--the finest homes, the finest college education, and the finest jobs in the government,"[11] were not without appeal to a post-war Hollywood itself increasingly open to East Coast influences. For the intellectual elite the lure of Hollywood was more than merely the superficial charms of Marilyn Monroe. By the early 1960s there were new charismatic political fictions to be endorsed, and the American cinema offered its co-operation. The construction of the post-war liberal hero is a subject for the next chapter, but the overt political location of this new figure can be seen in an examination of The Best Man (dist. United Artists, 1964).

It would be hard to imagine a film of more impeccably liberal credentials. Gore Vidal, former Democratic-Liberal Candidate for Congress and member of Kennedy's Advisory Committee for the Arts, adapted the screenplay from his Broadway success. The film was directed by Franklin Schaffner, who, like Vidal, had moved to films from television where he had directed, among others, Jacqueline Kennedy's Tour of the White House (1961). He had also directed the Broadway production of Allen Drury's Advise and Consent. Among the cast, Cliff Robertson had the year before played Kennedy as a war hero in P. T. 109 (Warners; dir. Leslie H. Martinson), while Henry Fonda was, of course, beyond repute as both an unemphatic liberal and a theatrical actor. The film is ostensibly a political melodrama about the selection of a Presidential candidate at a party convention. However, we are little interested in the process of selection as such, but more in the interplay between a number of political attitudes, personalized and polarized by the restricted situation the plot provides. In keeping with tradition, the film consciously does not name the party depicted, and this studied ambivalence is extended to the political issues it mentions: anti-Communism and integration, both bipartisan. Characters are instead differentiated by their attitudes to power and to politics as an activity, and these attitudes are seen as reflections of their personalities.

The central protagonist is William Russell (Fonda), the Stevenson-esque East Coast intellectual liberal. His central narrative position and his vulnerability automatically encourage the audience to endorse his viewpoint, and this tendency is reinforced by the evidence of his integrity. It is a different kind of integrity from Wayne's: an integrity of principle, by which his actions conform to an already articulated code, and seem laudable because he does what he has said he will do. As further confirmation, Russell is the most perceptive character in the film; that is, his judgments about other characters and relationships are consistently proved correct by the plot's development, a factual endorsement which permits the audience's confident acquiescence in his opinions. By agreeing with Russell, we the audience find ourselves better equipped to understand the relationships between the film's characters, and are also supplied with a prepared value-system with which to make judgments on them--judgments whose appropriateness will be retrospectively validated by the plot's outcome.

Through the perspective of Russell's liberal idealism we are shown three opposing political attitudes. Southern Governor T. T. Claypool (John Henry Faulk), who remarks to Cantwell (Cliff Robertson) as he accepts a coalition, "You may talk like a liberal, but at heart you're an American," is revealed as a hypocrite over integration. Cantwell himself, the States' Rights anti-Communist populist demagogue, is exposed as totally unscrupulous in his quest for power by his preparedness to perpetrate scandal about Russell and to intimidate or bribe delegates. Moreover, he is dramatically demonstrated as unacceptable because he does not understand character, as is revealed by his alienation of ex-President Hockstadter (Lee Tracy). As Russell puts it, he has "no sense of right or wrong," only an unscrupulous opportunism which is extremely dangerous because it is unrecognized. Cantwell believes in the righteousness of his cause because he believes in his own righteousness, and this position is attacked by Hockstadter:

> It's par for the course trying to fool the public, but it's pretty dangerous when you start fooling yourself.

The danger of self-delusion in politics requires that, from both Russell's and Hockstadter's positions, Cantwell be prevented from being nominated at all costs. The required qualities of integrity and self-awareness are emphasized by Cantwell's lack of them.

The third position opposed to Russell's is Hockstadter's pragmatic politics, which assumes that politics is a dirty game, and therefore that mud-slinging must be retaliated against. He extrapolates Acton's axiom backwards: "To want power is corruption already." His position, reflected by Russell's campaign manager, Jensen (Kevin McCarthy), is pragmatic, the difference between them being that Jensen, like Cantwell (and self-deluded like Cantwell), believes that ends justify means, but Hockstadter suggests "there are no ends." His is a defeated pragmatism, allowing no place for idealism in politics, which even Cantwell, in his perverse way, possesses. Hockstadter's attitude is contrasted with Russell's idealism over the issue of a counter-smear against Cantwell, and the ex-President's position is undermined not only by its inherent defeatism but also by the vindication of Russell's attitude when the counter-smear fails. A purely pragmatic, and therefore unprincipled, position can have its validity established only by its immediate success, and on this occasion its flaw is revealed by its failure. Hockstadter's attitude forces him to look on politics as no more than a game in which the rules are flexible and there are winners and losers. Thus he is uninterested in issues, which, from the standpoint of the film's endorsement of Russell, must be a criticism. The film suggests that Russell is the representative of a new politics of concern, and concern with issues. Hockstadter labels himself "the last of the great hicks," suggesting that his attitude is obsolete--a suggestion reinforced by the progression of the plot: his tactics fail, he dies.

It might be thought that Hockstadter's position is closer than Russell's to the practice of Liberal Realism, and that The Best Man should endorse the ex-President if it is to adhere to the liberal tradition. But it is necessary to differentiate between the practices of liberal politics and those of liberal drama. Martyring oneself in the name of idealism, as Russell does, is a central liberal dramatic tradition; it is the final device which cements the audience's sentimental adherence to the liberal hero, and diverts them away from an assessment in terms of winning or losing to a

more elevated recognition of the hero's moral superiority.
Russell compromises in practice to avoid compromising his
principles. In the personalized drama, martyrdom has its
own reward: his estranged wife returns to him during the
convention, endorsing his decision before he makes it. Her
evaluation, on the basis of his character, is a statement for
the audience from the only position the film has allowed it:
"Whatever you do, I'm sure it'll be the right thing."

Fonda in The Best Man is the political archetype of
the post-war liberal elitist tradition in perhaps its most precise cinematic formulation, and it is appropriate that it
should be Fonda, the martyr hero of Ford and Zanuck's
benevolent populism, who should play the part, expressing
the continuity between the two political styles. The Best
Man engages the same contradictions, and is caught in the
same paradox, as Young Mr. Lincoln and The Grapes of
Wrath: the assertion of the importance of a politics of issues from a vantage-point anchored firmly inside a politics
of individual images. Russell, the self-image of the East
Coast intellectual, questions his own stance as little as the
film suggests Cantwell does. Through the mechanics of
audience identification, the film is firmly attached to a politics of attitude and personality, while asserting its detachment from the self-delusions and hypocrisy of the fundamentalist tradition it caricatures in Cantwell and Claypool. It
bases its argument on the same kind of selective rationality
that protected Bell's "End of Ideology." Its most forcefully
presented proposition is Russell's claim, justifying the involvement of intellectuals in politics, that the problems now
faced are no longer simple, and require the understanding of
an expert. The representative practitioners of the new politics of the New Frontier are, despite their benevolence,
elitist and anti-democratic.

The undermining of the democratic process underlies
the plot structure of the film, in the opening condition that
the candidate nominated is bound to be elected President;
part of Hockstadter's analysis of the game of politics--
which Russell attacks--is structurally asserted to be true.
The democratic process has been invalidated by the conditions of the film, and the wisdom of leaving the choice up
to the people, in this case the delegates, is questioned by
their vulnerability to being swayed by Cantwell's disclosures
about Russell's previous mental breakdown. The film's conclusion appears to be that it is the responsibility of the intellectual to manipulate the people in order to produce the

desired electoral result. Politics is a game of manipulation, but the liberal, possessed of suitable principles, is allowed to play the game in the interests of his charges, the public. So Russell's solution is endorsed: he martyrs himself in order to destroy Cantwell, giving the nomination to the nonentity Merwin. His justification is:

> Men without faces tend to get elected President, and power or personal responsibility tend to fill in the features.

There is an inherent faith in the institutions of government which proposes that the position makes the man, and that an abandoning of the personality to the system's norms is all that is required for competent fulfillment of even the most exalted position. As the old President dies, a new one is created, emphasizing the continuity of the system's benevolent paternalism, and disguising the fact of manipulation through the illusion of the liberal compromise. The compromise result sustains Russell's heroism, allowing him both to be martyred and to win a principled personal victory in regaining the faith and trust of his wife.

OTHER MEN'S TERMS

At the same time that the liberal professional elite was institutionalizing its possession of power and its image, it threw a camouflage net over its activities. Part of that camouflage was the obscurantism which protected its professional activities from public scrutiny. More vital to the process, however, was its refusal systematically to define its own goals. Its Utopia was far off over the horizon, and while progress might slowly be made toward it--things were getting better, after all--it was not likely to come in sight in the near future. Pipe-dreams were not for practical men; instead, the "Liberal Realists" institutionalized the "limited objective," and policies of "containment." These verbal devices, and the assumptions behind them, were both cause and symptom of a basic premise of liberal orthodoxy: it never formulated its own terms of debate. Always conceding the ground rules of the argument to the other side, it could only hold out the negative goal of limiting the damage the opposition inflicted. Central to both the structure of intellectual liberalism, and to its crusade, was that it acknowledged its own failure to find an independent form of political expression.

The title with which the television courtroom drama series The Defenders opened, "Democracy is a very bad form of government, but all the others are so much worse,"[12] is in this sense a typical liberal conundrum. The abandonment of utopianism which Bell had associated with "The End of Ideology" led liberals to accept the need to compromise with imperfection. Such acceptance was implicit in the attitude of Realist historians such as George Kennan, Walt Rostow and Arthur M. Schlesinger, Jr., who in both their historical analysis and more importantly in their capacities as advisors to the government urged that "realities" be accepted: arguing for a politics which acknowledged the fact, if not the legitimacy, of spheres of influence. The terms of American diplomacy, they maintained, were dictated by external forces; the obligation was to provide the most adequate means of defense within those terms. The Cold War was seen to be the consequence of Russian refusal to accept American rules for international conduct. Since the opposition was not fighting by those rules, there was little point in their doing so. The Cold War had to be conducted as if it were a real war, and weapons stockpiled in enormous quantities instead of actually used. Kennedy's inaugural address contained one of those self-validating Catch-22s which could make sense only from a viewpoint which adopted the expedient course in accepting the unpalatable:

> We dare not tempt them with weakness. For only when our arms are sufficient beyond doubt can we be certain beyond doubt that they will never be employed. [13]

If only the Russians could be trusted, Liberal Realists could happily abandon their arsenals. But everyone knew the Russians could never be trusted, and so the unfortunate peace-loving liberals were locked into a cycle of having to do what they least wanted to do, and appeasing their consciences by proclaiming their reluctance to act--so long as everyone understood that reluctance would not stop them acting if they had to. The hypocritical rhetoric of the New Frontier policy of aggressive defense reached its nadir in the U.S. Army's description of the bombardment of Ben Tre:

> It became necessary to destroy the town in order to save it. [14]

There were notable advantages in accepting "reality."
By refusing to formulate the terms of its own debate, liberalism could never be defeated on its own terms. There
would, of course, be tactical gains and losses, but liberalism could avoid a more fundamental balance sheet of success
and failure, because it did not have definitive objectives
against which to measure results. Even a tactical victory
was never more than a temporary pleasant surprise: the
Cuban missile crisis, for example, only confirmed the need
to play the game of diplomacy by Russian rules. Since political controversy was always displaced onto the terms provided by others, the terminology of liberalism itself never
entered the lists. Its position was always defined as the
rational response to extremism. Since the debate was always centered on whether or not that extremism was irrational, the rationality of the liberal position was not up for
consideration. The politics of accommodation and displacement created for liberals a self-validating position that could
not be questioned within the framework of political debate.

Liberalism sought and secured a centrist position as
both opponent of and arbitrator between the ideologues of the
left and the backwoods bigots of the right. By enthusiastically acquiescing in the pursuit of happiness through material
accumulation, it also secured and redefined the idea of
equality:

> ... in the mass consumption society all groups can
> easily acquire the outward badges of status and
> erase the visible demarcations. [15]

Aided by this materialist concept of equality, liberalism acquired and transformed that central American fiction, the
myth of the man of goodwill. The complexities of a mass
consumption society demanded qualities other than those of
fundamentalist integrity. Instead it had need of a dispassionate managerial elite committed to securing the social
good through benevolent, progressive administration. Rationality, the balanced viewpoint, and objectivity became the
primary qualities of the men of goodwill, coinciding comfortably with the liberal professional self-definition. Following the common cultural tactic of an emergent ideological
tendency, liberalism annexed the existing mythical currency
and through it legitimized its own image.

That expert, professional claim to disinterest and
goodwill was ultimately based on a model of rationality that

derived from the identification of scientific proof with objective truth; that is, a truth whose validity had been established independent of the subjective act of its perception. Through the socialization of scientific discovery via technological invention the concept of objectivity acquired a social context and purpose: the betterment of the human condition, viewed in materialist, and hence economic, terms. The machine made life better because it made life easier. An ideological commitment to technological improvement was established as existing independently of the economic pressures which had brought it into being. Progress thus became not a journey to a goal, but an end in itself; an end, indeed, without an end-point, since the process of technological improvement could be regarded as indefinitely extendable, with the implicit social goal of equality established by material well-being. The core of the liberal emphasis on expertise lay in this axiom of social progress towards an eventual equality founded upon equal physical comfort, produced by the application of objective scientific knowledge. As with any consensual ideology, the predication of objective social good served to justify the claim to power of the expert elite.

REASONABLE BELIEFS

The mechanisms of displacement, by which liberalism avoided debating itself by always accepting the terms of others, were a reflection of the implicit concession it made to technological improvement. Liberals' commitment to material progress necessitated that technological advance be regarded as, in itself, a social goal. The tension in the liberal perspective was that the mechanics of technology were ideologically required to work for the betterment of man in society, and yet the imperatives of professional expertise and "pure research" insisted that they remain free from social control--for the simple reason that the machine was progressing at an ever-increasing rate towards a goal that could only be presumed, not guaranteed. It was comforting in 1950 to read Asimov's three laws of Robotics,[16] but there was other, more tangible evidence of the dangers of technological progress. Atomic weaponry questioned the benign potential of technology, but, perversely, required the ever more fervent assertion of that article of faith. The danger was again displaced: it lay not in the technology of nuclear destruction itself, but in man's capacity to employ it. Fear was diverted from the fact of the Bomb, which, of course, no rational man would ever use, to the possibility of that crazy finger on the button. The existence of such totalitarian weaponry gave credence to the need for eternal vigilance, and the need to compromise liberal idealism with the realism that accepted totalitarian forms of debate. Locked into their technological ideology, liberals located the threat as coming not from the Bomb, but from the fact that someone, specifically the Russians, might use it. The ascending helix of complex technological development was based on the assumption, which did not permit of questioning, that the machine was good for man. The problem, as seen by the liberal technocrat, was whether man was good enough to control the machine.

Perhaps nowhere did the liberal technocracy express its inherently schizoid nature so tellingly as in its attempts to resolve this fundamental dilemma. One solution, covertly practiced much more than it was openly articulated, was the adoption of a behaviorist psychology, which proposed applying the principles of a mechanistic, "objective" rationality to the study of man. This was a model of displacement at its most assertive: if man could be understood as if he were a machine, then the question of control became mechanically answered. Man was rendered redundant by default. Yet while this solution was to all practical purposes adopted in the automation of industrial processes and the application of military technology, it remained philosophically unacceptable to liberal idealists.

Instead, they sought perversely to assert man's superiority over the machine by stressing his irrationality or at least his capacity for irrational action. The unpredictability of human behavior became, for many liberals, a necessary, if somewhat uncomfortable, virtue. But such a fundamental contradiction required some mediating device to disguise and displace it. To counteract its insecurities, liberalism instituted the humanitarian concept of understanding, a word whose meaning crucially blurred the distinctions between compassion and comprehension. Understanding could, at the same time, accommodate a behaviorist model of mechanistic comprehension and an assertion of human uniqueness through a capacity for shared emotional response. Understanding is perhaps the most important single term in the liberal lexicon; a catch-all word whose semantic ambivalence can cover a multitude of inexact expressions in a haze of sentimental rhetoric. Understanding was an emotional quality

rather than an intellectual process. To understand people
meant to identify sympathetically with them; it was a form
of emotional acquisition of them, or of their problems. Understanding was a sentimental placebo for all ills and all
problems, for to be understood was to be absorbed into the
benevolence of the liberal consensus, and to be understanding was to be an active part of that consensus. Understanding was not an analytical activity; it was the very opposite,
a substitute for it which avoided the difficulties analysis
might reveal in a benign harmony of the rational and the
emotional. The liberal employment of the word played with
the dualistic meaning it gave "understanding" so that the rational basis of human understanding could be asserted at the
same time that its emotional nature could be exploited. The
process of understanding aimed to be all-inclusive, since the
understood object or person became predictable and consequently harmless, because that predictability permitted it to
be incorporated within the system of understanding that maintained the liberal status quo. In exchange for this emascula-
tion, the understood object was afforded a compassionate concern that revealed the centrality of a sentimental paternalism
to the understanding liberal elite--that paternalism itself being a consensual inheritance from the fundamentalist tradition.

    Certain areas of concern were, of course, more
problematic than others. Those groups or individuals who
refused to correspond with the liberal myth of men of goodwill had either to be forcibly placed within the orthodoxy, or
to have their unorthodoxy "understood" and explained. In
coming to terms with Nazism, McCarthyism or the psychopathic personality, liberalism most clearly revealed the
mechanisms it employed to sustain its humanistic vision,
and exposed their inadequacy. Liberal understanding wanted
not merely to answer the question of how such irrational political movements or personality traits had come about, but
also the question of why they had arisen, a question to which
no complete answer could be provided. Answers to the
question "how?" were available through the compilation of
sufficient data, but the question "why?" was much more
problematic, because it required the explanation of motive
in terms of a rationalist psychology that could not encompass
the irrational. For the liberal, the question "why?" was invariably rhetorical. When liberal historians asked how was
it possible for the Nazis to exterminate nine million people,
they were not primarily concerned with an explanation in
terms of the mechanics of execution or the bureaucracy of
the concentration camps, but with seeking to understand an

attitude to humanity and a psychology radically and frighten-
ingly different from the premises of their own.

The narrow limits to comprehension which their idea
of understanding as a process of emotional subjugation and
control afforded them inevitably prevented their coming to
terms with such aberrations as Nazism except by resolving
them in terms of individual psychopathology.   Liberal explanations could bracket off the psychopath from "normal"
society and declare him an aberration, but so long as he
remained unintegrated and beyond control--so long, that is,
as he evaded a rationalistic understanding--he threatened
the total system of that understanding.   A behaviorist psychological model might offer an explanation of irrationality
and propose medical means of removing the dysfunction, but
such a solution brought the liberal once more up against a
central dilemma in his philosophy: attempting to establish
some valid distinction between man and machine, even if
only on the level by which each was treated.

This individualization of the problem was, however,
the best practical solution liberalism could advance as a
way out of its dilemma.   It adhered to the consensual requirement of being all but all-embracing, and of labeling
those it excluded as being demonstrably "different, " socio-
pathic, less than completely human.   Having philosophically
rejected the idea of absolute evil, it strove all the more to
accommodate, or at least explain, the psychopathic "personality disorder" in terms which denied individual responsibility and spread the blame in rhetorical gestures of sentimental sympathy.   Here as elsewhere liberal orthodoxy found a
precarious balance between individualism and determinism,
which purported to grant free will to those who fell within
the benevolent conventions of its consensual framework, and
denied it to those who demonstrated an anarchic free will by
rejecting the restrictions of that framework.

THE INVENTION OF STANLEY KRAMER

If Stanley Kramer had not existed, he would have had to
have been invented as the most

> extreme example of thesis or
> message cinema.
>
> Andrew Sarris[17]

The psychopath proved as essential a figure to the post-war cinema as he was to the anti-ideologues of liberal realism. The popularization of psychiatry in the 1940s promoted the dramatic status of a character who could embody unregenerate evil in a fictional framework which sought to avoid populist conventions. Genre films might still resort to stereotypes for their Manichaean villains. For them the matter was relatively simple: just point to the nearest group of Mexican bandits, notorious gunfighters or monsters from outer space, have a couple of scenes in which they dispose of innocent civilians for their own amusement, and you have objective evil personified. But for the urban realist cinema, trading in images of paranoia it sought to explain but not to dismiss, there was a greater problem and a solution with much less precedent. The psychopath was created to avoid acknowledging a metaphysical notion of absolute evil that would have been contrary to the principles of understanding. The psychopath neatly provided an answer in being capable of irrational action in a rational society, and subject to a glib compassion for his inadequate humanity after he gets his just deserts in the last reel. The Adrian Scott/Edward Dmytryk tract on anti-Semitism, Crossfire (1947, RKO), ends with Robert Young looking down on the body of rabid bigot Robert Ryan. When someone asks if Ryan is dead, Young replies, "He's been dead a long time, only he didn't know it."[18] Understanding has become contempt for a character whose crime has been his contempt for others.

The psychopath personified liberalism's anxieties about its own rationality. In the immediate post-war period these anxieties revealed themselves mainly in the urban melodramas of film noir, but in the late 1950s the ideological function of the cinematic psychopath became increasingly clear as the cinema of social messages reached its zenith. Stanley Kramer, whose independent productions in the years around 1960 made him the arch-exponent of the film with the detachable theme, and won him the Irving Thalberg Award "for consistently high quality in filmmaking" in 1961, returned repeatedly to the psychopathic personality as a trigger for the liberal conscience. Kramer sought to elevate the cinema through its social significance, and while his relent-

less promotion of "meaningful" content over form has ensured
the rapid demise of his critical reputation he is nevertheless
a figure central to the emergence of the liberal consensus,
both in its thematic preoccupations and in its acquisition of
industrial power.

Kramer's habitual technique is to present an issue in
terms of an individual confrontation of characters the film
determines to be representative of opposed viewpoints, at the
same time purporting to dramatize a social problem and tell
a story. Pressure Point, produced by Kramer for United
Artists in 1962 and directed by Hubert Cornfield, exemplifies
this process in its handling of Kramer's recurrent topic of
racial conflict. Inside a framing device in which Peter Falk
plays a young prison psychiatrist unable to communicate with
a black prisoner, Sidney Poitier points a moral of goodwill
by narrating in flashback the story of his wartime failure to
cure an imprisoned psychopathic Nazi racist, played by Bobby
Darin. While Darin is not reduced to a position of complete
inarticulacy, this is no more than a device to conceal the
film's Manichaean characterization of good and evil. Darin's
speeches may well work to make white audiences uncomfortable by their closeness to their own unarticulated attitudes.
But by putting them in the mouth of an overtly unsympathetic
character, the spectator is not led to a position in which such
ideas can be openly raised and confronted. On the contrary,
they must be dismissed because they are depicted as part of
the intellectual property of a man persistently described and
pictured as a psychopath. The film posits a few individuals
as representative of general social positions, and then individualizes their problems, so that they no longer function
satisfactorily either as representatives of social groups or
as individuals in their own right. This form of audience involvement operates as a kind of emotional blackmail; a sympathetic Negro and an unsympathetic white are presented in
order to make the white liberal audience for whom the film
is presumably designed readjust their thinking on the subject
emotionally, not intellectually. Pressure Point reveals its
thematic opportunism more clearly than other films of the
liberal consensus because it matches it with an equal opportunism towards spatial relationships.

Pressure Point is filmed theatre. This much is apparent in the contrived use of sets, and in the dissolution of
the boundaries of spatial delineation. Sidney Poitier's office,
for example, can contain an elephant ridden by the twelve-
year-old Darin. Darin's fantasies are acted out in a non-

naturalistic manner designed to emphasize the fact that they are fantasies, which reinforces Poitier's plot role as psychiatrist and narrative role as interpreter of the action for the audience. The sets are constructed to make it possible to pan from Poitier's psychiatrist's room to Darin's father's butcher's shop through a pool of darkness, a proposition of theatrical space that echoes Arthur Miller's design for Death of a Salesman. 19 Composition, too, becomes a functionary of the drama, which is concentrated, through the use of deep-focus low- or high-angle medium close-ups, on the actors' delivery of dialogue. This emphasis on the actors, together with the artificiality of the settings, stresses the theatricality of the film, as well as its intention to make a significant statement. In the scene in Darin's cell, where the walls disappear with the ease of theatrical flats, the film most clearly reneges on the contract it has established with its audience over the presentation of space. Our guarantee of normative spatial perception is established by the conventional perspective in which we view recognizable objects like desks, walls or people, as delineators of space. Pressure Point offers us this guarantee, through the solidity of such objects, and then rejects that solidity while continuing to depict space under the terms of that guarantee. The contractual relationship between film and audience applies only when it is convenient for the film. The unilateral nature of the film's negotiation with the audience over the terms of its depiction of space precludes the possibility of the democratic presentation of a theme.

The crux of that presentation is Poitier, not only because he is the central figure in the narrative, but also because he is the narrator, and the interpreter of the events we are shown. He is, further, proven right in his analysis by the end of the story, when we learn that Darin was finally hanged for an ostentatiously psychopathic act. In placing Poitier in the position he occupies in the plot, fundamental aspects of the question of race relations have already been side-stepped, for here, as ever, Poitier represents the small minority of blacks who have escaped from the socio-economic oppression of their race to be accepted on a professional level with whites. The conflict has, by Poitier's education, been reduced purely to one of color, to the fact that he is black. This is to avoid, as blatantly as Kramer does in Guess Who's Coming to Dinner?, the question of Poitier's racial heritage. The social context to which the film refers is only that of the white world, and the racial problem is seen as entirely one-sided, a question of white men

accepting Negroes as their equals, * because, as portrayed
by Poitier, they self-evidently are.

By placing the Darin story in the Falk framing device, the film asserts that the important element in the
racial problem is merely one of skin pigmentation. Falk
is dealing with a Negro who hates all whites because his
mother was a prostitute who brought whites home, and his
father was lynched by whites for killing one of his mother's
tricks. The framing device presents this as being a parallel situation to Darin's, whose hatred of Negroes is based
on a set of political assumptions which Poitier is allowed
to define as psychopathic. Focusing on racial hatred rather
than its cause obliges the audience to assume, with the
film, that all causes are equally valid, or invalid, because
of the reduction of the issue to the level of individual manifestation of the effect. Thematic causality is reversed on
the assumption that the causal logic of the narrative will
sustain the thematic argument through its logical weaknesses.
The solution Falk proposes to adopt towards his Negro patient is to put on blackface, and Poitier agrees, announcing
that all human problems are simply ones of communication,
thereby asserting the myth of the man of goodwill and re-
taining the liberal analysis within an optimistic interpretation of bourgeois individualism. There is no irony in
Poitier, or in his proposed solution in terms of individual
personalities. For while he fails with Darin, it is only
because Darin is an extreme case.

Darin is a Nazi in 1942, in prison as a subversive,
and psychopathic. Thus anything he says is not only wrong
but dangerous to the fabric of American ideals, which
Poitier is forced to defend without context and in terms so
vague as to be meaningless:

> There's something so great about this country that
> you don't even know about it.

This does not engage Darin's argument that the ideal America is created on, that "all men are created equal," is a
self-evident lie. Poitier's response, and the ideology he
asserts (which applauds success, family, and the intellect),

---

*In Guess Who's Coming to Dinner? the same question is
given slightly different expression; that of a Negro accepting
that white men can accept Negroes as their equals.

wins by default--a default made possible by the framework
of the debate, which individualizes out of the general, and
then generalizes out of the individual, allowing two stages
for the omission of problematic areas, and a complete divorce from social context. By placing Poitier in a position
in which he may analyze Darin's racism on the individual
level of the film's dime-store psychology, he is reinforced
and Darin is undercut.

> More than I wanted to kill you, I wanted to help
> you, and that makes me more than a good man,
> that makes me a doctor.

Poitier is a black white liberal, whose ideal is that of the
doctor, the saver of lives without regard to his personal
feelings. But because he is speaking from a position of
historical confidence, telling the story which is in the past,
the danger and the physical confrontation that might be involved are circumscribed by our knowledge that Poitier lived
to tell the tale. The film uses history to its own ends. By
imposing its analytical chronology on the events it depicts,
it dictates the audience's attitude to those events. He who
controls the present (presentation) controls the past (history),
and he who controls the past controls the future (audience
response).

Poitier is the mediator of the film's paternalist analysis in his position as narrator, and its beneficiary in the
plot, from the prison doctor, Carl Benton Reid. "I fought
hard to get you this job, " says Reid, "don't let me down. "
It is Poitier who adds, "Because you're a Negro, " a statement which he can reverse at the end of the film to Falk,
on the film's presumption that there is no difference between their situations. But Poitier has been appointed prison psychiatrist not only by Reid in the plot, but in his casting by the makers of the film who, in common with Reid,
are white liberals making the Negro in their own image.
Poitier's analysis of Nazism, couched in terms of an individual psychopath manipulating others, is reinforced not only
by Darin's characterization, but by the film's inclusion of
newsreel footage of the Nazi entry into Paris. His social
analysis goes only so far as to refer to "The discontented--
socially, economically, or psychologically, " returning to an
emphasis on the problem as lying with individuals rather
than with social institutions, whose values are asserted
throughout. In this context it can be noted that the only act
of violence in the film is violence against property: the

Tick Tack Toe scene in the bar, where the violence perpetrated against the hostess is humiliation, not physical injury,
a violation of her being rather than her body. However, the
film regards what happens to her as an outrage of greater
significance than any act of physical violence which Darin
commits. Not only is it emphasized by the amount of screen
time given to it, but also by the script. After it, Poitier
narrates,

> That's when I realized that this man was not only
> sick but dangerous.

This emphasis given to an act of personal and not political
violence serves again to individualize and depoliticize a
problem whose roots have initially been determined as political by the film; Darin is in prison because he is a menace
to society.

    In the American cinema, the problem of dealing with
political questions has consistently been one of the manner
of the individualization of the issue. Kramer's approach
posits a universal truth that may be individually exemplified,
but such a method requires a predetermined definition of
what constitutes a political subject. The political subject is
distinguished as separate from the individuals whose story
presents an attitude towards it. The film exists as a linear
development of the predetermined attitude which has governed
its construction. An aesthetic split in the film's structure,
between the determining but independent attitude and the
dramatic logic which derives from the narrative individualization of that attitude, emerges. The attitude appears as a
detachable message--in Pressure Point that the racial problem is soluble through the application of the myth of men of
goodwill, which is tantamount to saying that it doesn't exist
--located in the speeches the characters make to each other.
Political attitude may become a mechanism by which to examine personality, but it can only function as such within
the framework of an assured political perspective. Both inside the cinema and in its wider manifestations, liberalism
secured that framework by defining itself as an idealist,
pragmatic reaction to situations it claimed to deplore, and
by insisting, as a result, that it could never be more than
a compromise with imperfection.

MARTYRS TO COMPROMISE

The notion of compromise was as central to the functioning of liberalism as the concept of understanding. Those
mechanisms of displacement by which liberalism avoided confronting itself were geared to producing a compromise solution, the best result possible in unfavorable circumstances.
Compromise disguised the real location of power, even from
those who held it. It preserved the appearance of an effective democratic political system, whose checks and balances
could be seen to operate because no one was getting his own
way. It gave authority to the voice of moderation. But as
a political objective, compromise was of more fundamental
importance than merely being the sum total of its superficial
effects. Liberal realism sought compromise as a means of
avoiding a confrontation with its insoluble fundamental dilemma: the opposition between individualism and determinism
expressed in the technological terms of man's relationship
with machines. To continue functioning, liberal realism required both forces to be in play at the same time; hence it
required that they not confront each other. Ultimately, the
liberal had to seek the liberal compromise not because of
his humanitarian beliefs, but for his own preservation, since
his sense of self-identity was founded on the notion of rational understanding which gives a human being dominance
over the machine. The preservation of that non-mechanistic,
non-determinist illusion became in effect the liberal definition of peace, for war was the subjection of humanity to the
destructive logic of the machine. To slip from the knife-
edge balance of the liberal compromise was to destroy the
illusion of independence from technology.

Progress and balance were the aims of the liberal
consensus; understanding and compromise were its tools;
failure was both its prime mover and its unconscious goal.
Compromise inherently acknowledged the failure of idealism;
Liberal Realism postulated it as an initial premise. Because liberalism refused systematically to define its goals,
it could not hope to measure its success except in the already compromised terms of its "limited objectives." Failure, on the other hand, was much more readily quantifiable,
since it could be determined by the success of others.
Liberalism sought failure as a protective cloak; it maintained
the illusion, necessary to its political preservation, that it
was not in possession of political power. In needing failure
as its final, covert goal, liberalism acquired for itself the

role of permanent underdog. It is, for example, the success
of this defeatist strategy that has prevented recognition of the
dominance of the post-war liberal consensus in Hollywood.
As pursued by liberal directors, producers, stars or politicians, liberalism practiced martyrdom as fervently as Chris-
tianity ever had, and by doing so it secured its rationality as
being beyond dispute. Through its martyrs and through its
eager annexation of hopelessly lost causes liberalism sentimentally registered its faith in a vision of rational humanity
at the same time that it protected that vision from scrutiny.

Any system of consensual politics seeks stability as
its primary goal. The predominant post-war liberal consensus sought stability through the institutionalization of its own
inactivity, whether it chose to call that refusal to take assertive action "containment" or "consolidation." In asserting its own rationality, liberalism elevated the notion of debate to the point where it substituted for action. For the
liberal, debating an issue became sufficient in itself; open-
mindedness came to replace decision-making, while events
might be allowed to run their course. The tensions within
liberalism thus never needed to be resolved. Contemplating
the irrational served at the same time to validate liberal social analysis and to provide a way out of liberalism's greatest dilemma; it accommodated what it could not encompass
within its rationalist vision by endlessly debating it, thus
formulating it in its own terms. What could not be accommodated in practice was displaced into theory in a quintes-
sential liberal movement, a shifting of the pieces around,
like castling in chess, which preserved the appearance of
activity without accomplishing anything that was positive in
itself. The particular was always referred back to the general, which was never precisely defined, but rather assumed
as common ground.

Most importantly, this process served to reinforce
and validate that acquisitiveness which liberalism displaced
from the material world into the world of sentiment. Liberalism strove to "understand" any attitude outside itself,
in order to include it within its accommodating world. What
was "understood" was not just rendered harmless, it was
acquired and thus made available as an alternative position
within the diverse liberal perspective. The goal was to pour
oil on troubled waters, to calm issues down so that they
could be acquired by men of goodwill for rational debate,
and if pollution ensued, that, too, had its advantages, since
the energy and pace of anger or ideological confrontation

were slowed down and slurred in the thicker waters of procedural, theoretical, or semantic disputation. Displacement of confrontation was the liberal objective; like an octopus it spread its tentacles to enclose and suffocate any fundamental set of oppositions.

It delighted most of all in revising the past. History was subject to its sentimental acquisitiveness, serving to reveal the benefits of liberal management to the present generation by comparison, and also permitting liberal rhetoric to maintain in its tone a sense of lost innocence, a regretful nostalgia for a past presumed simpler. Liberals could in this way see themselves as martyrs not only to the terminology of others, but also to their own rationality, which prevented them adopting the simplistic viewpoints their opponents survived with, and which had also been available to earlier generations not burdened with the administration of such complex social institutions. Isolationism had been replaced with a reluctant eternal vigilance, which required that the innocent optimism of earlier American dreams be sacrificed to the continuing need for self-protection. The blue skies of Carvel were now never without the vapor trails of B-52s--just in case. The liberal professional guardians were aware of their own unwanted but necessary protective role.

The emphasis in American foreign policy from 1941 onwards was on the necessary sacrifice of American isolationist self-interest to the preservation of fundamental ideals and the inalienable human rights upon which American democracy had been postulated. Liberal paternalists, who could not recover their own innocence, sought to preserve it elsewhere, above all in their image of the apolitical Vietnamese or South American peasant who wished only to till his land in peace, while benevolent humanitarians made his political decisions for him. The self-validating circle of liberal martyrdom completed itself in this ideal image of simple men pursuing a happiness no longer available to the technocratic elite who sacrificed their own contentment in order to provide the stability these simple men required. Government was a heavy burden willingly shouldered in hopes of a better future for all.

Thus liberalism concentrated its efforts on understanding the past and providing for the future, while paying as little practical attention as possible to the distasteful problems of the present, which were always seen in a perspective provided by some other viewpoint. This pervasive

nostalgia permitted those practical problems to be solved
through the application of a technological solution, whose
moral virtue was always predetermined and which could always be retrospectively justified by its expedient effectiveness, and the inevitability of the compromise with imperfection. Whether intentionally or not, the liberal political perspective was perfectly equipped to justify the assumptions of
the technological imperative, and the applications of a technocratic solution, whether in the development of atomic energy or the Vietnamese defoliation program. Liberalism
comprised a series of interlocking, mutually validating self-
definitions which secured its own ends by admitting of its
ultimate ineffectiveness, and martyring itself to its own unquestioning belief in the rationality of compromise.

REFERENCES

1. Budd Schulberg, On the Waterfront: A Screenplay, ed.
    Matthew J. Bruccoli (Carbondale, Illinois, 1980), pp.
    103-104. The monologue is quoted by Jake La Motta
    (Robert De Niro) in the final scene of Raging Bull (dir.
    Martin Scorsese, 1981).

2. John Cohen, ed., The Essential Lenny Bruce (London,
    1975), p. 238.

3. Daniel Bell, The End of Ideology (New York, 1960),
    p. 373.

4. Dwight D. Eisenhower, Farewell Address. Congres-
    sional Record, February 16, 1961. Reprinted in Rob-
    ert Allen Skotheim and Michael McGiffert eds., Amer-
    ican Social Thought: Sources and Interpretations, Vol-
    ume 2: Since the Civil War (Reading, Massachusetts,
    1972), pp. 407, 408.

5. Leslie Fiedler, An End to Innocence (Boston, 1955).

6. Sidney Hook, Heresy, Yes--Conspiracy, No! (New
    York, pamphlet published by the American Committee
    for Cultural Freedom, undated), p. 14.

7. Eisenhower, Farewell Address, in Skotheim and
    McGiffert, p. 408.

8. American Committee for Cultural Freedom statement

quoted in New York Times, March 9, 1953. Quoted in Christopher Lasch, The Agony of the American Left (Harmondsworth, 1973), pp. 85-86.

9. Noam Chomsky, American Power and the New Mandarins (Harmondsworth, 1969).

10. Norman Mailer, The Presidential Papers (Harmondsworth, 1968), p. 202.

11. Senator Joseph McCarthy, speech at Wheeling, West Virginia, February 9, 1950. Printed in Skotheim and McGiffert, p. 401.

12. An hour-long series on CBS running from 1961-64, created by Reginald Rose and starring E. G. Marshall and Robert Reed as a father-son team of lawyers, The Defenders was notable both for its insistent liberal sentiments and for being the first courtroom drama series in which the central characters would occasionally lose their cases.

13. John F. Kennedy, Inaugural Address, Congressional Record, January 20, 1961. Reprinted in Daniel J. Boorstin, ed., An American Primer (Chicago, 1968), p. 940.

14. Unattributed statement, quoted in Philip Jones Griffiths, Vietnam Inc. (London, 1971), p. 84.

15. Bell, The End of Ideology, p. 119.

16. Isaac Asimov, "I Robot," in I Robot (London, 1968. First published in book form in 1950).

17. Andrew Sarris, The American Cinema (New York, 1968), p. 260.

18. Michael Wood, America in the Movies (New York, 1975), p. 138.

19. In 1952 Kramer produced a stylistically similar film version of Death of a Salesman, directed by Laszlo Benedek.

CHAPTER 9

RHETORIC WITHOUT A CAUSE:
THE LIBERAL CINEMA

> The very fact that it's impos-
> sible may work to our advan-
> tage.
>
> Fredric March (Karel Cernik)
> in Man on a Tightrope (1953,
> Twentieth Century-Fox; dir.
> Elia Kazan)
>
> "We lost. We always lose."
>
> Yul Brynner (Chris) in The
> Magnificent Seven (1960, United
> Artists; dir. John Sturges)

DISPLACED PERSONS

The pre-war fundamentalist consensus had constituted
a political cinema without ever acknowledging the fact. Hollywood's overtly propagandist role during the Second World
War had emphasized to filmmakers the political significance
of their activities. Once made, the point was not forgotten.

> Our industry today is more aware than ever before
> that movies are one of the most powerful forms of
> expression and persuasion. There is, moreover,
> complete agreement that the motion picture must
> continue as an articulate force in the postwar
> world so that it can contribute vitally to the de-
> velopment of permanent peace, prosperity, progress
> and security on a global basis. It means that the
> motion picture has definitely broadened its scope of

257

> activity to include many more themes which can be
> presented in a dramatic and entertaining manner. 1

The practical application of this new political consciousness
was not restricted only to the brief outburst of committed
left-wing melodrama whose creative talents were so savagely
crippled by the House Committee on Un-American Activities.
Other, more cautious men were following a safe distance behind this vanguard, both thematically and stylistically.   Social Realism survived right-wing attempts to stifle it by compromising.   Dore Schary led the way in his reaction to the
Waldorf Statement.   Lillian Ross reported him as saying that
he disagreed with the decision his company had reached, but
that he would not resign over it.

> I don't believe you should quit under fire.   Anyway,
> I like making pictures.   I want to stay in the in-
> dustry.   I like it. 2

Not quitting under fire was a convenient principle to justify
the compromise.   Liberals accepted the imperatives of loyalty to the industry.   In turn, it accommodated their conscience.   When in 1952, Gary Cooper, archetype of the populist consensus and H. U. A. C. friendly witness, won the Best
Actor Academy Award for High Noon, Hollywood's liberal
compromise was institutionalized.   Despite the roar and
bluster of the H. U. A. C. hearings, and despite the more
permanent humiliations and injustices that were being wrought
by blacklisting procedures, the liberal consensus had by the
early 1950s largely secured for itself the conventional structures of American cinematic narrative, and had recast them
in its own image, to its own ends.

    The principal agent of this change was a gradual re-
definition of the hero's dramatic function and his relationship
to the audience.   The film noir had renegotiated the protagonist's social role, emphasizing his existential uncertainty
and alienation from an increasingly complex society.   But,
either by locking the film's viewpoint rigidly to the perceptions of the central character (The Lady in the Lake, The
Lady from Shanghai) or by providing a non-participating
leading figure through whom he could explain himself to the
audience (Virginia Huston in Out of the Past, Lauren Bacall
in Dark Passage), the films carried the spectator into a
sentimental understanding of the protagonist's insecurities.

    The individualist hero lost his innocence in the last

half of the 1940s, and found himself engaged in an ever more perilous struggle to secure the once-guaranteed happy ending. The ideological security of the homogeneous hero was increasingly questioned, reducing the extent to which Wayne's connection between moral and physical authority could be made by others. The social realist school of the late 1940s generated characters whose heroism was defined by a fundamental moral rectitude they lacked the physical capacity to back up (Van Heflin in Act of Violence, John Ireland in All the King's Men), or by leanings towards martyrdom (John Garfield in Body and Soul, Dana Andrews in Boomerang!). Mythic perfection gave way to human frailty as drama in the liberal consensus assumed the function genre had previously fulfilled for fundamentalists. The hero became a victim of the need to defy generic conventions in the name of greater dramatic force and complexity, and an emphasized psychological realism. The phenomenon of loser as hero came with the dominance of a liberal realism which regarded Wayne's easy optimism as simplistic and dishonest. By the mid-1950s liberal heroism had produced its own prototype, Brando and Newman, raised in a different school of acting and committed to the neurotic presentation of their characters' flaws. But initially doubts about narrative certainty were indicated by the replacement of the calm craggy assurance of Wayne's facial features by the self-questioning faces of James Stewart, Van Heflin, or Gregory Peck.

Peck, as Johnny Ringo in one of the first Westerns in the new mold, The Gunfighter (1950, Twentieth Century-Fox; dir. Henry King, prod. Nunnally Johnson) is a fated man, his fate written in the hollows of his cheeks and in his sunken, glazed eyes. * Defeated by his appearance in the opening shot, Peck exactly mirrors the failure of the liberal reworking of the modes of the consensus. Although the film alleges to deal in "realities," in its examination of the bad man from a psychological viewpoint and its theme of creating a future by coming to terms with the past, it adopts without reflection mechanisms of the consensus other than those relating to the hero. The iconic elements of the film

---

*At the time, however, the most remarked-on feature of Peck's appearance was his mustache. Spyros Skouras blamed the film's relative commercial failure on this modification of Peck's physiognomy, and maintained that Johnson and King's insistence on this "realistic" detail had cost him $1 million. [3]

which identify it as a Western are not possessed of an independent meaning, but function rather as textural figures providing a familiar moral and physical landscape as a backdrop
to the central drama.   The old timers, the saloon, the shots
in the opening credits of Ringo riding through mountain country, the schoolmarm wife, the old respectable women, do no
more than contribute to the context of the action, and are
possessed of no specific meaning outside that given to them
by the script.   In the different context of another script the
Skip Homeier figure, Hunt, could be Audie Murphy, Ricky
Nelson or one of the Bowery Boys.   He has a pre-existent
manner, physical style, attitude and approach to other characters, but these take on a precise significance within the
structure provided by a plot.   Reinforced by similar figures
in different genres (e.g., Richard Widmark in Kiss of Death,
Twentieth-Century Fox; dir. Henry Hathaway, 1947), he is
like the supporting characters in Casablanca--a type, but not
an archetype possessed of a meaning independent of the specific narrative involved.

The Gunfighter is thematically concerned with coming
to terms with the past, and creating a future by accepting
the realities of the past in the present.   That theme, and
its presentation through an individual's attempt to exorcise
the guilt of his own past, places it within the mainstream of
liberal narratives.   All is contained within an unconsidered
traditional melodramatic structure which has overriding control over the themes; the possibility of resolution exists only
for the morally pure, and the prefigured end is fated in
Peck's eyes.   Liberal heroes die or fail not only because
the liberal sees himself as a martyr, but also because he
seeks only to make minor alterations to the structure of
melodrama, which serve only to undermine the position of
the central character.   The liberal hero is a flawed man
because liberal realism dictates that men are flawed and
heroes are men who have come to terms with their flaws.
But the characters around him continue to act as if they
still lived in a determinist world, where his heroism could
be assumed as readily as the villain's evil or the puritanism of the Ladies' League.   The hero is fatally undermined
by his being the only character in the melodrama subject to
the weakness of "realistic" psychological examination; and
because the melodramatic structure has been affected only in
its portrayal of the hero, it remains bound by narrative conventions hardly different from those of Griffith.   It is necessary for flawed men to die, because only the morally pure
can attain the resolution offered by a film's final shot.   The

liberal film is caught up in its own contradictions, both in its observations about imperfect reality and the inevitable defeat of its heroes, and in its refusal to consider the possibility of significant, revolutionary change in the narrative forms it practices.

Regardless of this weakness, the liberal consensus succeeded in tying the audience emotionally to a different kind of hero; passive, defensive, unwilling or unable to take the initiative himself, but prepared and capable of committing himself to action in defense of a principle, and, if necessary, of sacrificing himself to it. As an earlier generation of audiences had had their loyalties bound to populist heroes by their dynamic narrative centrality, so the liberal consensus proposed that they accept as heroes those figures in the drama who revealed their emotional vulnerability. The liberal hero remained one of Us, but instead of gaining the audience's affection by presenting it with a perfected image of itself, he secured its sentimental loyalty by his structural position in the narrative. Revealing to the spectator a greater emotional and dramatic depth than any of the characters around him, he also appeared to possess a greater substance. His vulnerability made it possible for the audience to establish a deeper emotional relationship with him than with the stereotypes who surrounded him. Hence he became a character who no longer needed to assert himself dynamically as the center of the film through action and his ability to hold the center of a medium shot. Rather he clung to the audience in emphatic close-ups. In the process, the liberal hero altered the audience's self-definition: if he was one of Us, we the audience must be more like him. The cinematic mirror now chose to reflect an audience which was slowly abandoning its earlier populist faith in all-embracing communalism, and instead viewing the world as a hostile environment in which the individual felt increasingly alienated and helpless. A deeper sentimental attachment to principle seemed one way of replacing their lost security of meaning.

The liberal hero commonly faces a dilemma of divided loyalties. By the film's resolution that dilemma has been reduced to a straightforward moral choice, but in the process of getting there the audience has been securely attached to the protagonist not through the external dynamic of his interaction with others, but through the internal dynamic of his moral debate with himself. Jenny's moral security in Love Story is not inherently different from John

Wayne's, but it is less central because there is in such moral security less for the audience actively to attach itself to. The insecure or uncertain hero permitted the audience a more positive sentimental function; instead of a hero they could only endorse, and who gave them nothing to worry about except whether he would be strong enough to achieve his already defined objective, the liberal cinema offered them heroes whose very heroism they could be unsure of-- superficially more complex and ambiguous figures who need- ed their emotional support to make it through the film. * The determinism of the liberal narrative was thus disguised by evoking the sentimental complicity of the spectator in its enactment. The audience was seldom permitted just to watch the liberal hero. They had to understand him as well.

Frequently this obligation led to a revisionist approach to generic conventions in the name of thematic significance and an increased psychological "realism." Rather than re- maining a self-sufficient body of formal structures, genre was now seen as an exploitable tool, a collection of icons and motifs to which a narrative, and more importantly a theme, could be attached. Liberal directors with a theat- rical heritage found genre an unacceptable framework, since its conventions of character and plot were felt to be anti- psychological, inhibiting the dramatically convincing develop- ment of characters in Freudian terms. As a result, much of their work was anti-generic, in that they used generic surfaces to construct films which were "about" subjects quite outside the genre's conventional concerns. Breaking conventions in order to be more "realistic" was considered an act of assertion against the formulaic nature of genre by at least some directors of the liberal consensus.

I go for very realistic endings, very hard endings,

---

*This was a phenomenon as much of the star system as it was of the dramatic hero. The star as perfected common man was largely replaced by a public image of the star as victim--of his (or, more commonly, her) fame, of the in- creasingly decried commercial corruption of Hollywood, and of the need to comply with an artificial public image. The loser-as-star could best achieve immortality by dying: James Dean and Marilyn Monroe are, of course, the two most evi- dent examples of this phenomenon, though Judy Garland's career charts the course from innocence to destruction more precisely than either of theirs.

uncompromising endings on my films. There are
no happy endings on my films, and twice I had to
change, go back and re-shoot the end of a film.
The endings were so uncompromising, the audience
loved the film right up to the end and then they
hated it because of what happened.... The second
time was a film called <u>Trapped</u> [1949], about Treasury agents and counterfeiting, a pretty good picture
in fact, and it was kind of a turning point in my
career because I'd been making a lot of B-pictures
and doing them very efficiently and very lousily,
no personal stamp at all, nothing of my own personality is in them and I finally decided I would
make a change, and make my own film for once....
The producer of the film [Bryan Foy] got it started
at Eagle Lion and transferred his office to Warner
Brothers and I never saw him again.... While we
were writing the script, we came to a sequence that
always happens in all these kinds of films, where
the Treasury agent is unarmed, he's in the den of
the villains, who are all heavily armed, and the
'phone call comes through tipping them off as to
who he really is, and he's in a lot of trouble, and
the writer [Earl Felton] and I were trying to figure
out how we were going to get him out of this spot.
Well, of course, there's always the way, you turn
the table over and knock out the light and the next
scene he's out of the door. And I said, you know,
come on, we can't do that now, let's do something
honest. You know what would happen. They'd kill
him. You're a Treasury agent, bang! We thought
it was a great idea. When we wrote it I gave the
pages to the producer who was still at the studio
at the time and a few days later I said to him,
"What do you think of the ending?", and he said
"Terrific ending, kid, terrific, great." So we
went ahead and shot it, and that's the hero of the
picture, and it's not the end of the film. So when
I had my rough cut and had the first showing for
the producer, he loved it, up till the point where
this fellow got shot, and I thought we'd shot him,
too! He jumped out of his chair and said, "My
God, what have you done?" I was flabbergasted.
He said, "You've killed your leading man!", and I
said "Yeah," and he said, "You can't do a thing
like that. It's a disaster!" I said, "Didn't you
read the script?", and he said "No." He said,

> "We can't release the picture this way," so you
> see the film now, you know what happens? He
> turns over the table....4

The displacement of generic concerns that resulted
from the liberal cinema's stress on psychological realism
and thematic significance may be illustrated by examining a
later film of Fleischer's, Between Heaven and Hell (1956,
Twentieth-Century Fox).   Although set in the Pacific theatre
of World War II and iconographically a war film, Between
Heaven and Hell is "about" social conditions in the Southern
States and the maturing of the central character (played by
Robert Wagner) into a liberal hero.   At the start of the
film, Wagner is afflicted with battle fatigue, in the form of
an uncontrollable trembling after an action.   Importantly,
this psychological stress reaction does not interfere with
his capacity to perform heroically.   He is never presented
as a coward.   Instead, his fatigue operates as a device to
generate audience sympathy on two levels.   Firstly, he is
established as morally approvable by his generically acceptable conventional heroics: scaling a cliff to throw grenades
into a well-protected Japanese machine-gun nest, and making
a daring run from a forward post to the main base to warn
the Americans of a Japanese advance and arrange the rescue
of wounded Buddy Ebsen.   Secondly, his psychological vulnerability makes him emotionally accessible to the audience,
as well as presenting him as having physical manifestations
of a conscience--although Wagner is questioning not the validity of war as such, but the blind authoritarianism of the
Army, and, at the same time, the social patterns of the Old
South, where he and the film's other characters come from.

Most of the first half of the film is presented in three
prolonged flashbacks, establishing Wagner's background as a
landowner who has mistreated his sharecroppers before the
war, showing his behavior in combat, his growing sympathy
with the G.I.s who used to be his sharecroppers, and his
growing estrangement from the officers who were his social
associates in the States.   This is brought to a climax by a
patrol led by Mark Damon, the Lieutenant who used to be
Wagner's best friend in the States.   Damon reveals his personal cowardice by sending two of the soldiers into a clearing which he, Wagner and they know is likely to be held by
Japanese waiting in ambush.   The two soldiers are killed,
and Wagner attacks Damon for his cowardice.   The film's
main narrative begins with Wagner's sentencing: he is reduced to private and sent to a forward position held by a

group of misfits commanded by the psychotic and homosexual Captain Broderick Crawford.

The film draws parallels between the oppressive authoritarianism of the Army officers, particularly Damon and Crawford, and the injustices of the sharecropping system. Importantly, however, this is always done at a personal level. Wagner realizes the iniquity of his previous activities through his relations with the men he was exploiting, and the discovery that they are just like him. The Army's cruelty is not suggested as being institutional; it results from the personal weakness of the individuals given responsibility beyond their capabilities. Crawford is presented as a sergeant given unwelcome promotion: "They busted both of us. You to private, and me to Captain," he tells Wagner. His psychosis is indicated by his suggested homosexual relationship with the two machine-gun-toting young privates who act as his personal bodyguard (as much from his own men as from the Japanese), and by the extreme lengths he goes to to avoid putting himself in danger. He is willing to sacrifice his men for his own safety, and he refuses to wear his Captain's uniform, since it makes him an obvious target for enemy snipers.

The narrative is tightly constructed as a social parable. The Lieutenant is Wagner's friend from home, two of his G.I. friends are his ex-sharecroppers, his commanding officer is another landowner acquaintance. Each of these characters is thus provided with a dual function, in which their actions in the war can also be read as interchangeable with their behavior at home; a parallel established by the peculiar flashback structure of the story, which sacrifices any sense of a temporal continuum to the dramatically significant juxtaposition of events taken out of time. The Lieutenant exploits his men rather than confront himself. The sharecroppers fatalistically follow orders that lead to their deaths. When Wagner strikes Damon, he is not protesting against the Lieutenant's personal incompetence and the Army's authoritarian structure, he is making a symbolic stand on his attitude to the Old South's social system. [5]

Between Heaven and Hell not only contains a displacement in its subject matter, but also a displacement in the relationship between character and action. Each of Wagner's actions has a symbolic significance detached from its position in the plot. His shaking is not discussed as a reaction to the battle as such; rather, it is presented as a physical

manifestation of a flaw in his character, which disappears
when he resolves that flaw. The flaw, of course, is his
treatment of his sharecroppers, and once he protests his
intention of creating a new social order on his return to the
South, his shaking disappears. Finally convinced by his
conversation with the wounded Ebsen--they talk of the post-
war future in which Wagner will avoid class exploitation and
go duck shooting with his wartime buddies--he is able to
stand up with determination writ large in his facial expression and resolve embodied in the firm stance of his newly
competent body. Standing at the edge of their jungle clearing, supported by the assertive tones of the music track,
Wagner works the bolt action of his rifle to eject a spent
shell with a coordination of man and weapon that immediately iconographically identifies him as the self-assured
hero because of the complete confidence of his stance.
This moment in which Wagner adopts the mantle of heroic
certainty guarantees the success of his subsequent action.
For Fleischer, as for Ford or Wayne, the posture of heroism is sufficient to establish a matrix of mutual validation
between character and plot.

Wagner's experience in war is significant not for itself, but for the effect it will have on him after the film is
over. His actions are important only because of their
causes or consequences. Hence the film can be read as
suggesting that war is cathartic and socially cleansing. The
liberal vision of war as personally revolting as an experience
but capable of inducing social improvements is endorsed.
Wagner tells the wounded Ebsen he's beat. Ebsen replies,
"The nice thing about being beat is, all you can do is get
up off the ground." The war has dismantled Wagner's social
limitations and barriers and left him beat. Not until that
happened could he get up and be the different, resolved man
we see in the final scenes: resolved to save Ebsen by his
heroic action as a symbolic act inaugurating his commitment
to a new and more just society. Once his commitment to
this liberal optimism is made, it cannot be gainsaid by circumstance. The advancing Japanese he runs through put up
only a token resistance to Wagner's progress; they cannot
be permitted the arbitrary power of short-circuiting the narrative progression by a stray bullet.* Character determines

---

*Which was, of course, what Fleischer wanted to do in his
ending for Trapped. The difference lies in the more rigid
operation of generic codes in the earlier film,   (cont.)

action not only by selecting the actions the characters perform, but by ensuring that their outcome is commensurate
with the characters' relative moral stature.

JUST DESERTS

> "I'm a realist. I don't believe
> in coincidence. Especially when
> it happens more than once."
>
> Hume Croyn (Humsey) in Brute
> Force (1947; dir. Jules Dassin)

          The perverse consequence of the liberal cinema's em-
phasis on character over action was that liberal "realist"
narratives found themselves even more firmly attached to
melodramatic structures than the populist consensus had been.
The necessity for the manipulation of plot events to be conducted without disrupting the surface plausibility of the
narrative--that is to say, that the characters must appear to
function as independent entities and not as symbols, so that
the story can be read as "realistic" and not as allegorical--
enormously increases the importance of coincidence as a
plot device. Coincidence is an inevitable tool of film narrative, if for no other reason than the structural limitations
provided by the temporal abbreviation of any film plot. But
it can be used in a variety of ways, particularly with regard
to the extent to which it is emphasized as plot device. Hitchcock, for example, relies heavily in his plot construction on
the most unlikely of coincidences to express both his determinist outlook and the arbitrary nature of cinematic narrative. By his equally arbitrary use of coincidence, Sirk produces in his audience an awareness of generic convention as
manipulative, and offers a critique of melodrama through his

----

which reduce the agent-hero (John Hoyt) to no more than a
cipher of the plot, which could be resolved in any of several
ways (the ending imposed by Bryan Foy makes no sense at
all). Between Heaven and Hell, on the other hand, is so
closely constructed around the development of Wagner's character that the resolution of his moral dilemma must provoke
the resolution of the plot.

practice of it. The liberal filmmakers, however, begin with
different intentions, and consequently employ coincidence to
different ends. For them coincidence is elevated to the level
of moral inevitability, and in conjunction with the identification
of character as the embodiment of attitude it forms the final
confirmation of the system of closure which their narrative
model operates. In Between Heaven and Hell, Broderick
Crawford signals that he has regained sufficient self-knowledge
to recognize his previous corruption by putting on his Captain's uniform. He is, of course, immediately shot by a
sniper.

The moral inevitability of coincidence functions at its
crudest in a film like Arena (MGM, 1953; dir. Fleischer).
In the liberal tradition by which the hero becomes an adult
during the film, while his best friend dies a moral adolescent, Arena belongs to the Western sub-genre of rodeo films.
Its central character, Gig Young, is in the conventional generic position of aging rodeo star being challenged for his
position of preeminence by a younger man, and being offered
the choice between a declining career in the rodeo and a
stable and prosperous life ranching. His best friend, Harry
Morgan, is a former star now working as a clown and suffering from a knee injury that occasionally immobilizes him.
Despite all the evidence the film provides, Young is unable
to decide to retire until aided by coincidence. He arranges
to ride the toughest Brahma bull--the conventional climax of
the rodeo film--seeking proof of his continued ability. The
bull throws him almost immediately, but that in itself is insufficient. Morgan, the clown, draws the bull away from
Young, but as he does so his injured knee lets him down
and he cannot escape from the bull's charge. In keeping
with his pathetic stature in the plot, he is gored and
killed, dying in order that Young, and the audience, should
get the message.

Arena presents an obvious example of coincidence as
the implement of resolution and the tool through which morality will assert itself to provide plot and audience with the
"correct" conclusion. Morgan's knee fails him at the crucial
moment because his life is wrong--the reverse of Robert
Wagner's ability to assert himself at the crucial moment of
Between Heaven and Hell because his life is now right. The
operation of melodramatic coincidence is just as essential to
liberal films of greater superficial complexity.

The crucial plot device of The Boston Strangler takes

place in a lift. Henry Fonda and George Kennedy are leaving the hospital after interviewing the victim of the Strangler's most recent attack, having gathered two pieces of information: that her attacker left a plastic ruler behind, and that she bit his hand. The lift stops; enter an attendant and Tony Curtis, with bandanged hand and complaining of having lost his ruler. Without exchanging looks, Fonda and Kennedy get out of the lift and walk out of the hospital. Only when they have got to their car does Kennedy look at Fonda and say, "My God, I'm afraid to breathe."

The reaction of the two characters is vital to the successful operation of the scene. Only by registering their incredulity at the coincidence, and prolonging it as they silently walk through the hospital can the film convince the audience of the scene's plausibility. That plausibility is essential not only to the film's status as a fictional reconstruction of actual events, but also to the narrative function the scene has in moving the film's preoccupation from the details of police procedure to the character study of a psychopath. The coincidence is still an inevitable moral judgment on Curtis, but its construction seeks to disguise the extent to which the narrative hinges on its arbitrariness.

A CERTAIN INSECURITY

In their hostile revisions of generic structures, liberal filmmakers criticized the forms of previous American cinema without attacking the central institution on which they had been based: the relationship between film and audience. In fact, by emphasizing their own "realism," they strengthened the unilateral nature of that relationship, and did no more than substitute a new set of dramatic conventions for the earlier generic ones. Three variants of the liberal hero, open to multiple combination, emerged from this emphasis. The first, exemplified by Fonda in The Best Man, was the hero as victim and martyr, sacrificing himself for a larger principle. The second type, like Wagner in Between Heaven and Hell, became a moral adult through his education in the course of the film. The third variant of the liberal hero was the professional, the expert figure marked out by his specialized skills. In all three types, the impulse to psychological realism in the central character did more than simply distance him from the supporting

figures. As the fundamentalist man of integrity was revised
into the liberal man of principle, his natural bonds to the
small community he protected changed into moral obligations
to a larger society and to abstract ethical beliefs--an alteration indicated by the drift away from the Western to the contemporary urban location in the late 1940s.

The principled professional hero began to emerge in
the wartime propaganda films, in which his relationship to
the society for which he was fighting was necessarily distant,
while his involvement with the mechanisms of warfare was
emphasized. In the immediate post-war period he was frequently a newspaperman, seeking either an abstract notion of
truth or a more concrete act of social justice. James Stewart in Call Northside 777 (1948, Twentieth Century–Fox; dir.
Henry Hathaway) is for the first half of the film in a dilemma of responsibility between his professional practice, which
brought him to the story in the first place, and his growing
conviction that Frank Wiecek (Richard Conte) is innocent.
His loyalties, good copy and the principles of justice, find
resolution in his newspaper's crusade for Wiecek's pardon,
finally brought about through the agency of a newly developed
technology.

Elsewhere in the semi-documentary movement, the
professional hero assumed a corporate identity, being embodied in an institution rather than a crusading individual.
The movement's obsession with technology encouraged this
corporatism, almost always (The House on 42nd Street,
Walk East on Beacon, The F. B. I. Story) attached to a federal law enforcement agency. If there was not a typical
semi-documentary plot, there was at least a typical plot
resolution, dependent upon the combined activities of professional guardians employing a superior technology to protect society from those who would harm it, and to defend or
uphold an abstract social principle in a particular case. The
role of guardian was always emphasized. The plots' representative citizens were unable to protect themselves, while
the larger society was ill-defined. The city replaced the
small town as principle replaced integrity, and the individual
or corporate hero no longer required a generalized sense of
moral justification for his actions, but rather specific skills
he might employ for an accepted notion of the general good
embodied in the welfare of the film's oppressed and helpless
victims.

The consensual formulation defined itself with increasing clarity in the process of being constantly restated. By the time of its complete articulation in The Magnificent Seven (1960, United Artists; dir. John Sturges), for example, the hero had been replaced by a group. Bound together by their profession of mutually necessary skills and combating a force either numerically superior (in Westerns) or previously un-comprehended (in science fiction films), they could defeat it only by the application of a technological prowess--a know-how--unavailable to their opponents and incomprehensible to their audiences. Moreover, they were acting in defense of an explicitly political principle, most commonly the right to self-determination. Armed with principle, they could oper-ate a stricter moral absolutism than the optimistic resolu-tion of the fundamentalist consensus had ever required. The theme of lost innocence which Andrew Dowdy remarks on in the anti-Communist films of the early 1950s[6] was pervasive. The "realistic" abandonment of Capraesque all-inclusive hap-py endings now meant that redemption or reform were op-tions seldom open to the Manichaean villains of the post-war world, while professionalism by itself was an insufficient heroic quality. Those characters who most clearly under-stood the principles for which they were fighting were the ones most likely to survive the final denouement, along with those who most completely represented the ideals for which the battle was being fought.

In The Magnificent Seven the purely professional fig-ures (Brad Dexter, Robert Vaughn, James Coburn), who have their own motives for fighting (profit, proving their courage, or an escape from aimlessness) are killed, while the char-acters who understand the villagers' situation (Yul Brynner and Steve McQueen) survive the battle with their knowledge reinforced, along with Horst Buchholz, who learned the neces-sity of some purpose greater than professional display during the film. All the professional figures are aware of having lost a sense of community they could not recover. McQueen describes their situation as "Home, none; wife, none; kids, none; prospects, zero," and Charles Bronson explains to the village children that it takes more courage than he has to work a farm. Buchholz receives his moral education and decides to stay with his girl in the village, while Bronson's death both represents the sacrifice required of professional guardians and sentimentally exemplifies Brynner's melan-cholic liberal conclusion, "Only the farmers won. We lost. We always lose."

With the advent of a superior technology as an aid to

heroism, the need for the perfection of physical abilities diminished. The elder generation of populist heroes could be allowed to grow old more or less gracefully--a development from which Stewart, in particular, benefited. His amiable bumbling became an increasing asset as he was allowed to demonstrate a shrewd mind behind it. In Call Northside 777 he spends much of his time searching through his pockets in an apparently absentminded fashion for pieces of paper, displaying a physical vulnerability--except in moments of extreme tension--that was to be the defining characteristic of the new liberal heroes of the 1950s. This element of physical insecurity was an important ingredient in the justification of the new hero. It suggested that he was capable of some self-doubt, both about his physical capacity and his moral rectitude, which served to intensify his achievement when he was successful, reinforce his moral decision when he chose to make a stand, and provide grounds for sympathy when he failed.

The initial archetype of the new liberal method of heroic portrayal came from a somewhat unexpected source: Gary Cooper. However, Cooper's performance as Sheriff Will Kane in High Noon (1952; prod. Stanley Kramer, dir. Fred Zinnemann) contained the two key elements of later liberal acting style--masochism and inarticulacy--as well as reflecting the comparative ease with which the liberal consensus absorbed not only the conventions but also the personalities of the previous period. Wayne, of course, could never be accommodated; the development of the liberal consensus would leave him an island, entire unto himself-- which was exactly why his cinema appeared to be political when all around others were just making movies. But Stewart and Cooper had always carried an element of uncertainty in their performing styles, a point they had to establish, or a position they had to secure (e. g., in their films for Capra), which made them available to liberal manipulation. Cooper frowns all the way through High Noon; not his quizzical relaxed and amused frown of The Westerner (1940; prod. Samuel Goldwyn, dir. William Wyler), but a much more heavily borne and ostentatiously serious expression. This frown, which sets the tone for the film's repeated medium close-ups, is the dominant insight that we are offered into Kane's character. High Noon pursues its seriousness relentlessly; not only is there not a single joke in the film, there is no light relief of any kind. Since Cooper doesn't smile, no one else does either. The expression serves another function: it substitutes for a discussion of Kane's moral dilemma. The title song poses that dilemma: he is "torn 'twixt love and duty"--or so we are supposed, on the strength of Cooper's facial expression and two scenes, to believe. But his course of action is never in doubt, since the narrative is constructed solely as an escalation to a final crisis. The audience, with the townspeople, sit around waiting for something to happen, knowing that only Kane can cause the action by reacting to an inevitable event--the arrival of the train that brings Frank Miller. Repeatedly, and with greater frequency as the climax approaches and the sides have been firmly drawn, the film cuts between clocks and observers, watching and waiting, simply because there is nothing else for it to do. Everything is now arranged, and nothing of consequence can take place until the antagonist arrives.

Cooper's scenes of doubt reinforce his heroic status, because he makes the right decision. His uncertainty, carried in his face, becomes his justification. In the first scene, in the buggy outside town, he makes a decision to stay in town, which permits the film to continue. But that decision is not argued, simply stated, and its justification is provided by the continuation of the narrative. High Noon is a static film, composed substantially of shots from fixed camera positions. It is defined visually in terms of the opposition between two shots: the close-up of the clock, where the sole movement, of the clock's hands, serves to measure only the passage of time; and the long shot of the railway line, which dissects space geometrically and denies the possibility of spatial movement altogether--we do not, importantly, witness the arrival of the train from this position.

The first scene of doubt is visually perhaps the most uncomfortable in the whole film, since it takes place outside the town, in a landscape where those correlatives of stasis do not apply, and where movement is normative. Despite Zinnemann's best attempts with a side tracking camera on the horse and buggy, he cannot obliterate the possibility of spatial progression from the shots outside the town as he so effectively does elsewhere. The scene opens up a possibility which is enormously uncomfortable for the film, since it requires a more mobile manner of shooting than that presented elsewhere. With the end of this scene and the discarding of this narrative possibility the film can return to its elimination of significant spatial relationships in compositional patterns of tight medium shots and close-ups, where characters communicate across the space that divides them rather than through it.

The scene in the church is the most pointed example of this tendency. Since each speaker represents a particular political viewpoint, and is there to express a single opinion, he operates as a discrete spatial entity, separated, when speaking, from those around him. The community is united only in the establishing shot, and is divided into individuals by close-up. Medium shots have no significant place in the film's conception of its human relations, since the possibility of change is an inherent assumption of the tension implied by a medium shot. The polarities High Noon establishes do not admit of the possibility of change, so the medium shot, particularly the two-shot which balances its participants equally, has no function in the moral/political ambit of the film. The long shot/close-up polarity, between railway line and clock, serves the film's reduction of its static situation into an opposition of attitudes embodied in characters much more satisfactorily than the ambiguities of the medium shot could do. Medium shots in High Noon have no other function than the interlude of spatial presentation between long shot and close-up. Where possible, as in the hotel room scene between Grace Kelly and Katy Jurado, they are converted into close-ups by positioning one character in medium close-up on one side of the screen while the other is full length on the opposite side of the room and frame, and the composition determines that they cannot interact across the space between them, since they cannot move without disturbing the composition.

The second scene of Kane's apparent self-questioning takes place in the stable, when Lloyd Bridges encourages him to leave. Cooper admits that he has been considering it, and that he is afraid, but then announces firmly that he is going to stay, and dismisses his hesitation as the result of tiredness. Again, Kane's decision, and the motivation behind it, is not presented; Kane has in fact made his decision before the scene begins, and we are offered only his facial expression as evidence of the existence of any remaining irresolution. The characters around Cooper serve to provide excuse for his self-explanation; importantly, their discussions avoid or misinterpret the real motive for his actions, which is left to be tacitly understood by the audience and, finally, by Grace Kelly.

As with the ending of The Alamo, the ending of High Noon is the closing of a circle of mutually validating structures that seals in the film's interpretation of its own events. Cooper's heroism is rooted in a belief in the overriding im-

portance of an abstract principle, to the potential sacrifice
of his life or his marriage. The price of a place in the
community is of small concern in comparison. Hence his
throwing down of his badge of office is the final observation
of his value-system, which the film unquestionably seeks to
endorse. His final action impresses on both his audiences,
in the town and in the cinema, that he is rejecting the community as unworthy of him, because it does not live up to
his own standards. The film exploits the distance it creates
between Cooper and the town's citizens to enhance his moral
rectitude and justify his contemptuous dismissal. What
makes High Noon a pivotal film in the re-orientation of the
cinematic consensus is the combination of the archetypal
liberal hero concerned above all with a self-justification of
his own actions, and the rejection of the pluralism implied
by a community composed of individual viewpoints. Moral
choice may be open to the characters of a drama, but it
does not exist for the audience, because the mutually validating structures that both tell and interpret the story ensure that we are informed whether a particular choice or
action was right or wrong. The moral constraints on narrative provided by the Hays Code were intended to eliminate
any such ambiguity. Its legacy of moral authoritarianism
outlived its particular formulations and concerns, because it
took its effect through the mechanics of cinematic storytelling, and the narrative structures it gave birth to were not
re-examined by most of the filmmakers who would have dis-
puted their specific strictures. The mechanics and the idioms of the American cinematic consensus were not changed
as its political attitudes were realigned; only its vocabulary
was modified.

A METHOD FOR REBELLION

What Stewart and Cooper had suggested was expanded
in the 1950s into a total acting style by the new stars of the
Method school, most evidently Marlon Brando. Although
Zinnemann had directed the film debuts of both Brando (The
Men, 1950) and Montgomery Clift (The Search, 1948), the
Method's most prominent and sympathetic directorial initia-
tor was Elia Kazan. In the late 1940s, Darryl Zanuck's substitution of Kazan for John Ford as the preferred director for his
contemporary social dramas[7] charted the producer's drift from
naïve populist to naïve liberal sentimentality. Kazan, one of

the founders of the Actors' Studio, saw the Method as providing "a surface realism and strong feelings underneath."[8] The two were inextricably related. Both found their generative source in a form of applied Freudian psychoanalysis that sought to supply the actor with an understanding of his character's motivation. That understanding informed a set of physical mannerisms which both indicated his submerged emotions and provided the "surface realism." The resulting overtly mannered performance then functioned as a "naturalistic" code for the expression of verbally unarticulated feelings. Kazan insisted on the emotional "realism" of the end product:

> Streetcar is the first non-sentimental picture we have made over here. It is a landmark. Its issues are not oversimplified, and you're not in there "rooting for somebody"--all that old shit the motion picture industry is built upon. There is no hero, no heroine; the people are people, some dross, some gold, with faults and virtues--and for a while you are muddled about them, the way you would be in life.[9]

Exactly which issues were not simplified Kazan did not make clear. The undercurrent of homosexuality and Williams' explicit language were certainly excised, and, at the behest of the Legion of Decency, Stanley's rape of Blanche was all but removed.

The excisions, however, permitted Kazan to assume a posture that was central not only to the liberal hero, but to the liberal artist compromising himself with an adulterating commercialism. Kazan could become the victimized martyr hero of his own struggles with a philistine establishment; losing ensured that he retained his artistic integrity, since it was he who was compromised in the compromising of the text. Hollywood's liberal artists seemed masochistically determined to engineer untenable positions for themselves in order that their capacity to soak up punishment might be applauded. It was an experience they also frequently inflicted on their leading men, and no one responded better to it than Brando, whose mumbling was always most justified after a beating. Kazan himself was the most able exponent of this perverse strategy, and demonstrated it to perfection in his dealings with H. U. A. C.

Kazan was called to testify in January 1952. Initially

he testified in executive session, [10] admitting his brief membership of the Communist Party in the 1930s, but refusing to name others. In April he appeared again, this time with a prepared statement which did name names (all of which were already known to the Committee), and which also contained a lengthy apologia for his career. Citing names was a necessary tokenism if he wished to stay in work. His curriculum vitae was not, and what exacerbated the Left's hostile reaction to Kazan's behavior was the self-congratulatory tone in which it was made. He even went so far as to place an advertisement in the New York Times the day after the second hearing, repeating portions of his statement to the Committee. In it, he attempted to pose his situation as being akin to the liberal hero's dilemma of divided loyalties:

> I believe that Communist activities confront the
> people of this country with an unprecedented and
> exceptionally tough problem. That is, how to pro-
> tect ourselves from a dangerous and alien conspir-
> acy and still keep the free, open, healthy way of
> life that gives us self-respect.

The dilemma, however, could be resolved into a simple moral choice--to reveal or withhold information:

> I believe that the American people can solve this
> problem wisely only if they have the facts about
> Communism. All the facts.

Then the decision was clear:

> ... I believe that any American who is in posses-
> sion of such facts has the obligation to make them
> known, either to the public or to the appropriate
> Government agency. [11]

Kazan's political activities are relevant to an assessment of his work if for no other reason than that he associated the two, and provided a political description of his work. He projected himself as a victim of the reactionary right and a scapegoat for what he termed "the ritualistic left." He insisted he was speaking out because of his anger at the way he had been criticized and "booted out of the Party"[12] sixteen years before. He seemed to see himself as a justified martyr to both extremisms, suffering for his maintenance of a balanced viewpoint. If Kazan's sincere hypocrisy found him no allies elsewhere, it was an attitude applauded by the

Hollywood establishment. Like John Huston or Gene Kelly, Kazan was a valuable financial property who received studio protection against the reactionaries who would bar him from employment. He made himself a martyr at little cost to his career.

Kazan's artistic and political compromises helped make Method acting respectable. Hollywood's "first non-sentimental picture" had sufficient industry kudos to win Academy Awards for Vivien Leigh, Karl Malden and Kim Hunter, and a nomination for Brando. Viva Zapata! which Kazan presented to the Committee as "an anti-Communist picture,"13 gained Brando another nomination, and Anthony Quinn an Oscar as Best Supporting Actor. On the Waterfront cleaned up at the 1954 Academy ceremonies: it won seven Oscars, including Best Picture, Best Direction, and Best Actor for Brando in his fourth nomination in as many years. Three of the five nominations for Best Supporting Actor went to Actors' Studio players in the film: Rod Steiger, Lee J. Cobb, and Karl Malden. The Method presented an image of rebelliousness that substituted a mannered non-conformity for political radicalism. The idea of rebellion was displaced from the specifically political context it had been provided with at Enterprise Studios* into a rebellion against the conventional mores of Hollywood and stardom. Brando and Kazan in particular became archetypes of the Rebel as Artist:** Brando through his off-screen behavior, Kazan through his insistence on independence from studio control and the "controversial" subject matter of his films. This was an internal rebellion the industry could entirely accommodate within the attitudinal realignment forced on it by its changing economic circumstances.

---

*Enterprise Studios, formed by producer David Loew in 1947, around a group of left-wing talents including producer Bob Roberts, John Garfield, Robert Rossen, Abraham Polonsky, Robert Aldrich, Robert Parrish and Don Weis. The company's two most successful films were Body and Soul (dir. Rossen; 1947) and Force of Evil (dir. Polonsky; 1948). Originally distributing through United Artists, it transferred to M. G. M. in 1948 but, partially because of its "reckless working methods,"15 it went bankrupt in 1949.

**The subtitle of Bob Thomas' biography of Brando is "Portrait of the Rebel as Artist."

The political nature of this rebellion was distilled in Kazan's second film with Brando, <u>Viva Zapata!</u>14 Produced by Zanuck from a screenplay by John Steinbeck, the film was a project Kazan had nurtured since 1943, before he first went to Hollywood. At the time of its release, there was some controversy over the film's historical accuracy, centered on the dramatic crux of its interpretation of Zapata, his renunciation of power in Mexico City. Kazan described the appeal of his and Steinbeck's interpretation:

> What fascinated us about Zapata was one nakedly dramatic act. In the moment of victory, he turned his back on power. In that moment, in the capital with his ragged troops, Zapata could have made himself president, dictator, caudillo. Instead, abruptly and without explanation, he rode back to his village....
>
> Thinking thus--not of politics but of human behavior--we saw Zapata clearly. In his moment of decision, this taciturn, untaught leader must have felt, freshly and deeply, the impact of the ancient law: power corrupts. And so he refused power. 16

That quotation indicates the nature of Kazan and Steinbeck's concerns. Like <u>The Best Man</u>, <u>Viva Zapata!</u> is not concerned with politics, but with attitudes to power expressed dramatically through personality. Like the other film, it invokes Acton's familiar maxim, demonstrates the corrupting nature of power, has its hero display his incorruptibility by renouncing power, and glorifies his consequent martyrdom.

In <u>Viva Zapata!</u> the corruption of power is exemplified by Diaz, Huerta and Eufemio, Zapata's brother (Anthony Quinn), who use it for personal gain; by Madero (Harold Gordon), the liberal idealist who is murdered for his naïveté; and by Fernando (Joseph Wiseman), the "man with the typewriter," who

> typifies the men who use the just grievances of the people for their own ends, who shift and twist their course, betray any friend or principle or promise to get power and keep it.

and who Kazan explicitly identified as representing the

"Communist mentality."[17] Zapata (Brando) himself recognizes the corrupting effect of power when he re-enacts a scene he played with Diaz at the beginning of the film.   One of the peasants has spoken back to him angrily, as he did to Diaz.   He begins to circle the peasant's name on a list, exactly as Diaz did.   Suddenly he realizes what is happening, and decides to leave.   When Fernando pleads, "Zapata--in the name of all we fought for, don't leave here!", he replies, "In the name of all we fought for, I'm going."[18] Zapata's action is justified dramatically: power has corrupted him to the extent that he can act like the corrupt Diaz against whom he rebelled, and the similarity of their actions persuades him to abandon power.   But it is presented as a political act, and one, moreover, whose contemporary relevance Kazan insisted on.

> Another man might have made other choices and
> emphases with an eye to interpretation.   I thought
> John's angle had great value for our thinking today
> and I was proud to direct it. [19]

The question of the film's historical accuracy is essentially irrelevant to the issues it raises.   It is rather the manner in which its credo about the nature of power is presented which is important--a question of dramatic and visual style.   In the scene which immediately follows Zapata's renunciation of power, he confronts Eufemio, who has seized land and another man's wife as reward for his generalship in the revolution.   They argue, Eufemio leaves, and Zapata makes his most explicit statement about the nature of revolutionary power to the men with him, who include the woman's husband.

> Emiliano looks at the men around him.   He speaks,
> in an atmosphere charged with murder.   He is
> talking about the land, but he's also referring to
> the woman.

> EMILIANO: This land is yours.   But you'll have
> to protect it.   It won't be yours long
> if you don't protect it.   And if neces-
> sary, with your lives.   And your chil-
> dren with their lives.   Don't discount
> your enemies.   They'll be back.   But
> if your house is burned, build it again.
> If your corn is destroyed, replant.   If
> your children die, bear more.   And if

they drive us out of the valleys we
will live on the sides of the mountains.
But we will live.

(now he looks at the husband for a sentence or two)

About leaders.   You've looked for
leaders.   For strong men without
faults.   There aren't any.   There are
only men like yourselves.   They
change.   They desert.   They die.
There's no leader but yourselves. 20

The speech in itself contains, as Dan Georgakas points out,
"a revolutionary vision."21   But that vision is destroyed by
its dramatic context and its visual presentation.   The tension in the scene is created by the "atmosphere charged
with murder."   Immediately after it, the husband and Eufemio kill each other.   The relation that the script makes
explicit between communal property (the land) and individual
property (the wife) contains the generalizations of the speech
within its specific dramatic context, which is the confrontation between Eufemio and the husband.   The individual context of sacrifice for the revolution is then expressed by Zapata's reaction to his brother's death.

More importantly, Zapata's comments on the nature
of revolutionary leadership are undermined by the visual presentation of the speech.   The peasants are grouped around
Zapata, sitting at his feet, listening reverently to his words
of wisdom, their hats in their hands.   Fordian Expressionist
lighting and the choice of camera angles--a low angle over-
the-peasants' shoulder shot onto Zapata, and a reverse high
angle onto them--emphasizes both their passivity and the
paternalist teacher-pupil relationship between them and Zapata.   There is no suggestion offered in the scene that they
either accept or understand the generalizations Zapata is offering them.   There is, instead, a melancholia implicit in
their saddened faces about the corrupting influence of power
on the individual--in this case, Eufemio.   For the rest of
the film, Zapata remains both their hero and their leader,
their viewpoint endorsed by the film's dramatization of his
individual story.   The personalizing of the drama, in each
scene as well as in the overall narrative, diverts attention
away from the political and toward the personal significance
of any event it depicts.   After his death, in the banal final
image of the white horse on the hillside (which Kazan attrib-

utes to Zanuck)[22] Zapata becomes a heroic symbol of the
rebellious struggle against authoritarianism, a transformation which displaces his practical failure into his success as
myth.   He becomes an inspiration to the peasants to continue
the fight, but does so not in a presentation that expounds
some idea of permanent revolution, but in one which rather
assumes the continuing failure of the peasants, like Zapata,
to gain power and hold it, and which presents Acton's maxim
as an insoluble Catch-22.   Their continuing struggle is thus
not aimed at any possible victory, it is just a kind of mythologized reflex reaction to their inevitable oppression.

In his introduction to the published screenplay, Robert
E. Morsberger suggests that Camus' distinction between the
rebel as "an independent nonconformist protesting regimenta-
tion and oppression" and the revolutionary "who speaks of
liberty but establishes terror"[23] is the relevant context in
which to view Viva Zapata!   It is a loaded distinction.
Camus' rebel is an individual, acting as such, rejecting communal allegiance in principle, as he acknowledges the inevitable corruption of power.   The rebel is the natural object of
the personalized drama.   To take a generalized issue and
express it in individual terms necessarily places emphasis
on the role of the individual, who is, within the traditional
narrative framework of the American cinema, not susceptible
to presentation as one man in and of a mass.   Even within
that context, the nature of Zapata's rebellion is restricted.
Consistently, he is forced to act.   He does not seek leadership, it is thrust upon him by others who insist on his abilities.   His only assertive act in the film is his renunciation
of power.   Throughout, he is a figure who abdicates responsibility.   He never seeks control, so he can always be victim to external forces and circumstances which he can only
affect by reaction.   The peasants' passivity only reflects his
own.   The audience is attached to the character through his
vulnerability--particularly in such scenes as his wedding
night exchange with Josepha (Jean Peters), when he demands
she teach him to read.   We cannot criticize Zapata because
we are offered no other major character who provides a different viewpoint we can endorse.   Zapata is typical of the
liberal hero in that he dominates the narrative while himself
being dominated by the events of the plot.   The liberal loser
hero achieves his centrality in the narrative not by his innate ability to dominate the plot, but through the filmmakers'
benevolent permission.   In the name of drama, they
intercede for him with the camera to the exclusion

of more naturally dominant or more successful characters. *

Kazan saw <u>Viva Zapata!</u> as being autobiographical:

> ... the figure of Zapata was particularly attractive
> to me, because after he got all the power that
> comes with triumph, he didn't know what to do with
> it or where to put it or where to exert it. He felt
> about things as I was beginning to feel about my
> own situation. 24

He also recognized his next film with Brando, <u>On the Water-
front</u>, as having a similar correspondence with his own life:

> Terry Malloy felt as I did. He felt ashamed and
> proud of himself at the same time. He wavered
> between the two, and he also felt hurt by the fact
> that people--his own friends--were rejecting him.
> He also felt that it was a necessary act. He felt
> like a fool, but proud of himself because he found
> out that he was better than the other people around
> him. That kind of ambivalence. 25

The similarity between Brando's character in <u>On the Water-
front</u> and Kazan** was that they were both initially reluctant
informers. Terry was perhaps better protected by Kazan's
paternalism towards the character than Kazan was himself,
but it is not difficult to find the obvious parallels between
Terry's testifying to the Federal Crime Commission on
waterfront corruption and Kazan's justification of his own
action before H. U. A. C. The defense was certainly the
same; one of the Federal investigators tells Terry,

> It'll be worth it if we can tell the waterfront story
> the way the people have a right to hear it. 26

---

*The essential paternalism of the liberal filmmakers' attitude
to their central characters was never more concisely summarized than in the title of the Paul Newman/Robert Wise
biography of boxer Rocky Graziano, <u>Somebody Up There
Likes Me</u> (MGM, 1956).

**And, indeed, Budd Schulberg, the scriptwriter, who had
also testified as a friendly witness before the Committee.

Brando's Terry Malloy, authorized by his Oscar, became the definitive archetype of the new liberal hero of the 1950s; prey to the film's events and protected by its makers (who were his intellectual superiors), he was given time to confront a moral dilemma and find the approved solution. His vulnerability, expressed as an inarticulacy which replaced dialogue with gesture, offered the audience a gradual, cumulative sentimental engagement with him, via his growing attachment to conventional ideas of love (Eva Marie Saint) and morality (Karl Malden), finally vindicated by his ability to take a beating and still stand up.

Through this treatment of the hero Kazan was able, in East of Eden (1955) and Splendor in the Grass (1961), to criticize that central institution of the populist consensus, the small town. The heartland of the American family was here revealed, with the aid of psychoanalysis, to be the seed-bed of American fundamentalist hypocrisy. That hypocrisy was expressed as a hysterical didacticism through the caricatured extremes of mannerist acting style Kazan provoked from Raymond Massey, Warren Beatty and Pat Hingle in particular. Kazan's assertion of the rights of the young to be confused, and their melodramatic need to be misunderstood, was ultimately tied to a didactic shooting style which he had slowly been formulating, but which reached full fruition with his use of CinemaScope. He had earlier confessed to the influence of Ford, which is evident in Viva Zapata!

> I used to run Ford's pictures all during that time
> the making of Pinky, like Young Mr. Lincoln. And
> I noticed that he left the scene with the assassina-
> tion in a long shot.... And I thought how much
> more effective it is to let the imagination go. And
> I began to study those long shots where he tells
> everything. And I realized that I did that on
> stage.... Then I made up my mind to make a
> picture with as many long shots as possible. [27]

The long shot, which establishes space rather than articulates it, became one of the two main props of Kazan's construction of images. The other was the close-up:

> A long shot is one of the greatest forms of expres-
> sion in a movie. And the other great form is a
> close-up. A medium shot is valuable but they are
> often literal ... a long shot often can achieve po-
> etry. In a close shot the camera works like a
> microscope; it is a penetrating device. [28]

By Splendor in the Grass Kazan had substantially eliminated
the medium shot from his compositional repertoire, except
as an occasional transitional device from long shot to close-
up. It revealed a disinterest on his part in the revealing of
interaction between characters in spatial terms, the possibility that the medium shot offered more clearly than any other.
His polarized composition, between the "poetic" shot which
"let the imagination go" and the close-up which fixed interpretation, was typical of those stage-trained directors of his
generation and television-influenced directors who came after
them.

> The screen is the exact equivalent of the stage
> rectangle, and the mainspring of Kazan's direction
> is an accentuation of the phenomenon of the pros-
> cenium. [29]

What Kazan was providing was an inflexible, theatrical
space, unimportant in itself, and only significant in providing
an arena for his actors to work their emotional wiles on the
audience. Although it was not unique to him, Kazan mobi-
lized this "poetic"--more accurately, theatrical--concept of
space more exclusively around the expressive polarities of
long shot and close-up than anyone else.   Actors were
trapped, immobile, in shots where their movement would
ruin the composition, and hence the purpose, of the shot.
Where it had been an ideological imperative in the populist
consensus, stasis became an aesthetic, compositional imperative in the liberal consensus.   The unilateral viewpoint was
imposed by the restrictions on the presentation of an event,
which locked the audience into the "poetic" generalizations of
the long shot and the specific emphatic detail provided by the
close-up.   The ambivalence of the medium shot, in providing
two or more equally balanced objects or characters for the
audience to select between, was eliminated.   Kazan's medium
shots, indeed, consistently excluded spatial flexibility, by
pressing their characters against walls or otherwise enclos-
ing them.   In the "I coulda been a contender" scene between
Terry and Charley Malloy (Rod Steiger) in the back of Charley's car, for example, the possibility of spatial interaction
between the two characters is completely eliminated.   They
simply sit side by side, facing the front of the screen.   The
tension in the scene comes from the acting and the plot, not
from any possibilities of spatial development.

Elsewhere he achieves the same effect by wasting
space.   The medium shots in the party scenes in Splendor
in the Grass are all shot with the top half of the frame

empty above the heads of the participants, who crowd in on
each other to prevent characters moving within individual
shots.   The composition focuses attention on a small area of
the frame, effectively making the shot a close-up.   In this
film in particular, Kazan elevates the idea of spatial entrapment to a controlling compositional principle, diagrammatically revealed in one raked overhead shot down onto the roofless
interior of a small car, in which Toots (Gary Lockwood) is
pinning down and groping a reluctant Deanie (Natalie Wood).
As the actors are trapped within the frame, so the characters are trapped within their limited comprehension of their
relationships, and within the confines of their small enclosed
Kansas town.

In discussing what he does with his camera, Kazan
makes his priorities explicit:

> I never work out long shot, medium shot, close
> shot, reverse angle and all that; that doesn't mean
> anything; if you do that there's no use getting good
> actors because there's no surprises; if you're going
> to squeeze them into a straitjacket of that form I
> think you should get marionettes.

> I'm not a great guy for moving the camera.   I
> nail it down a lot.   I don't like it when it moves
> too much ... and I love a set thing because you're
> not aware of the camera. [30]

Here is a fairly clear statement that the director's primary
concern is with the actors, and that composition should be an
adjunct to the main thematic weapon of performance.

SUPERIOR TECHNOLOGY

The origins of this attitude to composition are to be
found in the technical improvement in film stocks, lighting
and lenses in the late 1930s and early 1940s, which made
possible a different articulation of space from that previously determined by the limitations on the camera's depth of
field. *   While deep focus photography appeared to liberate

---

*It was those limitations, of course, which had made the
medium shot plasticly the most flexible in its vocabulary.

the audience from the tyranny of a differential focusing of
their attention, in practice it proposed a re-evaluation of
their understanding of the image. The presumptions of
"Hollywood cutting" were deliberately maintained by Orson
Welles and Gregg Toland in Citizen Kane (R.K.O., 1941) in
so far as they wished

> actions to flow smoothly into each other by means
> of imperceptible transitions, with intercutting and
> inserts to be eliminated as completely as possible

in order to create "a fluidity of effect in storytelling."[31]
But the technical devices they employed to produce the deep
focus effect not only emphasized "the living, breathing presence of the characters,"[32] but also the composed nature of
the image itself. Whether in the early work of Welles of
the contemporaneous films of William Wyler, the principal
effect was to draw attention away from the image as a purely functional unit of the narrative towards its own principles
of composition. While the space of a shot was rendered in
more depth, it nevertheless became more immobile, since
movement was restricted by the essentially static compositions that abound in Citizen Kane or Wuthering Heights (1939;
prod. Samuel Goldwyn, dir. Wyler). Gregg Toland's comments clearly establish that this reassessment of the role of
the image came with an alteration in the attitude to acting
(Citizen Kane introduced a new company of stage and radio
actors to the screen), but not a re-evaluation of the nature
of cinematic narrative as such.[33] Subsequently Welles' predilection for visual pyrotechnics led him to polarize the possibilities of composition and camera movement, most apparently in Touch of Evil (Universal-International, 1958), again
substantially eliminating the function of the medium shot.

While the post-war cinema adopted the perceptual
framework of the populist consensus, it did so with the unavoidable awareness of the new order proposed by deep focus. Composition in High Noon, for example, is a thematic
weapon, a post facto device for reinforcing the moral line of
the film's argument. Zinnemann has described the shot which
rises from a medium close-up on Cooper to crane out to an
overview of his standing alone in the deserted main street as
pivotal to the film. The shot is, of course, merely making
the point that Cooper is alone, but it does demonstrate the
film's denial of the relevance of a spatial flexibility to its
unilateral communication. The crane out, which might open
up possibilities, in fact closes them down: there is nowhere
to go when we get to the top of the crane, nothing else in

sight that we can cut to to move the action in a different
direction. The shot supports the single-minded narrative as
the narrative supports Cooper, without reservation or the
presentation of alternative courses of action as valid.

Welles' goal in Kane appears to have been the creation of a fluid area of specifically dramatic space in which
characters could combatively establish themselves. Certainly, an image-oriented "realism" was not an implicit goal,
but rather something critically tagged-on, principally by
Bazin's idiosyncratic relation of American deep-focus with
the quite separate practices of the Neo-Realist movement.
Yet the naturalistic goal of neo-realism did come to coa-
lesce, quite independently from any traceable influence from
Bazin, with the compositional aesthetic practiced initially by
Welles. Their meeting point was an attitude to performance.
The imported theatrical acting styles of the 1940s and 1950s
--the Mercury Theatre, the Group Theatre, the Actors'
Studio--shared the loosely-defined aim of a realism in performance, which came to substitute for the "realism" of
characters in space that was central to Ford's and Capra's
populist aesthetic. That "realism in performance" must
necessarily lack precise definition, since it was largely a
question of the coming together of disparate personnel who
found a common artistic aim in so vague an idea. Zinnemann's The Search (M. G. M. /Praesens Film, 1948), for
example, was an early conscious imitation of neo-realism,
its central role being taken by "unknown" Montgomery Clift.
In describing the project in an article for Sight and Sound
in Autumn 1948, Zinnemann spelled out the educative purpose
of the film, and the need to compromise with the American
audience's expectations.

> The important element in such an undertaking is,
> of course, the fact that the story and its details
> must be conceived on the spot; second, that the
> inner truth of the subject matter is of such para-
> mount importance that it must not be sacrificed to
> ulterior considerations such as star names and
> conventional treatment.
>
> Our primary concern was ... to dramatize con-
> temporary history for the large American audience
> and to make them understand in emotional terms
> what the outside world looks like today....
>
> All of us realised, of course, that it would be

> necessary to soften the truth to a certain extent,
> because to show things as they really were would
> have meant--at least in our sincere opinion--that
> the American audience would have lost any desire
> to face it, used as they have been to seeing a
> sentimentalized world. 34

Dramatization, education in emotional terms, compromise
and benevolence, all concisely articulated along with the importance of improvisation and the rejection of conventions of
presentation.

    An authentic background combined with unglamorized
performances and a changed image structure to present a
new normative set of narrative conventions that added up to
a new kind of "realism." Central to that aesthetic was a
new relationship between camera and actor. The camera
was no longer industrially subservient to the actor, obliged
to provide as many glamorous close-ups as the studio contract required. It was also not aesthetically dominant, in
that it could not create the performance simply by movement and cutting. Instead, its function was as witness to
the actor's performance, emphasizing the detailed authenticity of his emotional response to the events of the plot.
But if it was a witness to the performance, it was also its
keeper. The actor as a professional evoker of emotion was
both exalted and trapped by the camera, which sought to
bolster the expressive realism of his performance by its
recording of it--polarized, as in Kazan's cutting or Welles'
or Zinnemann's composition, between location realism in the
long shot and mannerist realism in the close-up. The camera composed the actors, but effectively reduced their available sphere of movement to either expressive detail (Brando's
"business" with Saint's glove in their first love scene in <u>On
the Waterfront</u>), or expansive, proscenium-filling gestures.

    CinemaScope, an inherently wide-angle deep focus
technique, encouraged the abolition of the medium shot in
emphasizing the actors. As Henry Koster put it,

> With CinemaScope, a director is at last free of
> the camera and has an unparalleled chance to
> demonstrate his ability to move actors logically
> and dramatically.... Now he doesn't have to wor-
> ry about "dolly shots" and "pan shots" and "boom
> shots" and all the other camera movements; he is
> free to concentrate on his chief task of drawing
> superb performances from his players.

    ... Instead of moving the camera into the actor to
get a closeup, I stage their movements so that they
walk into the closeup. In that respect it is like the
stage--you must arrange the action so that the audience's attention will be focused on the center of
attraction.

    ... In brief, CinemaScope makes the movie direc-
tor less dependent upon the cameraman and the
film editor.[35]

Koster's was a strange ambition: to abandon the
cameraman and editor in favor of a return to theatricality--
to replace construction with composition. The aesthetic goal
combined with a commercial one: the static camera and the
sequence shot cut production costs as well as reducing the
function of the medium shot. A two-shot which had occupied
the image area of the Academy ratio left large portions of
the 'Scope frame unused; the medium shot only became a
viable aesthetic strategy for those directors, like Ray, Min-
nelli, Sirk and Preminger, who had an architectural sense
of spatial presentation, and knew what they wanted to do with
the frame, rather than just seeking to fill the image area.[36]

The consensus, however, adopted the relative crudity
of Koster's stress on performance and static composition,
coalescing as they did with the tendency over the previous
decade (with a hiatus during the war) to emphasize those two
elements. The stress on composition as the static presentation of balance between narrative elements within the frame
fitted conveniently with the ideological imperatives of liberal
realism. An emotional attachment achieved through performance was grafted onto the assertion of a politically loaded
message in the narrative, in exactly the way that Zinnemann
proposed in his comments on The Search. As an agent of
reinforcement, the stress on composition as a separate element endorsed not only the actor as professional, but also
the director as artist. Where populist construction sought
to obliterate the evidence of the director's intervention, liberal composition sought to emphasize the director's contribution without interrupting the narrative flow. It endorsed the
director as artist, granting him, in extreme cases such as
Welles', the distinction of possessing a "visual style" in the
manner of a painter. Whether used for that purpose or not,
composition served status ends at a time when the cinema
was undergoing both status promotion and economic demotion
as a result of television's emergence as a more popular

form.   Directors consciously emphasizing their theatrical connections and compositional abilities achieved thereby a degree of professional self-endorsement.

That, however, was a heavily displaced goal, if it was a conscious goal at all.   Similarly, while the liberal rhetoricians abandoned the populist ideal of a naturalistic space created by normative perspective, and substituted an opportunistic dramatic space which obeyed theatrical laws of scene change, that was also seldom their deliberate aim.   Rather it was a natural tendency linked to their aspirations, and, in many cases, their theatrical backgrounds.   The conscious goal was to create a drama of social significance, which would elevate the cinema to the social and artistic status of the theatre.   In a film like Pressure Point it coincided with contemporaneous developments in the theatrical presentation of space which were themselves influenced by cinematic traditions--most obviously, the malleable space of Arthur Miller's theatre.

THE LIMITS OF SELF-AWARENESS

Miller's theatre also produced, in the figure of Willy Loman in Death of a Salesman (1949), the prototype for postwar liberal protagonists.   He was obliged to possess a carefully limited degree of self-awareness if he was to function adequately as a dramatic character.

> Had Willy Loman, in Death of a Salesman, been
> unaware of his separation from values that endure
> he would have died contentedly while polishing his
> car, probably on a Sunday afternoon with a ball
> game coming over the radio.   But he was agonized
> by his awareness of being in a false position, so
> constantly haunted by the hollowness of all he had
> placed his faith in, so aware, in short, that he
> must somehow be filled in spirit or fly apart that
> he staked his life on the ultimate assertion. . . .
> That he had not the intellectual assertion to ver-
> balize his situation is not the same thing as saying
> that he lacked awareness. [37]

This distinction between articulacy and self-awareness was endemic to liberal dramaturgy.   Liberal heroes from

The Gunfighter to Paul Newman's characterizations in Stuart
Rosenberg's Cool Hand Luke (1967) and W. U. S. A. (1970) have
to be caught at a precisely chosen level of understanding by
which they are aware of their discontent and can register the
unsatisfactory nature of their position, but cannot articulate
it clearly enough to be able to do anything about it.   In that
position they are infinitely vulnerable to exploitation by the
vicissitudes of the plot, and exposed to the audience's sympathy within the drama.   That sympathy is handed down from
a position of superior knowledge granted to the spectator by
the filmmakers' practice of the consensual relationship between film and audience.   The hero is conventionally tragic-
ally innocent, both in intention and understanding, so that he
is entirely acted upon by forces outside his control, which
ultimately ensure his demise.   The liberal film thus rendered
its heroes helpless victims, while establishing a superior
knowledge, usually granted to the audience, as the source of
future salvation.   Politically, such heroes were therefore
destined to be always ineffective, never more than vehicles
of an already defeated protest, no more than "social bandits"[38] like Brando's Zapata or Warren Beatty's Clyde Bar-
row.

     Criminality as social protest was not, of course,
something new to Hollywood, having been the mainstay of the
crime film of the early 1930s.   But where I Am a Fugitive
from a Chain Gang (1932, Warners; dir. Mervyn Le Roy) or
Scarface (1932; prod. Howard Hughes, dir. Howard Hawks)
had offered opportunities for genuine social criticism by their
at least partial endorsement of the hero, The Asphalt Jungle
(1950, M. G. M. ; dir. John Huston) and its imitators offered
their central characters a different kind of support--the
crutch of understanding.   The criminal heroes of the Big
Caper films were all, like late 1940s social realist psychopaths, psychologically crippled in one way or another.   That
was why they did what they did, and the explanation was an
important part of their characterization.   No one took part
in a robbery just for the money; it was always for what they
thought the money would buy them.   At its most positive--
in The Asphalt Jungle--criminality was seen as a defensive
reaction against society in general, and the corrupt or inflexible police in particular.   The thieves' combined actions
against the law were informed with their "better" characteristics; those, like mutual trust and teamwork, which should
be of value to society--as they would be in a war film or
"professional" Western.   It was their aberrations that
caused their downfall--Doc (Sam Jaffe) is caught because
he stays too long in a diner watching a young girl dancing.

At its most understanding--in In Cold Blood (1967,
Columbia; prod. /scr. /dir. Richard Brooks)--the senseless
violence of Perry (Robert Blake) and Dick (Scott Wilson) is
finally overridden by their much more senseless execution.
Perry and Dick are victims--of their environment (viewed
in bleak, institutional, characterless surroundings that de-
prive them of an opportunity for individuality), of their bad
luck (the circumstances of their capture), of their own limited awareness and understanding (the search for buried
treasure, the mistaken belief in the Clutters' wealth that
leads them to commit the crime in the first place).   They
are provided with a matrix of excuses which pose as explanations for their actions; "society," on the other hand, is not.
"Will it change anything?" a young reporter asks Paul Stewart, the film's Capote figure and spokesman for Brooks'
moral sensibility before the execution.   "It never has," he
replies.   The moral equation is reinforced by the presentation of death: there is a concern with the detailed mechanics of the hangings that is quite absent from the presentation
of the Clutters' deaths, which take place expressionistically
concealed by the flashlight illumination of the scene and
largely out of view.   Moreover, they are presented in flashback, as part of an explanation, without the immediacy of
the film's present tense.   Both these factors blunt their
emotional, and hence their moral, impact.   Although we
cannot identify with Perry and Dick as we can with Bonnie
and Clyde, we are induced, by their helplessness after their
arrest, to feel complicit in the greater (because unexcused)
crime of their execution.   Yet we, and our spokesman Paul
Stewart, are as powerless to prevent it as Perry and Dick
themselves.   Instead of feeling helplessly innocent, we are
now permitted the even greater, typically liberal, sentimental luxury of feeling helplessly guilty.

REFERENCES

1.   Murray Silverstone, President of Fox International
     Corporation, speech on January 6, 1946.   Quoted in
     Ruth Inglis, Freedom of the Movies, p. 12.

2.   Lillian Ross, article in The New Yorker, quoted in
     John Cogley, Report on Blacklisting: 1: The Movies
     (New York, 1955), p. 75.

3.   Tom Stempel, Screenwriter: The Life and Times of
     Nunnally Johnson, pp. 128-129.

4. Richard Fleischer, seminar at Exeter University, 1970.

5. The film was based on Francis Gwaltney's novel, The Day the Century Ended, which dealt explicitly with this theme. The title referred to the death of the Wagner character's father, which symbolized the end of the old exploitative sharecropping system.

6. Andrew Dowdy, The Films of the Fifties, pp. 29-31.

7. A direct substitution in the case of Pinky (1949), where Kazan replaced Ford after the first few days of shooting.

8. Elia Kazan, in Michael Ciment, Kazan on Kazan (London, 1973), p. 38.

9. Quoted in Bob Thomas, Brando: Portrait of the Rebel as an Artist (London, 1975), p. 74.

10. That testimony has never been made public. See Eric Bentley, ed., Thirty Years of Treason, pp. 482-495.

11. Bentley, p. 482.

12. Ciment, p. 84.

13. Bentley, p. 494.

14. Although made after A Streetcar Named Desire, it was released a month earlier than Streetcar in the United States, in February 1952.

15. John Baxter, Sixty Years of Hollywood (London, 1973), p. 158.

16. Elia Kazan, letter to The Saturday Review (New York), April 5, 1952.

17. Kazan, letter to The Saturday Review, April 5, 1952.

18. John Steinbeck, Viva Zapata!: The Original Screenplay by John Steinbeck, ed. Robert E. Morsberger (New York, 1975), pp. 101-102.

19. Elia Kazan, letter to The Saturday Review, May 24, 1952.

20. Steinbeck, p. 104.

21. Dan Georgakas, "Still Good After All These Years," in Cineaste, Vol. VII, No. 2, p. 16.

22. Ciment, p. 97.

23. Robert E. Morsberger, "Introduction," in Steinbeck, p. xi.

24. Ciment, p. 89.

25. Ciment, p. 110.

26. Schulberg, On the Waterfront, p. 93.

27. Ciment, p. 61. The film he then made was Panic in the Streets (1950).

28. Unpublished American Film Institute Seminar with Elia Kazan.

29. Jean-Luc Godard, "Panic in the Streets," in Tom Milne, ed., Godard on Godard, p. 20.

30. Unpublished American Film Institute Seminar with Elia Kazan.

31. Patrick L. Ogle, "Technological and Aesthetic Influences upon the Development of Deep Focus Cinematography in the United States," in Screen, Vol. 13, no. 1. Reprinted in Screen Reader, p. 94.

32. Review of Citizen Kane in American Cinematographer, May 1941, p. 222. Quoted in Ogle, p. 82.

33. See Ogle, pp. 92-98.

34. Fred Zinnemann, "Different Perspectives," in Sight and Sound, Autumn 1948. Reprinted in Richard Koszarski, ed., Hollywood Directors 1941-1976 (London, 1977), p. 144.

35. Henry Koster, "Directing in CinemaScope," in New Screen Techniques (New York, 1953). Reprinted in Koszarski, pp. 193-195. Koster was the director of Twentieth Century-Fox's first film in CinemaScope, The Robe (1953).

36. See Charles Barr, "CinemaScope: Before and After," in Film Quarterly, Vol. 16, No. 4. Reprinted in Gerald Mast and Marshall Cohen, Film Theory and Criticism, pp. 120-146.

37. Arthur Miller, Preface to Death of a Salesman, quoted in Sheila Huftel, Arthur Miller: The Burning Glass (London, 1965), pp. 110-111.

38. "... social banditry, though a protest, is a modest and unrevolutionary protest ... The Bandit is a pre-political phenomenon." E. J. Hobsbawm, Primitive Rebels (New York, 1959), pp. 24, 27. Quoted in Peter Biskind, "Ripping Off Zapata: Revolution Hollywood Style," in Cineaste, Vol. VII, No. 2.

INTERLUDE

THE APOCALYPSE: "THERE IS NO END TO THIS STORY"--
ROBERT ALDRICH--SAM FULLER

> It would be better to fire real
> shots over the heads of the
> audience, and have real casual-
> ties in the theatre. --Sam Fuller

Robert Aldrich and Sam Fuller make films which attack their audiences.   Violence is an implicit part of their
movies, for the conflicting reasons that it is commercially
acceptable and that it can cause the audience, during their
experience of the film, to reconsider their relationship with
characters more immediately than anything else.   As political filmmakers, both men implicitly recognize that the immediate battleground is not some topic external to the cinema that their film might be "about," but the audience's relationship to the film itself.   Violence--action--is more than
simply a means of expressing the cinema's aesthetic uniqueness in using motion to define existence.   It is also a tool
with which to attack the audience's comfortable complicity in
their sentimental anaesthetization.   It serves the goal--
loosely defined but common to all the directors of Dissent--
of creating a form of cinematic narrative that does not hold
its audience in contempt, and leaves it something to do.

Thus far, and in their thematic preoccupations with
American violence, survival and death, Aldrich and Fuller
are in agreement.   They also share an attitude to genre,
which recognizes both its convenience and its limitations as
a form.   The second paradox: to create an open text you
must first make plain its systems of closure. Working within
the rigid confines of genre is one means of exposing conventional forms.   By making public those conventions, by putting

297

them on the table where anyone who wants can look at how their films work, they may expose the limitations of conventional narrative to the audience and subvert their conventional conclusions. In their re-evaluation of generic form, they have practiced--along with the other directors of Dissent--a defensive exclusiveness, a preoccupation with self that has revealed itself in the ruthless and vigorous selfishness with which they have defined their politics, and has led them to stress the personal psychological importance of an attitude to professional activity that they share with their films' protagonists. That is one reason why no one else's narrative protagonists are ever as convincing.

They share, in other words, an attitude to performance. A man may define himself to himself by the way in which he does what he does. Characters can be as exclusively concerned as they are themselves with the competent fulfilment of a limited professional task. But that, they insist, gives them no guarantees. It is an ability you require to get into the game, but in itself it is neither heroic nor does it provide any surety that you won't get taken out of the game by random chance. Aldrich and Fuller, among others, begin with an attitude to generic performance, to their own and their characters' professionalism, that derives from Hawks and Walsh, but they omit their mentors' conclusive certainty. This much they have in common. Their stylistic practices, however, are at variance.

Robert Aldrich is a survivor. In interviews he talks frequently of the need to "stay at the table, stay in the game." His characters share the same concerns: egotistically, they are a lot more interested in staying alive than they are in what the audience thinks of them. Few people curry favor in Aldrich; those who do (Keith Carradine in Emperor of the North, Ronald Fraser all the time) are written off by characters and audience alike as jerks. Usually, though, they make it to the end of the movie. Life's like that. In some of his films, it's impossible to tell who the hero is supposed to be: in Flight of the Phoenix you keep wanting, expecting, it to be Jimmy Stewart because that's what Jimmy Stewart always is, but he keeps letting you down. In other films--Kiss Me Deadly--there isn't a hero; they're all jerks. Too Late the Hero sums it all up: there is no narrative logic in the selection of who lives and who dies. Professional ability or the heroic action guarantees you nothing, not even an on-screen death--Flight of the Phoenix, Ulzana's Raid. Anyone can achieve heroic dignity

--even the psychopath Slim Grissom at the end of The Grissom Gang. Being able to stand up assertively, work the
bolt action of your rifle and start acting like a hero with
Frank De Vol's martial music supporting your pose, is
available to any character. It's not enough.

    The kind of physical competence his characters pos-
sess is shared by the films themselves. Fluency of movement is an assumed quality of Aldrich's work. Shots flow
into each other with an exactness in the cutting derived both
from Aldrich's obsessive concern with the pacing of his narrative, and from his working method of using two cameras
to gain time and control.

> I find that you lose maybe five or ten percent on
> absolute right composition but you gain fifty per-
> cent on the fluidity of cutting and the chance to
> change the pace of the picture. [1]

But as physical competence is a necessary but not sufficient
qualification for character survival, so the shot-to-shot fluency is a necessary requirement of the economical narrative
but no guarantee of narrative resolution. Given Aldrich's
thematic concerns, a comfortable resolution is rarely de-
sirable or even possible.

    His films are smooth progressions centered on indi-
viduals, because the individual sees himself as the center of
the universe, and life is nothing more than a progression
towards death. Aldrich works within the tight American narrative because it inherently asserts his individualist premises.
The intensity of his individualist focus means that the death
of his protagonist(s) is apocalyptic. And yet Aldrich is faced
with the irony of the cinema's enclosure: that after the apocalypse, the audience is still alive. From the imposed false
resolution of Attack, through the incomplete ending of Kiss
Me Deadly--where two characters are left staggering into the
sea while a nuclear explosion takes place behind them--to
The Dirty Dozen, where three characters survive the end of
the film in a totally arbitrary, unsatisfactory manner, or
Flight of the Phoenix, where the survivors are met at the
end by a group of oilriggers who completely fail to grasp
the nature of their experience, the endings of Aldrich's films
have forced their audience to confront both the unilateral,
one-dimensional nature of his characters' egotistic definition
of existence, and the absurdity of living after the apocalypse
of their death. The irony of survival is made explicit by

the vulgarity of the jingoistic music that accompanies his endings.

Aldrich's films have always been explicitly political, but they have been so within the framework of generic preconceptions and narrative forms. Put it this way:

Eddie Albert is Nixon![2]

If you don't see the sign in Ed Lauter's office (in The Longest Yard) that says "When the going gets tough, the tough get going," you'll probably miss the point. Aldrich removes the props of explanation, sympathy or motive from his narratives, and confronts his audience with the facts of the American cinema, out of which they must make what they will. The mocking tone of his attacks on their sensibility is his acknowledgment of the likelihood that they will miss the point. As early as Kiss Me Deadly he disposed of the hero. As late as The Choirboys it is still necessary to insist that his films do not endorse their characters.

The French release version of Sam Fuller's Pickup on South Street removed all references to the politics of the plot, and converted the Communist spies smuggling secrets on microfilm into conventional gangsters dealing in drugs. The film's politics, then, reside in its dialogue. So what?

Fuller's films are constructed around a number of oppositions.

I like to get a conflict, whereby a character is going one way and a situation is going the other way, and there is a clash.[3]

Fuller's films treat war as an extended metaphor for life. The consistent structure of his films revolves around a binary opposition. Two self-declared armies wage an ideological dialogue war over politics or America, while the central protagonist establishes a separate opposition between himself as the mobile, active, motivating force which triggers the inherently unstable dynamism of the director's fluid tracking shots, and the armies' High Command which embodies stasis, dialogue explication and argument, and the temporary fixed-camera stability of rational discussion.

There are, then, two contradictory elements consis-

tently at work within a Fuller film.   His doomed characters
revel in verbal contradictions that display the facility of language to be rationally irrational.   A soldier in China Gate
declares:

> This is the life for me, even if I have to die to
> live it.

He is, of course, promptly killed.   In Pickup on South
Street, Mo, the unfulfilled mother figure who peddles ties
and information, announces to her executioner,

> I have to go on making a living so I can die.

Acknowledging one's contradictions through their verbaliza-
tion is a sure-fire way of undermining one's identity, and
ensuring one's death.   The newspaper headline announcing
Chief Fowler's suicide in Underworld U. S. A. reads:

> POLICE CHIEF KILLS SELF TO AVOID INVESTI-
> GATION

The contradictions within Fuller's characters abound: as
double-agents or mercenaries, his protagonists are dependent for their situational effectiveness on a strong sense of
self-identity; as extreme individualists, they rely for that
sense on a loyalty to something or someone outside themselves.   Without a place in a social system, without a rank
in the army, his psychopathic heroes go mad (Johnny Barrett in Shock Corridor).   Without their psychopathic drive
their existence has no purpose.   They die (Tolly Devlin in
Underworld U. S. A.).   The only characters who survive his
films are those who can, despite the contradictions of their
existence, "just put one foot in front of the other and take
the next step. " Only his early heroes--Skip McCoy in
Pickup, O'Meara in Run of the Arrow--manage to attain
this state of existentialist grace, manage to sustain the balance between the psychopathic and the rational, and their
sustaining it does not provide a resolution to the story.

Run of the Arrow concludes with the caption:

> The end of this story can only be written by you.

In Pickup, there is no resolution of the contradiction between
Skip's location outside society and his mercenary plot function as hero.   As he and Cathy leave Captain Dan Tiger's
office, Tiger tells him,

> You'll always be a two-bit purse-snatcher. I give
> you thirty days before I pick you up with your hand
> in somebody else's pocket.

Cathy's reply, the closing line of the film, indicates the instability of the present balance: "You wanna bet?"   In the
later films, the heroes die, heroism as a human possibility
is assassinated, and the remaining characters left standing
at the end of the film have to find a way of picking up the
pieces and carrying on moving.   Only the ability to move
proves a Fuller character is alive.

Fuller is a political filmmaker not because his films
dwell on the issues of overt politics (in the main they do
not), but because of the matrix of contradictions he explores.
The state of war is his metaphor for life because the conflicts within war mirror and express in action the inner conflicts of his characters, each of whom is at war with himself.   Those irresolvable conflicts, between love and revenge,
between patriotism and the mercenary impulse, give rise to
the positive but dangerous dynamism of his protagonists.
Without such a conflict, peripheral characters are static
exemplars of the modes of thinking Mailer acutely describes
as totalitarian: Connors and Driscoll in Underworld U.S.A.,
who accept the condition of war as inevitable and tolerable;
Driscoll in Run of the Arrow, who engineers the unnecessary
conflict; the Communist and Nazi High Commands in Pickup
and Verboten!

Fuller represents the extreme point in the cinema of
the anarchic strain of American individualist democracy.   But
to therefore tie him to the radical right, as Phil Hardy does
through his employment of Hofstadter's theory of the Paranoid
Style, [4] is to miss the point of Fuller's political argument almost entirely.   Fuller is a paranoiac in one sense only: he
corresponds to William Burroughs' definition of a paranoiac
as someone "who has just found out what's going on."   Hardy
points out some of the contradictions within Fuller's films,
and then uses the fact that these contradictions are not resolved as evidence for his claim that Fuller is not an intellectual.   But not only is the point of Fuller's journalistic
exposés to reveal those contradictions, he also emphasizes,
through the stylistic contradictions of his anti-naturalist
(Manny Farber calls it art brut) use of the camera as kino-
fist, that the contradictions he depicts are not resolvable.
There are no neat answers, no happy endings; indeed, most
of the time there are no endings to Fuller's films at all--

"This story has no end"--because his films exist only in the present.

Within Hardy's terms, a paranoiac is someone incapable of resolutions in the real world, who therefore imposes a single, inflexible theoretical unity--a single focus--on the arbitrariness of externalities. Fuller does exactly the opposite. He promotes resolutions (like death) at every stage in his films. He accepts and operates a dialectical process by which his resolutions always exist in the permanency of the present tense of his films. But once acknowledging the existence of a dialectical process by which his syntheses are constantly mutating into theses, Fuller refuses to concede that there is an end-point to this process. If he were to, then the final captions of his films--"The end of this story will be told by you"--would be a meaningless begging of the question. They are not if the audience admit Fuller's vision of the cinema as an educative process--film and audience synthesize to create a new thesis. As Franz puts it in Verboten!,

"I saw a film. I didn't know, I didn't know."

At this point, the constant operation of a process of dialectical change fixed in the permanency of the present tense, Fuller unites a European model of change with Fitzgerald's definition of intelligence with the ease of his film's cultural allusions.

REFERENCES

1. Aldrich, in interview with Pierre Sauvage, in Movie 23, p. 61.

2. Aldrich, in Movie 23, p. 62. He is referring to The Longest Yard (GB title: The Mean Machine).

3. Interview in Cinema, no. 5, p. 8.

4. Phil Hardy, Samuel Fuller (London, 1970), pp. 18-22.

CHAPTER 10

MERE ANARCHY: THE CINEMA OF DISINTEGRATION

> Things fall apart; the centre cannot hold;
> Mere anarchy is loosed upon the world,
> The blood-dimmed tide is loosed, and everywhere
> The ceremony of innocence is drowned;
> The best lack all conviction, while the worst
> Are full of passionate intensity.
>
> W. B. Yeats, "The Second Coming"

A CINEMA OF NARCISSISM

Notwithstanding his occasional illusions of omnipotence, the narcissist depends on others to validate his self-esteem. He cannot live without an admiring audience. His apparent freedom from family ties and institutional constraints does not free him to stand alone or to glory in his individuality. On the contrary, it contributes to his insecurity, which he can overcome only by seeing his "grandiose self" reflected in the attentions of others, or by attaching himself to those who radiate celebrity, power and charisma. For the narcissist, the world is a mirror, whereas the rugged individualist saw it

304

as an empty wilderness to be
shaped to his own design.

Christopher Lasch, The Culture
of Narcissism[1]

The abandonment of the Production Code and the establishment of a ratings system in its place symbolized the
changed ideological status of the American cinema. The
companies' reluctant acknowledgment that cinemagoing was
no longer a majority activity tacitly encouraged a redefinition of Hollywood's presentation of America to itself. Although it remained the most prestigious and remunerative
form of popular entertainment for the individual celebrities
it employed, by 1968 the cinema had ceased to be the dominant source of its audiences' self-projections. The simple
fact that fewer films were being produced reduced the conventional security provided by the repetition of generic and
narrative patterns. When only half a dozen westerns were
made in any year, the genre no longer existed except self-
consciously as history and material for revision. The decline in Hollywood's material base, in terms of both volume
of production and audience size, inevitably made each act of
production more considered, while audiences, too, chose
more deliberately from a smaller range. In both its production and consumption, the American cinema became, for
the first time, acutely self-conscious. The consensual
role it had adopted for the previous forty years was now the
prerogative of television, which readily undertook the function of ideological confirmation not only because of the size
of its audiences but also because of its ability to integrate
the reporting of the "real" world of news and current affairs
with the construction of fictions of social harmony in a continuous flow of programming. Going to the movies was primarily an activity of the young, but even for them it was
subsidiary to other cultural forms manufactured more specifically for their consumption. The industry of "youth culture," particularly music, developed during the 1950s and
'60s out of the growing affluence of a new group of consumers, towards whom the record industry directed itself almost exclusively. Both television and music production
gravitated towards Los Angeles, but for neither of them was
Hollywood any more than an obsolete prototype for their own
commercial activities, and a peripheral concern in the present.

Deprived of its cultural centrality by television, the
film industry found itself adrift between the new electronic

instrument of consensus and the alternative forms of expression aimed at the largest section of its own market. One possibility open to it was not to endorse the prevailing ideology. A more overtly political cinema seemed not merely possible but opportune in the charged atmosphere of the late 1960s, but its no longer being a central instrument of ideological expression also fractured the basis on which political expression was possible. The manifest content of any individual film no longer clearly functioned as part of a larger system (of studio, genre, or formal articulation) and instead stood by itself, as a statement without a secure context. Whatever its meaning, its ideological status had become insecure to an extent that was clearly not true of, say, a film of the 1950s. It might, then, mean anything, both in terms of its explicit content and in the way it could be interpreted. Robert Altman's refusal in interviews to discuss the meaning of his films is indicative of a larger ambiguity that has obscured the ideological significance of the American cinema in the last decade. The pervasive incoherence of many '70s films may be seen as a response to their ambiguous status, a status which makes their analysis as ideologically representative objects a much more provisional activity than before.

In the event, the promises of the late 1960s were as unfulfilled in Hollywood as they were elsewhere. No American political cinema of any substance emerged in a decade mainly marked by the avoidance of issues. If every American film in the 1970s was, in some sense, about Vietnam, they were all so obliquely. Hollywood's conventional structures were no more capable of manufacturing fictions about defeat on such a scale than was the rest of the American ideological apparatus able to accommodate the ignominious failure of the liberal technological dream in South East Asia. Instead, the film industry chose to ignore what might have been the central cultural issue of the period. Nevertheless, Vietnam manifested itself in the pervasive uncertainties of every aspect of film production in the decade, for the ideological legacy of the war appeared above all to have been to induce a persistent insecurity in a culture that was previously supremely self-confident. The failures of '60s radicalism and the disillusionment with politics in the aftermath of Watergate contributed to an abandonment of clear social objectives and encouraged the retreat into the self that is the most readily observable trait of American culture in the last ten years. Despite a pattern of continued commercial success, the history of Hollywood since 1967 has been marked more clearly by disintegration and the obsessions of narcissism than it has by anything else.

The period began in uncertainty, mainly because of the major companies' abiding commitment to blockbuster economics and their continued reluctance to adapt to the reality of differentiated audiences. The panic caused by the box-office catastrophes of 1969-72, when the seven major studios lost $250m between them, 2 and the subsequent search for "the fourteen-year old director"3 that called itself the "Hollywood Renaissance" indicated the depth of the film industry's loss of self-confidence. No longer protected by its consensual function, the industry found itself commercially obliged to make product for a younger and apparently anti-authoritarian audience that its senior personnel made little pretense of understanding:

> they would say, get me a writer, any writer, as long as he's under thirty, as long as he knows what, you know, what these young people want. 4

The studios' enormous losses in 1968-70 were the result of a massive over-investment in productions designed to appeal to a family audience. The major successes of the period, however, were films like <u>Bonnie and Clyde,</u> <u>The Graduate</u> (both 1967), and <u>Easy Rider</u> (1969), low-budget, independent productions whose appeal was specifically to the younger audience, for whom they provided identification figures in rebellion against some form of authority.

The films re-enacted the traditional concerns and structures of the liberal cinema, fusing a pursuit of individual identity with a vague social protest. "A man went looking for America," the posters for <u>Easy Rider</u> read, "and couldn't find it anywhere." But they offered a significant redefinition of liberal practice in the narcissistic bravura that displayed itself in their selfconscious stylishness. <u>The Graduate</u> celebrated its own mannerisms as enthusiastically as it relished Dustin Hoffman's aimless adolescent rebellion. In its predilection for fast zooms, discontinuous editing and detached song sequences constructed as if they were advertisements, the film registered its opposition to earlier liberal narratives in much the same way as Hoffman resisted the activities of his parents' generation: both were predominantly a matter of superficial style rather than content.

<u>Bonnie and Clyde</u> was less ornate, and more coherent in reconstructing the limited liberal hero as a narcissist. Director Arthur Penn had earlier dealt in the territory of adapting Western myth to liberal concerns: in <u>The Left-Handed Gun</u> (1958) he had presented Paul Newman as Billy

the Kid, liberal loser in search of an analyst, the audience.
With <u>Mickey One</u> (1964), he had self-consciously sought to
inaugurate an American Art cinema that would explore the
relationship between image and self. <u>Bonnie and Clyde</u> took
the process one stage further, and dealt in the deliberate
creation of a stylistic myth both by the characters within the
film and by the narrative. It extended the liberal cinema's
preoccupation with the loser by finally elevating him from
the merely heroic to the immortal.

Bonnie (Faye Dunaway) and Clyde (Warren Beatty) are
immediately set apart from their surroundings by their physical appearance, their carriage, and their attitude to each
other. The opening scene, reinforced by the jaunty hillbilly
soundtrack, enlists the audience's emotional support for them.
They are presented as contemporary figures moved out of
time, and, indeed, out of conventional character concerns.
Bonnie's sexual desire for Clyde, established before the first
robbery by the explicit intercutting between his gun, the
twitching match in his mouth, and her Coke bottle, is converted immediately after it into a quest for mythic status
which Clyde pursues relentlessly for the rest of the film.
His impotence is part explanation, part narrative convenience
to displace the film's principal concern from their relationship with each other to the achievement of their shared goal.
Bonnie swaps sexual satisfaction for the alternative excite-
ment of adventure and fame. It serves at the same time to
humanize Clyde (he is privately vulnerable, imperfect, and
in need of our--and Bonnie's--support) and to glamorize him
(his intentions and aims are expanded, not contracted, by his
disability). The circle of Penn's facile psychology* is completed by the scene near the end in which Bonnie reads Clyde
her published "Story of Bonnie and Clyde." The poem is the
final statement of their mythic status. The script refers to
it as Clyde's

> Realisation that he has made it, that he is the stuff
> of legend, that he is now an important figure. [6]

--and Bonnie has achieved it for him. At this point in the
narrative, he overcomes his impotence, and they make love

---

*Penn's rather than that of the scriptwriters, David Newman
and Robert Benton, whose original draft of the poem-reading
scene had Bonnie acquiescing in her limited, mythic satisfaction.

for the first time. Once incarnated as myths, they can behave just like "normal" people: their subsequent assassination can then be presented as a tragic irony, in which they
are victimized for their non-conformity by a vindictive society.

     The emergent heroic archetypes of the "New Holly-
wood"--Hoffman, Beatty, Redford, Nicholson--no longer
bothered to justify their anti-social activity, nor, as often
as not, were they punished for it. Butch Cassidy and the
Sundance Kid (1969) withholds its death sentence on Redford
and Newman by a final freeze-frame. Rather than plead for
the audience's sympathy as Brando had done, they charmed
them with an easy, self-deprecating grace. Their characteristic gesture was an ingratiating, eye-twinkling half-smile
offering access to the performer rather than to the character. The stars of the 1970s effected a redefinition of the
nature of stardom, made possible by the changed commercial basis of their activity. The disintegration of the studios
as production centers granted the star an independence and
economic power commensurate with his or her value as a
commodity, but it also permitted a limited withdrawal from
the obligation to perform a manufactured persona. Redford
withdrew to Utah, Woody Allen preferred to play clarinet in
New York rather than collect an Oscar in Los Angeles.
Hollywood ceased to be the settled community fostered by
the studios, and was replaced by a more transient and apparently more accessible agglomeration of people whose involvement with the film industry might be only temporary.
Stars sought and bought the right to a public privacy that
had not been available to earlier generations.

     At the same time, however, the absence of a studio
publicity machine increased the need for self-promotion,
particularly in an expanding media market ever-hungry for
celebrity. Television in particular possessed in its novel
game and chat show structures mechanisms which dissolved
the boundaries between fact and fiction, individual and persona. Game shows provided the ideal instrument to make
Andy Warhol's dream that everyone should be a star for
fifteen minutes come true, while the chat show formula
similarly demanded of its participants that they perform
themselves in public. Television's promotion of celebrity
as a commodity juxtaposed in the public attention figures
from completely different worlds, whose only meeting place
was in the media that brought them together as personalities
for mass consumption without regard to their profession.

For the same reasons that Henry Kissinger felt compelled to retain an agent, film stars found their social and political attitudes in demand as media fodder. In an even more overtly narcissistic practice, the mechanisms of celebrity created a category of personality whose profession consisted in their being famous by, in a revealing usage, "appearing on television." Appearance for its own sake was a recognizable feature of the 1960s, when stylistic experimentation had been a gesture of social rebellion. As with much of the new culture of the 1960s, the following decade retained its forms but not its purpose. Appearance and the concern with image pervaded political activity, assuming as much or more apparent importance than the issue of dispute. The vacuousness of a politics of narcissim reached its nadir, perhaps, in the debilitating spectacle of the 1980 Presidential election, where the public search for charismatic leadership was answered by two hollow and unconvincing creations of the media, in whose images at times even their publicists seemed not to believe. It was entirely fitting that a decade so committed to the display of the fabricated self should culminate in the election to the White House of a retired actor who smiled ingratiatingly every time he forgot his lines.

By the same token that politics turned to show business for its characters, Hollywood no longer took it upon itself to breed its own stars or pillage them simply from Broadway. Rock singers, football players and the ubiquitous television "personalities" became likely material for promotion to what remained the highest titular rank of media aristocracy, Movie Star. The star system was changed in ways more important than its mode of acquisition. Encouraged by the mechanisms of media celebrity into public postures of narcissistic display, stars assumed ever-greater importance in the packaging and construction of films because they seemed the only stable element in an environment of almost complete commercial unpredictability. While they claimed greater freedom from the industrial machinery, stars also became more central to its workings as their "bankability" came to be the major determinant affecting whether or not a film was produced. Under the commercial pressure they now exerted, the nature of Hollywood's fictions changed. The liberal image of the star as professional became increasingly untenable in the post-Watergate disillusionment; Steve McQueen's mechanical perfection (Bullitt, The Thomas Crown Affair) was replaced by Gene Hackman's insecure passage through plots whose significance he could never quite discover (Night Moves, The Conversation). The star's previous obligation to make sense of the narrative for the audience was converted to an essentially anarchic celebration of spontaneity, of both character behavior and improvisatory performance.

No longer required to practice consensual formulations, the American cinema's narrative coherence disintegrated. In almost every respect, Hollywood films of the 1970s have placed a much lower stress on the need to be coherent than in any previous period. The cohesive function of genre, as already noted, has been replaced by a self-conscious generic revisionism, practiced with more or less nostalgia for previous certainties. The obligation to relate a determinist linear narrative has also evaporated. In the wake of stylistically self-conscious films like The Graduate, M*A*S*H (1970) or Catch-22 (1970) the American cinema of the 1970s has described situations more frequently than it has told stories, and the role of the star in creating this phenomenon has been crucial. Within the films themselves, the activity of stardom has altered from being the expression of persona as an integral part of a coherent text to being a largely separable form of role-playing. Woody Allen's persistent willingness to desert his fiction and perform himself directly at the audience is only an extreme version of a more general situation in which films are constructed around situations designed to display their principal salable commodities, their stars. Where James Stewart enacted The Glenn Miller Story (1954), Diana Ross performs discrete melodramatic incidents as well as songs from the life of Billie Holiday in Lady Sings the Blues (1972), which display Ross more effectively than they narrate Holiday, while the responsibility for narrative is awarded to the secondary characters.

Where, for Hawks, the performances of Bogart and Bacall served to question the restrictions of linear narrative, in the New Hollywood a star's enactment of him- or herself has become sufficient justification for a movie, and performance has assumed the cohesive function previously fulfilled by narrative. The result may vary from the self-congratulatory to the self-denigrating, but it is always narcissistic. At one extreme, the films of Burt Reynolds celebrate his appearance and his mannerisms with almost total disregard for plot or characterization; all they seek to provide their audience with is two hours of Reynolds driving cars, making jokes, having fistfights and getting laid. At the other, perhaps, are the films of John Cassavetes, where the celebration of performance similarly takes precedence over dramatic structure.   In A Woman Under the Influence (1974), for example, performance is privileged to the extent that Peter Falk is allowed to repeat an improvisation word for word.   Long takes, almost exclusively shot with telephoto lenses, concentrate attention on individual performances placed in opposition to each other.   Falk and Gina Rowlands compete for the screen's attention, performing for most of the time in separate frames.   Equally, the film refuses to construct its dramatic options in the manner of any conventional scene construction or statements of character relationships.   Instead, each scene lasts as long as the performance can sustain it, and then gives way to a disconnected incident.   The scene of Rowlands' nervous collapse, for example, is played out in long takes, each of which registers a stage in the escalation of her breakdown.   But each cut marks a temporal ellipsis, since the second shot picks up the performance at a different moment in its progress from the end of the previous shot.   It is as extreme an example of the abandonment of Hollywood's principles of continuity in favor of an exclusive concentration on surface mannerisms as one might expect to find.

The opposition between one or more charismatic central performances and an impulse to narrative on the part of minor characters has been a consistent pattern in the American cinema of the 1970s.   The road movies of the early 1970s exemplify it in almost diagrammatic form.   In the pattern of Easy Rider, they depict a pair or trio of characters passing through scenes on a journey which lasts the length of the movie and gets nowhere.   The minor characters they encounter are placed in the restricted circumstances of a fixed location and a conventional obligation to furthering a narrative, which usually (e. g. , Scarecrow, 1973; dir. Jerry Schatzberg) turns out not to be that of the film.   The protagonists, on the other hand, remain free to move on when they choose, confident that the film will stay with them (Five Easy Pieces, 1970; dir. Bob Rafaelson). If as characters their movement appears pointless ("where are we going?" is a question they repeatedly ask each other), as figures in a fictional structure they are enabled, by the amount of screen time they occupy, to reveal themselves in ways that will ingratiate them with their audience.

The separable nature of such performances permitted stars to perform antisocial activities with impunity.   Beatty, O'Neal, Newman and Redford among others regularly charmed

their audiences into acquiescing in criminal activities, revealing the extent to which the obligatory moral certainties
of the Production Code's linear narratives had been discarded in favor of a self-regarding opportunism which allowed performers to act as they pleased, as free from social conventions as they were from narrative responsibilities. Bonnie and Clyde and Butch Cassidy and the Sundance
Kid present criminal activity as play for its protagonists and
its audience. The game is repeatedly spoiled by "society"
insisting on the seriousness of their actions. When it is not
the subject of Bonnie and Clyde's near-slapstick comedy,
"society" is seen as stupidly vindictive, engaging in a grotesque overkill of retaliation for the robbers' flaunting of
its conventions. Sheriff Hamer (Denver Pyle) responds to
his humiliation by the gang by hunting them down and merci-
lessly executing Bonnie and Clyde. Ivan Moss (Dub Taylor)
betrays them because Bonnie encouraged C. W. (Michael J.
Pollard) to have himself tattooed. The interplay of comedy
(in which the gang is always seen to laugh) and violence (in
which the gang is always seen to suffer) enforces the audience's emotional attachment to them, and renders other minor characters victims either of the film's comedy or its
moral condemnation. The ingratiating nature of the central
performances allows the spectator no viewpoint other than
that of the characters themselves, and the narcissistic display of style as its own justification obliges the audience to
make its judgments on the appearances with which Beatty
and Dunaway are so obsessed.

     The apparently inevitable result of such fictional
structures is a thematic preoccupation with questions of
identity. Without the security of a determinist linear narrative or the behavioral certainties of a sympathetic dramatic structure, any character's presence on the screen
has become provisional upon his or her ability to sustain
it by performance. Frequently, such performances have
appeared as processes of self-examination, whether as re-
creations of adolescent experience (American Graffiti) or
more self-consciously existentialist investigations (The Conversation). John L. Mason advances the idea that the prominence of themes of identity can be partially explained by the
fact that identity crisis is a phenomenon of adolescence, the
age gap comprising the largest sector of the audience. [7]
Christopher Lasch argues more broadly that the obsessive
concern with the self is a broader cultural issue, whose preoccupations in the past two decades have replaced the sexual
neuroses of orthodox Freudian psychology. [8] Whatever ele-

ments combine to provide its explanation, it is in any case
clear that a cinema which justifies its protagonist's right to
stay in the picture by his capacity to examine his right to
stay in the picture is practicing an overt form of narcissism
in its relationship with its audience. Ben Gazzara, in Cassavetes' The Killing of a Chinese Bookie (1976), occupies the
place of the protagonist in a film noir world, but refuses
either to further or to investigate the narrative he is provided with, preferring, at one point, to sing "I can't give
you anything but love" into a telephone.

        Commercially a figure peripheral to the Hollywood
mainstream, frequently financing his films through his acting in other people's, Cassavetes has nevertheless maintained a central place in the orthodox critical history of the
1970s. This disjunction between critical and commercial
centrality is hardly new: the voluminous critical attention
paid to Orson Welles has never been justified by the relatively meager box-office receipts of his films, while there
is hardly an article written on the oeuvre of Robert Steven-
son, the most consistently profitable director in the history
of Hollywood. What has, however, changed in recent years
is the commercial value of a critical reputation. Cassavetes',
Bob Rafaelson's, or Monte Hellman's ability to keep producing films, under however adverse circumstances, is indicative
at least of the existence of an American art cinema market.
More important, perhaps, is the continued commercial viability, throughout the 1970s, of Robert Altman, despite the
fact that none of his 11 films between M*A*S*H and Popeye
(1980) were box-office successes. 9 Perhaps more clearly
than any other American director in the decade Altman has
practiced a "personal cinema" constructed around particular
emphases in performance and an immediately recognizable
visual and aural style. His continuing career as both director and producer in the face of such sustained commercial
failure indicates the potential value of a critical reputation
in "staying at the table." It also reveals the extent to which
self-consciousness is now an integral part of Hollywood's activity, pursued and deliberately practiced by the generation
of filmmakers who emerged to prominence in the 1970s. The
"Movie Brat" generation's self-consciousness concerns both
the role they play as directors, and their apparently felt obligation to possess thematic or stylistic idiosyncrasies that
will qualify them for the status of auteur. The 1970s is the
first decade in which film criticism can be said to have had
a significant influence on Hollywood production. On occasion
the influence may be said to be direct. Most of the Movie

Brats are products of the film schools or university film
courses which burgeoned in the late 1960s and early '70s. [10]
Some of them--Martin Scorsese, Paul Schrader--taught in
them, and these directors' films consciously display their
knowledge of film history by a matrix of references and
homages to earlier films.   More indirectly, criticism has
substantially enhanced the status of the director.   In 1968,
the year after the American Film Institute was founded, Andrew Sarris published his auteurist tabulation, The American
Cinema, [11] and if the auteurist approach found little favor with
the older generation whose artistry it sought to recognize, it
did provide a model by which Hollywood could be discussed
as art, and directors brought up in its precepts could see
themselves in the role of artist.   Film criticism's extraordinary dependence on the interview has furthered this self-
conscious promotion of the director as Artist and as Star,
to the point where, in 1980, Steven Spielberg released a re-
edited "Special Edition" of Close Encounters of the Third
Kind.   If the recognition of the American cinema as a subject of serious study was a by-product of the cultural radicalism of the late 1960s, it was at least partially responsible for giving birth to the curious phenomenon of the Hollywood Art Film, which eagerly absorbed European influences
to proclaim its self-consciousness as a diluted Modernism,
and the incoherence of most of its narrative as an indicator
of its artistic integrity.

PACKAGING CONCEPTS

     The fragmentation of production coincided with the
merger of the major distribution companies with larger corporate groupings.   The period from 1966, when Gulf and
Western took over Paramount, to 1969, when Kinney National
Services merged with Warner-Seven Arts, saw an upheaval
in company ownership more substantial even that that of the
early 1930s.   The majors diversified, predominantly into
other media, or were absorbed into conglomerates attracted
by their undervalued stock, their film libraries and their
real estate.   However, the reorganization of the industry
that followed diversification was a less fundamental change
than that provoked by the Paramount decrees.   By and large,
it extended the effects of divorcement.   The merger with
other media concerns, particularly the record industry, was
in a sense only an extrapolation of the majors' post-

Paramount commitment to a power-base in distribution rather
than production, and the growth of independent production
completed a process begun in the early 1950s.

Hollywood's acquisition by conglomerates has, to a
degree, merely been the swapping of one set of distant mas-
ters for another. The new landlords of the Dream Factory,
like their predecessors, have pursued the primary motivation of profit; on occasion obtained by slum clearance projects like Kirk Kerkorian's sale of M. G. M. assets to build
a Las Vegas hotel, or the urban renewal program of Century City on the back lot of the Fox studios. But if Hollywood has shrunk physically under corporate ownership, with
its volume of production declining from 196 features in 1969
to 106 in 1978, 12 its business remains much the same, and
in one respect only have the new patterns of ownership made
a significant difference to the way it conducts that business.
The role of the mogul has been abolished: Hollywood's recent studio executives are men under different influences
from those of Warner or Cohn. They share a trait common
among corporate management, of frequent mobility of employment. Where Mayer ruled M. G. M. from 1924 to 1951,
the studio saw six different studio heads in the years between 1968 and 1979. Only Warner Brothers and Universal
had the same management team throughout the decade, 13
while career structures like that of David Picker are increasingly the norm. Picker became President of United
Artists in 1969, left to go into independent production in
1973, became head of production at Paramount in 1975, and
returned to independent production for Lorimar in 1977.
This pattern of short tenure in senior management helped
to remove the last vestiges of any identifiable studio styles.
By the mid-1970s the post-Paramount attitude of regarding
each production as a one-off event had reached a point where
none of the majors any longer possessed a recognizable identity either in its personnel or its product.

The corporate acquisitions and the economic crises
of the late 1960s occasioned the removal of the old guard.
Box-office failures combined with the spectacles of the
counter-culture (Haight-Ashbury, Chicago, Woodstock) to
offer further evidence that Hollywood's liberal consensus
was no longer adequate to the demands of a more youthful
and volatile audience. The accepted explanation was that
the industry had lost contact with its audience because
there were too many old men with too much control over
production to encourage the right material. In response,

Hollywood engaged in an unparalleled wave of parricide. Its most conspicuous victims were the last surviving moguls. Jack Warner sold his interest in the studio in 1967[14] to embark on a notably unsuccessful career in independent production. Darryl Zanuck lost the last in a series of proxy fights at Fox, and retired in 1971.[15] Between 1966 and 1973 all the majors acquired new, much younger production heads, drawn as often as not from outside the immediate confines of Hollywood. The more public search for the kid genius director concealed a more enduring palace revolution giving power to a younger generation of executives whose previous careers were most likely to have been in television, talent agencies or "creative management."* If the personnel changed, the professional ethos remained the same. Heads of production continued to insist on their ability to gauge an unstable public taste, and to argue that the nature of the industry militated against predictable profit margins.

In other areas of its financial operations, the new Hollywood was more susceptible to corporate influence. The long-term response to the financial crisis of the late 1960s was for the majors to withdraw further from direct involvement in production, concentrate on financing and distribution, and find more ways of hedging their bets over investment. Tax shelter finance became an important source of production funding in the early 1970s when bank capital was more cautious about investment in films, and it probably saved Columbia from collapse.[16] Occasionally two companies would jointly finance a large-scale production, sharing distribution rights. Of greater significance was the practice of pre-selling films to exhibitors by demanding non-refundable guarantees in advance of screenings, passing the loss on unsuccessful blockbusters like A Bridge Too Far (1977) and 1941 (1979) onto the owners of the empty theatres. In mid-decade the majors began to recognize and capitalize on the value of ancillary markets to the point where television sales in particular were commonly negotiated in advance of production, and their revenues taken into account in calculating budgets. Such mechanisms of distributor protection

*e.g., James Aubrey, former head of CBS-TV, who became President of MGM in 1969; Ted Ashley, former agent at William Morris and founder of the Ashley Famous Agency, who took over production at Warner Bros in 1977; David Begelman, co-founder with Freddie Fields of Creative Management Associates, who became Columbia's production chief in 1973.

meant that, at least for them, a film might show profit without drawing audiences. Their regular distribution fee, of 30 per cent of rentals, guaranteed them healthy windfall profits on "supergrossers," while also delaying the point at which every film was deemed to have broken even, after which the distributor would have to pay the film's producers a percentage of the profits.

Distributors negotiated from a position of strength to ensure their own stability, if necessary at the expense of exhibitors and producers alike.   Theatre owners and television companies might have to carry the can for occasional unexpected box-office failures, but producers were more consistently penalized by overhead charges, punitive deductions for going over budget and interest charges while the film was recouping its costs. [17] Although the commonly accepted notional figure for a film breaking even is 2.5 times its negative cost, on occasion distributor manipulation of figures prevented a film declaring profit up to a point well in excess of its notional break-even level.   In December 1979 Fox declared that Alien, with a negative cost of $11m, had so far earned $48m in worldwide rentals and was still $2.5m in deficit. [18] The net result of these distributor practices has been a pattern of broadly stable and increasing profitability for all the majors during the decade.   By 1980, Ned Tanen, President of Universal Theatrical Pictures, was confident enough in both the certainty of profit and the uncertainty as to how it would be earned to declare,

> ... the business projections we make for each year usually end up correct within one or two percentage points.   We end up where we thought we were going to be, but we never, ever get there the way we thought we were going to get there. [19]

Stabilized distribution economics and a mobile corporate bureaucracy are the real legacies of the crisis of the late 1960s, not, whatever Francis Ford Coppola's good intentions, greater freedom for the individual filmmaker.

The dominance of the major distributors suggests that the influence of the smaller production or production-distribution companies has been exaggerated by writers in pursuit of critical genealogies rather than economics.   In itself, the Hollywood Renaissance of 1969-71 was an inconsequential event: in search of the profitable youth film and uncertain where to find it, the studios floated independent

production companies with radical intentions (in particular
BBS and Pressman-Williams)[20] by agreeing to distribute
their product, and themselves backed a few small-budget
first features by young directors. After Easy Rider, these
were almost uniformly unsuccessful: the few "anti-
Establishment" successes at the turn of the decade were
either large-budget productions such as Little Big Man or
Carnal Knowledge, or, like Midnight Cowboy and M*A*S*H,
were made by older and more established directors.

The illusion of the Hollywood Renaissance has, on the
other hand, been of more consequence in formulating the received history of the 1970s, largely because of the allegedly
crucial influence of one man, Roger Corman, in sponsoring
the first efforts of the majority of directors who attained
critical prominence in the rest of the decade. Michael Pye
and Linda Myles, in particular, have promoted Corman's
centrality to the American cinema of the 1970s, in their
book The Movie Brats.[21] His record of success is not to
be denied: Bogdanovich, Coppola, Scorsese, Kershner,
Nicholson and Wexler all got their breaks via Corman,
while his company, New World, was the prototype for Coppola's American Zeotrope, which itself sponsored Lucas.
But Corman is (in almost any terms, but particularly economically) a peripheral figure in the film industry. Whatever claims to critical attention he may have, the nature of
Corman's low-budget operation inevitably places it outside
the orbit of the major companies, on whose omissions and
miscalculations it is to a large degree dependent. Like his
mentors Sam Arkoff and James B. Nicholson of American
International Pictures, Corman's stock-in trade has been the
exploitation of otherwise unrequited demand, whether that be
as producer of biker movies or as American distributor of
Cries and Whispers. His reasons for employing young talent
have equally always been economic. Untried directors, actors and crew eager to make their first film are cheaper
than seasoned and unionized professionals. AIP, New World
and their imitators have largely taken over the function of
B-features as the training-ground for talent the majors will
later absorb.

Corman's historical importance stems from his commercial success in the period of the majors' greatest insecurity. But his working procedures were not a solution to
Hollywood's economic problems, because they did not provide
the majors with substantial enough product. In the early
1970s they were prepared to employ anyone, even Russ

Meyer, who might provide a clue to audience taste.   By mid-
decade, they had abandoned their scruples and committed
themselves to producing and distributing the kind of overtly
sensationalist material they had previously avoided, and independents like Corman could not compete in production values
with the likes of The Omen and Carrie (both Fox, 1976).
With the decline of low-budget production, Corman's critical
cultism and his commercial reputation began to ebb.

It may be that the most significant legacy of the brief
rise of the exploitation movie in the Hollywood Renaissance
was the majors' adoption of exhibition patterns that independents like AIP had been pioneering earlier in the decade.
Saturation booking, the simultaneous release of a film into a
large number of theatres at the same time, was a standard
practice among exploitation filmmakers, whose economics required the rapid recoupment of investment.   The majors began experimenting with it in the late 1960s, shortly before
they started to use national television advertising.   Strategies
of this kind greatly increased distribution costs by expanding
publicity budgets and print costs.   Where in 1960 a maximum
of 350 prints of a film might be made, [22] by the late '70s a
movie given blockbuster treatment might require as many as
1000 prints. [23]   Expenditure on publicity now regularly exceeds a film's negative costs (Fox spent $10.8 million mak-
ing Alien, and $15.7 million advertising it).   Such market-
ing mechanisms, available only to a limited number of films
at a time, inevitably reinforce the distributors' blockbuster
mentality.   The new economics revealed themselves clearly
enough in 1971, when the year's top-grossing film, Love
Story, earned more money in domestic rentals than the next
three highest-grossers combined.

As James Monaco has pointed out, [24] what is notable
about this economic strategy is that it is an essentially conservative response to a situation of limited audiences.   The
increased expenditure on publicity, with its tacit acknowledgment that it is possible to sell a film to the public, provides
a further mechanism of distributor control.   A low-budget
production like American Graffiti may produce phenomenal
profits when measured by the ratio of rental income to negative cost (in this case of 5000 per cent). [25]   But the decision
to sell the film vigorously enough to make such earnings possible lies with the distributors, whose preference remains for
the reliable investment.   American Graffiti's success bought
George Lucas a fourteen-fold increase in budget for his next
film, Star Wars, the most remunerative movie in Hollywood

history. By comparison to American Graffiti, it yielded a
mere 1855 per cent profit on investment. 26 But it was a
product more satisfactorily geared to the logic of a corporate economics seeking market stability than the much less
predictable earnings of Lucas' earlier film. Despite the
enormous cash-flow figures of individual films, the blockbuster approach to marketing is, like all distributor mechanisms, designed to guarantee commercial stability rather
than maximize profits. In this respect, it is in the grand
tradition of Hollywood economics, where a superficial extravagance conceals a fundamental conservatism.

In contrast to the calamities of 1969-71, relatively
few blockbusters have failed to cover their negative costs in
the later 1970s, given the protection for the distributor provided by exhibitors' advance guarantees. On the other hand,
blockbuster economics have a peculiar and apparently cycli-
cal habit of getting out of control. At the outset of the cycle, unexpectedly large profits accrue to one or more films,
provoking a wave of imitations formulaically repeating the
successful film's attractive "elements." Production and
marketing budgets expand in the attempt to produce more of
the same, to a point where investment in production exceeds
any possibility of recoupment, and companies suffer heavy
losses as a result of overproduction. Retrenchment, in the
form of limitations on budgets and a drop in the number of
films produced, follows until the cycle repeats itself with
another spectacular financial success provoking imitation.
From the crash of Cleopatra in 1963 the cycle has repeated
itself twice, reaching its critical stage in 1969-71 and 1980-
81. 27 The most recent crisis, involving films such as Hur-
ricane (1979), Raise the Titanic (1980), and most notoriously
Heaven's Gate (1981) has not, however, been nearly so severe
as the previous decade's, because the major distributors have
maintained a firmer grip over expenditure, on occasion simply
deciding to write off a $22 million investment in the produc-
tion of Sorcerer (1977) rather than plough an equivalent amount
into its promotion. The losses on individual films in 1980-81
were, in any case, occurring in a broadly buoyant market.
The crisis was provoked rather by a degree of laxity in the
supervision of a number of substantial projects and the box-
office failure of a cycle of disaster movies, rather than the
complete breakdown of producers' ability to predict public
taste. The conservative blockbuster approach, with its commitment to marketing rather than production, remains fundamentally sound.

To some extent, the differences between the production methods of exploitation movies and the packaging of blockbusters is merely a question of scale. In 1955 AIP was pioneering a process of commodity packaging by constructing a film around a title and an advertising campaign. The Beast from 10,000 Leagues has mutated into American Gigolo, initially constructed around a title and John Travolta (replaced, with a drastic cut in the budget, by Richard Gere). 28   The essential change has been the mutation of the idea ("You bring me an idea," said Jack Berners. "Things are tight. We can't put a man on salary unless he's got an idea."29) into the concept ("That notion of the gigolo as a metaphor for the man who can't receive pleasure hit me and from that moment I had a metaphor that was uniquely representative of that problem.")30 The heavy emphasis on marketing strategies, combined with the absorption of distribution companies into multi-media conglomerates, has elevated the concept to a central place in contemporary Hollywood construction.   Movies no longer exist as autonomous industrial products, but are increasingly manufactured as one item in a multi-media package. Star Wars, with its toys, games and bubble-gum spin-offs, is only the extreme version of the conventional packaging of a concept as film, record, "novelization," and so on.   The use of pre-sold source material, in novel or play form, was hardly new in Hollywood, but producer Robert Evans set a precedent when he persuaded the publishers of Love Story to print 25,000 copies of the book by offering $25,000 for its promotion. 31   Integrated and jointly financed promotion campaigns became increasingly the norm in the late 1970s, by which time the hype had become almost an art-form in its own right.   The carefully orchestrated publicity campaign for Jaws ensured that the film's release just happened to coincide with widespread reporting of shark sightings around the American coast.   Timing in such complex campaigns could be crucial in other areas, too. The disaster for Star Wars had nothing to do with the film. It was in not having the children's toys in the stores in time for Christmas.

This process of multi-media packaging has effectively substituted for the studio in the placement of an individual film.   Instead of being part of a balanced cluster of films produced out of the same studio, it has become one of a group of products occupying different places in the media web.   Likely to be the most profitable individual element, the status of the movie has nevertheless been diminished by a need for formal compromise with the demands of other

products. In its construction, its producers have been obliged to consider the possibilities for its exploitation as a
series of linked but separate commodites, and to compile
their package accordingly.

As Hollywood terminology the package has a more
specific meaning relating to the assembly of a production.
Stars, script (or concept), and less frequently a director or
producer, are "packaged" by a talent agency or an independent producer, and this package is then offered to one of the
majors for financial backing or a distribution deal. Apart
from its tendency to de-emphasize narrative, such an assembly procedure is no more novel than the pre-sold source,
but it is another function formerly performed by the studios
and now dispersed among a more amorphous body. Packages can be initiated by a wide variety of sources, and it is
contemporary Hollywood folk wisdom that more time and effort is spent in the arrangement of the packages than in the
resulting film, the process being made more complicated
than previous systems of production by the competing interests of the various individuals involved. As Joan Didion put
it in her essay "In Hollywood,"

> ... to understand whose picture it is one needs to
> look not particularly at the script but at the deal
> memo. [32]

She provides an acute analysis of the aesthetics of
the deal:

> The action itself is the art form, and is described
> in aesthetic terms: "A very imaginative deal,"
> they say, or, "He writes the most creative deals
> in the business." ... The action is everything, ...
> the picture itself is in many ways only the action's
> by-product. [33]

The deal mentality is the result of uncertainty; many
more films obtain money for development costs than go into
production, and each individual, to stay in reasonably frequent work, needs to be involved in several projects at the
same time in the expectation that one of them will come to
fruition. This is particularly true for independent producers, whose income generally comes from profits rather than
project development money, and who must therefore gamble
on as many deals as he or she can keep going. Deal psychology has also facilitated--as well as in part being caused

by--the predominance of agents in contemporary production. The speculative and negotiating skills needed by the producer as deal-maker have much more in common with those of the talent agent than they do with the organizational and financial abilities required by a studio producer. Since the deal was inaugurated by Arthur Krim and Robert Benjamin of United Artists in 1951, the dividing line between agent and producer has become ever thinner, and the occasions on which the agent has become the producer more common. The most grandiose version of this occurred in 1962, when MCA was forced by the Department of Justice to abandon its talent agency activities and took over Universal,[34] but the list of former agents who have become producers or heads of production is almost endless, and it is these figures who supply and maintain the deal mentality, and the insecurity it breeds.

While Didion's recognition of the substantial irrelevance of the final product to the processes of its packaging is further evidence of the New Hollywood's narcissism and incoherence, it should not in itself be seen as evidence of a decline. Packaging is no more detrimental to film production than the modes of organization it has replaced; those, like James Monaco and Pauline Kael,[35] who insist on seeing it as such have essentially failed to recognize that Hollywood never existed to make films, but rather to make people go to the movies. Like the studio system, the goal of packaging is the production of entertainment; like the studio system, packaging functions as an arrangement for reducing emphasis on the role of the content in what is being sold. The logic of media conglomeration has widened the marketplace in which the product is sold. It is now as tangibly on offer in book- and toy-stores as it is in movie theatres. In the process, its nature has changed.

The aesthetics of the deal have combined curiously with the critical enhancement of the director's status to produce, in the work of Spielberg, Lucas, De Palma and Milius, films which at the same time demonstrate a "personal cinema" through their mannerisms and operate the mechanistic structures that James Monaco has aptly identified as those of an "entertainment machine,"[36] much less concerned than earlier movies with telling their audience a story. Repeated assertions that the story is seldom a central element in deal-making indicate the extent to which narrative has been dethroned. Steven Spielberg suggests,

> What interests me more than anything else is the
> idea. If a person can tell me the idea in twenty-
> five words or less, it's going to make a pretty
> good movie. [37]

But it is unlikely to be a film in which narrative reaches
any great level of complexity, something which is clearly
true of all Spielberg's films, which comprise situations allowing for plenty of spectacle but little plot development.

The speed with which narrative declined as a force
in the movies in the 1970s may be indicated by looking at
the decade's one contribution to Hollywood's repertoire of
genres, the disaster film. Disaster movies are contemporary, debased epics, but more importantly they represent
the archetypal package vehicle, the instrument the majors
found for spending their money on predictably appealing
spectacle. As a genre, they share neither an iconographic
nor a narrative consistency, but rather an assembly of elements: stars in emotional conflict, sustained in crisis by a
physically restricting situation. Airport, the first success
of the disaster cycle, established a conventional pattern by
which the audience is attached to the narrative by its concern for individual characters. Later variants overtly dis-
located the competing elements that Airport successfully held
in tension. Airport and its sequels maintain a linear (if
circular) narrative: the survival of its characters is attached to the fate of the aircraft. All of them survive or
perish together, however big or small their billing. The
Poseidon Adventure (1973) is much more selective. Not
only does its situation manage to dispose of all the minor
characters (they are drowned en masse 45 minutes into the
film), but it also permits spectacle to be detached from any
plot obligation. Random incident determines the fate of individual characters: Shelley Winters has a heart attack,
Stella Stevens falls into a burning oil slick. Since the plot
itself cannot develop--either some or all of these characters
will survive or they won't--relations between characters are
required to fill in the gaps between the film's spectacular
occurrences. Because the situation supplies them with so
little to sustain dialogue ("how do we get out of here?",
"where do we go next?") and the need to make the right
choice to stay in the movie, they have to talk about something else. Hence the amount of time given over to discussing how fat Winters is, and the unprovoked bellligerent
exchanges between Gene Hackman and Ernest Borgnine.

The result is an overt and unintegrated application of sentiment, most apparent in Winters when for no good reason she
remarks to her husband, Jack Albertson, "Manny, how long
is it since we told each other I love you?" At her death
she repeats the same function with a more explicitly symbolic purpose, as she gives Hackman the Jewish sign for Life
she has brought for her grandson. Separable incidents such
as these provide an arbitrary and imposed meaning for the
action, which otherwise remains spectacularly independent of
significance.

Irwin Allen's next production, The Towering Inferno
(1974, Fox and Warner Bros, a package assembled by Creative Management Associates), carries the process further,
eliminating narrative altogether and substituting a game pattern of random incident and problem-solving for its characters. The film's introduction establishes a number of potentially complex character relationships with a thematic issue,
mainly revolving around the complicity of William Holden and
Richard Chamberlain in the breaching of safety codes. These
are hastily abandoned once the fire breaks out, and are used
instead to confirm characters' positions. Chamberlain becomes the film's bad guy, Holden's moral ambiguity is simply
forgotten in the confusion. Where in The Alamo the survivors represent the hope of the future, the best Holden can offer by way of moral summary at the end of The Towering
Inferno is, "All I can do is pray to God that I can stop this
from ever happening again." The film operates the mechanisms of earlier narrative forms--Jennifer Jones' cat becomes a sentimental object embodying loss when O. J. Simp-
son gives it to Fred Astaire at the end--but operates them
detached from a continuous narrative. The film is a series
of disconnected exchanges between characters interrupted by
the spectacle of the fire. Its packaging revolves round its
situation and its consortium of stars. Characters are paired
off in the introduction, offering a multiplicity of separate
stories which the film may or may not choose to develop.
The quantity on offer permits the film to dispose of some of
them at random: Robert Wagner's clandestine affair with
Susan Flannery ends abruptly when they become the first
victims of the fire; Jennifer Jones arbitrarily falls to her
death. Any character or story is available for sacrifice
without disrupting the spectacle, and the only guarantee for
survival is star status. * By the same token, individual

---

*Even this can be no security. Gene Hackman   (cont.)

scenes operate as separate and complete units in themselves, unconnected to the rest of the film. Paul Newman, Jones and two children spent ten minutes negotiating a demolished staircase, an incident quite detached from events occurring elsewhere and getting them, literally, nowhere. Immediately afterwards they discover their route down is barred, and have to climb up again.

The film revolves around creating incidents engineered by an arbitrary chance, such as the cement which blocks the door into the party room. No adequate explanation is offered for its presence, no justification required except that it provides grounds for another scene. Its placement is as fortuitous as that of the wall-light which Newman uses as a foothold to climb up to the pipeshaft in the same scene. Instead of seeking narrative continuity, the film is constructed like a set, with each group of characters isolated in their own area. What provides its coherence is not any sense of continuity or character development (the characters actually get simpler as the film progresses, and moral status is finally reduced to how well each character behaves when he or she stands in line for the bosun's chair), but the performances of its stars. Richard Dyer has commented on the importance of the stable camera and the stars' charisma in making the audience secure as they witness a disaster,[38] but the stars' performances have another function as well. They--particularly Newman and McQueen, but also Holden--are the only sources of coherence in a film whose content is concerned with collapse, destruction, and deconstruction. Against this, the stars' fulfillment of their industrial, commercial function directs the film away from a concern with loss, death, pain and money to a celebration of its performers, whose presence is necessary to justify and explain away everything else in the film. The audience witness performance as they witness spectacle, and since neither proposes causal relationships between consecutive events, they must accept arbitrariness in the film's plot progression.

---

sacrifices himself at the end of The Poseidon Adventure in a conventionally heroic gesture. In Earthquake Charlton Heston and Ava Gardner are swept away by floodwater in the final scene, conveniently saving Heston from choosing between Gardner, his wife, and Genevieve Bujold, his mistress. What star status does guarantee is survival until almost the end of the movie.

> The impression of arbitrariness in the reporting of
> disaster reinforces the arbitrary quality of experi-
> ence itself, and the absence of continuity in the
> coverage of events, as today's crisis yields to a
> new and unrelated crisis tomorrow, adds to the
> sense of historical discontinuity--the sense of liv-
> ing in a world in which the past holds out no guid-
> ance to the present and the future has become
> completely unpredictable. [39]

Although Christopher Lasch's remarks are primarily
directed against the news media, they apply equally to the
narrative structures of packaged blockbusters. A variety of
psycho-sociological explanations for the disaster movie phenomenon have been offered, [40] and they can readily enough be
identified as part of a larger conglomeration of films (including the science fiction packages which replaced them and horror films) which explore the bourgeois American hero's confrontation with the Unknown. This general emphasis seems
at first sight almost too easy to identify as a significant cinematic response to the circumstances of the 1970s. Specify-
ing what provokes such heroic insecurity is, however, rather
more difficult, particularly in a critical climate dominated by
psychosexual interpretations (the shark in Jaws as both phal-
lus and vagina dentata). [41] What has been less frequently
pointed out is the aptness of the disaster movie as a metaphor for the film industry's own situation. Faced, at the
beginning of the decade, with economic catastrophe and uncertainty about audience demand, Hollywood responded by
abandoning the structures of narrative continuity that had
previously served it so well, and inaugurating a cycle of
speculative investments in disaster in which the only security, for audience and industry alike, came from star performances. The Unknown in these films is not merely contained in their content, but also in the way they are put together out of separable elements. Later variants of the
package took the phenomenon to even greater extremes.
Close Encounters of the Third Kind makes no attempt to connect its scenes or explain itself. As a narrative it is incomprehensible, as a story it spends two-and-a-half hours
getting to the point at which a 1950s science fiction movie
would begin. The Unknown in the American cinema of the
1970s is, more than anything else, a matter of narrative
structure, a question of what commercial cinema should do
if it is not to tell stories. Both the initial problem and
its apparent solution came from the new instrument of
consensus, television.

TELEVISION AND THE NEW WASTE SPACE

If the immediate commercial impact of television has been exaggerated, its long-term, aesthetic effects have hardly been considered. In part this has been because of an unsurprising critical neglect: the products of television have generally been dismissed and, to a degree, television's existence as a more contemptible form has permitted the serious study of film, now lifted one rung from the bottom of the cultural ladder of respectability. It is also, however, related to the formal assumptions that have been made about the structures of television, and its apparent low-rent emulation of the movies. A one-hour episode of Starsky and Hutch is seen as imitating, in its formulaic narrative, a Republic B film, with little to suggest innovation. Television's influence on the cinema, either economically or aesthetically, is seen as impoverishing, and best abandoned for consideration of more amenable concerns. In fact, television's influence on the recent cinema has been decisive. First, by usurping the cinema's consensual role, it has obliged film, for the first time, to define itself and its function in opposition to a more popular medium. Secondly, it has promulgated new aesthetic structures, offering redefinitions of the presentation of space and the relationship of performance to narrative that the movies have been unable to ignore.

The impact of television on the American cinema was gradual: its first effects came with the employment in the late 1950s of directors, scriptwriters, and technicians who had served their apprenticeship in television drama rather than in B movies. Directors such as Penn, Ritt, Lumet and Frankenheimer saw the move into theatrical film as a liberation from the confines of a relatively inflexible medium, and the potential consequences of their training were largely concealed by the conservative nature of the areas of television from which they came. Television drama conformed, in the main, to the patterns of linear dramatic narrative acquired from Hollywood and Broadway. The cinema meant larger budgets, more sophisticated equipment, and, to some extent, a greater freedom of expression. Change, too, was tempered by the existence of a consensual rhetoric with which the new generation felt confortable: in their sentiments and mannerisms, Ritt's films are little different from the contemporaneous work of Kazan. Most importantly, the spatial polarity of long shot and close-up had been introduced by processes and personnel whose careers had been entirely within film production. The first TV generation merely reinforced that rhetoric with their own experience.

The radical aesthetic possibilities of television, the novel narrative, optical and spatial devices it invented, were also not immediately adopted by the cinema because these devices were initially developed in areas of television production that seemed outside Hollywood's interest--that were, indeed, commonly regarded as culturally the least redeemable of television's activities. It is an underrated truism that all television aspires to the condition of soap opera, since with soap opera television adopted from radio a genuinely new narrative form. The formal unit of television, as Raymond Williams has convincingly argued, [42] is not the individual program but the larger viewing block, whether that be afternoon or prime-time programming. The objective of programming is not to gain the audience's attention for a single program event, but rather to catch it for the station's evening output. In this respect, television seeks to engage its audience with an endless fictive experience, which is precisely the unique quality of soap opera narrative. The nature of so open-ended a narrative structure obliges it to avoid resolution; inevitably, therefore, it constructs itself around a situation involving multiple characters, each of whom can be involved in individual stories of varying duration, which can achieve individual resolution without affecting the overall structure. Small communities or institutions such as hospitals, newspapers, or even television studios lend themselves ideally to this kind of structure. Similarly, in these terms of narrative construction, there is no essential difference between the serial--soap opera proper, which tells a continuous, overlapping sequence of stories (e. g. Coronation Street, All My Children)--and the series, which involves a stable group of characters in discrete stories begun and concluded in a single episode (Rawhide, The Virginian, Starsky and Hutch). Unlike film serials of the 1940s, however, neither television series nor serial is permitted an eventual plot goal (the Rawhide cattle drive never ends), since to achieve a final resolution would be to conclude the series, potentially before the end of its financial viability. Narrative tension is, as a result, directed away from the overall conclusion towards the immediate event. The multiple-character narratives of disaster films imitate the structures of soap opera. Love Story, in beginning at its ending and displacing interest from the victim to the survivor, similarly employs the narrative devices of the TV series.

Television series commonly reveal the redundancy of their story-lines in their final "wrap-up" scenes which follow the conclusion of the episode's plot. The central characters are re-established in their normal milieu, and shown to be immune from the consequences of the narrative they have just participated in. This immunity from narrative pressure, which blesses every leading series character, has important consequences for the relationship between audience and television event. By discounting narrative resolution television privileges performance: this can be seen in its concern with pure performance events, such as game shows and sports events. The argument that most television is barren and banal is convincing only if it is presumed to be primarily a narrative form; if it is recognized that much of television's output is geared not to the telling of stories but to the presentation of performance, then the repetitious nature of its narrative structures becomes comprehensible and arguably beneficial.

The liberal consensus, like its populist predecessor, stressed narrative over performance. Both were primarily concerned with the consequences of their characters' actions, rather than with the nature of those actions themselves. The structures of television defer attention away from consequence. In soap opera there are no ultimate consequences because there are no ultimate goals, so the consequences of any individual action are reduced in importance. One formalist approach to narrative construction, favoured by Vladimir Propp and Joseph Breen alike, is to view the narrative as a series of choices offered to its various characters. Most analysis, from the Hays Code to Robin Wood, has sought to place those choices in a moral context and award praise or blame according to the consequences. But television structures have devalued consequence by eliminating its threat, and have instead focused attention on the process of choice, rather than on its results. Characters and audiences are required to make choices, but as they are immune from narrative, they are unaffected by the results of those choices. Television requires a constant flow of events and change, and as the consequences of choice are reduced, the obligation to choose, to engage the process of choice, becomes greater. The clearest illustration of this is perhaps in those infamous games shows of the 1960s in which contestants did not in fact receive the fabulous prizes they were seen to have won, but were instead paid a fee for their participation: what was then being presented was the illusion of material acquisition via choice (in answering questions, or guessing numbers) but what was actually offered to the audience was the performance of choice.

While Hollywood possessed a secure sense of narrative progression (and while television was still involved in the evolution of its own structures), film remained relatively untouched by these developments. Method acting, in its emphasis in practice on mannerist styles, placed noticeable and undue stress on performance for its own sake, and indeed the cinema of Dissent made much play with the oppositional nature of performance from a cinema predominantly committed to the integrated subservience of performance to narrative. But even under the liberal consensus these tensions were resolved within an overwhelmingly linear narrative comprehension. Clearly, the fact of the presence of Tracy, Hepburn and Poitier is central to the functioning of Guess Who's Coming to Dinner (the last substantial financial success of the unreconstructed liberal consensus), but they perform in the established consensual tradition as recognizable representatives of their audience, integrated into a narrative argument that manoeuvres itself, via them, towards its inevitable conclusion. By contrast, Elliott Gould's performance in Altman's California Split (1974) works constantly to disrupt the narrative that his co-star George Segal is attempting to construct. Gould's performance consists in discrete routines --the most obvious is his "one-armed piccolo-player" joke-- which prevent both Segal and the audience from building a coherent story. By the end of the film, when they go to Reno for the big poker game, Gould's interference has reached such a pitch that Segal orders him out of the game. The camera, revealingly, stays with Gould and leaves Segal to work out the story offscreen.

If television engineered the decline of narrative by its promotion of performance, it emphasized performance by its promotion of new spatial articulations. The space of television is more limited and less malleable than cinematic space, the result of the smaller size and restricted resolution of the image. Certain compositions and spatial arrangements suit the television image much more satisfactorily than others. In general, TV has little use for deep focus photography, since it resolves detail at a distance comparatively poorly. Conversely, both the shape and quality of the image are well suited to shots of individual figures, from waist shots to extreme close-ups. The conventional observation that television is a medium of close-ups does not, however, take the argument far enough. In particular, it is important to

recognize the general use of shallow planes of focus in the
television image. By comparison to cinema, and especially
Panavision, the television image concentrates the viewer's
attention on a single object, commonly shown in spatial isolation, to be regarded by itself rather than in its context.
TV manufactures what might be called a non-space, that is,
a context which contains no referents of its own, but merely
provides a neutral background in front of which objects are
placed. This is most evident in continuity studios, where a
fixed camera produces a standard chest-high close-up of the
presenter, with a cyclorama background providing a variety
of neutral colors. The construction of chat-show sets reveals
the same phenomenon. They provide spaces which resemble
nothing but the sets of other chat-shows. The layout of easy
chairs and an occasional table between them is not an attempt
to recreate a living room, but rather an arrangement designed
for the most convenient presentation by studio cameras of
close-ups of its participants, with the minimum furnishing
necessary for the presentation of an introductory full shot.

    This obviation of space has other consequences. The
shallow television image revises visual rhetoric. While
reverse-angle over-the-shoulder shots are still possible using
two TV cameras, they cannot readily be presented using wide-
angle or even normal lenses, since the cameras are liable to
fall within each other's visual field. The problem is solved
by the use of telephoto lenses, which remove the cameras
further from the performers and, by their inherently shal-
lower depth of field, tend to emphasize the limited, planar
focus of the TV image. The problem is also solved by the
use of frontal camera positions which divide the space of a
sound stage between the set, belonging to the performers,
and the spatial preserve of the cameras. Where the single
film camera could enter the set without photographing itself,
three or more simultaneously operating TV cameras are obliged to keep out of each other's fields of vision, and the requirements of this arrangement encourage the physical separation of cameras from performers along with strict demar-
cations of the areas in which each can operate. This, too,
inhibits the use of wide-angle shots, except for establishing
purposes. Together with the image's preference for close-
ups, the multiple camera arrangement encourages the use of
telephoto lenses to produce its images, and this, in turn, reinforces the propensity to shallow-focus images and the concentration on the single object.

    Such technological restrictions are of course only

directly applicable to live or electronically recorded television; largely because of the involvement of the major studios in television production since the mid 1950s, American TV has made greater use of filmed material than is common in other countries. Theoretically, the limitations I have mentioned do not apply to filmed material. But in practice the principal restriction, image size and resolution, remains in force, and the strategies of filmed material, though more flexible than studio-based recording techniques, follow similar broad patterns, particularly in the choice of lenses. Indeed, the multiple camera set-up has become a common arrangement in the production of both films-for-TV and feature films, recreating, in effect, the situation of the TV studio on the film set.

In much the same way that technological advances in the late 1930s made possible deep-focus cinematography and created a new idiom, the development of telephoto lenses under the impetus of television's necessity encouraged their use in the cinema. This trend, which became evident by the mid-1960s, was in contrast to the inherently wide-angle formulations of the CinemaScope process, and had to await the production of telephoto optics suitable to the widescreen system. The same held true for the other optical development for which television is responsible, the zoom lens. Although zooms existed prior to television, it provided the spur to their sophistication and improvement, since the zoom made possible recomposition without camera movement. This was of great benefit both to bulky studio TV cameras and in TV news-reporting, initially the preserve of lightweight 16mm cameras (the development of which was largely the result of television's demand for such equipment). The optical advances of both telephoto and zoom lenses were adopted by filmmakers although, as with other aesthetic effects of television, their impact was considerably delayed.

By the mid-1960s a visual aesthetic for television had been formulated, even if it was seldom consciously acknowledged. It provided a different, fundamentally simpler, articulation of images and space than that of the cinema. Its primary tool was the telephoto close-up, concentrating attention on a single object in a limited spatial context, but it had other ramifications. The arrangement of studio space encouraged the juxtaposition of shots taken with lenses of noticeably different focal lengths, so that a consistency of perspective presentation was not, for television, the normative convention that it was in the cinema of both consensuses.

The deep-focus quality of wide-angle lenses became subordinate to their more functional role in presenting the maximum view of a limited space, and images of quite different natures, from wide-angle to telephoto shots, were juxtaposed without significant implication.

Television discarded another of Hollywood's basic conventions. In classical Hollywood narrative, characters do not address the camera/audience directly. Our gaze is seldom met by characters in the fiction, a convention which allows the audience unselfconscious access to a fiction declaring its own transparency. Television on the other hand, constantly addresses its viewer directly and, in news programs at least, employs direct address as an instrument of transparency. We are more convinced that what we see is not a fiction but a neutral rendering of events by the newscaster's ability to look us in the eye as he or she informs us. This form of direct address is itself made possible by the simplicity of televisual space. The viewer does not have the perceptual problem of resolving two separate but equally visually complex spaces--the corporeal space he occupies and the space on the screen. Instead, he is presented with an abstraction of space on the screen (the announcer against a flat background), which is integrated into the visually evident space of the room in which his TV set is located. The cinema, by taking place in the dark, renders the spectator's corporeal space visually insecure and undetailed, and then substitutes for that space a recognizable space on the screen. Television inverts this relationship by inserting simple images into the pre-existing context of the known corporeal space of the viewer's home. The simplicity of television space permits a form of direct address which is derived from TV's industrial origins in radio rather than from the cinema. In much television programming sound is the more important instrument of communication while the image--of a newscaster, or in a chat show--is substantially redundant.

The possibility of direct address stresses performance, and on occasion obliges it. The newscaster provides a performance of a series of events normally assumed to exist independently of his performance of them. The convention of direct address is one example of the stress on performance required by the simplicity of television space. As television simplfies space, it also simplifies narrative, since it cannot articulate the complexity of spatial relationships which is so central a tool of the cinema. This, as much as the formulaic nature of television production, results in the repetitious banality of its narrative constructions. All television space is safe space, permitting the production of performances separable from the narratives that facilitate but do not contain them. Televisual space is inherently narcissistic in its prvileging of performance.

The second ramification of television's simplified image structure is an increase in the rate of cutting. The simpler an image is, the less time is needed to observe it fully--simply a reversal of the logic of deep focus. Deprived of the possibility of visual complexity, television promotes an aesthetic of temporal density of images, involving much faster rates of cutting than were conventional in the cinema. The rapid juxtaposition of images, combined with the use of varied perspectives among those images, has the effect of decreasing spatial perception. The occupation of space becomes less significant, because both the space being presented and the occupation of it are more provisional because more temporary. At the same time the television image is itself highly mobile. The camera zooms, tracks, pans, tilts almost incessantly, keeping the image in motion in order to counteract its limited information. As a result of this obligation to movement, recomposing the image becomes an end in itself, no longer subservient to the dramatic requirements of the action it is representing. The camera instead seeks a visceral endorsement of the action on the part of the viewer by providing, through mobile images and rapid cutting, an immediacy of sensory response to the image stream rather than a cohesive contribution to the narrative. The time span of television is shorter than that of cinema, not only in its programming units, but, and in many ways more consequentially, in the duration and stability of its images. These qualities of television are the more evident the shorter the temporal unit they are located within; and most evident of all in credit sequences and advertisements, where the necessity of immediate impact (a pressure exerted on all television to a much greater extent than in more modulated cinema narratives) is greatest.

It was inevitable that the movies would eventually incorporate elements of this aesthetic into their own practices, especially since in many respects TV's spatial presumptions concurred with the abandonment by the prevailing liberal consensus of the medium shot in favor of the polarity of long shot and close-up. Although it is possible to find earlier sporadic examples of their uses, Hollywood did not adopt the devices of perspective dislocation, rapid rates of cutting

and the zoom lens until they coincided with an appropriate
cultural conjunction, in the image-obsessed mid- to late-
1960s. Perhaps the earliest consistent practitioner was
Richard Lester, the first figure of a second generation of
TV-trained directors, whose experience had included non-
dramatic television production and, probably even more
significant, advertising. His films with the Beatles, A
Hard Day's Night and Help!, stressed this quality of images chosen for immediate, sensory impact, and cohered
that mechanism into a style which was linked to the presentation of music. Lester's films inaugurated the youth
film cycle, separating such films off from the much more
conventionally structured rock 'n' roll and beach party
films of the previous decade, or the stereotyped musical
vehicles for Presley and his imitators. Music in Lester's
films functioned not as a non-narrative interlude but as an
anti-narrative event, which rendered its films' plots both
irrelevant and absurd, and emphasized performance to the
absolute exclusion of plot progression. As a result they
were regarded, and in a sense dismissed, as comedies (the
comedy has always had a more contingent relationship to
narrative than any other cinematic form). To that extent,
although they inaugurated a cycle and served as the prototype for a style, they did not provide a narrative model for
its employment. That distinction probably belongs to The
Graduate, where the stylistic anarchy of the Beatles films
was attached to a content overtly concerned with breaching
social convention. Although the pyrotechnics of The Graduate's editing have not survived even in Nichols' own work
(e. g. , Day of the Dolphin, 1973), the spatial and temporal
revisions of cinematic structure they indicated have remained
as central a feature of the uncertain cinema of the 1970s as
the intensity of emphasis on performance.

NO ENTRY: OUTSIDE THE UNAVAILABLE TEXT

The economic importance of a film's sale to television became a significant factor in production accounting during the 1970s, and an element in multi-media packaging.
But the effect of a sale to television is not limited to a budget calculation. TV sales have been one of a number of en-
couragements not to make films in black and white. Where
the competition with television was a reason for the widespread use of color from the early 1950s, Hollywood's ac-

climatization to the rival medium's demands since the introduction of color TV has made the decision to film in color
an almost automatic one, with exceptions being the result of
specific aesthetic decision by the filmmakers.

The prospect of sales to television has also affected
composition. Its economic importance may well have proved
a significant influence in the decline of extreme widescreen
processes and the partial standardization of the Panavision
ratio of 1:1.85. This, at least, is a format that can accommodate the dual composition necessary if a film is to be
designed with television in mind. Television will accommodate barely half of the full CinemaScope frame, and compositions which occupy the whole width of the frame are muti-
lated by the reduction required by TV, as a screening of any
of Nicholas Ray's 'Scope films demonstrates all too painfully.
The common solution, when the problem is not ignored completely, is a mode of dual composition which frames for both
screen shapes, concentrating the significant material of the
shot in the area encompassed by the television frame. Alternatively, the cinema frame is masked to eliminate the top
and bottom of the eventual TV image. Either method implies that up to half the picture area is narratively super-
fluous, and the space it is presenting is redundant.

The new waste space has become a significant element in American cinematic construction during the 1970s,
at least in part the invention of television's necessity. The
influence of that necessity is not, however, simply a matter
of reducing the precision of composition within the cinema
frame. The provisional nature of that frame reduces the
narrative role of spatial articulation. If the frame is industrially encouraged to compose itself so that half the
space in it is redundant to the narrative, the film will have
to turn to structural devices other than the articulation of
space in order to establish its coherence. When, at the
same time, developments in optical technology have concentrated on lenses that present space in perspectives perceptually different to those of the human eye, the narrative
centrality of spatial articulation becomes even more tenuous.
Extreme telephoto and wide-angle lenses appear to distort
perspective to an extent that requires the audience to recognize the space they present as irredeemably different from
space as perceived outside the cinema. The zoom lens
takes this process further by for the first time devising a
movement of the image which is impossible for the human
eye: increasing or decreasing the size of an object in the

image field without physical movement. When these technological advances and the encouragement to redundant space
brought about by television were connected to a consensual
image system that itself declined the use of space as a
major signifying system, the pressure on filmmakers to construct scenes around some principle other than spatial cohe-
sion became irresistible.

The importance of this development cannot be over-
emphasized. "Classical" Hollywood narrative, and the consensus that it practiced, was above all defined by its articulation of space and its benevolent placement of the spectator both inside and outside the dramatic arena it presented.
Even in its presentation of safe performance space, it invited the audience's participation: the camera almost always
dances with Gene Kelly. This location of the audience both
inside and outside the fiction (identifying with the characters
but possessed of superior knowledge to them) was posited on
the representation of cinematic space as a dramatic arena
which the spectator, via the camera, could enter and move
through with impunity. Hollywood's representation of space
denied the spectator's voyeurism. Once that system of representation was fractured by new optics and the stress on
performance, the audience could no longer be presented with
images they could innocently consume. The viewer became
voyeur to the performer's narcissism and the pattern of audience response made possible by the unity of inside and outside was broken. Viewers merely witnessed fictions from
an increasing distance down a telephoto lens, or else found
themselves trapped inside the fiction, under constant threat
from its distorted images. The liberal polarity between
close-up and long shot veered towards a further extreme in
the opposition of telephoto and wide-angle lens. Normative
perspective, a central prop of classical Hollywood narrative,
became a thing of the past.

The camera itself, along with performers and spectators, became more self-conscious. One result of this,
evident in the films of Bogdanovich, Kubrick, Spielberg and
Polanski among others, was the appearance of an essentially
separable aesthetic of photographic beauty. Shots claimed
their place in films like Close Encounters, Barry Lyndon
and Chinatown through their appearance as attractive images
rather than through their narrative function. Through the
use of special effects, ultra-fast lenses and processes such
as Chem Tone, the pictures themselves, rather than their
content, become the object of spectacle. While in one sense

this emphasis on photographic beauty (and its enhancement of the cinematographer's status) is simply a variant of the traditional Hollywood principle of "putting money on the screen," it does so in a way that once again works against the images' contribution to a coherent and developing narrative.

Francis Ford Coppola's two Godfather films exhibit an intense fascination with the polished surfaces of dark wood. Reflection, chiaroscuro, and the isolation of figures in the frame by surrounding them with blackness are the dominant visual devices. The films are also extremely static, consisting in long takes from a normally immobile camera. *
The scenes of the Senate Investigating Committee hearings in Godfather II, for example, are all shot from a single fixed camera position. The film cuts between alternating shots of each half of the courtroom, even presenting close-ups from this single viewpoint slightly above and to the side of the action. The extreme restrictions Coppola imposes on the audience's visual access to the scene exclude them from a comfortable sense of participation in the action, and locate them firmly on the outside of the fictive world in which the film's performance is being staged. Although the static quality of Coppola's compositions is consistent across his films (e. g., The Conversation), it is at its most evident in the studied immobility of Godfather II. Throughout the half of the film which deals with Michael Corleone the limitation on the spectator's viewpoint, so noticeable in the Senate Committee scene, is maintained. Frequently the camera is placed on one side of a room and left to cut along limited angles for the duration of the scene. The film denies the audience physical access to the events they witness, and that denial contributes significantly to the incomprehensibility of its narrative. The film refuses to explain its plot, and leaves the audience to find their own way through it.

Godfather II is constructed around the opposition between a chronological series of events from the early life of Vito Corleone (Robert De Niro), and a much more complete sequential narrative of a power struggle between his son Michael (Al Pacino) and a rival crime organization. Several

---

*The predominance of dark static images in both films may well account for the unexpectedly small audiences Coppola's rearranged version, Mario Puzo's The Godfather: The Complete Novel for Television, drew when NBC screened it in November 1977. 43

critics have found in this structure a dialectic which demonstrates "that the benefits of the family structure and the hope
for community have been destroyed by capitalism."44 If it
is a dialectical structure, then it is one in which half the
synthesis is extremely simple. While the Michael half of
the film is riddled with plot, cross-plot and sub-plot, Vito's
elliptical story is transparent, despite--or perhaps because
of--its dialogue being largely in Italian.* Orphaned by ven-
detta, he arrives in America aged nine. Sixteen years later,
he is married with his first son and encounters Fanucci, the
Black Hand. Some time after this, he is initiated into petty
crime. Later (long enough for him to have had two more
sons), Fanucci demands a commission on Vito's criminal
profits and Vito instead makes him "an offer he don't refuse."
An indeterminate time after that, we see him solving domestic disputes in Little Italy and establishing his olive oil im-
porting business. Our last sight of him is on a family visit
to Sicily, where he kills his parents' murderer. Each of
these episodes is separated in time, although by precisely
how long can only be determined by guessing at the ages of
his children. Equally, there is no reference to the transitional events that occur between episodic scenes. In particular, no explanation is provided for Vito's rise to community
power after the killing of Fanucci. The scenes, bathed in
warm soft-focus browns, present instead an idyllic image of
familial affection in strong visual contrast to the pervasive
cold darkness of Michael's habitat. What is omitted, by way
of explication, from Vito's story is as important to its placement in relation to Michael's as what we do see. The absence of any critique of Vito, and its substitution by nostalgic image-making, encourages us to see his acts of violence
against Fanucci and Don Ciccio as justified and liberating.
Similarly, Robert De Niro's performance as Vito is gestural-
ly ingratiating for the audience: he smiles a good deal, is
demonstrably affectionate with his children ("Michael, your
father loves you very much," he says when he takes the baby
in his arms after killing Fanucci), and performs physically
heroic actions whose morality nothing else in his story permits us to question. By contrast, Al Pacino alienates the
audience by his distant reserve from the characters around
him and by his lack of physical grace.

---

*Vito's scenes are also somewhat more mobile, but even
here Coppola indulges his Griffith-like inclination to present
tableaux.

Michael's half of the film is not merely inaccessible through its central performance or its bleak and frequently very dark images. It has a plot of Byzantine complexity to which the audience is allowed no clear access. The mutual loyalties of various characters--Hyman Roth, Frankie Pentangeli, Fredo, even Tom Hagen--are in doubt until the final resolution, when all those convicted of disloyalty are killed. Senator Geary's involvement with the death of the Las Vegas prostitute is not accounted for. Only Michael seems to know what is going on, and he vouchsafes that information neither to other characters nor to the audience: (he tells Roth that Pentageli tried to kill him, and Pentageli that it was Roth). We witness a complex story constructed around a central character unwilling to keep us informed of its progress, but apparently capable of acts of immense and unseen power (as when Pentageli immediately changes his decision to testify on the appearance, with Michael, of his Italian brother). Michael's psychology is inaccessible to the spectator, while his father's is transparent. Michael's exercise of power, on the other hand, is conspicuously indicated, while Vito's takes place in the spaces between the episodes we witness--his only authoritarian act, against the landlord, is the opportunity for the film's one comic scene.

The audience devotes most of its attention to attempting to follow the plot of Michael's story, comprehending the transparent Vito episodes as relief from the confusions of the rest of the film. The juxtapositions between the two stories clearly are meaningful, but they are meaningful primarily as straightforward contrasts, both in behavior and in terms of their images. The synthesis they produce is straightforward enough: the familial warmth provided by Vito has been replaced by Michael's coldness, the harmonious colors of New York and Sicily twisted into the garish bleakness of Nevada. The proposed dialectic of the film's binary structure is no more than a dualistic opposition between a cold incomprehensible present and an imagined simpler and roseate past.

The other aspect of the film which needs some elaboration is Michael's function as the primary agent of the narrative. For the bulk of the film--two of its three hours--he is the central character and mediator of its story: every scene is occasioned by him. At the same time, however, his motives are not explained to us, nor does he make any attempt to ingratiate himself in the audience's emotions. We are, at the least, kept a severe distance from the central character, and left in doubt as to his intentions, or indeed what he is

actually doing for much of the time. That in itself contributes to our isolation and uncertainty, but it is compounded
by the events which close the film. After the deaths of Roth,
Pentangeli and Fredo we see, in long shot, Michael standing
at the window of his Nevada house, looking out to the lake
where Fredo has just been killed. The film dissolves to a
scene at Vito's house in 1941, in which Michael, to general
consternation, announces he has just enlisted in the Marines.
Thematically it is resonant: when Tom tells Michael, "Many
times he [Vito] and I have talked about your future" (presumably as head of the Family), Michael replies, "I have
my own plans for my future." Fredo, whom Michael will
later/has just killed, is the only person who offers him any
support, and the scene also includes Sonny's introduction to
the family of Carlo Rizzi, who marries Connie at the beginning of The Godfather, and who is murdered on Michael's
orders at its end. Set on Vito's birthday, the scene can be
read as portending the consequences of Michael's independence
from the family. Of the characters who appear in it, only
Michael, Tom and Connie are alive at the end of Godfather
II. Even here, in a way quite contrary to his earlier/later
behavior, Michael is denying the multilayered concept of
family propounded by Vito and Sonny. Yet, thematically
rich as it is, its placement is only available to those
members of the audience who have seen The Godfather,
Three of its principal characters, Sonny, Carlo and Luca
Brazzi, do not appear elsewhere in the film. Without such
prior knowledge, it can only be read as revealing a contrast between an earlier selfless and patriotic Michael and
the cold, repressed figure we have been studying for the
last three hours; a reading which contradicts the thematic
resonances a detailed knowledge of The Godfather would
give us. This peculiar construction, along with the scene's
chronological distance from any of the other events in the
film (Vito's set in the 1920s, Michael's between 1958 and
1960), presents considerable difficulties in deciding how it
should be regarded. These difficulties are compounded by
what follows: the scene dissolves to a reprise of the final
shot of the last Vito sequence, with Vito and a four-year-
old Michael waving from the window of a Sicilian train; this
dissolves to Michael in 1960, sitting alone in the garden at
Nevada. The camera tracks from waist shot to close-up,
at the same time as the light on the camera side of his
face is reduced, leaving him half in shadow. Are we, from
this final image, to regard the two previous sequences as
Michael's memories? If so, and it is a plausible enough
implication despite the distance we have been kept from him,

344 / One-Way Ticket to Palookaville

ought this to affect our reading of all the Vito scenes, since one of them is referred to specifically by the exact repetition of a previous shot? Should we then see all the Vito scenes as perceived through Michael, and locate the nostalgic perspective that pervades them as his?* If so, then why is such an interpretation signaled only once, and at the end of the film. And if not, how are we to place the end? Perhaps as a commentary by the film on Michael's alienation, and on the irrecoverable bridge between Michael as primary agent of the fiction and ourselves as consumers of it? The problem is that even if the ending is a statement about inaccessibility, it is itself inaccessible.

The films of Robert Altman practice an alternative, and more complex, response to the facts of spatial dislocation and separable performance. His rigorous use of telephoto lenses to provide a separate, extra-fictional place for the spectator offers the most sustained and recognizable visual style in the contemporary American cinema. The observer is distanced from the action by an unbridgeable optical divide which presents the actor/characters in a space obedient to different laws from those governing that which the audience inhabit. Far from being the instrument of mediation between performers and characters, the camera itself becomes an independent performer, enacting a narrative distinct from that in which the characters are located, but only marginally concerned with explaining itself to its audience. The camera constitutes a separate narrative force, prepared and occasionally eager to abandon characters for reasons which are not disclosed to the audience. In The Long Goodbye (1972), a camera which is almost constantly mobile possesses no loyalty to its central character. At one point the film has acquired a certain amount of plot momentum occasioned by Marlowe's jorney to Mexico to search for the corpse of Terry Lennox. We see him get off a bus, and follow him in an indolent pan as he crosses the main square. He bends down to perform his single ubiquitous act of physical skill, the ability to strike a match on any surface. At this moment, Altman performs one of his ironic deconstructions of conventional Hollywood rhetoric, the cut on action.

---

*The shot of Michael clearly can have this function. It was used in the TV versions to open each of the four parts, implying that the entire story is told as Michael's recollection.

The camera cuts to a slightly closer shot from an almost identical angle; the effect is of a jump cut, arbitrarily disrupting the visual field with no clear intent. Marlowe, half stopped in his movement, continues to cross the square, but no sooner has the camera again begun to pan right than it gradually zooms in, eliminating Marlow from the right of the shot, and focusing instead on a pair of copulating dogs. Marlowe's apparent commitment to a lateral, linear and plot-motivated movement has been dismissed by the camera in favor of the detached performance of these canine extras.

Altman applies similar strategies of disposal throughout The Long Goodbye. Earlier, there is a conversation scene between Marlowe and Roger Wade on the beach side of the Wades' Malibu house. The conversation itself is a series of failed engagements, attempts at conversation that short-circuit each other:

Wade:	You don't get to grow a face like mine I guess unless you know a lot about men's faces.
Marlowe:	What about ladies' faces?
Wade:	What about ladies' faces?
Marlowe:	I don't know.
Wade:	Well why d'you ask?
Marlowe:	I was just wondering.
Wade:	Christ, you're a real dingaling, you know. You're some phony. What you say doesn't quite make sense.

No plot information is provided, and the characters' mutual incomprehension is verbally enacted. At the same time, the camera takes a dispassionate, almost cynical attitude to their attempts at coherence, observing the dialogue in a series of loosely matched arcs and zooms whose movement is unmotivated by either dialogue or action. During this process, it has established a second subject of attention for the audience by its frequent reference back to a bottle of Acquavit embedded in a bottle of ice that stands on the table between the two characters. We are distracted from the conversation into puzzling over what the camera is looking at. Eventually the camera, having failed to explain the bottle, exhausts the possibilities of movement around the couple and abandons the conversation by zooming past Marlowe's shoulder to the sea, dissolving into the next sequence.

In scenes such as this the camera adopts an essentially antagonistic attitude towards its characters. Instead of indulging their activities and locating the object of our attention within their motivated plot actions, it refuses to take an interest in them unless they are doing something of immediate interest. Characters are then required to perform for the camera, frequently in competition with each other for the camera's attention. The only thing, indeed, that can guarantee the camera's attention is a specific act of performance: Ronnee Blakeley's songs in Nashville, for example. The camera itself denies any obligation to guide the audience through a plot, preferring Gould's performances to Segal's attempts at narrative in California Split.

Altman's rigorous elimination of spatial coordinates in his exclusive employment of telephoto and zoom lenses and his emphasis on the separable performance of both characters and camera has led him into two kinds of narrative practice. A number of his films (McCabe and Mrs. Miller, The Long Goodbye, Thieves Like Us, Buffalo Bill and the Indians) deconstruct Hollywood's central genres, emphasizing that the ethical as well as the spatial precepts around which they have been constructed no longer apply. Buffalo Bill (1976) begins with an Indian attack on settlers, which is revealed to be not even a performance, but a rehearsal for the Wild West Show. The Western's open landscape is circumscribed within the Show's encampment, in which the whole film takes place, and its geographical location is never stated. The film does not so much seek to revise history (as its alternative title, Sitting Bull's History Lesson might suggest) by presenting an accurate version of mythologized figures, as explore the process of myth-making itself. Of the film's alternative heroes Bill (Paul Newman) blusters and is manipulated, while Sitting Bull is diminutive and speaks only through his interpreter. The film shows Bill imposing an inadequate version of history on events, but does not offer an alternative to it, since its events are contained within the arena of the Show.

Similarly, The Long Goodbye offers a critique of the private eye's morality. Most of Marlowe's (Elliott Gould) troubles stem from his attempts to conform to an ethical

code which is not entirely self-serving, in a world where
every other character pursues his own interests to the exclusion of any other consideration. Marlowe's morality is
as conspicuous and as out of date as his car. It is also,
the film implies, ultimately as narcissistic as the behavior
of any of the other characters, since Marlowe's externally-
directed morality can only have any wider validity if other
characters recognize its terms of reference, which they
don't. Marlowe acts for himself as much as anyone else in
the film does; his final shooting of Terry Lennox demonstrates
the point. No one, except Marlowe, has been damaged by
Terry's betrayal. Nothing except Marlowe's irrelevant sense
of morality benefits from his death. Marlowe imposes the
conventional morality of a Hays Code ending on the film,
which declares its absurdity by playing "Hooray for Hollywood" over its closing shot. Altman's exercises in generic
revisionism, unlike those of Dick Richards, for example,
are anything but nostalgic musings over lost narrative certainties. Instead, the films declare the contemporary irrelevance of Hollywood's traditional approaches, but they
fail to offer a concrete substitute.

Altman's other vehicle has been the multiple character
structures of Nashville, A Wedding, and to a lesser extent
Three Women, Quintet and Popeye. This structure closely
resembles soap opera, in that rather than constructing a
plot, he presents a many-faceted situation loosely bound together by a sequence of consecutive events. The minimal
plot line is continually disrupted by individual acts of performance, while the audience are confronted with more characters than they can adequately place in relation to each
other. Their difficulties are enhanced by the characters'
common lack of interest in communicating to the audience,
a feature of Altman's technique that reaches its extreme in
Robin Williams' incomprehensible accent and dialogue in
Popeye. Kept outside the action by its impenetrability, the
audience are free to construct the action as they wish, and
to supply whatever meaning they care to. Nashville may
and may not be a political film; that, Altman's construction
proposes, is up to the individual spectator to decide for him
or herself. The structure of the films themselves becomes
infinitely revisable: in its television version, Nashville was
a four-part eight-hour film, and that in itself was simply a
different selection from the 70 hours of material Altman and
his crew filmed. [45] Like the juxtapositions in Godfather II
and the characters in Close Encounters, the structure of
Nashville repeatedly declares "We think this means some-

thing. We think it is important," but refuses to suggest
what that meaning and importance might be. The emphasis
of such a structure on separable performances which may
be included or omitted without disrupting the film as a whole
results in a product whose elements are completely detachable from each other, and to which the only available audience response is itself a sense of detachment. At the same
time the film completely dispenses with its need for an audience and becomes completely mutable, allowing its spectators to make whatever they want of it. Altman creates a
cinema of multiple options, both for himself and his audience,
but in the process abandons any possibility of a fixity of
meaning.

NO EXIT: INSIDE THE PSYCHOPATHIC TEXT

If one response to the collapse of a sense of spatial
security in American films was to distance the audience
from the screen, the alternative reaction was to trap them
inside the fiction and make them victims of its images. In
the 1970s point-of-view the shot has become a standard rather
than an occasional device. Even in a film so concerned with
visual stability as The Towering Inferno the audience's first
sight of the Tower is through a subjective shot from Fred
Astaire's point of view. Subjectivity is a logical condition of
narcissism, and the more widespread use of subjective shots
is a natural enough phenomenon of an increasingly self-
conscious and self-referential cinema. The disintegration of
consensual Hollywood space has forced spectators as well as
filmmakers to consider, even if only incidentally, how they
are placed in relation to what they see and how the images
they witness come to be present on the screen. No longer
offered a secure relationship to those images, the audience
must now frequently negotiate a narrative perspective out of
conflicting subjective viewpoints.

In Jaws, we witness the attacks on swimmers from
the shark's point-of-view. We perceive from the point of
view of the threat at the same time that we are otherwise
identified with and frightened for the victims of the threat.
The camera becomes a weapon directed at both the characters in the fiction and the audience, since the menacing object is not itself visible to us except through its own subjectivity. The act of looking becomes an act of menace,

not only for the characters who are under threat from the
audience's gaze, but also for the audience, who have no control over their gaze and cannot fix their viewpoint securely
because they are not offered a reverse angle on the threatening object. It is this tendency not to supply the complemen-
tary objective locating shot which makes the subjective camera position so threatening to its audience. They can no
longer trust in the benevolence of the image any more than
they can in the laws of physics (Carrie) or anatomy (The
Exorcist). When the detached subjective shot is used as a
structuring principle, as in Halloween (1978; dir. John Car-
penter), it deprives the audience of any firm position from
which to view the fiction. Throughout Halloween we never
see the mad killer, but we always see his attacks on his
victims from his own viewpoint. Instead of being able to
see and recognize the threat, we only see its consequences
without being able to know its purpose. As a result, we
have no option but to accept Donald Pleasence's description
of the killer as the embodiment of pure evil with whom we
are distressingly visually identified. The only way, indeed,
that this notion can be sustained is if the audience is deprived of a sight of the madman. The curious nature of
the point-of-view shot is precisely that it excludes any psychological knowledge of the character whose viewpoint it
represents. In The Parallax View (1974; dir. Alan Pakula)
Warren Beatty undergoes a psychological test which measures his reactions to a sequence of words and still photo-
graphs. The audience sees the sequence uninterrupted and
in its entirety--effectively we take the test as well. But
neither we nor Beatty are ever informed of how he did, and
we learn nothing of his reactions, since we do not witness
them. The only way in which Halloween can sustain its notion of pure evil is if we do not see the madman, since any
context or knowledge of his material presence would provide
us with evidence for making relative judgments. The one
place in which the audience can be located in Halloween without the fiction disintegrating is inside the head of the madman. Once we see him, the terror is at an end, because
we have been able to place him, and he is no longer an unknown threat.

Alternatively, the act of looking may be threatening
because everything we look at may threaten us. In Race
with the Devil (1975; dir. Jack Starrett) two bourgeois cou-
ples are isolated inside their motor home as they gradually
realize that everyone they meet is a member of a Satanic
cult intent on killing them. To look out of the window is to

look on menace, and the film structures itself around the
provisional safety offered inside the trailer and the pervasive
unknown threat outside.

Voyeurism and the threat in looking are two areas in
which recent American cinema reveals its indebtedness to
Hitchcock. A third area of his influence has been in the
use of strategies of suspense in narrative construction.
Hitchcock defined suspense as "the opposite of surprise,"[46]
a condition in which the audience waits for the inevitable to
happen without knowing exactly what form it will take. When
Richard Dreyfuss swims down to the sunken boat in Jaws,
the audience know (partially through music cues) that something shocking will appear on the screen, and that knowledge
enhances the shock when the severed head does appear in the
porthole. Homages to Hitchcock and his mechanisms of audience manipulation abound in the American cinema of the
1970s, as much in films celebrating the encounter with the
Unknown (Close Encounters quite gratuitously restages part
of the climax of North by Northwest when Dreyfuss and
Melinda Dillon are climbing the mountain) as in the purely
imitative later films of Brian De Palma (Dressed to Kill is
the most extreme example). As important as the direct
borrowing of techniques and the restaging of scenes from
Hitchcock's films is the widespread adoption of a game form
in suspense narratives in place of a previous attachment to
story development. Halloween and its successors describe
non-developing situations: all that can happen is that the
madman will commit so many murders before the end of the
film. The game becomes the ingenuity with which these can
be presented: Paramount's President Michael Eisner described Friday the 13th as having "some of the most creative killings I've ever seen on screen."[47] A game form
is implicit in suspense films, since much of the film's activity is in delaying the inevitable. Given the collapse in
narrative security the emergence of the game structure as
a central phenomenon of American cinema in the 1970s is
not in the least surprising.

Robin Wood has argued that "the astonishing evolution
of the horror film" is one of the "two keys to understanding
the development of the Hollywood cinema in the seventies."[48]
But although the horror film is a natural vehicle for devices
of insecurity and audience manipulation, to single the genre
out in the way Wood does diverts attention away from the
broad thematic and structural elements it has in common
with other areas of contemporary American cinema. Horror

films can make particular use of the external threat directed
against an audience by an interior perspective, but so does
a film like Close Encounters, where the central character,
whose ambition is "to know that it's really happening," seeks
to embrace the Unknown rather than defeat it. So, equally,
do paranoid political thrillers like Three Days of the Condor,
The Parallax View and All the President's Men, in which the
unknown is a corporate entity working to hinder the protagonist's perception of the plot. The horror film makes use,
but not exclusive use, of the psychopath, whose function in
the 1970s has largely shifted from that ascribed him by the
liberal consensus to one of providing a convenient solution
to a problem of characterization in a period of increasing
moral ambiguity. The psychopath, as represented in Halloween, is the personficiation of pure evil, an abstract articulation of a metaphysical concept that the film at no point discusses, but merely states as unambiguously as Darth Vadar
is presented as the embodiment of evil in Star Wars. A
sense of moral ambiguity has, in these cases, resulted in
the statement of moral positions in extreme terms, and liberal agnosticism has given way to a Manichaean expression
of good and evil, in which the unknown appears as an irresistible and incomprehensible force of immense power.
Against this barely revised figure of populist demonology is
pitted the bourgeois hero, but the decline of cinematic benevolence means that he is as likely to lose without even understanding the rules of the game (Race with the Devil, The
Omen) as he is to defeat the forces of evil (Jaws, Star Wars,
Raiders of the Lost Ark).

In the 1970s the paranoid hero has ceased to be a
figure belonging solely to the horror genre, but may now inhabit any film making extensive use of a closed interior perspective. Robin Wood has pointed out that, whatever its
other generic borrowings, Taxi Driver (1976; dir. Martin
Scorsese) is a horror film. This is not because of the
presence of the psychopath, but because the psychopathic vision is the only perspective it offers on its narrative. As
in Halloween, we witness the subjective perception of a character we know to be mad and dangerous. But unlike Halloween, where Donald Pleasence at least explains what is going
on, we see nothing else. If Taxi Driver is the archetypal incoherent narrative of the 1970s, it is so because the sole
agent of its narrative, Travis Bickle, is a psychopath unable
to explain himself to anyone.

The film allows its audience no other point of purchase

on the excremental city it presents. Visually, our one point of fixity in the images of a constantly mobile urban landscape is the taxi itself. Early in the film, we see a series of close-ups of details of the cab--the hood, the wing mirror --fixed completely still in the frame while out-of-focus lights move past in the background. In the opening shot of the film, we see the cab moving through the frame with a rigid, linear certainty in contrast to the turmoil of the ever-variable lights and steam through which it cuts. The taxi does not move erratically; alone among the objects and people in Taxi Driver, it offers the possibility of stable progression in a straight line. But it is emblematic of the film's narrative confusions. The straight line, which previously encouraged narrative progression, in fact leads nowhere: Travis traverses the same territory night after night, merely going round the block, to return to his starting point in the 58th St. warehouse. The taxi-ride, normally no more than a linking motif between distinct but more important narrative arenas, becomes the central and fixed space of the film: it is via the taxi that Travis meets all the significant Others of the film. Only at two points in the film does the cab move out of its normal pattern of stable motion; when he accelerates rapidly away from the Palantine headquarters to avoid confronting Tom (Albert Brooks) over Betsy (Cybill Shepherd) and when he brakes sharply to avoid hitting Iris (Jodie Foster). Only women can interrupt the stately progression of the always immaculate cab through and somehow above the squalid city. Conversely, interrupting this movement is to violate Bickle's privacy and force him to enact a relationship.

Twice in the film we leave our obsessional concern with the obsessional Bickle; on both occasions to relate the two women to another man: Betsy in the first half of her first scene with Tom, Iris in the "Scar" scene with Sport (Harvey Keitel). But neither of these scenes provides us with an alternative viewpoint--Bickle is, indeed, observing both encounters from a distance. Neither scene presents a viable alternative to our return to Bickle, in large part because of the limited performances of the two other men: Tom serves a merely comic function as the butt of Betsy's jokes (anticipating the brothel-keeper, he cannot function with only the thumb and little finger of his hand), while Sport's cooing to Iris is evasive and inaudible. Normalcy then exists in the film only so far as it exists in the taxi. Other characters are no more able to articulate their responses to the city than is Bickle: even Palantine (Leonard Harris) says nothing, and says it as clumsily as Wizard (Peter Boyle).

Bickle occupies the film's privileged center: our attention is held on him not only via his apparently explicatory interior monologue, but also as the possessor of the film's few stable frame centers. Scenes are cued by his arrival, frequently through an otherwise redundant tracking movement which "finds" Travis for us (as in the first shot of the subsequently static scene in the coffee shop with Betsy). In other inherently static (and largely incidental) scenes, we witness more intricate versions of this same privileged centrality afforded by the camera to Bickle, in the way that it integrates our viewpoint with his. In the first night-time coffee-shop scene with the other drivers, their conversation is deemed irrelevant not simply by Bickle's disengagement from and disruption of it, but also by the camera's lateral track left to right across the group to Bickle, in which the camera pushes them out of frame to concentrate our attention first on Bickle, and then on his subjectivity. The sequence ends with a slow zoom in on his fizzing Seltzer glass in a shot which must be read as Bickle's point of view (whatever irrelevant protestations that it is also an incidental homage to Godard). 49 Of more consequence, though, is the interpolated shot of the other occupants of the coffee-shop, several black pimps, who are viewed in a short low wide-angle curved track, in which they stare back with inactive hostility at where we might expect Bickle to be. Clearly this shot is not literally subjective: it does not align itself with Bickle's spatial viewpoint. But it is intercut with a shot of Bickle looking, obliging us to read it as the target of his gaze, and, even more, requiring us to accept Bickle's power to move the camera.

A similar shot sequence occurs in the second night-time coffee-shop scene with the other drivers. Again the scene is cued by Bickle's arrival: the film cuts between a group shot of the drivers at a table and Bickle's entry via a ticket barrier. Until Bickle arrives at the table, we are "entertained" by tales of Wizard's sexual exploits and of dwarfs, at the same time alienating us from the characters' grossness and confirming in peripheral detail Bickle's view of the city as grotesque. Travis, never secure in a group or in a group shot containing more than two people, takes us away from the scene as soon as he arrives, by leaving with Wizard to talk outside in the street. As they leave the coffee-shop, they pass a group of young blacks strutting noisily down the street. One, with a gold-lamé vest, cane and goatee beard, is singled out for our attention by another short curved track, intercut with a similar movement around

Bickle. It is a movement of potential, menacing engagement, which links the camera's aggressive movement to a threat from Bickle, a pattern finally endorsed in the film's climax. The rest of the scene consists in a pair of shots presenting Travis and Wizard, once they have stabilized themselves by Wizard's cab. But the imbalance of our viewpoint is enacted here, in a pattern repeated frequently in the various static two-character scenes elsewhere in the film. One of the shots is full-length, presenting both characters: it is in this shot that Wizard expounds his nebulous philosophy. The other, however, is a medium close-up of Bickle, locating him as its sole point of interest, and encouraging our identification with his mocking dismissal of Wizard's remarks. Bickle is granted an attention that other characters are denied.

The most extreme example is his monologue at the camera (or at a point just to the right of the camera) in his room: "You talkin' to me?" Bickle, then, is both the narrative focus of the film and its focusing agent: we either look at him or look with him, and he alone possesses the power to move the camera. This is revealed most clearly in the overhead shot behind Travis at Palantine's Columbus Circle speech. As Bickle begins to move through the crowd towards the podium, the camera follows. Crowd extras move out of the way to left and right when Bickle comes level with them: whether to grant him passage, or the camera, it is impossible to say.

There is nothing particularly novel in the protagonist's exercising such authority over the frame, nor in his capacity to mobilize the camera. That, indeed, is a conventional "heroic" function, and is one of the two principal ways that the film grants Bickle a formal heroic status (the other being De Niro's gestural codes). What is disconcerting, however, is the extent of the camera's concession of authority to Bickle, particularly in the light of his inability to organize a narrative. Not merely is he verbally inarticulate, his performance is inconsistent, switching from loquacious and ingratiating fan (of Palantine and Betsy) to introvert and menacing voyeur (in the two scenes described, in the cab with Scorsese, and in the subjective shot in the hotel room where he points the .38 out of the window at a female couple below), to concerned moral adult (over breakfast with Iris). Quite simply, Bickle does not know how to behave. Worse, he does not know that he does not know. At one level, this manifests itself in the date with Betsy; at another, in the interchangeable nature of the targets of his

violence. The inconsistency of his behavior permeates the
entire film: the audience are subject to and victim of random
and unexplained incident (Bickle firing directly at us in the
target range). Because of the camera's identification with
Bickle, it is equally subject to and victim of random and unexplained camera movement. Bickle cannot guide us through
the narrative, because he doesn't know where it's going.
What he does do is to chart its escalation from his initial
position of hoping that "someday a real rain will come and
wash all the scum off the streets" to demanding of Palantine
that someone take action to "clean up this whole mess here
and just flush it right down the fuckin' toilet," to assuming
the role himself. He does this at the same time that he
charts an escalation from latent to fantastic to explicit violence, when he fulfils the destiny predicted for him by the
King Kong Company badge on his jacket.

The audience face the absence of a normalizing
perspective--a perspective other than Bickle's which could
ratify or place his in context, at the same time that they are
forced to identify him (and identify with him) as both heroic
and demonstrably psychopathic. We see the city ("whores,
skunk pussies, buggers, queens, fairies, dopers, junkies
... sick, venal") only from the perspective of Bickle's moving cab cruising the streets, and we are unable to differentiate hookers from passers-by. Obliged to adopt his viewpoint, we are presented with nowhere from which to view
his actions, and no framework in which to place them, since
we cannot anticipate the narrative's progression, left as it
is in the hands of a character who confesses and demonstrates his need to "get organize-ized." Only after the
film's climactic blood-letting are we offered an external
point of purchase on the action, in the subjectless track
over the letter and newspaper clippings, and the appearance
on the soundtrack of a second interior voice, Iris' father re-
citing the text of his letter to Travis. Consistently the
film's reviewers and critics have claimed the ending as
ironic, 50 yet there is nothing in its presentation to signal
it as such. We are presented with a series of external
validating references (the newspaper clippings, the diagram
of the final carnage that confirms the overhead shot of the
killings, the external voice) which might offer a second
perspective on the events we have witnessed. But because
the tracking shot that presents us with this information has
no subject, we cannot attach the information to any character in the fiction or determine what moral response we
should make to it. Instead, it serves to convert Bickle's

enactment of psychosis into public fantasy, and extend the
moral vacuum beyond Bickle himself to the limits of the
film's world.   The remaining scenes do little to counter
this impression: Travis, back at work and more integrated
with his fellow cabbies than we have seen him before, has
a final encounter with Betsy, in which she is recognized as
a hollow illusion, seen not as whole but only as a reflection,
a face suspended among the night lights.   We still see from
Bickle's viewpoint, in which he is the confident possessor of
certainty, and she hesitant as to how she should behave.
The final images of the film are unreadable: Travis darting
a glance into the mirror suggests a possible menace still in
him, but whether as psychopath, vigilante or simply cabbie
is not evident.   His face is caught briefly in the mirror before he turns it to reflect instead more of the city lights,
and the end credits roll over multi-layered shots of the city
at night.   An ambiguity exists in these final images, but it
is not penetrable because of our limited access to viewpoints
other than Bickle's.   The urge to read the film's coda as
ironic is the product of audience or critical unwillingness to
accept its apparent meaning: the endorsement of the psychopath hero.

OUT OF TIME

        Locking the audience into an interior perspective is
not necessarily threatening.   The fantasy film, like the horror movie, cannot be adequately constructed as a genre solely in terms of its plot and thematic preoccupations.   It is
equally determined by its manipulation of space and time,
and represents the other side of the horror film's coin.
Where the horror film traps its audience in a disintegrating
interior space menaced by an antagonistic force external to
that space, the fantasy film presents an interior space that
has no threats made against it, and thus is rendered perfectly safe.   The safe space of the fantasy film is situated
outside history (Star Wars) and, being unrestricted by any
external threat, is capable of infinite expansion.   Luke Sky-
walker and his companions demonstrate the security of fantasy space by the ease with which they fix their position in
space by reading the two-dimensional displays on their space-
ship consoles.   Like Bob Dylan in Peckinpah's Pat Garrett
and Billy the Kid, they can live anywhere and leave anywhere
too, moving from planet to planet with impunity because Star

<u>Wars</u> will always re-locate them in benevolent environments, and tell the audience where they are. The gift of mobility secures the safety of fantasy space, a phenomenon best demonstrated by George Lucas' non-science fiction fantasy film, <u>American Graffiti</u> (1973).

The safe space in <u>American Graffiti</u> is in a moving car, listening to the radio. There, anything can happen without danger: John (Paul le Mat) and Carol (Mackenzie Phillips) can bridge the generation gap without ruining his image, Curt (Richard Dreyfuss) can join the Pharaohs and fall in love with a girl from <u>Citizen Kane</u>. Lucas sets the film in a period of innocence, before Kennedy's assassination, Vietnam, and the history of the '60s. This safe time, together with the safe space of the cruising cars, permits its characters to perform without responsibility or causal relations. Inside the moving cars, actions have no consequences: in contrast to <u>Rebel without a Cause</u>, Bob Falfa (Harrison Ford) and Laurie (Cindy Williams) walk away unharmed from the wreck after the drag race.

<u>American Graffiti</u> might more conventionally be described as nostalgic, but nostalgia is only a form of fantasy. Nostalgia consists in a particular relation to history, in which objects are displaced from their material context in time and relocated in another framework detached from their original position. <u>American Graffiti</u> is no more set in 1962 than <u>Star Wars</u> is set "In a distant galaxy long long ago and far far away." It is set in 1973, fixed there by the style of its images and performances, and creates a fantastic version of Modesto, California by its nostalgic consumption of objects loosely belonging to the period it claims to represent. Nostalgia collapses into sentiment in the film's last shot, when it arbitrarily attempts to revise itself by entering history with a deterministic account of its characters' subsequent lives. The nature of the film is suddenly and drastically changed. Instead of remaining within the safe space of the fantasy movie, where privileged characters can produce noncausal performances, it suddenly claims that this night has been a formative experience, a dramaturgy which will lead to change in the external world. Curt escapes the closed world which will kill John and stifle Steve (Ron Howard) by going to college and becoming a writer in Canada, presumably to escape the draft. In a vestige of the liberal tradition, Terry the Toad (Charlie Martin Smith) is killed in Vietnam because he is physically inept with a motor scooter.

Nostalgia has pervaded the American cinema of the 1970s as a leitmotif of narrative uncertainty. In the films of Dick Richards, for example, it seems as if the authenticity of the costumes and the labels on the tin cans is used as a substitute for coherent story development. The Culpepper Cattle Company (1972) resolves itself by a familiar device in films which make some initial attempt to reconsider the presuppositions of their genre. It collapses into generic conventionality, with the bad guys developing consciences and saving the wagon train. The same strategy of collapse can be found in Coma's (1978; dir. Michael Crighton) abandonment of its assertive heroine (Genevieve Bujold) and in the gradual conversion of Alice Doesn't Live Here Anymore (1974; dir. Martin Scorsese) from a film about Ellen Burstyn's independence into a "woman's picture." At the beginning of the film, she and her neighbor fantasize about Robert Redford. At the end, she gets Kris Kristofferson.

Another of Richards' contributions to the decade's generic nostalgia, Farewell My Lovely (1975), offers an alternative response in employing the insecurities of film noir. The investigative narrative and its archetypal heroes, the private eye and the journalist, emerged in 1974 as figures for post-Watergate fictions. Their heroic status was compromised by their inability to bring their narratives to a successful resolution (Chinatown, The Parallax View); instead, the films beguiled their audiences with the notion that the central characters were as confused about the plot as they were. The employment of noir fixtures was a self-conscious justification for narrative confusion. The audience was presented with a recognizable terrain inhabited by objects and lighting codes remembered from earlier films, and this evocation of displaced objects directed attention away from plot to the image and the central performances of bewilderment and uncertainty.

The resort to nostalgic conventions and the unconvinced re-enactment of generic patterns is indicative of the more general collapse of temporal coherence in films of the 1970s. Wherever else in American culture the sense of historical continuity has come under attack,[51] Hollywood has measured its deterioration in the growing failure to construct coherent linear narratives. Temporal connection, the primary tool of narrative causality, has been increasingly abandoned in favor of structures that declare their incoherence. Dog Soldiers (1978; dir. Karel Reisz) is in many respects (its presentation of space for example) notable for the old-

fashioned conventionality of its construction. But it makes
no attempt to place its characters in time, either historically
(the film might be set in 1971 like the book on which it is
based, or it might not), or in their movements from scene
to scene. Instead, there is an assumption of simultaneity:
the audience is forced to assume that the disparate events
affecting the two principal characters occur at more or less
the same time if it is to construct a comprehensible narrative sequence--a task which the film passively declares is
not its responsibility. As it progresses, Dog Soldiers de-
generates into a chase movie and its central conception of
splitting the post-Vietnam American hero into two individually inadequate and mutually dependent characters collapses.
By the climax both have become capable of heroic action,
the motivation for which remains inaccessible to the audience, since neither character has previously offered a rationale for his actions. Ray (Nick Nolte) declares at one
point, "I don't always have to have a reason for the shit I
do," and the unmodulated performances of both Nolte and
Michael Moriarty provide the spectator with no evidence of
their motivations.

Where the American cinema of the consensus developed its mechanisms of construction around a requirement
to produce narratives that were rigid in their linear determinism, the cinema of disintegration has commonly abandoned the attempts to tell stories at all, providing rather a
sequence of events arbitrarily connected by the fact of their
being edited together. From this the audience may construct as much of a story as they feel capable of. This
loss of confidence in the ability to construct a sequential
narrative time reveals itself most clearly in a reluctance
to provide an ending. Star Wars does not just announce
that it is not set in the conventionally remote future of science fiction but in the distant past. At its end it declares
that it is the fourth episode in a series of nine.

More normally, Hollywood's recent products have refused to provide a sense of resolution in their conclusion,
and have abandoned their central protagonists to an ambiguous fate. Gene Hackman seems particularly prone to this
discomfiture. In Night Moves (1975; dir. Arthur Penn), he
is left wounded in a disabled boat which describes circles
in an otherwise empty ocean. The Conversation (1974; dir.
Francis Ford Coppola) closes with him playing the saxophone
in the apartment he has just demolished. While the conclusion of Penn's film is clearly open to metaphorical interpre-

tation, the end of The Conversation is merely ambiguous,
available to signify anything. Coppola is notorious for the
difficulty he has in ending his films, Apocalypse Now (1979)
being merely the most spectacular and extravagant example.
But the reluctance of Hollywood's contemporary self-conscious
auteurs to provide endings which locate the meaning of their
films is remarkably consistent. One might argue that the
ambiguity of the final "God Bless America" sequence of Michael Cimino's The Deerhunter (1978) is an economic necessity, since a film which refuses to declare its attitude to
American involvement in Vietnam is a safer box-office bet
than one which does. One might argue that it allows the
audience a choice of interpretation, or that it reflects the
ambivalence of American response to the war. What it undoubtedly does do is to leave the film open as a text for an
endless critical game-playing over its ideological implications, which may well guarantee Cimino's dubious status as
an auteur simply by the weight of paper devoted to him. As
part of a more general tendency, the contemporary emphasis
on an aesthetics of performance would suggest that, since
"Robert De Niro is The Deerhunter," whatever Robert De
Niro does has the support of the film.

    The privileging of performance which is so consistent
a feature of the Hollywood product in itself disrupts the temporal continuity of a causal narrative. In performance structures, what a performer does at the end of his or her routine
is no more significant than what he or she has done at any
other point. The openness of Altman's (or, to a lesser extent, Coppola's) films to almost infinite restructuring is evidence of this, and endorses the argument that a fixity of
meaning simply is not present in these inherently incomplete
texts. By not telling a story (but rather offering several incomplete stories for the spectator to choose from), such
films cannot be said to occupy narrative time. It is, then,
hardly surprising that so little of the American cinema of the
1970s has concerned itself with an investigation of temporal
structure, preferring instead to abandon time as a fictive
concern either by the resort to nostalgia or by making narrative construction entirely the responsibility of the audience.

    One of the few consistent exceptions to this general
practice has been Sam Peckinpah's reassessment of the primary cinematic myths of America. Peckinpah's critical
neglect during the decade has been curious: dismissed for
his apparent political conservatism and misogyny and condemned for his depiction of violence, Peckinpah has never-

theless conducted the most complex revision of cinematic
temporal structures since Welles (or perhaps Griffith), and
provided a functioning solution to the problem of joining inside and outside while operating firmly within the new post-
television aesthetic. Peckinpah's films, however pessimistic
their thematic conclusions might be, present some of the few
coherent discussions of the pervasive phenomenon of incoherence in the contemporary American cinema and, contrary to
most critical assumption, reconsider the problematic nature
of heroism in a universe where morality can no longer be
straightforwardly attached to physical decorum.

His early films (up to The Getaway, 1972) play on the
extent to which their central characters exist as heroic out-
siders because of their opposition to temporal progress.
One advertising slogan for The Wild Bunch (1969) was, "The
land had changed. They hadn't." It was equally applicable
to the two gunfighters in Ride the High Country, Tyreen in
Major Dundee, Cable Hogue and Junior and Ace Bonner. Usually aging men running out of space in which to act because
time (progress) has made them redundant, Peckinpah's early
heroes engage in some futile, romantic, and usually fatal
gesture of rebellion, a sub-Hemingway stance which has
clung as firmly to Peckinpah's public persona as it once did
to John Huston's.

His later films, however, have questioned the traditional mechanisms of heroism. His central characters lack
moral certainty, and they are also deprived of the guarantee
of heroic status their performances might bring them elsewhere. Pat Garrett and Billy the Kid (1973) does not concern
itself primarily with Billy, whose mythic status is secure before the film begins, and who has nothing to achieve except
its confirmation by his death. Instead Peckinpah concentrates attention on Garrett, who falls victim to the moral
incompatibility of his desire to survive to be "rich, old and
grey" and his need for individual independence. As a mythic
force, Billy remains immune from narrative pressure, a
situation reinforced by the industrial status of Kristofferson's
performance. His physical movement is unaffected by the
events of the film, and he relaxes into a separable activity
of role-playing which represents both Billy the Kid and Kris
Kristofferson, country-rock star. By contrast, James Coburn demonstrates his entrapment within the narrative, and
his vulnerability to historical processes by becoming stiffer
and more pained in his movements as the film progresses.
Garrett's tragedy lies in his gradual discovery that a pro-

fessional commitment to a linear course of action guarantees
neither the loyalty and respect of his corporate employers
nor the moral endorsement of the film and its spectators.

Peckinpah's subsequent films all assume the moral
vacuum Garrett discovers. Bring Me the Head of Alfredo
Garcia (1974), The Killer Elite (1975) and Cross of Iron
(1977) occupy an anarchic terrain in which betrayal is endemic and heroism is inevitably compromised. Their central
characters all function within a framework which assumes
that their personal objectives will prove incompatible with
those of the larger external forces which have determined
the circumstances the film presents. For the protagonists,
any action is permissible in the quest for survival, from
the mutilation of a corpse to the murder of a child, but
such figures can no longer hope for the sympathy of their
audience. Nor, increasingly, do they seek it; Steiner (James
Coburn) has no attachments to anything outside his platoon,
and no rationale for his behavior except survival in what he
describes to the Russian boy they take prisoner as No Man's
Land. None of the characters in Cross of Iron enact positions which the audience can endorse, since the conventional
yardsticks of morality by which they might be judged are not
contained within the film. Steiner's brutal laughter, which
closes the film over images of dead children, is an acceptance of the arbitrariness of the war the film depicts, and of
the film's depiction of it.

Peckinpah's films match their deconstruction of moral
certainty with an equally deliberate deconstruction of the
spatial and temporal certainties within which such a moral
certainty might exist. The films realize the condition of
arbitrariness rather than merely depicting it, and force the
audience to experience the condition of their characters by
paralleling the characters' moral situation with the physical,
perceptual situation of the audience. At its broadest, this
process is signalled by Garcia's beginning and ending on a
frozen frame: cinematic time is displayed as an arbitrary
construct, which the film is free to play with as it wishes,
and which the audience must simply endure acceptingly.
Where, in his earlier films, Peckinpah employed slow motion to render ambiguous the spectator's response to a brutal action by revealing its grace, his later films employ it
to reveal the arbitrariness with which the film travels
through the gate of the projector. Slow motion ceases to
indicate a significant event, as it did in The Wild Bunch,
but rather to divert the audience's attention to incidental

physical trajectories, such as the arc described by the spent shells ejected from a sub-machine gun. Peckinpah repeatedly demonstrates the moral incompatibility of cause and effect; Cross of Iron returns again and again to intercut shots of explosions and artillery shells being ejected. This is a description of process, established by a kind of angle-reverse angle cutting, but one which is only made possible by the recognition that the cinema constructs its space according to unique laws which enforce a relation between two consecutive images.

As juxtaposition constructs significant space, it also enforces temporal progression. The tank battle in Cross of Iron enacts in microcosm the narrative process of Garcia. The sequence begins with a series of static shots of the Russian tanks, cut together in an accelerating montage which animates the tanks themselves into movement. The film constructs not only its own moral landscape, but also its own momentum, which arbitrarily obliges or interrupts the movement of its characters. Peckinpah's aesthetic is constructed around the acknowledgment that the American cinema of the 1970s can place any two shots together and create an arbitrary meaning through the creation of an arbitrary space and time. It is an aesthetic that makes no concessions to the audience, who are offered fewer and fewer positions they may comfortably adopt, either spatially, temporally, or ethically. In Cross of Iron, the spectator becomes a redundant witness to a process completely out of his or her control.

In Peckinpah's films, the audience's only recourse is to a morality external to the film itself. In this deliberate anarchy is the most coherent statement of the endemic incoherence of contemporary American cinema. The collapse of consensual structures has led the American film into an apparently unavoidable oppositional stance to the primary source of consensus, television. The best hope it has offered has been the suggestion that it is possible to survive a disaster movie, but the heroic status of survivors, from Travis Bickle to Rolf Steiner, is uncertain to say the least. Even the most closely argued of these films oblige the audience to keep a distance from the screen which threatens them. The juvenile attempts at consensus via a conservative engagement in fantasy have merely produced a reactionary cinema of escapism that re-enacts Hollywood's simplest generic and heroic archetypes without the context that once gave them meaning. The more complex articulations of Coppola or Altman limit themselves by their exclusion of the audience, and their refusal to offer a fixed meaning. The nihilism of this response achieves its most deliberate formulation in the anarchy of Peckinpah's world.

REFERENCES

1. Christopher Lasch, The Culture of Narcissism (London, 1980), pp. 37-38.

2. Garth Jowett, Film: The Democratic Art, p. 484.

3. Tom Mankiewicz, in interview with John L. Mason, in John L. Mason, The Identity Crisis Theme in American Feature Films, 1960-1969 (New York, 1977), p. 357.

4. Tom Mankiewicz, in Mason, p. 357.

5. Robin Wood, Arthur Penn (London, 1967), p. 45.

6. Quoted in John G. Cawelti, ed., Focus on Bonnie and Clyde (New Jersey, 1973), p. 161.

7. Mason, The Identity Crisis Theme in American Feature Films, Ch. 1.

8. Lasch, The Culture of Narcissism, pp. 71-103.

9. David Pirie, "The Deal," in David Pirie, ed., Anatomy of the Movies (London, 1981), p. 50.

10. Linda B. Greensfelder, ed., The American Film Institute's Guide to College Film Courses, 1970/71 (Chicago, 1970).

11. Andrew Sarris, The American Cinema, Directors and Directions, 1929-1968 (New York, 1968).

12. Andrew Laskos, "The Hollywood Majors," in David Pirie, ed., Anatomy of the Movies, p. 38.

13. Laskos in Pirie, ed., p. 30.

14. Robert H. Stanley, The Celluloid Empire (New York, 1978), p. 262.

15. Mel Gussow, Zanuck: "Don't Say Yes Until I've Finished Talking" (New York, 1980), pp. 318-323.

16. Stanley, The Celluloid Empire, p. 241.

17. Laskos in Pirie, ed., pp. 34-35.

18. Laskos in Pirie, ed., p. 136.

19. Mike Bygrave, "The New Moguls," in Pirie, ed., p. 77.

20. James Monaco, American Film Now (New York, 1979), p. 116.

21. Michael Pye and Linda Myles, The Movie Brats: How the Film Generation Took Over Hollywood (London, 1979).

22. Michael Conant, Antitrust in the Motion Picture Industry, (Berkeley, 1960), p. 59.

23. B. J. Franklin, "Promotion and Release," in Pirie, ed., p. 97.

24. Monaco, American Film Now, p. 394.

25. Monaco, p. 394.

26. David Pirie, "The Deal," in Pirie, ed., p. 53.

27. David Gordon, "Why the Movie Majors Are Major," Sight and Sound, Vol. 42, No. 4 (Autumn, 1973), pp. 194-196.; Alan Stanbrook, "Hollywood's Crashing Epics," Sight and Sound, Vol. 50, No. 2 (Spring 1981), pp. 84-85.

28. "Gigolos: Paul Schrader Interviewed by Mitch Tuchman," Film Comment, Vol. 16, No. 2 (March-April 1980), p. 52.

29. F. Scott Fitzgerald, "A Man in the Way," in The Pat Hobby Stories (Harmondsworth, 1967), p. 36.

30. "Gigolos: Paul Schrader Interviewed by Mitch Tuchman," p. 50.

31. Robert Evans, "Confessions of a Kid Mogul," in Pirie, ed., p. 85.

32. Joan Didion, "In Hollywood," in The White Album (Harmondsworth, 1981), p. 165.

33. Joan Didion, The White Album, pp. 160, 162.

34. Robert Sklar, Movie-Made America (New York, 1975), p. 287.

35. James Monaco, American Film Now, pp. 46-80; Pauline Kael, "On the Future of Movies," New Yorker, August 5, 1974.

36. James Monaco, American Film Now, Ch. 3.

37. American Film Institute Seminar, quoted in David Thompson, "Screenwriters and Screenwriting," in Pirie, ed., p. 144.

38. Richard Dyer, "The Towering Inferno," Movie 21, pp. 30-34.

39. Lasch, The Culture of Narcissism, p. 130.

40. H. Schlechter and C. Molesson, "It's Not Nice to Fool Mother Nature: The Disaster Movie and Technological Guilt," Journal of American Culture, Vol. 1, No. 1 (1978), pp. 44-50.

41. Stephen Heath, "Jaws, Ideology and Film Theory," Times Higher Education Supplement, March 26, 1976.

42. Raymond Williams, Television: Technology and Cultural Form (London, 1974), pp. 86-96.

43. Monaco, American Film Now, p. 346.

44. John Hess, "Godfather II: A Deal Coppola Couldn't Refuse," Jump Cut, No. 7 (May-June, 1975), reprinted in Bill Nichols, Movies and Methods (Berkeley, 1976), p. 82. See also Robert Philip Kolker, A Cinema of Loneliness (New York, 1980), pp. 159-193. Although Coppola's comments in interviews might seem to support this interpretation, his willingness to unpack the dialectic and rearrange the events of the two films in strict chronological order for the television version casts some doubt on his commitment to it.

45. Connie Byrne and William O. Lopez, "Nashville--An Interview 'Documentary'," Film Quarterly, Winter 1975-76, p. 24.

46. Quoted in Monaco, American Film Now, p. 69.

47. Quoted in Andrew Laskos, "The Hollywood Majors," in Pirie, ed., p. 15.

48. Robin Wood, "The Incoherent Text: Narrative in the 70s," Movie 27/28, p. 25.

49. e. g., Robin Wood, "The Incoherent Text," p. 30.

50. Wood, "The Incoherent Text," p. 33; Kolker, A Cinema of Loneliness, p. 250.

51. Lasch, The Culture of Narcissism, pp. 28-33.

INTERLUDE

THE MULTIPLE REVISIONIST AND THE DETACHED
NARCISSIST: DON SIEGEL AND CLINT EASTWOOD

The increasingly provisional nature of cinematic
structures in contemporary Hollywood in many respects
echoes the practices of the filmmakers of Dissent.   In
interviews, Scorsese is fond of declaring that his tracking shots borrow from Fuller's.   But the disintegration of
consensus has eliminated the context in which Fuller might
register his dissent through his mobile camera, leaving
only the empty form for Scorsese to imitate.   The most
successful dissident in the early 1970s was Don Siegel,
whose films displayed a dialectical tension generated by
their mutable surface appearance.   In Dirty Harry and
Charley Varrick Siegel revises and renegotiates relationships between character and audience, time and space, by
filtering our perceptions of the narrative through a set of
alternative perspectives on the film's surface tension.   One
perspective is generated by the tunnel vision of the protagonist's urge to move through the plot, while a counter-
movement is proposed by the camera's provision of a variety of viewpoints on the same action.   At its simplest,
there are three verbal explanations as to why Clint Eastwood is called Dirty Harry.

In the Mount Davidson Park sequence in Dirty Harry,
Siegel discusses viewpoint with the audience.   Eastwood,
held under the gun of the as-yet invisible Scorpio (Andy
Robinson), is told to "Turn and face the cross.   Come on.
Put your nose right up against the cement."   The film cuts
to a subjective shot from Eastwood's point-of-view; a shot
which establishes the audience's inability to identify themselves with Eastwood's perspective.   From this viewpoint
we can, literally, see nothing.   The screen is filled with
the dark grey concrete of the massive cross.   Cut to the

extreme alternative: from the top of the cross, we look
down through the night fog onto the two small figures, in-
discernible in detail. Become too detached, and you lose
the relativity of the story. Cut to the ideal position: from
slightly above and to the left of Robinson, we watch him
complete his advance towards Eastwood, and strike him
with the butt of his submachine-gun. We see as we want
to see: from a comfortably removed closeness which ensures our protection while not inhibiting our vision. But
in negotiating this viewpoint, the shots Siegel presents require us to accept such a perspective not only on the action, but also on the characters. In Dirty Harry the camera examines and discards the possibility of aligning itself
with Eastwood; by doing so, it provides the audience with
the same opportunity.

Siegel's camera does not dispute the solidity of space;
that is, however, a tangential issue. Rather it offers a set
of multiple perspectives on that space. Each viewpoint possesses its own validity, and each provides a different interpretation of the events it records. This use of the camera
does not determine the events recorded, only the relationship
that exists between those events and the audience, which the
camera mediates--whether in the diagrammatic form of the
scene in Dirty Harry in which the black man beats up Robinson (seen from both their points-of-view and a "neutral,"
"objective" position), or in the more complex office scenes
among five or six characters. Such scenes, where the camera cuts between a multiplicity of fixed viewpoints, do more
than provide an additional source of information with which
the audience may fix the "meaning" of an action or reaction,
and its "significance" within the narrative. They question
the notion of "meaning" within the context of a character's
or camera's perspective, which governs its interpretation.
Siegel revises the presentation of spatial reality by demonstrating the way events may be viewed differently, depending
on his characters' varying physical and psychological locations.

The construction of the Kezar stadium sequence in
Dirty Harry makes the point that a character's perspective
is not necessarily related to a subjective shot from his
point-of-view. Siegel in fact demonstrates the exact reverse. After Eastwood has shot Robinson and is walking
towards him, we see each character as they see themselves: Robinson, lying on the ground, cringing in panic,
shot from an unstable hand-held camera whose insecurity

of image intensifies Robinson's own; Eastwood, advancing relentlessly, his jawline set as firmly as he is set in center-
frame of a stable, low-angle composition.   The two shots
correspond approximately to point-of-view shots, but they
embody the vision of the characters in them, not of the character from whose position they are taken.   The extreme moment of this presentation comes when Eastwood treads on
Robinson's wound: we see the action, and Robinson's facial
reaction, from Eastwood's viewpoint.   The parallel intensity
of their psychotic states is measured by this shot, while the
next perspective, the helicopter shot which soars out from a
medium shot of the two figures, isolates them as indistin-
guishable points of light in the middle of a deserted football
stadium, surrounded by blackness.   Tied together indissolubly
by the previous sequence, these two psychopaths have no social dimension.   Their unilateral perspectives exclude the
acknowledgment of other people's activity, other people's
viewpoints.   Harry is separated from Scorpio only by his
badge, the plot's equivalent of their relative billing on the
cast list.   It is, however, exactly this notion of alternative
perspectives that Siegel's use of the camera stresses.   A
different viewpoint provides you with a different story.   With
the Kezar stadium sequence, the film has apparently ended.
It begins again with the introduction of the District Attorney's
viewpoint, in a scene constructed of three medium shots and
three close-ups, which present with equal emphasis conflicting notions of justice.

Siegel's films emphasize acts of looking, leading to a
discussion of the privileged nature of the audience's position.
In Dirty Harry we see through the telescopic sights of Scorpio's rifle, and Callaghan's (Eastwood) binoculars.   These
privileges have their disadvantages: the subjective shot offers only a limited perspective, and may cause us to miss
the action: Harry is looking in the wrong place when Scorpio appears on the roof.   Looking too closely, through a
telephoto lens, for example, may distort our perspective
and omit a context which changes the nature of what we are
seeing: the opening sequence, where the grass-edged swimming pool, in which Scorpio's first victim is swimming, is
revealed by the zoom out to be on top of a multi-story building in the middle of the city.   Siegel's characters consistently discuss the nature of appearances, what they can and can't
see, and how deceptive a surface appearance may be (e. g. ,
The Beguiled).

The tunnel vision of protagonists like Harry Callaghan

is, however, far from a solely negative quality. Their
limited viewpoint provides them with the single-mindedness
with which to energize the narrative. For the Eastwood of
Coogan's Bluff and Dirty Harry, the capacity (resulting from
his narrow field of view) to hold the center of a moving
frame and carry the camera with that movement becomes
the sole definition of his "heroic" status; a definition derived from a formal practice, not from a moral argument.
In Dirty Harry, Eastwood is established as protagonist/
"hero" in the credit sequence, in which he does nothing
significant except to move and look. The positive narrative
virtues given him by his tunnel vision might otherwise be
described as professionalism. Siegel's protagonists are be-
haviorists: the Police Chief (John Larch) acknowledges this
when describing Scorpio:

> These sick guys have behavior patterns. We know
> for a fact they rob the very same store three,
> four times in a row. Must appeal to their super-
> ego or something.

It is not necessary to understand motivation, it is only necessary to anticipate the likely result (Siegel's own attitude to his
psychopaths). His "heroes" solve problems and play percentages: Harry rescues the "jumper" in the suicide sequence
not by discussing what led him to this precipice, but by describing what's likely to happen when he hits the concrete below, and provoking Anthony Zerbe into attacking him by telling him,

> Always happens with you guys, you know. At the
> last minute you always want to grab onto somebody,
> take somebody with you.

Contrasted to Eastwood's power to energize the narrative,
consider Henry Fonda, the Commissioner in Madigan, pushed
progressively towards stasis and ineffectuality by his developing tolerance. Unable adequately to cope with the grief of
Madigan's widow (Inger Stevens), he can only leave the film
muttering, "There's never a right thing to say."

   Dirty Harry is the culmination of a particular period
of Siegel's stylistic and structural concerns. Callaghan is,
like the McQueen archetype in Hell Is for Heroes, the psychopathic center of the film: characters and multiple viewpoints revolve around him as the most consistent mobile possessor of frame center. His limitations as an isolated indi-

vidual are explored in a visual world which forces him into
relationships with other characters that he finds uncomfortable.   Pinned up against a brick wall (by Siegel) and questioned about motivation (by Chico's wife), he can only reply
"I don't know.   I really don't."   Faced at the end of the
film with the increased isolation provided by his successful
completion of his goal--by what ought, if he were the un-
questioned hero, to be the culmination of his heroic endeavor
--he has to reject his increasingly tenuous attachment to a
social order with which he has, during the course of the
film, become incompatible.   He throws away his badge of
social office, the camera zooms out in one of Siegel's ambivalent tension-releasing final shots.   No resolution has
been provided.

By contrast, Siegel's later films present a more adjusted character operating as the pivotal center of the narrative, confronting a society whose notions of order are
questioned by arbitrary and unstable events.   Charley Varrick is named after its sole survivor, a character who
makes no claims to heroic status, only to the pursuit of a
self-centered, rational, and strictly limited goal.   Having
accidentally stolen $750,000 of Mafia money, all he wants
to do is avoid being killed.   Varrick (Walter Matthau) is
absorbed in the present; the other characters die because
they ignore the present in their contemplation of future advantage.   Charley Varrick, The Black Windmill, and Telefon may be seen as revised and less direct statements of
the thematic of Invasion of the Body Snatchers, Siegel's
most politically explicit movie.   The revision is caused by
an alteration of situation through time: the paranoiac edge
of much of the subversive culture of the 1950s and 1960s
(Fuller, Sirk) no longer has the cutting edge it did when
attacking the secure complacency of Eisenhower's America.
The post-liberal, post-Easy Rider audience assumes character rebellion against authoritarian power.   The glowingly-
lit figure of Kevin McCarthy, standing in the middle of a
crowded freeway shouting, "You could be next!" might seem
ludicrously overstated to an audience intimately concerned
with its own "cool."

The later films' thematic emerges through a different, less overt process of consolidation of visual presentation and repetition of theme.   Siegel's films have become
less emphatic, more prosaic, as the logic of multiple perspectives has been extended into an assumption of equal
validity for any character on the screen.   Varrick and

Molly, the Mafia killer (Joe Don Baker), treat Jewell Everett (Sheree North), the passport-maker, with equal seriousness, though in an entirely different manner. Siegel's presentation of their behavior towards her establishes an interaction among the three characters, although they never appear together in a scene. In Telefon, there is an even more extreme example. Patrick Magee is demonstrating to Charles Bronson the hypnotic trigger implanted in the Telefon agents. A soldier is serving tea. Magee intones the trigger phrase, and the soldier immediately reaches for a pistol in a box on the table, and begins firing at Magee. The pistol is empty, but he continues clicking the trigger until he is removed. In presentation, his action, and with it his understanding of what is taking place (which ignores the fact that the gun is empty), is validated equally with Bronson's astonishment and Magee's restrained amusement. Each course of action adopted by each character is simply an alternative to what each other character is doing. The particular choice may be more or less rational, and more or less interesting; the two do not, of course, coincide. But characters can use objects and events for quite different purposes with equal validity; the most blatant examples in Siegel are cultural jokes: the Robert Frost poem that triggers the Telefon agents, "The Sound of Music" in The Black Windmill.

Operating a spatial system of multiple perspectives, in which the point of the audience's view is not fixed, Siegel's films require another element to unify them, both internally and as a body of work. That is provided by his management of time, which at the same time relates his work to the generic conventions of melodramatic form and is his most obvious auteurist contribution to the crime film genre. Siegel's characters are constantly placed under a pressure generated by time: Madigan (Richard Widmark) has forty-eight hours in which to catch Benesch (Steve Inhat); Dancer (Eli Wallach) and Julian (Robert Keith) have until 4:00 p.m. to deliver the recovered heroin (in The Line Up); Miles Bennel (Kevin McCarthy) has for as long as he can stay awake to escape from the Body Snatchers; J. B. Books has an imprecisely defined but limited time left to live (in The Shootist). Temporal pressure displaces and underwrites spatial unity. The chase in Madigan after Benesch has taken Madigan's and Bonaro's (Harry Guardino) guns is compiled of spatially unrelated shots of the characters moving through separate areas in the same time. It is a possibility established by the definition of space provided by the opening shot of the film: a crane up from the subway line to the two detectives (who discuss time: "Eight days, already," announces Bonaro, referring to his giving up smoking, while time is signified by the word "Friday" overprinted on the screen). They then move off, with the camera panning and following, until they enter Benesch's apartment building.

Time controls narrative development, space is flexible: hence the importance of telephones in Siegel's stories as a way of stressing narrative connection simultaneously with spatial dislocation. In space, the telephone can be a physical weapon to keep people apart, the purpose for which Susan Clark uses it in warding off Eastwood's advances in Coogan's Bluff--at the same time that the narrative connection of the phone introduces time as another defense for her: someone is coming to see her in five minutes. It can also revise the idea of communication as a movement through time in space. Frequently, Siegel shoots telephone conversations in which a character gestures as expansively as if he were having a conversation with the other party present (e.g., Robinson in Charley Varrick). What Siegel also makes plain, by the other party's reactions, is their unawareness of this gesticulation. In Siegel's world, discontinuity is only a 'phone call away--a point stressed by his detailed presentation of the circumstances of the Telefon agents immediately prior to Pleasence's triggering them.

The pressure of time cements Siegel's narratives, forcing their causality by the strict emphasis on the constant present, which at the same time provides for the instability of the present moment. His psychopathic heroes attempt to impose their own causality on this unstable world where the frame may break up at any moment, where they (and we) must wait for mechanical objects to complete their functions before the narrative can progress, and where surface appearances are relentlessly decreed to be mutable. His pivotal heroes recognize that multiple perspectives lead to multiple conditions: every decision is based on another one. This establishes a new causality, which requires that to succeed they must be single-minded professionals, playing percentages based on their experience, anticipating possibilities which other possibilities might produce. On such a basis they attempt to maintain a precarious balance within this insecure world, sufficiently aware of its instability not to seek permanency. At the end of Telefon, Bronson and Lee Remick leave the frame for a "Happy Hour" motel.

Siegel's films stress their surface tension by the pressure of time on the characters and, as a determining factor of the films' construction (particularly through editing), on the audience. At the same time as they operate a linear, unilateral plot, they also emphasize, through the presentation of multiple perspectives on an event, the mutability of the surface appearances through which that tension is maintained. However, Siegel's sense of temporal pressure itself depends on an expectation of narrative development. Performances unencumbered by an obligation to narrative coherence refuse to accommodate themselves to Siegel's dialectics of time and space. In the telephoto close-up, the only dissenter can be the star.

"Who wants to see Clint Eastwood play anything?"
--Clint Eastwood.[1]

At the beginning of The Eiger Sanction a spy is murdered. Just before his death, he swallows the microfilm he has been carrying. His assassin cuts his throat to get the film. It was Eastwood's original intention that the murdered spy should be played by his mentor, Don Siegel. It would have been a joke that Eastwood, Siegel, and very few other people would have understood, but I suspect that would have merely added to Eastwood's pleasure. Eastwood is perhaps the supreme narcissist of the contemporary American cinema. His films display an elitism that at times threatens to exclude his audience altogether. The Eiger Sanction's Dr. Jonathan Hemlock, professor of art and part-time government hit-man, undertakes his assassinations to finance his private collection of original paintings, which he exhibits only to himself. In Play Misty for Me Eastwood and his barman (Siegel again) play an intriguing board game called "Cry Bastard." Its rules are not explained, but Eastwood always wins, since the object of the game turns out to be to attract the attention of any single woman in the bar. At its most physically apparent, Eastwood's elitist detachment from the camera and the other characters is measured by the frequency with which he turns his back on them. This is often (e.g., any of the scenes with Pope [Gregory Walcott] in The Eiger Sanction) a prelude to his punching them in Eastwood's unique and particularly dismissive way. He always punches downwards, his fist moving in a descending arc from the level of his shoulder, regardless of the height of his victims. The outcome is assured by the gesture; Eastwood's contempt for the other character is already registered by his facial expression, and the dismissive punch confirms his judgment. Eastwood has not lost a fistfight in his screen career.

The game in Misty might stand as a metaphor for Eastwood's consistent relations with the audience. His films are above all self-indulgent games he plays with himself, a point his audience seems repeatedly to miss by continuing to turn up at the box-office in millions. As a result, Eastwood is privileged with an almost unique freedom from economic pressure in his choice of projects, which allows him to carry on making the most expensive home movies in the world. In the case of Misty it was, literally, that: the setting for Jessica Walter's climactic attack on Eastwood's image was his own house in Carmel. The principal motive for his making The Eiger Sanction appears to have been to develop his interest in mountaineering, although it also provides him with the opportunity to develop his most outrageous character to date. A director who is prepared quite gratuitously to make his principal villain a mincing effeminate homosexual with a dog called Faggot is obviously not overtly concerned with his audience's sensibilities. Eastwood quite explicitly detaches himself from his audience and declines any obligation to communicate with them. In his first scene, the improbable Dr. Hemlock addresses the cinema audience directly when he tells his students,

> If we've learned nothing else this year, I hope you've learned the stupidity of the statement that art belongs to the world, because art belongs to the cultured, who can appreciate it. The majority of the great unwashed does not fit into this category and neither, I'm sorry to say, do most of you.

He cannot get much more explicit than that.

Eastwood's career in the 1970s divides into two distinct halves, depending on whether he directs himself or not. Eastwood quite clearly regards his screen persona as a marketable commodity and detaches himself as completely from that commodity as he does from his audience. Those films which state the commodity (Thunderbolt and Lightfoot, The Enforcer, Every Which Way But Loose) he donates to other, younger directors whose careers he is interested in fostering. The films he has directed himself constitute a sustained revision of his screen image conducted mainly for his own benefit. The least interesting of these exercises have been his two Westerns. High Plains Drifter effectively disposes of The Man With No Name by revealing him to be a ghost incapable of any adequate integration into an American narrative. The Outlaw Josey Wales is a conservative engagement with the traditional Western, more or less a remake of Rio Bravo on the move, except that Eastwood maintains his detachment from any obligation to others by abandoning his companions for no reason, and then equally arbitrarily returning to them.

His contemporary films offer somewhat more complex exercises in perceptual reorganization, in which he observes the disintegrative effects of technology on narrative development. In The Gauntlet he exposes the notion of redemption through action as absurd, since his initial characterization as a washed-up drunk detective is so thoroughly unconvincing. The emotional development of the narrative is abruptly curtailed by an equally arbitrary act of performance. Eastwood's objective in the film is to transport Sondra Locke from Las Vegas to Phoenix despite the concerted attempts of the police and the Mafia to prevent him. In the process and against their better judgments they develop a romantic attachment which is resolved in a scene in a motel room shortly before the denouement. Locke makes two phone calls, one to her bookmaker to bet all her savings on the success of their mission--at odds that will make them almost as much money as a Clint Eastwood film, the other to her mother to tell her she's found Mr. Right and is about to get married. For Eastwood, resolution is only a 'phone call away, but all it will do is close down one aspect of the film. The rest of the film, in which they survive being shot at by the entire Phoenix police force, is an impossible foregone conclusion. Eastwood encourages the film to collapse into its separate component parts with as much evident enthusiasm as he records the demolition of Locke's Las Vegas house by police gunfire.

This fragmentation is a narrative version of the visual territory he explored in Play Misty for Me. That film comprises two incompatible spaces, inhabited by its two principal females. Donna Mills, with whom Eastwood is seeking a "serious" relationship, lives in a timeless telephoto world of cigarette and shampoo advertisements, voice-over songs in artifically lush "natural" landscapes and Eastwood's detached verbal performance as a disc jockey. Jessica Walter occupies a vivid three-dimensional world of deep-focus frames, dynamic movement and narrative development. The two are, of course, completely incompatible; Walter ends up attempting to kill both Mills and Eastwood, who is left at the end of the film with the realization that his entry into Walter's three-dimensional space (he has just punched her over the side of a cliff) has irredeemably compromised the telephoto aesthetic he had shared with Mills. The film provides no solution to Eastwood's problems in occupying space. It merely recognizes the divergent logics inherent in the lenses it employs.

Eastwood's occupation of three-dimensional space is, of course, central to the appeal of his films. A good deal of The Eiger Sanction is occupied by shots revealing that it really is Clint Eastwood hanging by a rope over a three thousand-foot drop, and not a stuntman or a process shot. But the clearest demonstration of his own centrality to the construction of a space in which narrative movement (however fragmented) is possible is, curiously, the one film in which he is absent. Breezy traverses a similar landscape to Play Misty for Me--the California lifestyles of Eastwood's home town, Carmel. It depicts an impossible romance that nothing in the film can challenge because none of its characters can establish a strong enough sense of time or space to resist the seductive sentimentality of its advertising images. William Holden is frequently embarrassed by his enclosure in extreme telephoto shots on empty beaches, and keeps looking at his watch in the hope of salvation, but finally succumbs to Kay Lenz's amorphous sense of time and place as the only one on offer.

> Holden: I don't know, if we're lucky we might
> last a year.
> Lenz: A year. Just think of it Frank, a whole
> year.

Where less ironic narcissists have inserted themselves into a narrative to reveal a vacuum (Warren Beatty in Shampoo and Heaven Can Wait, for example), Eastwood removes himself to produce the same effect, revealing the extent to which he understands that permanence is unavailable to a cinema incapable of articulating coherent space. Eastwood's films may be no more responsible than those of Coppola or Scorsese, but they are a good deal more entertaining.

REFERENCE

1. Quoted in Iain Johnstone, The Man with No Name: The Biography of Clint Eastwood (London, 1981), p. 75.

SELECTIVE BIBLIOGRAPHY

Adair, Gilbert. Hollywood's Vietnam. London: Proteus, 1981.

Allsop, Kenneth. The Bootleggers. London: Hutchinson, 1961.

Althusser, Louis. Lenin and Philosophy and Other Essays. London: New Left, 1971.

Altman, Charles F. "Psychoanalysis and Cinema: The Imaginary Discourse," Quarterly Review of Film Studies, Vol. 2, No. 2.

Andrew, J. Dudley. The Major Film Theories: An Introduction. London: Oxford University Press, 1976.

Balio, Tino. United Artists: The Company Built by the Stars. Madison: University of Wisconsin Press, 1976.

_____, ed. The American Film Industry. Madison: University of Wisconsin Press, 1976.

Barr, Charles. "CinemaScope, Before and After," Film Quarterly, Vol. 16, No. 4.

Barthes, Roland. Mythologies. London: Granada, 1973.

_____. Image-Music-Text. London: Fontana, 1977.

Baxter, John. Hollywood in the Thirties. London: Tantivy, 1968.

_____. The Cinema of John Ford. London: Tantivy, 1971.

_____. Hollywood in the Sixties. London: Tantivy, 1972.

381

_____. <u>Sixty Years of Hollywood</u>.   London: Tantivy, 1973.

Baxter, Peter.   "On the History and Ideology of Film Lighting," <u>Screen</u>,   Vol. 16, No. 3.

Bazin, André. <u>What Is Cinema?</u>   Berkeley and Los Angeles: University of California Press, 1967, 1971.   2 vols.

Behlmer, Rudy, ed. <u>Memo from David O. Selznick</u>.   New York: Viking, 1972.

Bell, Daniel. <u>The End of Ideology</u>.   New York: Free Press, 1960.

Bellour, Raymond.   "The Obvious and the Code," <u>Screen</u>, Vol. 15, No. 4.

_____.   "The Unattainable Text," <u>Screen</u>, Vol. 16, No. 3.

Belton, John. <u>The Hollywood Professionals Vol. III</u>.   London: Tantivy, 1974.

Belton, John, and Lyle Tector.   "The Bionic Eye: The Aesthetics of the Zoom," <u>Film Comment</u>, Vol. 16, No. 5.

Benjamin, Walter. <u>Illuminations</u>.   London: Fontana, 1973.

Bennett, Tony, Susan Boyd-Bowman, Colin Mercer, and Janet Woolacott, eds. <u>Popular Television and Film</u>.   London: British Film Institute, 1981.

Bentley, Eric, ed. <u>Thirty Years of Treason: Excerpts from Hearings Before the House Committee on Un-American Activities, 1938-1968</u>.   New York: Viking, 1971.

Bergman, Andrew. <u>We're in the Money: Depression America and Its Films</u>.   New York: Harper & Row, 1972.

Bessie, Alvah. <u>Inquisition in Eden</u>.   New York: Macmillan, 1965.

_____.   "Jail, Freedom, and the Screenwriting Profession," <u>Film Comment</u>, Vol. 3, No. 4.

Biskind, Peter. "Ripping Off Zapata: Revolution Hollywood Style," Cineaste, Vol. 7, No. 2.

Bogdanovich, Peter. John Ford. London: Studio Vista, 1968.

Boorstin, Daniel J., ed. An American Primer. Chicago: University of Chicago Press, 1968.

Bordwell, David, and Kristin Thompson. Film Art: An Introduction. Reading, Mass.: Addison-Wesley, 1979.

Braudy, Leo. The World in a Frame: What We See in Films. New York: Anchor, 1976.

Brenner, Marie. Going Hollywood: An Insider's Look at Power and Pretense in the Movie Business. New York: Delacorte, 1978.

Browne, Nick. "The Spectator-in-the-Text: The Rhetoric of Stagecoach," Film Quarterly, Vol. 29, No. 2.

Bruccoli, Matthew, ed. On the Waterfront: A Screenplay by Budd Schulberg. Carbondale: Southern Illinois University Press, 1980.

Budd, Michael. "A Home in the Wilderness: Visual Imagery in John Ford's Westerns," Cinema Journal, Vol. 16, No. 1.

Buscombe, Edward. "Ideas of Authorship," Screen, Vol. 14, No. 3.

_____. "Notes on Columbia Pictures Corporation, 1926-1941," Screen, Vol. 16, No. 3.

Butler, Terence. Crucified Heroes: The Films of Sam Peckinpah. London: Fraser, 1979.

Cahiers du Cinéma editors. "John Ford's Young Mr. Lincoln," Screen, Vol. 13, No. 3.

Calder, Jenni. There Must Be a Lone Ranger: The Myth and Reality of the American Wild West. London: Hamish Hamilton, 1974.

Cameron, Ian, ed. MOVIE Reader. London: November, 1973.

Campbell, Russell. "The Ideology of the Social Consciousness Movie," Quarterly Review of Film Studies, Vol. 3, No. 1.

Capra, Frank. The Name Above the Title: An Autobiography. New York: Macmillan, 1971.

Carmen, Ira H. Movies, Censorship, and the Law. Ann Arbor: University of Michigan Press, 1966.

Caughie, John, ed. Theories of Authorship. London: Routledge & Kegan Paul, 1981.

Cavell, Stanley. The World Viewed. New York: Viking, 1971.

Cawelti, John G. The Six-Gun Mystique. Bowling Green, Ohio: Bowling Green University Popular Press, 1975.

_____, ed. Focus on Bonnie and Clyde. Englewood Cliffs, N.J.: Prentice-Hall, 1973.

Cawkwell, Tim, and John M. Smith, eds. The World Encyclopedia of Film. New York: Galahad, 1972.

Ceplair, Larry, and Steven Englund. The Inquisition in Hollywood: Politics in the Film Community 1930-1960. New York: Anchor/Doubleday, 1980.

Chaney, David. Fictions and Ceremonies: Representations of Popular Experience. London: Arnold, 1979.

Chomsky, Noam. American Power and the New Mandarins. Harmondsworth, Eng.: Penguin, 1969.

Ciment, Michael. Kazan on Kazan. London: Secker & Warburg, 1973.

Clarens, Carlos. "Hooverville West: The Hollywood G-Man, 1934-1945," Film Comment, Vol. 10, No. 6.

Cogley, John. Report on Blacklisting. Vol. I: The Movies. Vol. II: Radio and Television. New York: Fund for the Republic, 1965.

Cohen, John, ed. The Essential Lenny Bruce. London: Granada, 1980.

Collins, Gary. "Kazan in the Fifties, " in The Velvet Light Trap 11.

Combs, Richard, ed. Robert Aldrich. London: British Film Institute, 1978.

Commager, Henry Steele. The American Mind: An Interpretation of American Thought and Character Since the 1880's. New Haven: Yale University Press, 1950.

Comolli, Jean-Louis, and Jean Narboni. "Cinema/Ideology/ Criticism (I), " Screen, Vol. 12, No. 1.

Conant, Michael. Antitrust in the Motion Picture Industry. Berkeley: University of California Press, 1960.

Corliss, Richard. The Hollywood Screenwriters. New York: Avon, 1972.

_____. Talking Pictures: Screenwriters of Hollywood. London: David and Charles, 1975.

_____. "The Legion of Decency, " Film Comment, Vol. 4, No. 4.

Cripps, Thomas. "The Future Film Historian: Less Art and More Craft, " Cinema Journal, Vol. 14, No. 2.

Crowther, Bosley. The Lion's Share: The Story of an Entertainment Empire. New York: Dutton, 1957.

Curran, James, Michael Gurevitch, and Janet Woolacott, eds. Mass Communication and Society. London: Arnold, 1977.

Dardis, Tom. Some Time in the Sun: The Hollywood Years of Fitzgerald, Faulkner, Nathanael West, Aldous Huxley, and James Agee. London: Deutsch, 1976.

Davies, Philip, and Brian Neve, eds. Cinema, Politics and Society in America. Manchester, Eng.: Manchester University Press, 1981.

Davis, Dave, and Neal Goldberg. "Organizing the Screen Writers Guild: An Interview with John Howard Lawson, " Cineaste, Vol. 8, No. 2.

Dayan, Daniel. "The Tutor Code of Classical Cinema," Film Quarterly, Vol. 28, No. 1.

De Lauretis, Teresa, and Stephen Heath, eds. The Cinematic Apparatus. London: Macmillan, 1980.

Deming, Barbara. Running Away from Myself: A Dream Portrait of America Drawn from the Films of the Forties. New York: Grossman, 1969.

De Saussure, Ferdinand. Course in General Linguistics. London: Fontana, 1974.

De Tocqueville, Alexis. Democracy in America. New York: Harper & Row, 1966.

Didion, Joan. Slouching Towards Bethlehem. Harmondsworth, Eng.: Penguin, 1974.

_____. The White Album. Harmondsworth, Eng.: Penguin, 1981.

Dowdy, Andrew. The Films of the Fifties: The American State of Mind. New York: Morrow, 1975.

Downing, David, and Gary Herman. Clint Eastwood: All-American Anti-Hero. London: Omnibus, 1977.

Dunne, John Gregory. The Studio. London: Allen, 1970.

Durgnat, Raymond. Films and Feelings. London: Faber and Faber, 1967.

_____. "King Vidor," Film Comment, Vol. 9, Nos. 4 and 5.

_____. "Genre: Populism and Social Realism," Film Comment, Vol. 11, No. 4.

Dyer, Richard. Stars. London: British Film Institute, 1979.

_____. "The Towering Inferno," in Movie 21.

_____. "Entertainment and Utopia," in Movie 24.

Eames, John Douglas. The MGM Story. London: Octopus, 1975.

Ellis, John, ed. Screen Reader I. London: Society for Education in Film and Television, 1977.

Elsaesser, Thomas. "Why Hollywood?" in Monogram 1.

_____. "Tales of Sound and Fury," in Monogram 4.

_____. "The Pathos of Failure," in Monogram 6.

Facey, Paul W. The Legion of Decency: A Sociological Analysis of the Emergence and Development of a Pressure Group. New York: Arno, 1974.

Farber, Manny. Negative Space. London: Studio Vista, 1971.

_____. "Raoul Walsh: 'He Used to Be a Big Shot,'" Sight and Sound, Vol. 43, No. 1.

Feuer, Jane. "The Self-Reflective Musical and the Myth of Entertainment," Quarterly Review of Film Studies, Vol. 2, No. 3.

Fielding, Raymond, ed. A Technological History of Motion Pictures and Television. Berkeley and Los Angeles: University of California Press, 1968.

Finch, Christopher, and Linda Rosenkrantz. Gone Hollywood. London: Weidenfeld & Nicolson, 1979.

Fitzgerald, F. Scott. The Last Tycoon. Harmondsworth, Eng.: Penguin, 1974.

_____. The Pat Hobby Stories. Harmondsworth, Eng.: Penguin, 1967.

Fitzgerald, Michael G. Universal Pictures. New York: Arlington, 1977.

Fordin, Hugh. The World of Entertainment: The Freed Unit at MGM. New York: Avon, 1975.

French, Philip. The Movie Moguls: An Informal History of the Hollywood Tycoons. London: Weidenfeld & Nicolson, 1969.

_____. Westerns. London: Secker & Warburg, 1973.

French, Warren. Filmguide to The Grapes of Wrath. Bloomington: Indiana University Press, 1973.

Frye, Northrop. Anatomy of Criticism. Princeton, N.J.: Princeton University Press, 1957.

Furhammer, Lief, and Folke Isaksson. Politics and Film. London: Studio Vista, 1971.

Gaddis, John L. The United States and the Origins of the Cold War. New York: Columbia University Press, 1972.

Garnham, Nicholas. Samuel Fuller. London: Secker & Warburg, 1971.

Gassner, John, and Dudley Nichols, eds. 20 Best Film Plays. New York: Crown, 1943.

Gelmis, Joseph. The Film Director as Superstar. London: Secker & Warburg, 1971.

Georgakas, Dan. "Still Good After All These Years," Cineaste, Vol. 7, No. 2.

Glatzer, Richard, and John Raeburn, eds. Frank Capra: The Man and His Films. Ann Arbor: University of Michigan Press, 1975.

Goffman, Erving. The Presentation of Self in Everyday Life. London: Lane, 1969.

_____. Interaction Ritual: Essays on Face-to-Face Behaviour. Harmondsworth, Eng.: Penguin, 1972.

_____. Frame Analysis. New York: Harper & Row, 1974.

Gomery, J. Douglas. "Writing the History of the American Film Industry: Warner Brothers and Sound," Screen, Vol. 17, No. 1.

_____. "Tri-Ergon, Tobis-Klangfilm, and the Coming of Sound," Cinema Journal, Vol. 16, No. 1.

_____. "The Picture Palace: Economic Sense or Hollywood Nonsense," Quarterly Review of Film Studies, Vol. 3, No. 1.

Goodlad, J. S. R. A Sociology of Popular Drama. London: Heinemann, 1971.

Goodman, Ezra. The Fifty-Year Decline and Fall of Hollywood. New York: Simon & Schuster, 1961.

Gordon, David. "Why the Movie Majors Are Major," Sight and Sound, Vol. 42, No. 4.

_____. "Mayer, Thalberg, and MGM," Sight and Sound, Vol. 45, No. 3.

Gow, Gordon. Hollywood in the Fifties. London: Tantivy, 1971.

Greensfelder, Linda B., ed. The American Film Institute's Guide to College Film Courses. Chicago: American Library Association for the American Film Institute, 1970.

Griffiths, Philip Jones. Vietnam Inc. London: Collier-Macmillan, 1971.

Guback, Thomas. The International Film Industry: Western Europe and America Since 1945. Bloomington: University of Indiana Press, 1969.

Gussow, Mel. Zanuck: Don't Say Yes Until I've Finished Talking. New York: Doubleday, 1971.

Handel, Leo A. Hollywood Looks at Its Audience: A Report of Film Audience Research. Urbana: University of Illinois Press, 1950.

Hanet, Kari. "The Narrative Text of Shock Corridor," Screen, Vol. 15, No. 4.

Hardy, Phil. Samuel Fuller. London: Studio Vista, 1970.

_____, ed. Raoul Walsh. Edinburgh: Edinburgh Film Festival, 1974.

_____, Claire Johnston, and Paul Willemen, eds. Psychoanalysis/Cinema/Avant-Garde. Edinburgh: Edinburgh Film Festival, 1976.

Harvey, Sylvia. May '68 and Film Culture. London: British Film Institute, 1978.

Haskell, Molly. "Howard Hawks--Masculine Feminine," Film Comment, Vol. 10, No. 2.

Heath, Stephen. Questions of Cinema. London: Macmillan, 1981.

_____. "Film and System: Terms of Analysis," Screen, Vol. 16, Nos. 1 & 2.

_____. "Jaws, Ideology and Film Theory," Times Higher Education Supplement, March 26, 1976.

Hellman, Lillian. Scoundrel Time. New York: Little, Brown, 1976.

Henderson, Brian. A Critique of Film Theory. New York: Dutton, 1980.

Hickey, Terry. "Accusations Against Charles Chaplin for Political and Moral Offences," Film Comment, Vol. 5, No. 4.

Higham, Charles. Hollywood Cameramen: Sources of Light. London: Thames and Hudson, 1970.

_____. Warner Brothers: A History of the Studio: Its Pictures, Stars and Personalities. New York: Scribner, 1975.

_____, and Joel Greenberg. Hollywood in the Forties. London: Tantivy, 1968.

Hirschhorn, Clive. The Warner Bros. Story. London: Octopus, 1979.

_____. The Hollywood Musical. London: Octopus, 1981.

Hofstadter, Richard. The Paranoid Style in American Politics. London: Cape, 1966.

_____. Anti-Intellectualism in American Life. New York: Knopf, 1970.

Huettig, Mae D. Economic Control of the Motion Picture Industry. Philadelphia: Pennsylvania University Press, 1944.

Huftel, Sheila. Arthur Miller: The Burning Glass. London: Allen, 1965.

Inglis, Ruth. Freedom of the Movies: A Report on Self-Regulation from the Commission on the Freedom of the Press. Chicago, 1947.

Ionescu, Ghita, and Ernest Gellner, eds. Populism, Its National Characteristics. London: Weidenfeld & Nicolson, 1969.

Jacobs, Diane. Hollywood Renaissance. New York: Barnes, 1977.

Jacobs, Lewis. The Rise of the American Film. New York: Harcourt Brace, 1939.

_____. "World War II and American Film," Cinema Journal, Vol. 7.

_____, ed. The Movies as Medium. New York: Farrar, Straus & Giroux, 1970.

Johnston, Claire, ed. The Work of Dorothy Arzner: Towards a Feminist Cinema. London: British Film Institute, 1975.

_____. History/Production/Memory. Edinburgh: Edinburgh Film Festival, 1977.

Johnstone, Iain. The Man with No Name: The Biography of Clint Eastwood. London: Plexus, 1981.

Jowett, Garth. Film: The Democratic Art. Boston: Little, Brown, 1976.

Kael, Pauline, Herman Mankiewicz, and Orson Welles. The Citizen Kane Book. London: Secker & Warburg, 1971.

Kahn, Gordon. Hollywood on Trial: The Story of the Ten Who Were Indicted. New York: Boni & Gaer, 1948.

Kaminsky, Stuart. Don Siegel, Director. New York: Curtis, 1974.

_____. American Film Genres. New York: Dell, 1974.

Kaplan, Max. Leisure: Theory and Policy. London: Wiley, 1975.

Karimi, Amir Massoud. Towards a Definition of the American Film Noir, 1941-1949. New York: Arno, 1976.

Karp, Alan. The Films of Robert Altman. Metuchen, N. J. : Scarecrow, 1981.

Karpf, Stephen. The Gangster Film, 1930-1940. New York: Arno, 1973.

Kass, Judith M. The Hollywood Professionals, Vol. IV. London: Tantivy, 1975.

_____. Robert Altman; An American Innovator. New York: CBS, 1978.

Katz, Ephraim. The International Film Encyclopedia. London: Macmillan, 1979.

Keyser, Les. Hollywood in the Seventies. New York: Barnes, 1981.

Kitses, Jim. Horizons West. London: Thames & Hudson, 1969.

Klingender, F. D. , and Stuart Legg. Money Behind the Screen. London: Lawrence & Wishart, 1937.

Kolker, Robert Philip. A Cinema of Loneliness. New York: Oxford University Press, 1980.

Koszarski, Richard. Hollywood Directors, Vol. I: 1914-1940; Vol. II: 1941-1976. London: Oxford University Press, 1976, 1977.

Lasch, Christopher. The Agony of the American Left. Harmondsworth, Eng. : Penguin, 1973.

_____. The Culture of Narcissism. London: Sphere, 1980.

Laslett, Peter, ed. John Locke: Two Treatises on Government. Cambridge: Cambridge University Press, 1960.

Lawson, John Howard. Film in the Battle of Ideas. New York: Masses and Mainstream, 1953.

_____. Film: The Creative Process. New York: Hill & Wang, 1964.

Levin, Martin, ed. Hollywood and the Great Fan Magazines. New York: Arbor, 1970.

Limbacher, James L. Four Aspects of the Film. New York: Brussel & Brussel, 1968.

Lindgren, Ernest. The Art of the Film. London: Allen & Unwin, 1948.

Lovell, Alan. Don Siegel: American Cinema. London: British Film Institute, 1975.

Lovell, Terry. Pictures of Reality. London: British Film Institute, 1980.

Luhr, William, and Peter Lehman. Authorship and Narrative in the Cinema: Issues in Contemporary Aesthetics and Criticism. New York: Putnam, 1977.

McArthur, Colin. Underworld USA. London: Secker & Warburg, 1972.

McBride, Joseph. Orson Welles. London: Secker & Warburg, 1972.

_____, ed. Focus on Howard Hawks. Englewood Cliffs, N.J.: Prentice-Hall, 1972.

McCann, Richard Dyer. Hollywood in Transition. Boston: Houghton Mifflin, 1962.

_____. "Film and Foreign Policy: The U.S.I.A. 1962-1967," Cinema Journal, Vol. 9.

McCarthy, Todd, and Charles Flynn, eds. Kings of the Bs: Working Within the Hollywood System. New York: Dutton, 1975.

McConnell, Frank D. The Spoken Seen: Film and the Romantic Imagination. Baltimore: Johns Hopkins University Press, 1975.

McCoy, Horace. I Should Have Stayed Home. Harmondsworth, Eng.: Penguin, 1966.

McLuhan, Marshall. Understanding Media. London: Routledge & Kegan Paul, 1964.

McQuail, Dennis, ed. Sociology of Mass Communication. Harmondsworth, Eng.: Penguin, 1972.

Mailer, Norman. The Presidential Papers. Harmondsworth, Eng.: Penguin, 1968.

Mairowitz, David Zane. The Radical Soap Opera: Roots of Failure in the American Left. Harmondsworth, Eng.: Penguin, 1976.

Manvell, Roger. Films and the Second World War. New York: Dell, 1974.

Martin, Olga. Hollywood's Movie Commandments. New York: Wilson, 1937.

Marwick, Arthur. Class: Image and Reality in Britain, France and the USA Since 1930. London: Collins, 1980.

Marx, Arthur. Goldwyn: The Man Behind the Myth. London: Bodley Head, 1976.

Marx, Samuel. Mayer and Thalberg: The Make-Believe Saints. London: Allen, 1976.

Mason, John L. The Identity Crisis Theme in American Feature Films, 1960-1969. New York: Arno, 1977.

Mast, Gerald. Film/Cinema/Movie. New York: Harper & Row, 1977.

_____, and Marshall Cohen, eds. Film Theory and Criticism: Introductory Readings. New York: Oxford University Press, 1974.

May, Lary. Screening Out the Past. New York: Oxford University Press, 1981.

Mayersberg, Paul. Hollywood, The Haunted House. Harmondsworth, Eng.: Penguin, 1967.

Metz, Christian. Film Language: A Semiotics of the Cinema. London: Oxford University Press, 1974.

_____. "The Imaginary Signifier," Screen, Vol. 14, No. 2.

Milne, Tom, ed. Godard on Godard. London: Secker & Warburg, 1972.

Moley, Raymond. The Hays Office. New York: Bobbs-Merrill, 1945.

Monaco, James. American Film Now. New York: New American Library, 1979.

Morsberger, Robert E. Viva Zapata!: The Original Screen-play by John Steinbeck. New York: Viking, 1975.

Mulvey, Laura. "Visual Pleasure and Narrative Cinema," Screen, Vol. 16, No. 2.

Munsterberg, Hugo. The Film: A Psychological Study. New York: Dover, 1972.

Nachbar, Jack, ed. Focus on the Western. Englewood Cliffs, N.J.: Prentice-Hall, 1974.

Neale, Stephen. Genre. London: British Film Institute, 1980.

Nichols, Bill, ed. Movies and Methods. Berkeley and Los Angeles: University of California Press, 1976.

Nye, Russell B. The Unembarrassed Muse: The Popular Arts in America. New York: Dial, 1970.

O'Connor, John E., and Martin A. Jackson, eds. American History/American Film. New York: Ungar, 1979.

Ogle, Patrick J. "Technological and Aesthetic Influences on the Development of Deep-Focus Cinematography in the United States," Screen, Vol. 13, No. 1.

Paine, Jeffrey Morton. The Simplification of American Life: Hollywood Films of the 1930's. New York: Arno, 1977.

Panofsky, Erwin. Meaning in the Visual Arts. New York: Doubleday, 1955.

Parrish, Robert. Growing Up in Hollywood. London: Bodley Head, 1976.

Paul, William. "Hollywood Harakiri: Notes on the Decline of an Industry and an Art," Film Comment, Vol. 13, No. 2.

Peary, Gerald, and Roger Shatzkin, eds. The Classic American Novel and the Movies. New York: Ungar, 1977.

_____. The Modern American Novel and the Movies. New York: Ungar, 1978.

Perkins, V. F. Film as Film: Understanding and Judging Movies. Harmondsworth, Eng.: Penguin, 1972.

Peterson, Merrill J. The Portable Thomas Jefferson. New York: Viking, 1975.

Pickard, Roy. The Hollywood Studios. London: Muller, 1978.

Pirie, David, ed. Anatomy of the Movies. London: Windward, 1981.

Place, J. A., and L. S. Peterson. "Some Visual Motifs of Film Noir," Film Comment, Vol. 10, No. 1.

Place, Janey. The Western Films of John Ford. Secaucus, N.J.: Citadel, 1973.

_____. "A Family in a Ford: The Grapes of Wrath," Film Comment, Vol. 12, No. 5.

Poirier, Richard. The Performing Self: Compositions and Decompositions in the Languages of Contemporary Life. London: Oxford University Press, 1971.

Potter, David M. People of Plenty: Economic Abundance and the American Character. Chicago: Chicago University Press, 1954.

Powdermaker, Hortense. Hollywood, the Dream Factory: An Anthropologist Looks at Hollywood. Boston: Little, Brown, 1950.

Pratley, Gerald. Otto Preminger. New York: Barnes, 1971.

Pye, Douglas. "Genre and Movies," in Movie 20.

_____. "John Ford and the Critics," in Movie 22.

_____. "Genre and History," in Movie 25.

Pye, Michael. Moguls. London: Temple Smith, 1980.

_____, and Linda Myles. The Movie Brats: How the Film Generation Took Over Hollywood. London: Faber & Faber, 1979.

Ramsaye, Terry. A Million and One Nights: A History of the Motion Picture. New York: Simon & Schuster, 1964.

Randall, Richard S. Censorship of the Movies: The Social and Political Control of a Mass Medium. Madison: University of Wisconsin Press, 1968.

Richards, Jeffrey. Visions of Yesterday. London: Routledge & Kegan Paul, 1973.

Roberts, Kenneth. Contemporary Society and the Growth of Leisure. London: Longmans, 1978.

Robinson, David. Hollywood in the Twenties. London: Tantivy, 1968.

Robinson, W. R., ed. Man and the Movies. Baton Rouge: Louisiana State University Press, 1967.

Rogin, Michael P. The Intellectuals and McCarthy. New York: Knopf, 1975.

Rosefelt, Reid. "Celluloid Sedition: The Strange Case of the Hollywood Ten," in The Velvet Light Trap 11.

Rosen, Philip. "Screen and the Marxist Project in Film Criticism," Quarterly Review of Film Studies, Vol. 2, No. 3.

Rosenbaum, Jonathan. "Improvisations and Interactions in Altmanville," Sight and Sound, Vol. 44, No. 2.

Rosenberg, Bernard, and David Manning White, eds. Mass Culture. New York: Free Press, 1957.

Rosenberg, Bernard, and Harry Silverstein. The Real Tinsel. New York: Macmillan, 1970.

Rosow, Eugene. Born to Lose: The Gangster Film in America. New York: Oxford University Press, 1978.

Ross, Lillian. Picture. London: Non-Fiction Book Club, 1952.

Rosten, Leo. Hollywood, the Movie Colony, the Movie Makers. New York: Harcourt Brace, 1941.

Salt, Barry. "Film Style and Technology in the 1930s," Film Quarterly, Vol. 30, No. 1.

_____. "Film Style and Technology in the 1940s," Film Quarterly, Vol. 31, No. 1.

Sarris, Andrew. The American Cinema: Directors and Directions. New York: Dutton, 1968.

_____. The John Ford Movie Mystery. London: Secker & Warburg, 1976.

_____. "Notes on the Auteur Theory in 1970," Film Comment, Vol. 6, No. 3.

_____. "Big Funerals: The Hollywood Gangster, 1927-1933," Film Comment, Vol. 13, No. 3.

_____. "Film Criticism in the Seventies," Film Comment, Vol. 14, No. 1.

_____, ed. Interviews with Film Directors. New York: Avon, 1967.

_____, ed. Hollywood Voices: Interviews with Film Directors. London: Secker & Warburg, 1971.

Sauvage, Pierre. "Interview with Robert Aldrich," Movie 23.

Schary, Dore. "Statement [on Blacklisting]," Film Comment, Vol. 3, No. 4.

Schatz, Thomas. Hollywood Genres: Formulas, Filmmaking and the Studio System. New York: Random House, 1981.

Schickel, Richard. The Disney Version. New York: Avon, 1969.

Schlechter, H., and C. Molessen. "It's Not Nice to Fool Mother Nature: The Disaster Movie and Technological Guilt," Journal of American Culture, Vol. 1, No. 1.

Schrader, Paul. "Notes on Film Noir," Film Comment, Vol. 8, No. 1.

Schulberg, Budd. What Makes Sammy Run? Harmondsworth, Eng.: Penguin, 1978.

Schumach, Murray. The Face on the Cutting Room Floor: The Story of Movie and Television Censorship. New York: Morrow, 1964.

Shadoian, Jack. Dreams and Dead Ends: The American Gangster/Crime Film. Cambridge, Mass.: MIT Press, 1977.

Shain, Russell Earl. An Analysis of Motion Pictures About War Released by the American Film Industry, 1930-1970. New York: Arno, 1976.

Shindler, Colin. Hollywood During the Great Depression. Unpublished Ph.D. thesis, Cambridge University, 1974.

_____. Hollywood Goes to War. London: Routledge & Kegan Paul, 1979.

Shipman, David. The Great Movie Stars: The Golden Years; The International Years. London: Hamlyn, 1970, 1972.

Short, K. R. M., ed. Feature Films as History. London: Croom Helm, 1981.

Silver, Alain. "Kiss Me Deadly: Evidence of a Style," Film Comment, Vol. 11, No. 2.

Sinclair, Upton. Upton Sinclair Presents William Fox. Los Angeles: Upton Sinclair, 1933.

Sklar, Robert. Movie-Made America. New York: Random House, 1975.

Slater, Philip. The Pursuit of Loneliness: American Culture at Breaking Point. Harmondsworth, Eng.: Penguin, 1971.

Smith, Henry Nash. Virgin Land. New York: Vintage, 1957.

Smith, Robert E. "Mann in the Dark: The Films Noirs of Anthony Mann," in Bright Lights 5.

Spellerberg, James. "Technology and Ideology in the Cinema," Quarterly Review of Film Studies, Vol. 2, No. 3.

Stanbrook, Alan. "Hollywood's Crashing Epics," Sight and Sound, Vol. 50, No. 2.

Stanley, Robert H. The Celluloid Empire. New York: Hastings House, 1978.

Steinberg, Cobbett. Reel Facts. New York: Vintage, 1978.

Stempel, Tom. Screenwriter: The Life and Times of Nunnally Johnson. New York: Barnes, 1980.

Stott, William. Documentary Expression and Thirties America. New York: Oxford University Press, 1973.

Stuart, Frederic. The Effects of Television on the Motion Picture and Radio Industries. New York: Arno, 1976.

Suid, Lawrence. Guts and Glory: Great American War Movies. Reading, Mass.: Addison-Wesley, 1978.

Tailleur, Roger. "Elia Kazan and the House Un-American Activities Committee" (translated by Alvah Bessie), Film Comment, Vol. 4, No. 1.

Talbot, Daniel, ed. Film: An Anthology. Berkeley: University of California Press, 1969.

Talbot, David, and Barbara Zheutlin. Creative Differences: Profiles of Hollywood Dissidents. Boston: South End, 1978.

Thomas, Bob. King Cohn: The Life and Times of Harry Cohn. London: Barrie & Rockcliff, 1967.

_____. Brando: Portrait of the Rebel as an Artist. London: Allen, 1975.

Thomas, Tony, and Aubrey Solomon. The Films of Twentieth Century-Fox. Secaucus, N.J.: Citadel, 1979.

Thompson, David. America in the Dark: Hollywood and the Gift of Unreality. London: Hutchinson, 1978.

Thorp, Margaret Farrand. America at the Movies. London: Faber & Faber, 1945.

Toeplitz, Jerzy. Hollywood and After: The Changing Face of Movies in America. London: Allen & Unwin, 1974.

Trumbo, Dalton. The Time of the Toad: A Study of the Inquisition in America. New York: Harper & Row, 1972.

Tuchman, Mitch. "Gigolos: Paul Schrader Interviewed," Film Comment, Vol. 16, No. 2.

Tudor, Andrew. Theories of Film. London: Secker & Warburg, 1974.

_____. Image and Influence: Studies in the Sociology of Film. London: Allen & Unwin, 1974.

_____. "The Many Mythologies of Realism," Screen, Vol. 13, No. 1.

Tunstall, Jeremy. The Media Are American: Anglo-American Media in the World. London: Constable, 1977.

Tyler, Parker. The Hollywood Hallucination. New York: Simon & Schuster, 1944.

_____. Magic and Myth of the Movies. New York: Holt, 1947.

_____. Sex Psyche Etcetera in the Film. Harmondsworth, Eng.: Penguin, 1971.

United States Temporary National Economic Committee. Investigation of Economic Power: Monograph 43.: The

Motion Picture Industry--A Pattern of Control. Washington, D. C.: U. S. Government Printing Office, 1941.

Vaughan, Robert. Only Victims: A Study of Showbusiness Blacklisting. New York: Putnam, 1972.

Vizzard, Jack. See No Evil: Life Inside a Hollywood Censor. New York: Simon & Schuster, 1970.

Walker, Alexander. The Celluloid Sacrifice. London: Michel Joseph, 1966.

_____. Stardom: The Hollywood Phenomenon. Harmondsworth, Eng.: Penguin, 1974.

Warshow, Robert. The Immediate Experience. New York: Doubleday, 1964.

Wasserman, Harry. "Ideological Conflict at the RKO Corral," in The Velvet Light Trap 11.

Wiles, Peter. "To Define Populism," Government and Opposition, Vol. 3, No. 2.

Will, David, and Peter Wollen, eds. Samuel Fuller. Edinburgh: Edinburgh Film Festival, 1969.

Will, David, and Paul Willemen, eds. Roger Corman: The Millenic Vision. Edinburgh: Edinburgh Film Festival, 1970.

Willemen, Paul. "On Realism in the Cinema," Screen, Vol. 13, No. 1.

Williams, Christopher, ed. Realism and the Cinema. London: Routledge & Kegan Paul, 1980.

Williams, Raymond. Television: Technology and Cultural Form. London: Fontana, 1974.

_____. Keywords: A Vocabulary of Culture and Society. London: Fontana, 1976.

_____. Culture. London: Fontana, 1981.

_____. "A Lecture on Realism," Screen, Vol. 18, No. 1.

Wolfenstein, Martha, and Nathan Leithes. The Movies: A Psychological Study. Glencoe, Ill.: Free Press, 1950.

Wollen, Peter. Signs and Meaning in the Cinema. London: Secker & Warburg, 1969.

_____. "Notes Towards a Structural Analysis of the Films of Samuel Fuller," in Cinema 3.

Wood, Michael. America in the Movies. New York: Dell, 1975.

Wood, Robin. Arthur Penn. London: Studio Vista, 1967.

_____. Howard Hawks. London: Secker & Warburg, 1968.

_____. Personal Views: Explorations in Film. London: Fraser, 1976.

_____. "To Have (Directed) and Have Not (Written)," Film Comment, Vol. 9, No. 3.

_____. "Art and Ideology," Film Comment, Vol. 11, No. 3.

_____. "Ideology, Genre, Auteur," Film Comment, Vol. 13, No. 1.

_____. "Smart-Ass and Cutie-Pie: Notes Towards an Evaluation of Altman," in Movie 21.

_____. "The Incoherent Text: Narrative in the 70s," Movie 27/28.

Wood, Robin, ed. American Nightmare: Essays on the Horror Film. Toronto: Festival of Festivals, 1979.

Wright, Will. Sixguns and Society. Berkeley and Los Angeles: University of California Press, 1975.

Zolotow, Maurice. John Wayne: Shooting Star. London: Allen, 1974.

INDEX